P9-EDS-634

Reminiscences of a Maynooth Professor

BY WALTER McDONALD

EDITED WITH A MEMOIR BY DENIS GWYNN

THE MERCIER PRESS
4 BRIDGE STREET, CORK

CONTENTS

BIOGRAPHICAL MEMOIR

By Professor Denis Gwynn

When Dr. Walter McDonald died, after a protracted illness, at Maynooth on May 2nd, 1920, he was only sixty-six. But he had been a professor at Maynooth for almost forty years, and he had been Prefect of the Dunboyne Establishment, its school of post-graduate studies, since 1888. During all those years he had been intimately concerned in many changes and much progress in the development of Maynooth. The present volume an abridgement of his published reminiscences has been prepared at the request of some of his old friends and students who desire that his memory should be clearly preserved.

It will seem surprising that the preparation of such a volume should be entrusted to a layman. I only knew Dr. McDonald during his later years, when I was still a student in Dublin. But he appointed me, shortly before his death, as his literary executor for all writings which were not of a theological nature; with the intention that I should publish his *Reminiscences of a Maynooth Professor*, and any other papers and essays or lectures which might seem suitable for permanent publication. When I was working in London in the late spring of 1920, he wrote to me the distressing news that his doctors told him that he had only a few more weeks to live. He had made arrangements for the disposal of his various unpublished theological writings; but he desired particularly to secure publication for the Reminiscences which he had been writing over a considerable period. He told me that he did not wish that any priest should be involved, as his literary executor, in the controversies which might be provoked by their publication. I offered to help him, if I could, in finding a publisher; and he then asked me at once to act as his literary executor for all his writings which, in his view, would not require ecclesiastical censorship.

His *Reminiscences of a Maynooth Professor* were accordingly published by Messrs. Jonathan Cape under my direction in 1925; and, although the book has long been out of print, it has been widely read. It dealt in part with certain personal controversies which had caused much unhappiness and mental distress to Dr. McDonald in his later years; but these are now long forgotten and are of little general interest. These contentious chapters were only part of a very remarkable volume of recollections, which gave a vivid picture of Maynooth during years of rapid progress and development. It has since been quoted often, as an indispensable source of contemporary information, in recent books such as Dr. Meehan's *Window on Maynooth*. Even in 1913, when he first started to write his reminiscences, Dr. McDonald could claim in his opening pages that 'I am now the oldest member – reckoning by length of service – of the College staff; the only remnant of that old order that passed away with the disendowment. I saw Dr. O'Hanlon in the flesh; Dr. Russell was President all my time as a student; I read under Murray, Crolly, and McCarthy, and sat at table, nearly opposite Dr. Murray for two years after I returned to the College as a professor. There were others of the old staff – Macaulay, Hackett, Molloy, Hammond, O'Rourke, Lennon – to tell me of the past. Any fragments of what they said, any stories of what they did, can hardly fail to be of interest, if I can but repeat and tell them, as simply, with love and reverence for those forerunners of ours, and for the dear old Alma Mater of whose life they are part, and whom so many true hearts fondly love.'

His devotion to Maynooth, and to the advancement of studies there, was an inspiration to generations of students at the Dunboyne, who included many of the Irish bishops during his lifetime and since. It was he, as Prefect of the Dunboyne, who was called upon to propose the formation of the Maynooth Union during the celebrations of the College's centenary in 1895. The address in which he outlined its purpose, and appealed for support, is included in the recently published collection of his papers, *The Manliness of St. Paul*. It gives expression to that wider conception of the function of Maynooth which he constantly expressed. At that time he had not yet encountered the difficulties of censorship which afterwards gave him a sense of frustration in his original writing. But his remarkably long tenure of the chair of Dogmatic Theology and of his position as Prefect of the Dunboyne Establishment, were never interrupted. Consequently his reminiscences enabled him to set down a record of his long experience at Maynooth, and a statement of the many causes that he had laboured to serve.

In 1913, some seven years before his death, he commenced writing his reminiscences. The greater part of his life, he wrote then, had already been 'spent here at Maynooth, which is the heart of the Irish Church, and therefore of the English-speaking Catholic world. A Californian friend of mine, a priest wo knows the American Church well, once told me that we in Ireland did not realise the position which we hold, as a centre of Catholic thought; did not know or bear in mind how many ears are strained, from the

Atlantic to the Pacific, day after day and year after year, to catch whatever message of faith or doctrine may be transmitted from the Irish shore. It is so, to an even greater extent, in Australia, which is practically an Irish Church, and in South Africa, of which the same may be said. This little island sent them the bishops and clergy that laid their foundations, broad and strong, the generous laity that *'Scalpri salubris ictibus et tunsione plurima* reared the fair structures that they are; so that for them, there are two *matres et magistrae* – Rome and Ireland. And however insignificant my life has been, it has been spent – forty years of it – at the heart of one of these.'

He had at that time been Prefect of the Dunboyne for almost twenty-five years. In June 1888 he had succeeded his friend Dr. O'Donnell, who then was appointed Bishop of Raphoe and who subsequently became Archbishop of Armagh, Primate of All Ireland, and Cardinal. 'During this quarter of a century,' wrote Dr. McDonald, 'I may be said to have lived my life; done the work that was given to me to do, and enjoyed the supreme good of doing it and of suffering for it. After my appointment, my uncle the Dean, writing to congratulate me, said that I had now the most desirable position in the Irish Church; which was not the whole truth, as I now think, after the experience of so many years. He should have designated it the most desirable position in the Irish Church or in any other; always, of course, provided you are able for its duties and not afraid of its responsibilities; when you will be likely to get into trouble, as I have done, but need not be unhappy.' Years of experience and devoted service had deepened his conviction of the wide extent of Irish influence throughout the Church, especially in the new Continents.

Walter McDonald's family, on both sides, had close connections with this Irish missionary apostolate. In his own youth, when he entered upon his early training for the priesthood, he had not the remotest thought of being trained for an academic vocation. He was born in June 1854 in Emil, in the parish of Mooncoin, County Kilkenny. He describes his father as 'a tenant farmer, holding sixty acres more or less, equal to something over a hundred acres statute measure.' His mother was 'one of the Carrolls of Pollrone, at that time the strongest farmers in the parish.' Both the Carrolls and the McDonalds had produced remarkable priests who served as missionaries in the distant new countries. One of his mother's brothers went out to San Francisco, soon after the first gold rush, and died there, of fever, after a few years. One of his father's brothers was Dean McDonald, a former president of St. Kieran's

College, Kilkenny, who paid for his education and enabled him to enter Maynooth. In his reminiscences Dr. McDonald writes very harshly of his father's thriftless ways, and his tendency to intemperance which placed a great strain on his mother. Some of his friends insist that these strictures upon his father were unfairly exaggerated. But it was well known that these early memories of the distress caused in his own family by occasional drinking were constantly in his mind. He often referred to them and they contributed to making him a prominent and earnest champion of the total abstinence movement in later years.

His earliest recollections, dating from the period soon after the great famine of 1845-47, illustrate vividly the immense changes that were to follow during his lifetime. He was only five when he was sent first to the local national school in 1859; three years later he went as a weekly boarder to a school in Carrick-on-Suir. He recalls how he used to come home each week-end to Emil, walking the seven miles there and back. On the Monday morning he would set out on foot 'with a basket in which I carried the bulk of the week's provisions – oatmeal, cake, eggs and butter. A supply of potatoes, sufficient to last some weeks, had already been sent on by cart; besides oatmeal for stirabout – our Irish word for porridge; and milk was bought daily in Carrick.' He was already regarded as the student of the family. But there was an almost complete lack of books. He inherited a small library from his uncle, another Father Walter McDonald, the parish priest of Templeorum; but even this brought him little more than some volumes of the *Dublin Penny Journal* and Alban Butler's *Lives of the Saints*. Even *Robinson Crusoe* had to be borrowed, as a rare treasure, from a friend. And he attributes some of his first lessons in 'the music of a sentence' to the ballads which he and his young friends would buy from pedlars. 'We read nothing and had nothing to read,' apart from the school texts, is his summing up of these earliest years. At the national school they had been taught the usual curriculum of 'reading, writing, arithmetic, geography, parsing and so on.' But even at Carrick he found no books to read; and the boys were not taught to write essays or even letters. His clearest recollection is that he had got to know 'every nook – almost every stone – in Carrick'; and of having loved nature study. He 'knew where the wild flowers blew and where the wild birds built their nests; there were few trees in the neighbourhood that I could not climb, and in the deepest water I was at my ease.'

Conditions were more encouraging when he went on to St. Kyran's College, Kilkenny, at the age of eleven. His uncle, who afterwards became Dean McDonald, was then president of the College, and he undertook to provide for his nephew's schooling. The College was still called St. Kyran's, but the name was changed later to St. Kieran's; and it has long been one of the chief Irish seminaries. In the eighteen-sixties it was divided into a senior department, reserved entirely for seminarists, and a junior department which included boys from Dublin and elsewhere, besides those who were intended to enter the seminary. Walter McDonald spent five years here; and his recollections are candidly critical, though by no means ungrateful. Within little more than twenty years of his arriving at St. Kyran's as a small boy, he was to be not only a professor at Maynooth but head of its post-graduate department. Yet he records that even at St. Kyran's, as a junior, he was taught little better than in his previous schools. 'We had indeed to write an essay now and then,' he recalls, 'which was a kind of exercise for me; but as we got no instruction as to how we should write, the results of our efforts must have been very crude.' He now had his first lessons in Latin and Greek and French, but his teacher was the prefect, who was 'a grown boy who had passed through the ordinary curriculum and was awaiting a place at Maynooth'. These prefects were paid very little for such teaching, but it 'gives them the first claim to the next vacancy at Maynooth.' Besides Latin and Greek and French, the prefects were expected to teach some geometry and algebra; but the system of teaching the classes was simply to 'work through so many pages of Latin or Greek Grammar, to be learnt by heart, and so many lines of a Latin or Greek author to translate. Parsing was treated as being no less important than translation, to define all the nouns and adjectives and to conjugate all the verbs, giving the rules of syntax in each case.'

Such teaching meant no more than seeing that each lesson was duly learned; but McDonald's recollection was that he did in this way learn grammar thoroughly, and he developed a retentive memory. He was thus able to keep well at the top of his class, though he had become a 'thoroughly idle lazy boy.' There were at least some books available for his reading. He even acquired some enthusiasm for the classics through reading Goldsmith's *Histories of Greece and Rome*. Reeve's *History of the Bible* also made him familiar with the great Bible stories. In more general reading he remembered chiefly Longfellow's *Evangeline* and some popular books bought from an itinerant bookseller such as T.D. Sullivan's *Speeches from the Dock,* and his brother, A.M. Sullivan's, *Story of Ireland*. He was sixteen when he left St. Kyran's in July 1870, as one of five candidates for matriculation at Maynooth. Only eleven years later he was to join the staff of Maynooth as one of its professors of theology; and it is not surprising that during his long association with Maynooth, the development of its library became one of his chief preoccupations.

In a retrospect on his five years of secondary schooling at St. Kyran's he stresses that 'from the literary point of view the great defect was a lack of attractive books, with time to read them. The teaching staff, too, was very defective; and this in turn was due, I fancy, to lack of means. Good professors require good pay; and as there was no endowment at St. Kyran's, while the pension was low, the President was forced to content himself with an inefficient staff, too few in numbers and not sufficiently prepared to teach. This lack of means – of endowment – was at the root of the whole misery. The College grounds and buildings, we used to hear, cost the diocese forty or fifty thousand pounds. It was a pity, if so, that they did not provide plainer buildings at half the cost, and put the other half into an endowment to maintain proper staff and equipment. For, with a staff thoroughly prepared and a sufficient library, you can have a College or University in any kind of tin or boarded shed; whereas the loveliest buildings are of no avail without cultivated brains to tenant and use them.'

Although his whole subsequent life was to be absorbed in intellectual pursuits, these school years at St. Kyran's had still failed to arouse his interest, even under the supervision of his uncle as its president. By his own account, he only 'just scraped through' the entrance examination for Maynooth. By good luck he knew part of the ode of Horace on which he was examined; but in the oral examination he gave such a poor performance that he was put back to the Humanity class, with the option of trying again for Rhetoric. Being painfully aware that he might fail altogether in a second attempt for Rhetoric, he decided to accept immediate admission to the lower class. Failure would not only disgrace his uncle, who had nominated him as a candidate; 'it certainly would have been the end of my studies for the priesthood,' he wrote long afterwards, 'and God alone knows what my life would have been.' As yet, he had not the remotest thought of even attempting any academic distinction. During his first year at Maynooth he 'remained the idle careless boy I had been at Kilkenny.' Discipline was more strict than what he had known hitherto, and some old customs still survived which were soon to disappear. For instance, all secular priests were still addressed as 'Mr.' unless they were doctors of divinity, and the word 'Father' was only used for friars. He noted afterwards that even in 1878 an obituary of Professor Crolly in the *Maynooth Calendar* described him as Mr. Crolly.

But an era of rapid transitions was just beginning, as a result of the Irish Church Act of 1871, which disestablished the Church of

Ireland and made other important changes. The Treasury supervision of Maynooth's accounts was now discontinued; and the whole government of Maynooth was handed over to the episcopal trustees, who at once assumed responsibility for enacting new statutes. One result was to reduce the burses that had previously been available to students out of Government funds; they now had to make good the difference themselves. This financial difficulty was so crippling in many cases that some students were given permission to shorten their courses. In this way Walter McDonald was allowed to 'jump' straight into the Logic class without having to pass through Rhetoric. Even so, he recalls that he began his second year at Maynooth 'pretty much as I had passed the first – quite careless and idle, without however indulging in any great irregularity.' His impressions of the teaching which prevailed in his student years are of special interest as showing the defects which he strove afterwards to overcome. While he complains repeatedly of the lack of text books, he speaks poorly of even the few text books that were available in some subjects. He attributes his first awakening of interest during his second year to existence of a text book in Logic, written in Latin by Professor Jennings, a former occupant of the chair. Though he became aware of its shortcomings later on, he learnt much from it. 'It gave me a firm grip of the construction of sentences. It was grammar, as much as logic – and more. There were of course syllogisms, with their rules, and words and figures with theirs; and sophisms; and certain criteria of certitude. I got through all this and liked it; knew what was in the text book, and was acquiring a new kind of command of Latin; all of which meant no little progress.' But in the next term, when he began Metaphysics in January, there was no text book, but only summaries of notes by one of the former Maynooth professors, Dr. Anglade; and even of these he could obtain no copy. On examining a copy in later years, he found that the notes seemed to be only 'a very bald rehash of Tourelli's treatise *De Deo,* which is in itself not very valuable. What a pity it was to see students at this poor *jejune* stuff, instead of a book, however poor; and above all, instead of a fairly good book – which might have been obtained rather easily.'

But his active critical faculty had now been aroused, and he had keen discussions with his fellow students. He began to 'tear to pieces not only the treatise of Anglade, but that of St. Sulpice, and even the sacred MSS., with the result that I did little more than criticise, and was in a very bad way when the midsummer examinations came around.' Luck helped him again, however. Dr. Molloy, who examined him, liked to pin students down to one special point, regardless of what they had learnt by heart. That suited Mc-Donald's own methods of study; and by showing some power of resistance he 'came off with flying colours.' Yet his general recollection of these critically formative years left him with the impression that 'there must have been something very wrong with the way in which we were taught philosophy, seeing that it failed so utterly to interest one like me.' In five years, he admitted readily that he never had a solid grounding in philosophy, and that this was one of his chief difficulties when he attempted to produce original work. He complains of having been kept 'to a dead grind of some old traditional statements of doctrine, proofs, and answers to objections; all very bald and imperfect – very unlike what one meets in the real world. Darwin was then revolutionising thought, but we overturned him in two or three brief sentences. Kant was a name of which we read in a paragraph of our books, with Fichte, Schelling, and Hegel, all visionaries.' The new leaders of materialist and agnostic thought, led by Huxley and Spencer, received even less attention. 'We were educated in a fool's paradise, as if we were still in the eighteenth, or even the sixteenth century.'

He was still only an 'average student,' and it was a surprise when he won a premium, 'though but among the thirds,' at the end of his second year. He had been working really hard at the course in Mathematics and Natural Philosophy. This included mechanics and astronomy and physics; but here, too, he recalls that he 'suffered a great deal from lack of teaching; for, in Mathematics especially, the professor examined us merely, but did not teach; and many short cuts were unknown to me.' His third year also included Ecclesiastical History; but here also he complains that there were 'no text books and we learned little or nothing. There were indeed in the divisional library some Histories of the Church in French; nineteen- or twenty-volumed works, into which we dipped now and then – those of us who could read French sufficiently well. But, as you may fancy, beginners at the subject were quite lost in forests of that kind.' More than any of the others, the professor of this subject at that time seemed to him incapable of teaching or arousing interest. He lacked perspective, so that 'every fact and date seemed of equal importance; and in that great panorama wherein so many thought and taught, and fought, and shaped the world or lost it, and died, the date of Luther's grandmother's birth, or the number of bishops who were present at some session or other of this council or that, was as engrossing as the struggles of Augustine or of Hildebrand.' The result was that his students neither read nor listened to his lectures on the history of the Church, 'nor did we care to read or listen.

It is not surprising that such criticisms of Maynooth's earlier conditions aroused resentment when Dr. McDonald's reminiscences were first published. There were still many who remembered the professors whom he criticised. But no one who knew him could misunderstand the earnestness of his desire to learn from the failures of the past and to insist upon improvement. With his entrance upon theological studies, in his fourth year at Maynooth, he found a distinct change. Text books were now available, and he had a professor who not only examined but taught. Dr. Molloy, who had recognised his capacity to think for himself, in his previous examination, was soon afterwards removed to Dublin, to become vice-rector of the Catholic University. He was succeeded by Dr. Walsh, who later became president of Maynooth and then Archbishop of Dublin. They were both men of outstanding ability and distinction. But McDonald insists that, even under their direction, his teaching had little cognisance of contemporary controversy. 'The only adversaries whom we recognised were the Protestants of these countries; Protestants, that is, of the old school, High Church men, Low Church men, Evangelicals and so on; all however Episcopalians; with a shot now and then at the Presbyterians, but little thought of the Congregationalists or Unitarians, or indeed, of the new rationalistic spirit which had begun already to wave over England and which has since become such a mighty force in all Protestant and most Catholic countries... We were behind our time; slaying foes that had been disabled or killed long ago, and unaware of, or closing our eyes to, the new method of attack; with the result that, while we were not in the least in danger of joining the Anglican or the Irish Protestant Church, some of us were painfully disturbed when we could no longer keep our eyes closed to the arguments of the Rationalists.'

Dr. McDonald's recollections of his professors at this period are critical, but he gives them full credit for their merits. Dr. Molloy, with many brilliant gifts, seemed to him to have frittered away his life on trifles. A year later, when he moved into the higher class, McDonald had two famous teachers, in Murray and Crolly. Murray, he insists, was 'clear, but then he did not go very deep'; and as he was 'more ultramontane than the Pope,' he 'had not sufficient sympathy with error to realise an adversary's position.' Murray used to say in jest that he personally never had the least temptation agains faith; and McDonald complains that he 'could not understand how a Catholic could have difficulty, not only about dogmas of faith but even about received teaching.' But at least Dr. Murray had collected a fine library of his own and he kept on adding to it every week on his visits to Dublin. McDonald recalls how his library 'overflowed to that of the Junior House; also to a reading-room sacred to the professor, which was then where the billiard room is now.' One of McDonald's first achievements at Maynooth was when he had been appointed librarian to the Junior House and he was required to dispose of that part of Dr. Murray's library. It had overflowed into this large room, which was being converted as a billiard room. Young McDonald put nearly all the books into the students library of St. Mary's division.

He remembers Murray's rooms as being 'quite bare of all but books, which were stored all round, in plain deal cases, well glazed. There was no carpet; nor pictures that I remember, except one of Suarez, such as may be found in the frontispiece of some old folio edition of his works.' Murray died while McDonald was still a student. So also did Crolly, whom McDonald remembers as a poor and confusing lecturer, though his books showed remarkable intellectual and literary abilities. In the Scripture course, which extended for some three years, McDonald found Dr. McCarthy similarly conservative and uninspiring. 'He was acquainted, no doubt, with the new theories of the German Rationalists; but they seemed to give him about as much trouble as the doctrine of the Mormons, or of the Koran, or the sacred books of the Buddhists. They were doctrines which never could take root in Ireland or trouble any one in these countries. In this respect he was simply a man of his time, in our College.'

These criticisms were written by Walter McDonald some forty years later, when he had become obsessed with the idea that Maynooth was in fact the training centre for priests who would minister in all parts of the world. When they went forth on this wider apostolate, they would live among peoples who did not share the Catholic faith, and who certainly would not share that sense of unquestioning conviction which dominated the Maynooth system in his own youth. He writes with real appreciation of their virtues, though he deplores their attitude towards contemporary life. 'The great strong, childlike faith of these men – *fides carbonarii*,' he writes, 'was just the thing which a preacher requires; and I have no doubt that they preached so well to us as to save most of us from any faith troubles. But it was not scientific; nor, however they may have preached, can they be allowed also the fame of first-rate professors. A great world-shaking movement had been in progress for some years in Germany; had even found support in England, as witness the Colenso episode; while our professors went calmly on their way, with a shrug at the most, or a sneer at a Church that could have any difficulty about dealing with the Colenso case. Dr. McCarthy had a fling now and then at Dean Alford or Dean Stanley, for throwing doubts on the inerrancy of the New Testament record; but we heard nothing of myths, or redactions, or later insertions, or of the Synoptic problem or of the many other commonplaces of modern Biblical criticism. Our strong, childlike faith kept us safe in the Middle Ages; which was well for such of us as could stay there always, but full of danger for any that could not.'

The professor of Irish appears as a specially pathetic figure, in these reminiscences. Dr. McDonald's recollections have acquired a special interest through subsequent developments. When he came to Maynooth as a student, Irish was still widely spoken in many dioceses. Even in his native County Kilkenny McDonald's father and mother were both native speakers; and many old people in the neighbourhood, when he was a child, could scarcely speak English. In later years Walter McDonald was to be the protagonist of Dr. O'Hickey when he was dismissed from the professorship of Irish at Maynooth, during the campaign to demand compulsory Irish in the new National University. In these early years he had shared the general indifference towards learning a language which was obviously dying. Nevertheless he attended classes given by the professor, an 'old man, white-haired and feeble; quite incapable of conducting a class,' and very different from the enthusiastic champions of the language who were appointed later. McDonald writes of him with real respect as a 'pious man zealous to hear confessions.' But he records sadly that 'being what he was, it was a pity that he did not remain on the mission – did not do anything rather than occupy in our College a chair for which he did not seem to have any other capacity than a speaking knowledge of the Irish language... he came to us for the greater part of the year; during which he never did more than call a student's name, ask him to read, then to translate; and to pass on to another man, to whom he gave the same command. This will tell you how the Irish language was taught at Maynooth College. I went into that class with an honest, though not very strong, intention of learning Irish; but gave up the effort after two or three lessons.

In contrast with these adverse criticisms, he pays a fine tribute to the Vincentian, Father Gowan, who taught preaching and the teaching of Christian doctrine. McDonald recalls him as 'a man of first rate ability' who 'preached not only with great earnestness but with true fire and eloquence.' He had a 'strong rough voice wherein there was no attempt to conceal the brogue, and he often gave an unfavourable impression first. But there were many of us whom he won over late or soon, and who came to look on that iron grey, rough, plain man not only with esteem but with admiration and reverence.' On the other hand the teaching of liturgy and sacred music was still sadly inadequate. 'The liturgy was taught by the Deans; the music by students of the College choir, or by nobody. Both were taught execrably or not at all; with the result that we left the College knowing indeed how to say the Divine Office and celebrate Mass; but with little or no knowledge of liturgy, and unable, most of us, to sing a Preface. Here again the Deans were at fault; and in the Liturgy they had a splendid subject, in teaching which they could, as Mr. O'Kane had done, rival the professors or even eclipse them. O'Kane, however, had no successor; and the Deans of my time earned nothing but contempt for the way in which they taught the Liturgy. As for Sacred Music, so little attention did it receive that it is no wonder the Requiem Office and High Mass for the Dead should be the abomination I have often heard; for which, instead of an honorarium, all concerned should of right receive a castigation.'[1]

These were the last years of Dr. Russell's presidency, and McDonald recalls his venerable figure, 'a tall spare, white haired, scholarly, priestly man whom everybody respected. He was one to be proud of, and we were proud of him.' His biography of the great Roman librarian and linguist Cardinal Mezzofanti had been translated into foreign languages; and he had been Newman's friend and confidant both before and after Newman's conversion. McDonald judges him to have been 'in many respects an admirable President; though he can hardly have been happy. For it now looks as if on becoming President, he committed the fault which so many men of his type commit – of giving up the line of work for which he was eminently suited, for one which did not suit him; a fault which always leads to misery and not infrequently to shipwreck. Before he became president, Dr. Russell had been professor of Ecclesiastical History; and knowing what we now know of him, through the revelations made by Fr. Russell (Fr. Matthew Russell, S.J., his nephew) he must have been almost ideally suited for that chair, and almost as ideally happy therein. On the other hand, he had not some qualities which were badly needed by a President of our College in his time – and at all times. He was by nature very loth to interfere with anyone, especially in a way to hurt one's feelings

1. The volume of his selected papers, entitled *The Manliness of St Paul* includes an impassioned protest against the frequent desecration of what he calls the 'Apocalypse Drama' of the Office for the Dead.

or cause pain; and if the impressions recorded in this book are anything like correct, he was called on to interfere, in a way which would be very likely to cause pain to many people. With his knowledge of books and of modern life, he must have known what the Church had need of in his day, and how much of that was lacking in the College of which he was the head. He can hardly have been unaware of the shortcomings of the Deans; of the imperfection of the different courses of study; of the disorder in the Bursar's department among the servants; and of the weakness of some of the professors. To remedy this he would have to admonish sharply, and even to report severely. This he could not do; so that one fears that the sad face which he always wore may have been due to a feeling that he was out of place – that he would have been much happier if he had remained in the chair of ecclesiastical history. And if he had remained there, or if his successor, Dr. Kelly, had not been taken away so young, what a difference it would have made to the fame of either, and to the fortunes of our College. Good Presidents are very well; but good Professors are so much more rare – and better.'

Dr. Russell received a notable tribute in Newman's *Apologia*, as having 'had perhaps more to do with my conversion than any one else... He sent me at different times several letters; he was always gentle, mild, unobtrusive, uncontroversial. He let me alone. He also gave me one or two books.' That was written in 1857; and Russell's connection with Newman's conversion was well known at Maynooth long before McDonald went there as a student. Yet Maynooth was still miserably unequipped with books for its own students. McDonald mentions a curious difficulty which arose in this respect during the three years of his theology course from 1873 to 1876. 'Books circulated among us freely,' he writes, 'poetry, history, essays, but not novels. At that time we used to appoint students as agents with the booksellers for books which those agents sold to us; and as these agents were supplied freely, and we had free access to their rooms, while they did not press for payment we bought some books or borrowed those which had been bought by others. Anyway we had a fair supply; and some of us made use of them. The credit system on which we worked led of course to very unpleasant results, as the agents were not able to meet the bookseller's bills. And so feeble were the superiors that, when this was brought to their notice, they could think of no remedy except forbid these agencies in future.' Apart from this haphazard purchase of books by students, he writes sadly that 'all this time the library at the disposal of students was poor and uninteresting. It contained Suarez, de Lugo, Billiart, the Salamanca Course;

besides many-volumed Histories of the Church and such things; but then we did not read much of Suarez or de Lugo, except here and there on some easy moral question; nor were we able to read them with interest... I read Carriere's treatise *De Matrimonio* with interest and profit right through; till I came to the rules for applying for dispensations; where I stopped, as our professor Dr. Murray told us that part of the subject was only for Bishops, Vicars General and others – such as we should not be for a long time.'

He found the divisional library 'of some use for Ecclesiastical History; of very little use for Theology; and of none, practically, for general reading.' When he asked permission for the privilege of reading in the College library during a special fortnight, when he would be left almost alone in the College as sacristan for the clergy retreat, he was told that the request was without precedent, and was sternly refused. Another recollection of these years reflects the severe discipline which still prevailed. During his second year's Divinity some of the students bought a football and began to kick it in St. Mary's grounds after dinner. A conference among the authorities ensued and they were informed that a football could not be allowed. One of the students 'who subsequently became a well known priest in Pennsylvania' kept the football in his own rooms for a year, until it was suddenly brought out again. This time the football was confiscated and McDonald comments 'that was the beginning and end of the football game in the College in my time. I wonder are there many other things now banned as innovations and dangerous which would turn out harmless enough on trial.' But he sums up his general recollections of his student years at Maynooth as having been 'almost ideally happy after I grew serious and began to work hard and to observe the rule.' A slight shadow of the future, he admits, fell on him in his last year, in the shape of loneliness on being partly separated from his class, when he was appointed monitor of St. Joseph's Division. But he concludes 'the independence of the life at Maynooth had a charm for me. I knew no fear, whether of professor or dean; and if called on, would have spoken truth, however unpleasant, to the College of Cardinals; for I had no notion that an honest well meaning man could be injured by anyone, and especially by any ecclesiastic.'

An interval of five years interrupted this happy phase of contentment and hard study, before he returned to Maynooth for the remainder of his life. He had completed his time in 1876, as the theology course had been reduced to three years, since the disendowment which had seriously curtailed the revenues of Maynooth. He was still a year under age for ordination, but he had received deacon's orders and was otherwise qualified to be ordained. His bishop, Dr. Moran (who soon afterwards went to Australia and there became the first Australian Cardinal), needed help for the diocesan seminary, St. Kieran's. McDonald was accordingly recalled from Maynooth before ordination and appointed dean at St. Kieran's. He was to have 'general charge of the whole College under the President and special charge of the lay house.' He was also to be a professor, of philosophy, besides having a class in English. Hitherto he had never expected any appointment other than pastoral work in his native diocese; and his recall from Maynooth before ordination suggested that Bishop Moran thought he would gain nothing by spending an additional year of study there. The change to St. Kieran's removed him at once from the happy companionship which he had enjoyed greatly at Maynooth. As dean at St. Kieran's he would be very isolated, all the more because he was only a deacon and was therefore separated from the rest of the staff and could not even go for walks with them. He found it 'an awful change from Maynooth,' and he wrote several times to his uncle, who was then Dean of Kilkenny, begging that he might be removed anywhere to the mission. But in fact Bishop Moran had already recognised his abilities, and he obtained from Rome a dispensation to permit his earlier ordination.

On October 14, 1876, he was ordained; and he continued as dean at St. Kieran's for four more years. Practical experience as a teacher induced him to specialise; and his gifts for teaching soon led to his lecturing the whole school and not only the lay house. After the first year he was relieved of administrative duties, and put in charge of the classes in Dogmatic Theology and Philosophy. He relied at first upon the notes he had brought from Maynooth, but he soon found them lacking in depth and he sought for wider sources. It was not merely, he wrote, 'that the notions I took away from (Maynooth) were often shallow; but what was worse, there was so much that I had not read at all and of which I had not even shallow notions.' Once again he craved for more books, and during this interlude at Kilkenny he got the President's permission to form a Literary Society, whose members paid a small annual subscription towards buying books. He thus formed the nucleus of a general library, and students began to give up part of their recreation to reading. About this time, also, Canon Smithwick died in his Dublin parish, and bequeathed all his books to St. Kieran's. McDonald had them placed at the disposal of the students. He adds significantly that it was through this bequest from Canon Smithwick that he first became acquainted with Thackeray, whose works were constantly with him afterwards, and also with Tennyson. In

Kilkenny also he had invaluable early practice in preaching and he prepared his sermons with great care, 'remembering Father Gowan's warnings against florid writing and exaggeration and un-truth of every kind.' He was reading as deeply as he could in all directions.

One result of these early years of intensive study was that he began to cut into his necessary hours of sleep, especially after he had been appointed chaplain to the Loreto convent, with an early Mass each morning. Insomnia affected his nerves; and by his own account, brought new psychological troubles and doubts even re-garding the foundations of faith. These neurotic fears, he wrote afterwards, 'have haunted and troubled me all my life, making it at times such a torture as only those can realise who have gone through the ordeal.' But his years at St. Kieran's made him happy in his work and he records gratefully that he 'retained the same spirit of fearlessness and independence that I had at Maynooth, conscious that I was working hard, and with at least average suc-cess.' He sent an essay to the *Dublin Review* which was rejected, and this cured him, for the time, of all ambition to publish origi-nal work. He had no thought of competing for a professorship at Maynooth, or anywhere else, and he was fully content with the prospect of continuing to teach at St. Kieran's 'until I should be appointed to some parish, first as a curate and then as parish priest.'

In the summer of 1881, when he was twenty-eight and had been ordained five years, he had begun his two months of holiday when his uncle Dean McDonald sent for him urgently. It was to say that Bishop Moran desired that he should compete for one of the chairs of theology which was then vacant at Maynooth. The concursus to elect a new professor was to be held within five weeks time. McDonald's recollections are characteristic, both of his humility and of his conviction that he should refuse no labour. The proposal cut across the whole plan he had formed of his future life, and he had moreover a poor opinion of his own abilities. But he set to work at once, and in October, 1881, he was appointed to the vacant chair. It meant leaving many good friends at St. Kieran's, but it was a relief to be free of having to give more than twenty hours of lectures every week, which left no time for private studies. 'Professors, if they are to be happy or efficient,' he insisted after-wards, 'must have plenty of time for private reading and writing too.' He was determined to live up to these convictions when he became a professor; but it is not surprising that, with his restricted training up to that time, he was soon involved in difficulties.

Returning to Maynooth after five years absence, he found Dr. Walsh installed as President. The Dunboyne Establishment for postgraduate students had been revived two years previously, with Dr. Murray as its Prefect. His two colleagues as professors of theology were Dr. O'Donnell, who was later to become Primate and Cardinal, and Dr. Healy who was to become Archbishop of Tuam. Dr. Macaulay was professor of Scripture and Dr. Gargan of Ecclesiastical History. There was surprisingly little social intercourse among the professors, and they lived in small groups, who were soon divided by the political controversies of the Land League and Parnell's agitation. McDonald's recollections of the staff at this time show that the older men inherited the Whig tradition and had no sympathy with either Parnell or the Land League. McDonald was soon siding with the younger group among whom Dr. O'Donnell was the leader, 'against the Gladstonians and the Respectables.' Four years later Dr. Walsh was to leave Maynooth and become Archbishop of Dublin. McDonald writes regretfully of his absorption in the administrative duties of the Presidency, which kept him from all original work. He considered that Dr. Walsh had the ability to 'write a solid book which would prepare men's minds for acceptance of the lines of reform needed in the Canon Laws as affecting the Irish Church. He had it in him to do the work that was needed, but chose to fritter away his time on the University question, Bimetallism, public addresses, and letters to the newspapers.' Nevertheless it was Dr. Walsh who brought to McDonald's attention a small text book which directed his studies to new fields. This short primer of Philosophy, by St. George Mivart, contained discussions of contemporary difficulties which 'stimulated me in a way I had never felt before. It was the beginning of a new life – the life which I have led ever since and which I am likely to lead while I live at all, the only life worth living, apart from the service of God, which may be found in any life to which He calls us, were it only in Milton's phrase to 'stand and wait'.'

In the years after his appointment as professor of theology, several important incidents affected the status and duties of professors. McDonald soon became associated with the assertion of academic duties and rights. Dr. Walsh was still president when the Royal University was established in 1882, and soon afterwards a number of fellowships in the Royal University were provided. Dr. Walsh insisted, with success, that three or four of these fellowships should be allotted to Maynooth, while the others went to the College in Stephens Green or to the Medical School in Cecilia Street. This had unexpected results in diverting some of the staff to such subjects as Moral Philosophy and English, which thus became better endowed than the professorships of theology. The arrangement was only provisional; but it produced some appointments which did not seem justified on grounds of academic distinction, and the younger professors, including McDonald, became concerned to demand a more effective system of making appointments. Their independent attitude was strengthened when the famous letter *Quidquid de Parnellio* denouncing the Land League, was issued from the Vatican after Mgr. Persico's mission of inquiry in Ireland. An appeal for subscriptions to a presentation to Parnell had just been issued, and some of the younger Maynooth professors decided to subscribe openly notwithstanding the Vatican letter. Five memebers of the staff, Drs. Hackett, Boylan, O'Donnell, O'Dea and McDonald, sent a joint subscription over their names, in a letter which was published in the *Freeman's Journal*. They were well aware that both Dr. Walsh and the vice-president, Dr. Carr, disapproved of their action; and the Trustees at their next meeting passed a resolution which was to be shown privately to the five signatories, though it was not to be entered upon the minute book of the College. Its purport, according to McDonald, was 'to the effect that members of the College staff are to abstrain from taking a side on public questions as to which the bishops of Ireland disagreed.' This demand involved a principle which was to concern McDonald and other professors deeply in later years. It became directly relevant during the agitation for compulsory Irish in the National University; and in that controversy Cardinal Logue declared publicly that Dr. O'Hickey was entirely free to advocate 'essential Irish, provided he did so temperately and respectfully.' But at this earlier stage such academic freedom for professors was by no means admitted. In his reminiscences McDonald comments 'and indeed why should not a professor at Maynooth be at liberty to take a side, publicly, on such a question, even though some of their Lordships might have advocated the contrary opinion? Think of a professor of Trinity College or Oxford being forbidden to avow himself a Liberal or a Conservative as long as the members of the Board were divided in their allegiance.'

In this demand for greater academic freedom for the staff, Dr. O'Donnell, het future Primate and Cardinal, was one of the most active reformers. Of the others in the same group, Dr. O'Dea became bishop of Galway. Dr. O'Donnell was concerned in another incident soon afterwards. Dr. Murray died and was succeeded as Prefect of the Dunboyne by Dr. Healy, who a year later was appointed coadjutor bishop of Clonfert. His promotion created a difficult situation, because all the three professors of theology were now very young priests. Even Dr. O'Donnell, the oldest of them, had been still a student only four years previously. They learned that Dr. Walsh, as president, had written to Dr. Murphy in Carlow, 'practically offering him the vacant position if he would take it.' On the advice of Father Boylan, the three young professors sent a formal letter to the Trustees of Maynooth, claiming that they had each won their chairs by concursus and that they should not be passed over in favour of anyone who had not given similar proof. They asked that the vacancy should at least be filled by a concursus, at which one of the three present professors would compete. Their protest prevailed and Dr. O'Donnell was appointed Prefect of the Dunboyne.

Later experience was to shake McDonald's earlier conviction that a concursus was the best method of finding the most suitable candidate. He notes that he had himself subsequently recommended the appointment of certain professors without a concursus; 'but this only on the recommendation of the Faculty which he would join, the members of which moreover would not be empowered to recommend for the vacant chair anyone who had not given proof, by published writings, of his fitness for the position.' His intervention against Dr. Murphy in this case had been specially significant, because they were old and intimate friends. But Dr. Murphy had not yet written or published even an article in the *Irish Ecclesiastical Record;* and his appointment as head of the Dunboyne in such circumstances could not have been defended. So Dr. O'Donnell became Prefect of the Dunboyne at the age of twenty-eight in 1884. But his abilities and distinction were so marked that in 1888 he was nominated to the See of Raphoe. He continued as its bishop until 1922, when he was made coadjutor to Cardinal Logue as Archbishop of Armagh, and after a few years succeeded him as Primate.

By the time of Dr. O'Donnell's promotion to Raphoe, McDonald had already made his mark so strongly that his succession as prefect of the Dunboyne was taken for granted. It was so generally assumed, that McDonald asked two of the most important bishops to propose and second him. His own bishop, Dr. Brownrigg, would not be able to attend the meeting of the Trustees; so he asked Archbishop Walsh, as a former president and colleague, and Archbishop Croke, to be his two sponsors. In retrospect, with his keen sense of independence, he regretted even that he had done so. 'This was the only occasion in my life,' he wrote in his *Reminiscences,* 'when I asked anyone to recommend me for promotion and I have since regretted – as I do still – that I asked then. Nor should I have done so were it not that I felt assured there was no question of appointing anyone but me.'

The Dunboyne Establishment had been originally founded, with very slender resources, to provide special courses of study for a small number of advanced students. It arose from the endowment left to Maynooth by Theobald Fitzwalter Butler, twelfth Baron Dunboyne, who died in May 1800. He had inherited the barony and considerable estates in 1786, on the death of his young nephew, the eleventh baron; and at that time he had been Bishop of Cork since 1763. His story illustrates vividly the temptations to apostasy which weighed upon Catholics under the penal laws. He had been an exemplary ruler of his See under the restrictions of the code; but his inheritance of the title and the estates created an opportunity to retain both in Catholic hands. He actually applied to Rome for a dispensation to resign his See and to marry, so that he might provide an heir. The request was of course refused; but Bishop Butler thereupon resigned, and publicly conformed to the Protestant Church in order to retain his civil rights. Before his death he repented of his apostasy and bequeathed to Maynooth his estates in County Meath, which provided an income of £1,000 a year, subject to an annuity of £200 for his widow. His will was immediately contested by the Protestant relatives, with allegations that he had been formally reconciled to the Catholic Church before he died. An extraordinary lawsuit ensued, in which the Protestants claimed that he had died a Catholic and so forfeited the estates, while the Catholics denied that he had been formally reconciled. Eventually a compromise was reached which was sanctioned by a special Act of Parliament in 1809. The Maynooth trustees received part of Lord Dunboyne's Meath estate, producing £500 a year, on payment of £1,000 to the other claimant. It was agreed with the Government that this income of nearly £500 a year should be devoted exclusively to the Dunboyne Establishment. The Government added a further £700 a year, so that twenty students could be maintained, with an endowment of £50 for each student. The first students appointed under these conditions were chosen in 1813 and a formal constitution for them was published in the statutes for 1820. Three years later a Prefect of the Dunboyne Establishment was appointed, but there were considerably less than twenty of these 'senior' students and the funds were spent largely on providing accommodation.

In 1878 a new constitution was established. Dr. McDonald as Prefect of the Dunboyne supplied for Archbishop Healy's centenary *History of Maynooth*, a summary of the revised constitution of the Establishment. He explains that the number of students entitled to the special allowance of £ 25 a year was restricted to ten, but that other 'students qualified by their studies for election to the Dunboyne House but not entitled to a Burse herein, may be admitted at the request of their Bishops as Dunboyne students on payment of the ordinary College pension.' They were to be selected by the Scholastic Council, with the usual power of veto by the President, and their selection was to be made in accordance with the already recognised claims of the provinces: but if any province had no suitable candidate the vacancy could be filled *pro tem* from another province. Students were eligible for the Dunboyne only on completing their fourth year of theology, and they must have got one premium in Theology and one in Sacred Scripture. The special studies to be pursued in the Dunboyne course were Dogmatic and Moral Theology, Canon Law and Ecclesiastical History, besides the Hebrew, French, German and Italian languages.

McDonald's appointment as Prefect was made the occasion for certain changes in the curriculum, which had his entire approval. Earlier occupants had been expected to lecture in Ecclesiastical History and also in Canon Law, besides teaching Theology. McDonald was exempted from teaching Ecclesiastical History, but he continued for some years to teach Canon Law, besides both Dogmatic and Moral Theology. After some years, when Maynooth was empowered to give degrees in theology, he was relieved also of teaching Canon Law. He observes that 'whereas in the old times the students had had but one professor, practically – not counting the professor of Hebrew who lectured once a week – now they had several.' They could by special arrangement take modern languages instead of theology, which was McDonald's chief concern. He soon succeeded in altering the system under which the Dunboyne students had been required to 'hold one of those dreary disputations every month.' He prevailed upon the Visitors to limit these disputations to one at the end of every term. He also reduced the programme of languages, believing that 'to force students of Theology while pursuing a postgraduate course to learn in addition several languages, is to make them attend lectures in which they take no interest, and for which they make no preparation – the very worst thing you can do with a man.' Before long, he had also introduced a change in the method of teaching, insisting that in the disputations which were held each day on the text books, the 'really important points' should be faced. Often, he writes, 'they did not know what was important; and sometimes, for lack of preparation, they found it easier to spend the hour on some old time wrangle, of no bearing whatever on modern life or thought.'

So McDonald began to intervene more actively in their discussions. He was soon 'confining the discussion in class to the more difficult questions, while leaving easier ones for private study.' After some years the discussions had developed into 'conferences.' Writing after 25 years experience, he said 'we still have some formal disputations towards the close of each term; but as a rule we make the class hour a conference, wherein the students are encouraged to propose any difficulties they may feel. And as difficulties are so common, and so much more easy to propose than to solve, the Prefect, whose duty it is to find a solution for all, has his work cut out for him; especially if he be resolved, as I have tried to be, never to ride off by confusing the issue or throwing dust in the eyes of his hearers.' He found this continual exercise in controversy thoroughly congenial, especially when he challenged ideas or theories which were generally accepted, and propounded new solutions which were not. It was 'good for both sides. Few professors, I fancy, have had anything like the advantage I have had, in hearing my teaching criticised in this way, year after year, by a number of clever young men, who, if they accepted it at all, did so only with great reluctance. I have always welcomed this criticism and tried to profit by it, lopping off or modifying any part of my teaching which I could not defend to the satisfaction of my own conscience.' He prided himself on ensuring that his students were always 'allowed and exercised the fullest liberty of opinion. They were, moreover, allowed to defend their opinions and criticise mine with perfect freedom; and if at times their arguments were met with undue ardour on my part, they understood, I hope, that the heat which I showed was evoked, not by any feeling of resentment, so much as by love of truth, joined to keen dislike of the old world prejudices, whereby as I have long believed, progress in philosophical and theological sciences is so much retarded.'

This vigorous enjoyment of controversy attracted him inevitably to problems arising out of the new discoveries of science, which appeared at that time to have much more revolutionary implications than they do now. He states his position broadly in his *Reminiscences*. 'Accordingly, as years went by on the Dunboyne Establishment, I realised more and more that it was not for me a question merely of learning what had been taught; but of harmonising it – as much of it as would harmonise – with itself, and with other truths which one has to accept as such. And as I could not begin with exegesis, history and philosophy, all at once; not at least with all those equally, extensively and minutely; I took up what came readiest to me; which, owing to my bent of mind and previous studies, was philosophy.' Explaining some of the difficulties which confronted him, he continues: 'And yet I must say, I found or seemed to find – that the main lines of the traditional arguments and conclusions could be retained; in many cases modified, no doubt; that when so modified, they received a new strength from the now so much clearer teaching of natural science on which they depend. Instead of rejecting incontinently the new knowledge of nature, I strove to see whether it might not be retained as a handmaid; and I am satisfied myself that it could. How far this satisfaction was justified, my writings must be left to show. But, of course, as I rejected any part of the traditional teaching, I was bound to come into conflict with the more conservative body of theologians; and as a pioneer in a humble way, was bound to suffer. That was anticipated, as part of the day's work; and as such I hope has been accepted.' He recalls how 'this double conflict – of science with traditional and official teaching and of criticism with the Bible – absorbed my attention for years, so that I had little time except, indeed, to keep myself satisfied, as a kind of outsider, with regard to the historical reliability, in the main, of the books of which the New Testament is composed. Keeping myself so satisfied, I devoted almost my whole attention to the science of theology, as such.'

This boldly independent attitude as a teacher, and the exciting methods of discussion with his students which he employed, were at all times well known to the Trustees of Maynooth. They appear to have imposed no restrictions upon either his subjects or his methods. They had special opportunities for observing his work, because the Trustees, after he became Prefect, had ordered that the old practice of publicly defending certain theses should be revived, as the concluding act of each year; 'so that every year we had to draw up a body of theses such as we might hope to defend against all comers – professors and others.' McDonald determined from the outset that the defence of such theses should be entirely unrestricted. He had himself 'reached the stage at which I was dissatisfied with much of the tradition – its conclusions, arguments, explanations; and I felt it cruel to expose young men to the ordeal of a public bombardment, against which, as I felt, they could no longer defend themselves on traditional lines. Such an exhibition would be, I thought, a disgrace to the Dunboyne Establishment, and to the science of theology of which it ought to be the home. And so, rightly or wrongly, I deemed myself bound in love of truth and honour, to have recourse to no chicanery or subterfuge; but to propose Catholic teaching such as I should represent it to real inquirers and adversaries, and to defend it only by such arguments and explanations as I should advance in conversation or controversy with them. This meant putting my own conscientious view of the question – whatever it was – before the students; and to leave no room for doubt, I drew up the theses, doing my best to outline therein the arguments wherewith I should defend them, and the solutions that I should give to the main difficulties which I felt myself. These collections of theses, sometimes amounting to near three hundred, were published regularly in the College Calendar.'

No one who reads McDonald's *Reminiscences* can fail to realise the enormous disadvantages under which he laboured in attempting such a personal effort. He was only thirty-five when he was appointed Prefect of the Dunboyne, and he had been a professor at Maynooth for only seven years before that appointment. During his previous years at Kilkenny, when he had never thought of becoming a professor of theology, he had no scope for deep study; and in his earlier years at Maynooth his own recollections show that he had not even begun to read seriously at that stage. He was further handicapped by the lack of a modern library; and he had very few opportunities for discussing his problems with specialists or experts. Yet he had already begun his efforts to 'purify and develop the science of theology,' and he never had any hesitation in challenging traditional views. It is not surprising that, when his opinions were set forth publicly in the collections of theses which were published in the College Calendar each year, they aroused opposition from some of his colleagues. The first serious trouble arose at the end of the academic year 1893-94, when the thesis *De Gratia*, which he had prepared for the public disputation in June 1894, had been printed and distributed to the professors of theology and to other members of the staff. The senior professor of Dogmatic Theology at this time was Dr. Coghlan[1], who subsequently became Bishop of Cork. He wrote formally to McDonald on Sunday, June 24, stating his objection:–

'Dear Dr. McDonald,
    The subject matter of this letter has caused me very great embarrassment. The doctrine which you enunciate in the chapter *De Modo Agendae Gratiae in Natura* seems to me clearly opposed to Faith. With this conviction on my mind I could not

1. After his appointment as Bishop of Cork, Dr. Coghlan regularly spelt his name as Cohalan.

allow the matter to pass unchallenged. I have accordingly referred the matter to the President. I would have given you earlier notice if I could have made up my mind what to do, or even if I were definitely determined to do anything in the matter. Yours faithfully,

Daniel Coghlan.'

A long controversy, which extended over years, was to follow upon this intervention by Dr. Coghlan, and the whole story is set out at great length in McDonald's *Reminiscences*. The President, Dr. Browne, came to see McDonald about the letter. McDonald advised him to consult the Council of Studies, which consisted chiefly of the professors of theology and he also asked that Dr. Coghlan should state precisely what theses, or parts, he considered objectionable. The Council then met and McDonald felt that he should not attend it. He was then shown the passages which had been underlined. He refused to withdraw them, as he could see nothing unorthodox in them. A compromise was then reached, allowing the disputation to be held, but omitting these particular theses from the College Calendar. McDonald considered that this compromise was a defeat for himself, because he felt that, if he could not teach these views in his class, 'There was nothing for it but to resign my chair; which I was resolved not to do without a struggle, not for myself alone but for the doctrine. I would have a definite doctrinal decision against me before I should resign; and I was not without hope that the authorities would be very slow to take up any definite position in the doctrinal question at issue.' A full statement of the dispute is to be found in McDonald's *Reminiscences,* and it would be impossible to attempt a summary here. To later readers, a most interesting aspect of the controversy is to note, on one side, the unflinching courage with which McDonald insisted upon the necessity of freedom to teach what he believed to be true, and on the other, the remarkable absence of any direct restraint upon his freedom by the Trustees. McDonald then set himself to write a series of papers 'into which, as I thought, I could put all I had to say on the subject.' But the papers soon expanded into a substantial book, which he published several years later, in 1898, under the title, *Motion, Its Origin and Conservation.*

The book was before long delated to Rome, and after some delay McDonald was ordered to withdraw it from publication. McDonald himself was fully aware of its limitations; and it is important to note his own candid admissions of its inadequacy. 'It was written,' he explains in his *Reminiscences,* 'under great difficulties; owing, in the first place, to vastness and complexity of the subject, which comprised all the physical sciences as well as metaphysics and theology. I could not of course pretend to any deep knowledge of any one of the physical sciences; but could, at most, show that the kinetic theory was advocated by all, or nearly all, the experts in these subjects; and indicate possibly, how they proposed hereby to explain some of the most striking phenomena. Even this, for one of my training, would be hard to do. Then there was the difficulty of getting help; as those who knew physics had no knowledge of, and little care for, metaphysics; while the metaphysicians and theologians were almost entirely ignorant of the new physics of which, at best, I might hope to teach something when my book was published... No wonder, then, that there are mistakes in the book; though, so far as I know, they are few and, with one exception, unimportant.'

Moreover, as he admitted freely, he was deliberately challenging 'active, extensive and powerful opposition from the metaphysicians and theologians.' Few professors in any country would have ventured to make such a daring attempt. It is vastly to the credit of Maynooth, as well as of McDonald himself, that his motives were never doubted, and that, in spite of the official condemnation of his book, he continued for the rest of his life as professor of theology and also Prefect of the Dunboyne Establishment. He never had any illusions about escaping opposition. 'I was about – there could be no denying it – to run counter to the *consensus theologorum*; to propound novel doctrine, on one of the most touchy points in all metaphysics and theology; to lecture Thomist and Molinist alike on the famous question *De Auxiliis*; to admonish them that they had all alike been arguing principles of physics which physicists have now discarded; and to tell them that it is no wonder they could not agree, and that each party could prove so conclusively that the other was wrong. What mercy or fair hearing had I to expect from either school?' With such anticipations clearly in mind, McDonald submitted advance proofs of his book to the censor and to others whose opinions he thought of special value. In the autumn of 1897, some months before the book appeared, he was invited to read a paper at the International Scientific Congress at Fribourg. He took that opportunity to proclaim openly his disputed views in a paper on *The Kinetic Theory of Activity*, which was duly published in the Proceedings of the Fribourg Congress, and also in the *Irish Ecclesiastical Record* for October 1897. He had thus given ample notice of what his forthcoming book would contain. The book appeared at the beginning of 1898. McDonald was soon informed that his colleague, Dr.

Coghlan, would publish in the *Irish Ecclesiastical Record* a series of articles challenging the orthodoxy of his views. But the prospect of such a controversy between two Maynooth professors seemed undesirable, and Dr. Coghlan's articles did not appear, although he returned to the same subject some eight years later in the summer of 1906.

The bishops had, however, learned of the impending controversy, and their Standing Committee decided in April 1898 that the matter should be referred to Rome. They sent him no formal letter of disapproval, or even direct instructions, but they deputed his friend and former colleague, Bishop O'Donnell, to write to him, on their behalf, as a personal friend. The letter instructed him that he should submit his book to the judgment of the Holy See as soon as he conveniently could; that he should abstain from teaching these doctrines pending a decision from Rome; and that he should privately impress upon any professors whom he knew to be favourable to the kinetic theory, that they also were to use similar reservations in their classes. Bishop O'Donnell's letter concluded, 'There was only one feeling at the meeting of the Episcopal Committee as to the learning and ability of the book, or as to the purpose and piety of the author. But in all the circumstances of the case the Bishops thought that the submission *by yourself* of this work to the Holy See is what any private friend ought to advise, or at least what a friendly body who had the responsibilities of the Bishops on their shoulders should direct. In writing to Cardinal Ledochowski it would be well, I take the liberty to say, to state your position in the College, and the inconvenience that would arise if the doctrine were taught for some years and the Holy See by any chance afterwards issued a *tolerari non potest*. This, without any mention of the Bishops, would seem to meet the requirements of the case. I have only to add that if one of themselves were concerned, there could not be more friendliness and esteem expressed than the Bishops evidenced at the meeting in your regard. In giving full effect to their Lordship's directions there does not appear to be any reason for the College body being told what has been done.'

McDonald himself, in publishing this letter in his *Reminiscences*, comments that 'if the book were to be submitted to Rome by order of the Bishops, I do not see how the orders could have been given in any more kindly, paternal, even friendly spirit than breathes through this letter. I felt this at the time; and ever since, however I may have differed with their Lordships, I have never had the least doubt whether as to the purity of their motives or as to the kindliness of their feelings towards myself personally.

It has often been a very real and grievous trouble to come into conflict with a body of men, all of whom have been so good and kind, and many of them so friendly.' Nevertheless he felt that the Bishops had placed him at a disadvantage in requiring that he should submit his book for a judicial pronouncement before it had time to be considered. It had, he knew, raised a 'new and very abstruse question.' The kinetic theory was 'new, at least to the schools of metaphysics and theology; and we know how theologians are startled by whatever wears even the appearance of novelty. If you take any new opinion and send it at once to Rome, what can you expect but condemnation? Whereas if discussion were permitted, so that it could be seen that there were some learned and pious men who did not regard the opinion in question as so very dangerous, possibly thought it the reverse, the officials at Rome would be much more tolerant.' A more troublesome result of the controversy was the prohibition of discussion of his theories by other professors, pending a decision from Rome. McDonald resented this prohibition at least as deeply as he did the suppression of his book. 'Who on earth,' he wrote afterwards, 'was going to read my book on Motion except philosophers and theologians? And apart from the most expert, how many would realise what my opinions were, or what the controversy was about? He was so accustomed to free criticism by his own students, and he had encouraged controversy so earnestly, that he could see no sense in disguising the fact that two professors might be shown to disagree.

With these objections in mind, he replied to Bishop O'Donnell's letter by asking for further instructions on certain points. He already expected condemnation of his book, if it were referred to Rome under such conditions. 'I was thinking of throwing up my chair,' he recalls, 'and with it the struggle for reform, if the decision of Rome should be unfavourable, as I feared and felt it would be.' The subsequent proceedings produced a protracted correspondence which is fully summarised in McDonald's *Reminiscences*. But the most interesting aspect, to a later generation for whom McDonald's pioneer work must already seem obsolete, lies in the relations between Maynooth and its extremely daring and earnest young Prefect of the Dunboyne. He had already been able to expound his theories in his address to the Congress in Fribourg, which was subsequently published in the *Irish Ecclesiastical Record*. He now referred the question to several distinguished theologians in Louvain, including Mgr. Mercier, to ask their views about what the probable attitude of Rome would be. The Dominican Père de Munnynck told him 'very frankly that my book would be condemned, and that in his opinion it deserved to be, as it was unorthodox in the sense of being opposed to some of the dogmas of faith.' Mgr. Mercier also gave him little encouragement, but he did not express the downright opposition of Père de Munnynck.

In fact the book was condemned by the Sacred Congregation of the Index on December 15, 1898. The decree was sent a month later by Cardinal Ledochowski to the Archbishop of Dublin, Dr. Walsh, who had been president of Maynooth during McDonald's early years as a professor. The Archbishop forwarded the decree to McDonald personally, 'very kindly and sympathetically.' It declared that the work entitled *'Motion, Its Origin and Conservation,'* was to be prohibited, but that the decree was to remain unpublished, 'out of regard for the fair name of Maynooth College, as well as in consideration of the right dispositions of mind displayed by the author.' The author was, however, to be required to 'withdraw from publication, as far as can be, all the copies of his book, to renounce the opinions therein contained and to abstain in future from further teaching the same.' The condemnation was none the less disappointing because it was expected, but McDonald at once 'made the recantation which was required of me, and promised to do my best to withdraw the book from circulation.' It had been published jointly by Burns and Oates in London and Browne and Nolan in Dublin, and he told the publishers quite openly what had happened. As he wrote afterwards, he 'was not prepared to show that I felt ashamed or disgraced. I hoped... and the hope has grown with me... that the day may come, perhaps long after I have passed away, when Maynooth College will be proud to claim the author of 'Motion' as one of her professors.' But whereas withdrawal of the book from circulation was easy, he was left without any clear direction as to what precise opinions it had been condemned, and what he was to avoid teaching in future. 'I was resolved,' he writes, 'to comply strictly with the commands of my ecclesiastical superiors. I was no less resolved to know precisely what I was to avoid, and to teach nothing but what I believed to be true.'

After much thought he sent to Cardinal Ledochowsky an explanatory letter, containing twenty-six of his disputed theses, and asked for directions. The Cardinal wrote back, after some three months interval, saying that it was unusual for the Index to make schedules of erroneous propositions. He had, however, submitted McDonald's theses to 'two grave consultors' and their animadversions were enclosed for his instruction. McDonald was gratified to find that these animadversions did not express any condemnation of his propositions as being 'directly opposed to revealed doctrines.' He saw that he was being confronted with the opinions of two Roman theologians, whom he suspected of having given only a perfunctory study to his views. Meanwhile he had discovered a number of essays and books by eminent authorities in France which appeared to support his own views; and he wrote again to Cardinal Ledochowski calling his attention to them. It was not surprising that the Cardinal, in a friendly reply, pointed out that he 'could not be expected to carry on a private theological controversy' and would only give his advice. That was, that he should refer the matter to the Irish bishops, and let them decide whether it should be settled by themselves or referred to Rome for an authoritative consideration.

He had risked a severe reprimand by attempting to enter into such a theological argument with the Holy See. He knew now that, if he accepted the Cardinal's kindly advice and referred the matter to the Bishops, his own position as a professor and as Prefect of the Dunboyne would be at stake if he did not simply accept their decision. Some of the younger bishops, including Archbishop Walsh and Bishop O'Donnell, had been his colleagues and friends at Maynooth. But Cardinal Logue belonged to an earlier generation, who were not accustomed to such assertions of independence from professors. McDonald's independence was the less likely to command the Cardinal's sympathy because Rome had already required him to withdraw a book which the Index had condemned. The reputation of Maynooth itself for orthodox teaching was obviously involved in any censure of one of its principal professors. But this last reply from Cardinal Ledochowski had referred McDonald directly to Cardinal Logue, and he now attempted persuasion nearer home. In a long letter to Cardinal Logue, he explained his difficulty in deciding whether the 'animadversions' represented an official decision against him, or whether they 'contained merely the private opinions of two theologians, who I have no doubt are men of learning and authority, but whose knowledge of this particular question might not be quite up to date.' He gave reasons for thinking that the document did, in fact, represent no more than such 'private opinions.' In concluding his letter to Cardinal Logue, he said clearly that 'while I am determined to do my best to get an authoritative decision on the whole question in dispute, I am also prepared to abide loyally, with the help of God, by the decision, whatever it may be.' Cardinal Logue replied briefly that these questions could not be considered during the summer vacation. At the end of the vacation, McDonald wrote again, enclosing his whole correspondence with Rome and asking for directions. Cardinal Logue now requested him to submit the whole dossier to Dr. Sheehan, the Bishops' secretary, for submission to the hierarchy at their next meeting. In October the bishops met at Maynooth, and the result of their consideration was then communicated orally to McDonald by Cardinal Logue. McDonald writes: 'They resolved to send the whole matter back to Rome, acting thus in their official capacity so as to secure an authoritative doctrinal decision. Meanwhile I was to promise not to teach what may be considered the doctrines peculiar to the Kinetic Theory. Cardinal Logue assured me that the Bishops had not hitherto pronounced any opinion on these doctrines in question, and promised to mention this to Cardinal Ledochowski when next he should have occasion to write to His Eminence.'

He could not have expected any other result. The bishops had refrained even from exhorting him to leave difficult questions alone. They were merely referring to Rome, for a decision, the abstruse questions which he insisted on raising. They undoubtedly admired his courage, and his fearless pursuit of researches which might so easily jeopardise his position as a professor. It was no secret that he lacked the academic training and experience which would seem indispensable for any such large undertaking as he had attempted. He had no direct support, nor even encouragement, from any prominent theologian; and he was provoking a direct conflict with the theologians in Rome which might easily compel him to resign his chair. Yet the bishops placed no obstacle in his way; and they referred his problems to Rome as those of one of their principal professors. They had not expressed adverse opinions, either on his teaching or on his action in demanding a decision upon it, although it obviously involved the reputation of Maynooth. So he began to prepare a full dissertation in support of his theses, in reply to the animadversions of the Roman consultors. He intended to show that their views were 'in conflict with views that had been propounded by some of the foremost experts in philosophy and theology.' He wrote to inform Cardinal Ledochowski of his intention; but he asked first whether the submission of such a dissertation 'would be deemed lacking in reverence for the Sacred Congregation.' His letter grew to a printed pamphlet of 46 pages, in addition to the 26 disputed theses which he had previously submitted.

He despatched this massive document to Rome in November 1899, and he heard nothing further until May 1900. The vice-president of Maynooth, Dr. O'Dea, then brought him an oral message from Cardinal Logue, and also the text of a letter from Cardinal Ledochowski. The letter stated that Cardinal Logue himself, after careful consideration and consultation, was to admonish Dr. McDonald if he thought it desirable, in case he should find 'that the doctrine which he has taught in his class at Maynooth College is not in conformity with Catholic teaching, and if need be that you should remove him from his chair.' McDonald states in his *Reminiscences* that the oral message from Cardinal Logue was 'to the effect, as I understood it, that it was the Cardinal's wish that, for the future, in explaining the co-operation of God and created agents, I should confine myself to putting before the students of my class the two systems traditionally advocated respectively by the Thomists and the Molinists.' McDonald asked then that his decision should be communicated to him in writing. Moreover he declared 'as far as I can remember, that I should scrupulously obey any such decision if it were given, or else resign my position in College.'

Both the Roman authorities and the Maynooth Trustees had deliberately avoided any announcement which might have brought discredit upon McDonald. They had done all that could be done to prevent any publication of the fact that his book had been condemned. But he had no intention of concealing the facts. He talked about the matter freely, while he set himself to produce some other book or work, that would fulfil his own demand that professors must produce original writing. He recalls that at one stage he thought he should write a formal letter to the Board 'to say that if I were to go on teaching, I could do so only on the lines set forth in my letter of June 20, 1901.' But on reflection he felt that he would only make himself a nuisance, as he had already stated his case. So he 'made up his mind to let things lie as they were, and to go on teaching on the lines which I had explained to the Trustees, making no parade and yet no concealment of this, and being prepared to abide by the consequences that might ensue.' He had not reckoned with the caution of official censors, to whom his future writings would have to be submitted; and in his *Reminiscenes* he writes bitterly of the frustration that they subsequently imposed. His complaints may indeed give a misleading impression to the general reader, as he protests that there was no Irish bishop who would give an *imprimatur* to his writings. In practice, under Canon Law, every priest or layman was obliged to submit for censorship any writings of doctrinal character; and the censors must be those appointed either by the bishop of the diocese where the author lives; or by the bishop in whose diocese the book is published; or where the book is printed. For a priest living at Maynooth, the choice was further restricted by the fact that he lived within the jurisdiction of Dublin; and both printer and publisher would normally be there also. No bishop could even offer an *imprimatur* unless the book was either written or printed or published in his diocese. And in practice no professor of Maynooth could well go outside the Dublin censorship, as Maynooth is within the archdiocese of Dublin. It is impossible now to judge the reasons which may have caused the censor's decisions. All the manuscripts of McDonald's unpublished books of a theological character were entrusted after his death to one of his most gifted former students. It is unlikely that after such a lapse of time, they would now be sufficiently up-to-date to be suitable for publication.

One book after another which McDonald wrote during these years was refused an *imprimatur,* and this continued refusal gave a sense of bitter frustration to his later years. In the first page of his *Reminiscences* he writes: 'It is February 1913, and not many days since I was told that a MS volume of *Notes and Queries in Sacramental Theology* which I submitted to one of the authorised censors of the diocese of Dublin, had not the least chance of getting a *Nihil Obstat,* as, in case it was published, it would be delated to Rome almost immediately, and as surely would almost as quickly be condemned there. It is the fifth volume of the kind which I have written during the last ten years: (1) *Theses on the Supernatural, Annotated;* (2) *On Virtues, their Nature and Specification;* (3) *On the Theological Virtues of Faith, Hope and Charity;* (4) *Essays on Religion and the Church;* and now (5) these *Notes and Queries;* besides my first book, *On Motion,* actually delated to the Index and condemned. Only *The Principles of Moral Science* has escaped; how, I do not know. I feel that if it were first presented to the Censor now, or for the last few years, it would not have any more chance of securing the *Nihil Obstat* than this last volume; nay, less.' He explains how he had written these *Notes and Queries* 'with great care, an eye always on the Censor, and a firm determination not to raise any question which I could not discuss without shocking even the most sensitive nerves.' Of course, he adds ironically, 'I ventured here and there on a sentence or paragraph on some side issue – at which the Censor might sniff, and in regard to which he might show himself a Censor, who, of course, does nothing at all if he does not delete something, or require it to be put in another – his own – way. It was all of no use; the book was found to be full of errors not merely in those special paragraphs on which I had ventured to enable the Censor to show how easily he could correct me, but running through the Notes on almost every page. They were wrong every way, even as regards most elementary dis-

tinctions; and through no doubt the general tendency was conservative, they were calculated, somehow, to disseminate a
critical and sceptical spirit.'

McDonald occupied during these years the most responsible teaching position at Maynooth; and his writings were a persistent effort
to make some worthy and original contribution from Maynooth to
theological studies. 'Surely,' he writes in the same passage, 'I
must be conceited and stupid – in theology; are not these five
volumes of mine – banned or even condemned – proof sufficient
and to spare? Yet I am not ashamed of them, nor sorry for having written them, though as the average man – who is not such a
fool – regards things, it is so much time – so much! fifteen or
twenty years more or less – thrown away. They were the best
years of my poor life, too, which, however conceitedly and foolishly, I dedicated honestly in the service of Theology and the
Church... The service itself is ample reward; *cui servire regnare
est*. But how much more than crown and sceptre it would be if
one heard her say occasionally, 'Well done! thou good and faithful'; or if she gave one some badge to wear in token of being
recognised as hers. Such rewards are for others; my best services she regards as disservice, so that, like another theologian
of our time – *parvum componere magnis* – I stand in the market
place all day idle. And yet the pen which I am not allowed to use
in the service of my mistress would perhaps, be welcomed heartily and rewarded handsomely by her enemies.'

This frustration of his efforts to produce published work hurt
him all the more keenly, because he had long regarded such original publication as the surest test of a professor's value to his
College. Two of the most interesting chapters in his *Reminiscences*
describe the 'Reforms in Studies' and 'Other College Improve-
ments' during his years on the teaching staff. In the autumn of
1894 the Faculty of Theology presented to the Trustees a report
which they had been asked to prepare on the conditions on which
degrees in theology might be conferred. Power to confer such degrees was granted in the year after the Maynooth centenary celebrations of 1895; and under the new arrangements, McDonald,
as senior professor and Prefect of the Dunboyne, was appointed
to preside at the examination boards. But the Trustees decided to
entrust these duties to the President of Maynooth, and McDonald
was instead made Prefect of Studies. 'There were no emoluments,' he writes, 'only trouble – attaching to the office; else,
perhaps I should not have got it. And I should have respectfully
declined accepting it, if their Lordships had consulted me before

making the appointment; not, however, because of any labour or trouble it would bring, or because there was no remuneration; but because I felt that, to fulfil his duties, a Prefect of Studies should have what I lacked – the confidence of the Trustees.' After a few years he resigned the office, and Dr. Mannix was appointed in his place until his appointment to Melbourne and no further appointment was made.

Another result of the centenary celebrations was that Rome gave power to Maynooth to confer additional degrees in philosophy and in Canon Law. McDonald had opposed the petition for such powers, on the ground that it would require a larger staff than Maynooth could provide. He believed that specialists would be better trained in Rome or in other universities. After twenty years experience he confessed to disappointment with the results, though, as he writes, 'no man living had as much personal interest in pretending' that the progress had been greater than it honestly seemed to him to have been. He was convinced that 'there must be something wrong' in the teaching system, which failed to produce a higher level, afer such a prolonged period of training. His own explanation, with full knowledge that it would provoke indignant denial from seminaries everywhere, was that 'our lack of success is due in very great measure to the use of Latin in our schools.' His argument must be read in full; and it certainly implied no disregard for the spirit of unity within the Church. But he believed particularly that the use of Latin for teaching was an impediment to the extension of theological science and research. 'Theology,' he writes, 'is regarded as an unprogressive science; or if it did make progress at one time, that was long ago – in the earlier or later medieval schools, wherein the science reached its full stature; dwindling later, except in so far as it is preserved in books, so that the best theologian is he who is best acquainted with the school tradition and is most ready to accept that as true. Against all this, my whole life has been one long protest, which will be continued while breath is left to me. The deposit of Catholic faith, it is true, was closed with the last of the apostles, but there never was and never can be any such closing of the science either of theology or philosophy; which must either make constant progress or become fossilised. The more one admires the fundamental principles of the scholastic philosophy – which may be reduced to this one, that scientific truth is objective, to be dug out from Nature – the more one is convinced that, as we progress in knowledge of nature, we are in position to advance in philosophical science: and who is there that does not realise that the science of philosophy and that of theo-

41

logy go hand in hand? If you desire that we should keep abreast of the time, but think we can do so while using Latin only in our schools, I can only give you the assurance of one whose whole life has been spent in those schools, that, hampered as we are with this dead language, we cannot attain or keep the position which you wish us to occupy. We are behind the times in many ways; mainly because our thoughts, from being clad in old-fashioned garments, have become themselves old-fashioned.'

One practical development with which McDonald was directly associated was the formation of the Maynooth Union which arose out of the centenary celebrations in 1895. He had himself urged that an appeal should be made to provide an endowment for the Maynooth library, instead of appealing for the tower and spire, which 'had to be euphemistically represented as the completion of the College chapel.' His plea for the Library failed to find support. But the idea of a Maynooth Union had been urged for many years by one of McDonalds contemporaries, Provost Lynch of Salford; and, when several other proposals for the centenary congress had been turned down, the Maynooth Union project was adopted as a more practical way of filling the time. His Address at the centenary, when he moved the resolution for the constituting a Maynooth Union, is included in his posthumous volume of essays *The Manliness of St. Paul.* The Union has flourished and grown greatly, since he wrote some sixty years ago that 'it has, I think, been the source of no little good to the College; not only in putting us into closer and more sympathetic touch with our old students, but in bringing us more into the open, so that the world can see more of what we are and of what we think and do.' He noted also that the character of the Union's meetings had changed considerably, and that the academic aspect of its proceedings had been almost discarded. McDonald himself had read the first academic paper and declared that it was a 'decided failure'; and he welcomed the subsequent policy of Dr. Mannix, who became the Union's first secretary, in choosing subjects of general and topical interest.

One early result of the Union's formation was that it contributed a grant of fifty pounds to each of the divisional libraries, to be spent on buying 'literary works.' This led to the concession of an annual grant of fifty pounds from the Trustees, to buy books for the students' libraries. McDonald notes that it was Archbishop Walsh who 'proposed and carried this grant; for, as he said to me in conversation, seeing that the Union had taken action, the Trustees could not very well refrain from doing as much. The happy result is that the students have in their own libraries – especially that in the Senior House – a very nice collection of works of literature, philosophy, theology and the kindred sciences.' About the same time also he recalls that some of the staff began to agitate for a better supply of reviews. It was agreed to pool the cost of taking such reviews and newspapers privately and thereby create a fund to buy a wider selection of periodicals for common use. Nearly all the community joined in this plan, and they soon obtained also from the Trustees an additional yearly allowance for literature of this kind. McDonald confesses to disappointment at finding that there was so little demand for what he called the 'scientific' periodicals, that should have been useful for each faculty. He had been himself 'largely responsible for creating or procuring these funds' and he had hoped to obtain through them a regular supply of the best reviews in theology and philosophy, Catholic or otherwise. But the money was spent rather on such reviews as the *Nineteenth Century* or the *Revue des Deux Mondes* and the *Spectator* and other weeklies; and some of the more serious-minded of the staff soon withdrew from the pool. But his greatest disappointment concerned the students, whom he had hoped to provide in this way with reviews and also with newspapers. He held strongly that secular priests should be trained to use newspapers during their seminary course. Having urged these suggestions at first without success, he wrote to 'many prominent seminaries – in England, America, France, Belgium, and even at Rome,' to enquire whether newspapers were there permitted. The replies were encouraging, a digest of them was submitted to the Trustees, who made a slight relaxation of the rule. They allowed the *Saturday Review,* but not yet the *Tablet* nor even the weekly edition of the *Times.* They would not allow even the *Freeman's Journal,* oldest of the Dublin daily newspapers and the recognised organ of Irish Catholics though they permitted *L'Univers* and *La Vera Roma,* as inducements to read foreign languages. Another innovation around this time was the introduction of literary and debating societies, which could not flourish previously owing to the lack of students' libraries.

In the system of appointing professors McDonald was to be directly concerned over many years. The principle of holding a concursus had only recently been admitted when he first obtained his professorship. But before long he found that the concursus system had its limitations, as the election was entrusted to a board who might have small qualification for deciding. The Council of Studies had to propose the question, and hear the answers, on whatever subject was concerned. 'We selected questions for examination – not of students but of candidates for chairs, on subjects of which the best of us knew little and some of us very little, and we reported on the answering of candidates who, if at all qualified for the chair, and if anxious to secure our votes, must have set themselves to talk down to the measure of our incapacity.' The examiners voted conscientiously and without fear or favour, and their votes were cast by ballot; but McDonald and others were keenly aware of their own lack of competence for voting in many cases. Even at its best, he concluded afterwards, 'The system of concursus for professorships is open to this objection, that it keeps away good men who may have made a name in the subject, and may therefore be unwilling to pit themselves against young men just from the schools, with fresh memories and nothing to lose by being worsted in the contest. The concursus system may get you the best students in the sense of the Latin alumnus, but not the best qualified men. Moreover, as against a student trained in our own schools, a man who had read elsewhere, however qualified, would be very much handicapped in an examination conducted here, just as our men would be at no less disadvantage in a similar examination conducted elsewhere.'

To meet this difficulty, a new statute, for which McDonald was largely responsible, was drawn up and approved by Propaganda. It provided that when a chair became vacant it 'could be filled without concursus or examination provided the members of the faculty in question, the President, and the Visitors, were satisfied that a man could be found who had proved himself fully qualified for the vacant position, and the President and members of the faculty were exhorted to bestir themselves, whenever a vacancy occurred, to find someone who might be recommended for appointment in this way, on merits of which he had already given proof.' He insists that in such exceptional selections he would 'pay no attention to college distinctions, nor to university degrees, whether obtained at home or elsewhere, nor to recommendations of any professors or experts, however eminent. The one test that is fairly reliable – though even this can be secured by craft – is a reputation based on published work of exceptional merit, and I for my part, should be deeply grieved and disappointed to find any man recommended for a professorship in any faculty on any other qualification.' His high ideals were reflected also in another statute which was adopted at his instigation. He wished that all professors should be appointed temporarily first; but he assumed that the probationary period would be at least seven years, to allow the young professor time to produce important original work. He held that the temporary appointment should not be renewed unless he had published some work which would bring credit to himself and to the College. In practice, he complained, the Trustees subsequently made the temporary appointments for three years; which enabled any professor to say that he had not time to produce important original work, before his appointment had to be made permanent.

While he insisted so strongly always upon the necessity of original work by professors, his own persistent and industrious efforts to produce published work were being frustrated time after time by the caution of ecclesiastical censors. It was inevitable that he should regard the censors with feelings of hostility. While he continued to hold the most responsible teaching position at Maynooth, the censors who prevented him from obtaining publication could not claim to have either his knowledge or his experience on technical matters. At the same time, his reputation for orthodoxy was obviously exposed to suspicions; and he made no secret of his inability to obtain an *imprimatur*. When he insisted all the more firmly that professors must be expected to produce published work, he was compelled inevitably to uphold the rights of professors to express independent views, and to claim security of tenure, even if their views incurred disapproval. By temperament he had always been a challenger of authority, though he never questioned its right to impose obedience within its proper sphere.

As the years passed and his personal efforts were thwarted by censorship, while his seniority at Maynooth became more evident, he acquired an attitude of instinctive criticism towards his superiors, and even towards the bishops. He felt that his peculiar situation required that he should set a special example of moral courage. The later chapters of his *Reminiscences* are largely occupied with minor controversies which he either incurred or deliberately provoked under these conditions. He desired to strengthen the rights of professors, and give them greater security in case they should incur temporary disapproval. Undaunted by the suspicions which hung around him since the condemnation of his book on *Motion*, and by the discouragement of being refused an *imprimatur* for his subsequent books, he made plans for the publication of a serious quarterly journal at Maynooth in collaboration with his colleagues. It materialised as the *Irish Theological Quarterly* in 1905.

He explains in his *Reminiscences* the general purpose that he had in view. 'I had long felt the want, in our College, of a journal wholly devoted to theological science in the best sense, a review, that is, in which the latest questions would be discussed, always with a reverent eye to ecclesiastical authority and scholastic tradition, but with a filial confidence, too, that one had nothing to fear from the authorities, even though they were to maintain, with a fair show of reason, that a school tradition, however venerable, could be no longer held. I felt that in Maynooth we were somewhat out of touch with life and were likely to remain so – to keep running on the old track made by our predecessors – unless we had a journal of our own to sustain by hard work and thought; that the very books that would come for review would be a constant source of light and a stimulus to work, and that in exchange for ours, we should get almost all the theological and philosophical reviews, and thereby be kept *au courant* with what was being said and done in the schools of theology the world over. I hoped for immediate profit to our faculty from this new supply of theological literature, and the added stimulus to work, nor was I without assurance that in good time we should do something for the science of theology; that it would develop, under our care, not so rapidly, of course, as other sciences, such as physics and chemistry, develop in their schools, but however slowly, that it would be steadily evolved. Every other branch of knowledge – every science, at least, that was taught in universities – had one or more journals devoted exclusively to its service, and was advanced thereby. So had theology, too, in Germany, where there were a number of theological reviews. Why should not we have one in English for our own school in the first place, and for the other theological schools of the English-speaking world?'

With these intentions, he discussed the project 'from time to time in conversation with colleagues – those especially who had spent a year abroad after appointment to their chairs.' They sympathised in principle, but foresaw the difficulties in obtaining freedom of control by censors. McDonald himself considered that the bishops should 'leave the control of it to others and be content with intervention now and then, if necessary, to correct grave mistakes, if made, and take measures against their repetition. I would not work in leading strings, being convinced that no really good work can be done that way, and the question was whether we should be allowed the liberty that, as I thought, was necessary for a review.' He foresaw no direct competition with the *Irish Ecclesiastical Record,* which never aspired to be an organ of theological studies. Towards the end of 1904 he consulted specially with Dr. MacRory, Dr. MacCaffrey and Dr. Toner. Ater some delay, a meeting was held in McDonald's rooms in March 1905, to discuss practical possibilities. It was attended by Drs. Coghlan, MacRory, Harty, MacCaffrey, Toner and McKenna, besides McDonald. By a vote of five to one it was decided that the review should be started, the only dissentient being Dr. Coghlan, who took no further part in the enterprise. To make practical arrangements a committee was then formed, consisting of Drs. MacRory and Harty (who subsequently became archbishops of Armagh and of Cashel) and Dr. MacCaffrey and McDonald. They were to share financial responsibility, besides being an editorial committee. The first immediate problem concerned censorship, and McDonald wrote accordingly to Archbishop Walsh of Dublin. He explained that there would be an editorial board to deal with five departments; Scientific Dogma, Historical Dogma, Moral Theology, Sacred Scripture, and Ecclesiastical History. The associate editors would be Drs. MacRory, Harty, MacCaffrey, Toner and McDonald. His letter explained that it had been agreed that 'no article in any way suspicious or dangerous will be inserted without having been submitted to each of the associates, and that no article will be published against the vote of any two of the body.' The Archbishop replied at first that he could not make any special arrangement for censorship 'without being deluged by applications for similar exceptional arrangements.' In October he was still unable to make any special concession about censorship; and a few days later he wrote to say that he found there was 'a difference of opinion among the bishops as to the wisdom of issuing' the new quarterly. He had already promised to become a subscriber, but he now asked that his name should not appear in any list of subscribers, as he would not wish to 'do anything that could be regarded as taking sides against the Bishops who disapprove of the intended publication.'

Notwithstanding these discouragements, the editorial committee went boldly ahead. The first issue of the *Irish Theological Quarterly* appeared in January 1906 under the censorship of Canon Dunne, the president of Holy Cross College Clonliffe, to whose courtesy and helpfulness McDonald pays full tribute. But within the same month they received a letter from the standing committee of the Bishops, expressing surprise that 'a theological journal should be published by the members of the Theological Faculty without seeking the consent and approval of the Trustees for the project.' It stated that 'the Bishops expect that the matter will be set right before the next meeting of the Trustees.' McDonald, replying on behalf of the editorial committee, explained that they had no wish to show disrespect to the Trustees, but that they had not been aware that they were 'bound either in obedience or in reverence to seek the consent and approval' of the Bishops for the publication. He pointed out that it was not published by the Faculty of Theology, which had never been consulted on the matter; and that the five editors were not aware that their membership of the Faculty precluded them, as individuals, from publishing theological works on their own responsibility. No direct instruction from the bishops followed: but Bishop O'Donell was again sent, as an old and intimate friend, to request McDonald orally to act as the Bishops desired. With real reluctance he refused; being convinced that the Quarterly would lose its value if it were made subject to direct control. The Quarterly continued to appear; but the committee had 'an uncomfortable feeling that we were under a cloud and disliked.' McDonald was generally regarded as the chief instigator of the project; but he was in fact only one of the five editors, and the others included the future Archbishops of Armagh and of Cashel, and Dr. MacCaffrey, a future President of Maynooth. He felt keenly, however, that he was himself the chief cause of suspicion, and in November, 1908, he heard rumours that he had been delated to Rome by some of the Bishops. He went at once to see Dr. Mannix as president, and was told by him of a recent letter from Cardinal Logue. The Cardinal complained that he was writing indiscreetly, and said that Rome had given direct authority for taking action against him. McDonald then stated that he felt he should withdraw from the *Theological Quarterly,* and he accordingly did so. The main work of editing and producing the review devolved thereafter upon Dr. MacRory.

After this disappointing experience with the *Theological Quarterly,* he turned to what he called his 'own line of work,' and produced 'three volumes: an Essay on the *Theological Virtues of Faith, Hope and Charity,* in continuation of my *Essay on Virtues, their Nature and Classification;* a collection of *Essays on Religion and the Church;* and a volume of *Notes and Queries in Sacramental Theology*.' None of these three works was ever published; and he did not even seek an *imprimatur* for the first two, 'knowing that a *Nihil Obstat* would be refused, as one or more commonly received opinions are rejected in each.' During these years also he interested himself increasingly in public questions concerning education and social reform, approaching all questions with an open mind, and with an instinctive attraction towards the less conservative view. The discussions about a new National University which should be acceptable to Catholics brought him into conflict with the attitude of most of the Irish bishops on two issues which involved very different considerations. Before the introduction of Birrell's Universities Act of 1908, McDonald had urged openly that the most effective and reasonable solution would be for Catholics to enter Trinity College in large numbers, as Catholics had done in certain Protestant universities in other countries. He maintained that they would very quickly be able to assert their own rights in the university; and also that they would benefit by contact with a different atmosphere in the university, which would compel them to learn more about their own religious faith. In this view he had in fact some support among the Bishops, though very little among the Catholic body in general.

On the other issue, he came into direct conflict with the bishops as a body, while he sided with the popular agitation which they opposed. An acute public controversy arose over the demand that an examination in the Irish language should be made compulsory for all students entering the new University. Memories of these old controversies have been obscured by later events; and it is seldom realised now that Archbishop Mannix, who was President of Maynooth until he went to Melbourne in 1913, as coadjutor to Archbishop Carr, was one of the strongest and most formidable opponents of compulsory Irish. The Bishops shared his view, and they passed a resolution opposing the demand for compulsory Irish. The popular agitation for compulsory Irish had by that time produced a tide of national enthusiasm, and among its foremost champions was Dr. O'Hickey, the professor of Irish at Maynooth. He threw himself into the campaign with a lamentable lack of discretion, and he denounced the bishops with a disregard for their dignity which was scarcely tolerable in a professor to Maynooth. His many platform speeches reached a climax when, at a students meeting, he declared that he could only 'commend the bishops to your earnest prayers.' Such outbursts could not have been ignored in any college, and Dr. O'Hickey was first reprimanded, and then dismissed from his chair.[1]

McDonald had never been prominently identified with the Irish language revival, though it always commanded his sympathy. But this dismissal of a professor for expressing disagreement with the Trustees of Maynooth, on a matter which did not concern either faith or morals, aroused his active sympathy at once. He put himself at O'Hickey's disposal as his adviser in Canon Law, and he persuaded him to appeal to Rome against his dismissal by the Bishops. This whole sad story is told at great length in McDonald's *Reminiscences,* which convey the impression that O'Hickey was ruthlessly and unfairly victimised by Dr. Mannix. In his defence of O'Hickey, McDonald pointed out that the Bishops complained of intemperate language in his public speeches, and he replied by quoting certain injudicious statements by particular Bishops in controversies where they had been engaged. He thus became more than ever suspect of trying to discredit the Hierarchy. It would be difficult today for any dispassionate reader to share McDonald's conviction that O'Hickey was unfairly censured, or even that his dismissal could have been avoided while he persisted in such denun-

1. See page 248.

ciations of his superiors. But McDonald's earnestness in his defence was all the more vehement, because he knew that he risked his own security as a professor by making himself O'Hickey's champion in a forlorn hope. The persistent suspicions of his orthodoxy always spurred him to open conflict; and his increasingly frequent troubles with the College authorities made him all the more determined to act courageously.

The dismissal of Dr. O'Hickey seemed to McDonald to involve the principle of security of tenure for professors, and their right to speak or write freely on public questions. By making himself O'Hickey's legal adviser in the appeal to Rome, he took risks which were apparent to everyone. Yet O'Hickey might have been better advised by some friend who took a more dispassionate view, and who had not McDonald's quixotic inclination to invite martyrdom. For some time, O'Hickey became a national hero among the advocates of compulsory Irish, while they swept the country when the Gaelic League was at its strongest. A public subscription was opened to pay the expenses of his appeal to Rome, but the appeal could never have succeeded and Dr. O'Hickey died a few years later, broken-hearted. At his funeral in County Waterford none of the leading champions of compulsory Irish attended, and Dr. McDonald's reminiscences give a melancholy description of that lonely end.

Having held his chair for so long and with such distinction, McDonald's security of tenure was scarcely in doubt; but these later years brought a sense of isolation, with the departure of old friends, and a growing consciousness of conflict with his superiors. It was generally assumed that he would always adopt the unpopular or unorthodox side in any controversy; yet his students could never feel sure which side he would take, in his conferences; and his influence with them was never greater. He was as eager as ever to provoke or to accept challenge from all quarters when he was teaching. And it was well known among the senior students that his personal efforts had been largely responsible for providing them with adequate libraries and reading rooms. When Dr. Mannix departed for Australia in 1913, as coadjutor to Archbishop Carr in Melbourne, the tension which had arisen during the O'Hickey case was notably relaxed. But the Labour disputes of 1913 provided a new distraction; and McDonald began to interest himself increasingly in social problems. He was one of the very few priests who had expressed sympathy for Larkin's Transport Union and for his advocacy of the 'sympathetic strike' by other unions. He felt very strongly that the trade unions were being unjustly crushed, and he refused to ride on the Dublin tramways during the dispute.

The prospect of Home Rule becoming operative in 1914 awakened his interest in many questions, especially concerning the future management of the schools which he thought must lead to a revolt against excessive clerical control. But the outbreak of war in Europe in 1914 cut across all immediate speculations: and McDonald became concerned with the moral principles which should govern Ireland's attitude towards participation in the war. He wrote two books during these war years, which set forth the ideas which he had been expounding to his students during that time; but neither book was published until the war was over. One was entitled *Some Ethical Aspects of the Social Question; Suggestions for Priests,* which did not appear until 1920. More controversial at time was his *Some Ethical Questions of Peace and War, with special Reference to Ireland,* which was published at the end of 1919. Both books received *imprimaturs* from the Westminster censor, being published in London by Burns and Oates.

In the pre-war years he had become a hero to the younger nationalists, for his defence of Dr. O'Hickey against his dismissal and for his support of the Land League; and his defence of cattle driving, as a legitimate reply to eviction, in an essay entitled 'The Hazel Switch.' He subsequently altered and recanted the views which he expounded in the 'Hazel Switch'; and his book on 'Peace and War' ran counter to the Sinn Fein agitation when it had acquired its greatest momentum after the rising of 1916. It provoked many hostile reviews, which in some instances descended to personal abuse. One writer particularly, whom he quotes in the closing chapter of his *Reminiscences,* declared that 'as the author of the notorious work *Motion,* condemned by the Church, he long since ceased to write or speak with authority as a Catholic theologian.' The same writer even asserted shamefully that 'ignorance, flippancy, vanity and personal animus – and perhaps Episcophobia, to coin a word – are the marks of this shallow pamphlet.' The word Episcophobia rankled with Dr. McDonald in these last months of his life. It was not he, but others, who had displayed fear of bishops by their unwillingness to state their opinions freely. In the last page of his *Reminiscences,* written when he knew that only a few weeks of life remained to him, he expressed the hope that his unpublished works would be found to be of value. 'I should dearly love to see these volumes published, but must pass away without hope of that. They might do a little to withstand the Revolution, which the official guardians of our religion will not see coming, or will endeavour to keep out with their broomsticks. Good men, animated by the best of motives, but so short-sighted, and so cruel too, in their religious blindness to such as cannot shut their eyes. So God permits – no doubt for wise purposes; blessed always be His holy will. Episcophobia! Yes I have faced Bishops and their Masters, being worsted in the conflict, and, as I believe, injured grievously. Not maliciously, however; the men who struck hardest at me did it in good faith. I do not blame them, nor desire to see them punished, however I may feel aggrieved.'

The volume entitled *The Manliness of St. Paul and other Essays,* published in Dublin by Clonmore and Reynolds in 1958, included a selection of lectures or pamphlets which were published before his death, besides various sermons, essays and newspaper articles. I have included in the present volume his lecture to Maynooth Students on 'How I Have Studied the Social Question', ad two contributions to the weekly Leader, about the ethics of the Sympathetic Strike.

I take this opportunity of answering the question which has often been asked, concerning a few minor omissions from the *Reminiscences,* when I arranged for their publication. Dr. McDonald left me absolute discretion in making any abridgment which might be necessary to ensure publication of the book. He knew that the full manuscript in its original form, would be longer than any publisher was likely to consider. It contained, for instance, the full text in Latin of his correspondence with the Sacred Congregation of the Index in Rome, besides his own translations of the Latin documents. I omitted almost all these Latin documents, and published only the English versions. I omitted also one of the later chapters, which expounded his views on the first World War in relation to Ireland; because this was only a summary of the much fuller statements of his views which he had published shortly before his death as *Some Ethical Considerations of Peace and War,* which went through several editions. The only other substantial omission which I made was a chapter concerning an old scandal in one of the western dioceses, when he had offered his services to defend a priest who had been dismissed by his Bishop without a canonical inquiry. This was the first of a series of instances where McDonald offered legal advice in Canon Law to priests who became involved in conflict with their bishops, and needed expert defence. In this particular case the priest was entirely unknown to him; and he had incurred dismissal for neglect of duty and for improper conduct, which provoked a general protest from the local people. But McDonald was at that time in charge of Canon Law classes at Maynooth, and he felt that the accused priest had not been given the benefit of the legal assistance to which he was entitled. His generous offer of help in such unhappy circumstances was thoroughly characteristic of Dr. McDonald even at that early stage of his career, as a very young professor. But the scandal was long forgotten, and I thought it advisable to refrain from reviving it. I therefore omitted this whole chapter, though it was so evidently creditable to his generous instincts.

Apart from these principal omissions, the *Reminiscences* were submitted by me, almost exactly in the form in which they were published, to Messrs. Burns and Oates in London, who had published his previous works, particularly at the end of his life. The publishers submitted the manuscript to the ecclesiastical censors for Westminster; though Dr. McDonald himself had insisted that it would not require an *imprimatur* after his death. I considered that, if the book were published without submission to censorship, there would be suspicions of its orthodoxy. But it was obviously unlikely to obtain an *imprimatur* in Ireland, because the book contained direct criticism of the actions of Irish Bishops in various matters. I therefore agreed that the censorship in Westminster should be asked to consider the book; and a detailed report arrived in due course. The censor took exception on theological grounds only to two passages in the final chapter, in which Dr. McDonald discussed his general view of the difficulties in presenting the Catholic Faith in a changing world. One of these passages contained only a few sentences; the other ran to two paragraphs. I at once agreed to omit both passages in deference to the censor's ruling, while noting that the censor expressly stated that the book gave no other reason for complaint on theological grounds. Nevertheless the Westminster censor strongly urged the London publishers to refrain from accepting the book for publication, on the ground that it criticised the Irish hierarchy, or individual Bishops, on many matters. He urged very reasonably that it was inadvisable that such criticisms should be published by an official Catholic publishing house in London. He also drew attention to certain passages in Dr. McDonald's detailed account of the controversy concerning Dr. O'Hickey's expulsion from the chair of Irish at Maynooth. He suggested that Dr. McDonald's version of these events might incur a risk of libel actions from certain persons whom he represented as having treated Dr. O'Hickey unfairly. On this matter also I agreed readily to make the suggested excisions; but Messrs. Burns and Oates were unwilling to publish the *Reminiscences*. I therefore brought the book, shortened by the omissions above indicated, to Mr. Jonathan Cape, and it was published by him in 1925.

In the present volume the *Reminiscences* have been abridged to about half the original length, because it would have been impossible to publish a reprint of the whole book at a price within reach of ordinary readers. But this Memoir has attempted to include a summary of the long and highly technical controversy with Rome concerning McDonald's book on Motion. The Memoir also conveys the main issues involved in Dr. O'Hickey's dismissal from the professorship of Irish at Maynooth, during the agitation for compulsory Irish in the new National University, in which Dr. O'Hickey took a sensationally active part. The other omissions from the Reminiscences, which have been made solely to produce a shorter version of manageable length, are his early recollections of childhood in county Kilkenny and his impressions of a much later visit to the United States. But I have kept intact the various chapters concerning Maynooth and the general progress of ecclesiastical education in Ireland, and other chapters concerning social and educational problems which are most likely to interest modern readers.

It is too early yet to estimate how far Dr. McDonald's views and efforts have found support in the decisions of the Vatican Council. But his demand that any priest should be informed of the grounds for suppressing his books and given the opportunity to defend himself has been definitely approved. His objection to the use of Latin in teaching and examinations in seminaries has gained wide support and approval. And his general ideas about the need for wider scope in clerical education have shown him to be a prophet in his day.

Denis Gwynn
May, 1966

MAYNOOTH: THE OLD ORDER (1870 – 1871)

In July, 1870, I was nominated one of five candidates for Matriculation at Maynooth College; whither we betook ourselves for examination towards the end of the next month. We all proposed for Logic, and were to be examined, principally, in two Latin and two Greek authors; those which I chose from the official list being Horace (*Odes* and the *Art of Poetry*) and some books of Tacitus, and in Greek certain books of the Iliad and Longinus, 'On the

54

Sublime'. We had been reading Horace and Longinus the preceding academic year; but the Iliad and the Tacitus were to be made up during the vacation; and it shows what a lazy happy-go-lucky boy I was, after five years in St. Kyran's that, after a feeble attempt, for a day or two, to prepare these texts at home, I threw them aside and took my chance. Owing, moreover, to the shallow method I had followed in preparing for class during the year, what knowledge I had acquired of Horace and Longinus evaporated quickly: so that on reaching Maynooth I found myself in anything but a comfortable position.

Fate, however, was kind. Candidates were actually examined only in one text in each language; and the Dean in charge, whose duty it was to select the passages, presented me with a paragraph in Longinus and one of the Odes of Horace – the two books of which I knew a little. Moreover, the monitor who took charge of us in what, in the College slang, was called the 'sweating hall' – where we were allowed to look over the texts for a few minutes before examination – came to my aid, with translations of both passages; so I was just able to pass muster. Whether it was that my written examination was bad, or that, even with all this luck and assistance, my answering at the oral was poor, after the vacation, I was put down to the Humanity Class; with an option of standing again for the higher class of Rhetoric. I had quite enough of examination, however, and was glad to get it at all; so I accepted what was offered me, and in this way matriculated for Humanity.

Often since have I shuddered to think what might have happened – how different my fate might have been – if I had been examined in the Iliad and Tacitus; and as, even with the aid supplied by the monitor, I could hardly have learned the translation within the few minutes of preparation allowed. And then the disgrace to my uncle, the President of St. Kyran's, to have nominated a nephew who was sent back. It certainly would have been the end of my studies for the priesthood; and God only knows what my life would have been.

For the next year – my first at Maynooth – my professors were Mr. O'Brien, for Latin, Greek and Algebra; Mr. O'Rourke, for English; and the Vice-President, Dr. Whitehead, who gave us lessons once a week in the Old Testament and in Catechism. Up to that time secular priests who were not Doctors of Divinity, were addressed officially – by their Bishops, as Mr.; not Father, which was the form used by the people. The title Mr. corresponds to the Latin Dominus, which is the style of the Roman Curia when addressing secular priests; the title Father being reserved for

Friars who are priests.

In the first years of my students' course at Maynooth, we used the official style, and spoke of Mr. Crolly, Mr. Walsh, Mr. Lennon, Mr. O'Brien, and so on. It was, I think, owing in no small part to the influence of Dr. Walsh, now Archbishop of Dublin, that we came to address those members of the staff who were not Doctors as Father.[1]

I am not sure that the change was for the better. It was, I think, an unauthorized assumption of a title that had been hitherto given exclusively to the Friars – at least in the style of those who were supposed to know, as we were. It was about the same time that the custom began to prevail in Ireland of addressing all Bishops as Most Reverend; for I remember well the formula whereby the episcopal indulgence was proclaimed in the Cathedral, Kilkenny; to wit 'The Right Rev. Father in God, Edward, by the grace of God and favour of the Apostolic See, Bishop of Ossory, grants to all here present, etc.' Since then, too, every priest who is not quite a young curate, has come to be addressed as Very Reverend; so that, as a national Church, we are given to that form of flattery which makes every captain a major or a colonel, and every sub-constable a sergeant. Would it not have been simpler, straighter, and better, to continue, as elsewhere, to give every one just what is his due?

During my first year at Maynooth I remained the idle, careless boy I had been at Kilkenny; doing little or no study, and caring little for the College rule. Not, indeed, that I was guilty of any great irregularity, such as drinking; I never saw any drink in the College during my course as a student. Apart from this, however, I did, practically, whatever I cared to do; and must have got a very indifferent report at the end of the year. I was but sixteen: and from Easter to the summer vacation of that year, we had to rise at five, with a fast till half-past eight, when we got breakfast. This discipline must have told severely on a lad so young; and I remember that towards the end of the year, I was very anaemic. But I had a splendid constitution, which pulled itself together after a week or two of summer vacation. It was the last year we were asked to rise at five; a change to six for the year round being made at the next meeting of the Board; to the joy of the Deans, I fancy, almost as much as that of the students.

1. Throughout a very interesting Obituary Notice of Professor Crolly, who died in January, 1878, the deceased is called Mr. Crolly. The Notice was written by Dr. Murray, and is published in the College Calendar (1878–79).

The professors did not press us – at least, not me. Mr. O'Brien I thought, and still think, a man of genius; who used to translate the Iliad and Hecuba for us into an English prose that was more than half poetic. He told us also of the myths of Greece, and made the texts interesting in other ways that were quite new to me. He did not, however, press us; nor did he make us do written work – no construing of unseen passages, of which we could get no translation; and no rendering of English into Latin and Greek. It happened that I was a favourite with him; because, I suppose, I was clever enough to take up and follow the hints he gave in class; but I made little or no progress in knowledge of Greek and Latin; and the same held of Algebra.

Our English lectures were of the poorest – were, indeed, but an examination of how we read in an English Grammar we had, by Hiley. There were no texts for analysis or criticism; a piece of declamation now and then; an occasional exercise in dictation; and little or no English composition. Dr. Whitehead's lectures on the Old Testament consisted in hearing three students repeat each a chapter of the Bible, word for word. This involved learning about twelve chapters during the year; as we might be called up on any of about four successive days. The lectures on Catechism were elaborate; or at least we thought them so; it must have been easy to make them appear so to youths of our condition.

Dr. Whitehead, who taught us Catechism and the Old Testament, deserves some special notice. He was medium-sized, somewhat hawk-featured, and very artificial, as you saw at once from his stilted speech and high-pitched voice. He began his career in the College as Professor of belles-lettres (English and French); after a year in that chair, passed on to that of Logic, Metaphysics, and Ethics; which he retained till 1845 – when he became Vice-President, and filled this office for twenty-six years – till 1871, I think, when he resigned, on the grounds of age and long service; taking in its place the position of Librarian, which was practically a sinecure. Rumour had it among us students, that he was disappointed when, in 1857, Dr. Russell was made President, over his head; and I think there is no doubt that he retired from the College on two occasions; once to America, to escape citation in connection with some dispute regarding family matters; and again to a cottage and little farm not far from Maynooth – near Leixlip – where he lived unknown to most of his colleagues.

He led somewhat the life of a hermit, especially towards the end, shutting himself up in his rooms and admitting no one; though he came to the common room for meals. He had a fine collection of books, mostly theological, which were sold by auction after his death. He made no will; lest, as the malicious said, he should in decency have to leave some bequest to the College; and the relatives who inherited whatever means he had, neglected to put a stone over his grave. Few, I think, if any, in the College know where he lies in our cemetery; and as there is no stone to mark the spot, I may say here that he is laid beside Mr. Crolly and nearer to the central cross, at the feet of Dr. O'Hanlon, who is out of his place in the order of time; as, when Dr. Callan was buried, Dr. Russell reserved for himself a place beside him.

Dr. Whitehead had a talent for writing Latin verse; and, if I mistake not, the hymn to St. Ita, in the supplement to the breviary, is from his pen. He was a friend of Dr. Butler's, Bishop of Limerick, who made him honorary Vicar-General of that diocese. When the foundation-stone of the new Chapel was laid, in 1874, we had a procession through the College grounds singing, among other pieces, a Latin hymn composed by Dr. Whitehead for the occasion. One who was on the staff when I was a student told me that it pleased and flattered Dr. Whithead to be asked to explain some obscure or knotty question in philosophy; a task which he would not undertake there and then, but would defer for two or three days, when, at a fixed hour, he would have an elaborate dissertation prepared. It was part of the formality of the man. He said Mass for us, in the Chapel of the Junior House, on two mornings of the week, and used to amuse us, and woke our mimicry by the way in which he declaimed the lessons of the Mass.

As I have such a poor account to give of the lectures we heard in English, it is fair to say that the Professor, Dr. O'Rourke, had very bad health almost the whole of his time on the staff. I knew him fairly well afterwards, when I joined the Community myself; and a better-mannered, more agreeable colleague one could not have. He was the only man I knew in my time to refuse a bishopric; (Dr. Russell, I believe, was actually appointed to some see in India, and got himself excused), as he actually received the brief from propaganda appointing him to the See of Clonfert. It was done, we understood, without his knowledge, through the influence of Cardinal Cullen, who was at that time guided in Western affairs by Dr. McEvilly, Bishop of Galway, whom Dr. MacHale did not like.

He left the College a good deal, very often from Saturday to Monday; and whenever he had a few days free, he went to friends in the West of Ireland. This meant that he was not engrossed in the business of his chair; nor did he seem to be able to read hard; so that his tenure of office, I fancy, must have been unhappy. He was a very handsome, dark-skinned man; dressed well; and if endowed with good health, might have had no small share of the world at his feet. As it was – with what health he had and taste for his work – it seemed as if he would have been happier anywhere than as a professor of subjects – he taught French as well as English – in which the students were very backward and which demanded, on the professor's part, a considerable expenditure of energy.

The discipline of the College, when I became a student, seems to me, as I look back now, to have been lax, and this, as I think, was due to the Deans, who were not what they should have been. Mr. O'Kane was ill and had his place supplied two years in succession, by one of the Dunboyne students; one, that is, who was in his third year on the Dunboyne, and therefore, ordained priest. For, at that time, it was only at the end of their second year on the Establishment students received the priesthood. The young man who took Mr. O'Kane's place had charge of the Junior House; which, in my first year, was ruled by Mr. O'Riorden, of the Diocese of Waterford; a very nice refined young priest, but lacking the strength of authority to keep us in control. Nor, as far as I could hear, was the Senior House anything better, though it had the benefit of the supervision of three Deans regularly appointed on the staff. The fact was that the students had no respect for those Deans; two of whom, at least – Mr. Quinn and Mr. Hammond – were men of very moderate ability, as they showed by the lectures they gave now and then. Mr. Hughes was better; but even he was a heavy, unwieldy man, who did not seem to put much heart into his work. Mr. Hammond was active, but lectured and spoke so badly that the students thought little of him. As a result of the whole, things went on badly. I never heard Mr. O'Kane speak, as he had practically retired before I matriculated; but those who had heard him used to tell of the beautiful lectures he gave, based often on the *Memoriale Vitæ Sacerdotalis*. The students respected him greatly; so that his retirement must have been a grievous loss to the College, in the way of discipline and religious instruction.

In the Junior House we had every Wednesday evening an experience of inefficiency on the part of a Dean, which, as I recall it now, was more than sad; it was deplorable. We assembled on that evening, in the prayer-hall, to hear an address from Mr. Quinn, on prayer, meditation, and clerical manners generally. It was a splendid opportunity, for the right kind of man; for we were all at heart pious, generous, and good; just at the time of life when boys need moulding and are most easily moulded. Mr. Quinn, however, was not the right man; as you could see at once by the reception he got, week after week. No wonder discipline went down under a man like him. The next year, Dr. MacCarthy – a pious and able man – became Dean of St. Columba's Division, in the same place; and, by meams of lectures such as Mr. Quinn was expected to give, produced a deep impression on the students. Incapacity, or inefficiency on the part of the Deans, was in my opinion, as I look back now, at the root of most of the irregularity which prevailed at that time in the College.

My first year as a student in Maynooth was remarkable, as being the last of the old order. The Irish Church Act came into force at the beginning of January, 1871, and with it the annual payment made by the Government to our College, ceased; so that we who matriculated after the Act became law, and who therefore had no vested rights, had to pay a pension of £ 30 a year, from the beginning of that January. Part of this pension, no doubt, was supplied by the Bishops; who themselves were allowed a certain number of free places provided by the interest on the capital sum paid over to the Trustees in redemption of the endowment hitherto provided annually. In this way some students got full free places; others two-thirds or half; I and my compeers got one-third, leaving us £ 20 to pay; a condition of things which made the new order unpleasantly different from the old.

At the same time the Government resigned all control of the College, whether in finance or in discipline. Hitherto the Bursar's accounts were submitted to a Treasury official every year for audit; and members of the College, students or masters, had a right of appeal from the Trustees to a body of Visitors appointed by the Government. Any change, moreover, in the College Statutes had to be submitted to Parliament and to obtain its sanction. In future the supreme Government belonged to the Trustees, subject, of course, to the Holy See; and whether they could or could not make new statutes of their own authority; as to which, I understand, there was, and is, some difference of opinion – they proceeded to do so. A committee of Bishops – of which two who had been members of the Vincentian Congregation of the Mission, Dr. Gillooly of Elphin and Dr. Lynch the coadjutor of Kildare and Leighlin, were the ruling spirits – drew up new rules and regulations; some of which, no doubt, were good, while others were afterwards given up. Each of the two Houses into which the College had been divided hitherto, was subdivided into two Divisions; with barriers between them; stone walls on the grounds and wooden partitions in the refectories. In the Junior House, for instance, a wall was built, and remains to this day, between the Rhetoric and Logic Houses; while the outward separation of the Divisions of the same House was completed by another wall connecting the gable of the Logic House with the boundary-wall or Parson Street. In the Senior House a strong wooden door was thrown across the cloister immediately beyond the passage into the Refectory, to debar access to and outlet from St. Mary's Division. The door may have been closed a few times, but soon was left open all day and all night; till at length it was removed, altogether. The place where it hung may be still traced by a staple which projects from the walls of the cloisters; while there is a socket to correspond on the floor underneath, and on the opposite wall a projecting stone against which the door pressed when it was closed. In the Senior Infirmary there were similar partitions, which, however, were continued up to the ceilings, on both corridors, and were provided with turning-tables for the passage of dishes and such things; while in the Senior Refectory a movable partition, long since removed altogether, was thrown across, about mid-way up the hall; with, of course, a central opening, to admit access to the upper portion of the Refectory.

Another considerable change affected the tradesmen who supplied our needs. Hitherto they took their places on the grounds, in the morning, after breakfast. The old hawthorn bush that stands inside the entrance-gate of the Junior House grounds was known as Mal's Bush, from the name of a celebrated character who took his stand there – Malachy Duggan, a tailor, who had amassed a nice little fortune. There were, I think, considerable abuses in connection with this mode of supply; as the tradesmen sometimes provided commodities which the rules did not allow. To facilitate inspection, the present Tradesmen's Hall – which had been the College Kitchen in old times, and where we had lectures in English during my first year – was given over to its present use; the students of the various divisions being allowed access to it once a week, on different days. It was a bad day for the tradesmen, who no longer made money as easily or as plentifully as of old; but, then, students who had to pay a pension, as we had, were not so well supplied with money as were those who preceded us, with free places during their entire course, besides scholarships of £ 20 a year for the last three or four years they spent in the College.

The subdivision of the House has been given up practically, nor as far as I knew, was it ever of any value. The evil against which it was meant to provide had its root elsewhere – in the character of the Deans. If they are efficient and respected, they will not find the Houses unwieldy; while they remained what they were, the subdivision did not improve matters. It was, I think, advisable to have two prayer-halls for the Senior House, as this enabled the Deans to give more homely, more pointed, and better lectures; and I am glad that this part of the arrangement has been retained.

It remains to add, with regard to the first year of my student's career at Maynooth, that I must have done some private reading, though I remember little of it. I know that I came across some of Scott's poems, which I read with avidity. We were bound to supply ourselves with a full Bible, Douay Version; so I probably read some of that, besides what I had to get up for class. The Library, too, of the Junior House comprised some English classics; besides historical dictionaries and similar works; and there were a number of miscellanea which Dr. Murray had sent there recently – by way of overflow from his own collection. Some of my class-fellows, moreover, had got some volumes of Dickens, with whom I had not been acquainted hitherto; and I may have read one or two volumes of his; though if I did, surely I should remember. I remember Scott's *Lord of the Isles*, and that's all.

MAYNOOTH: PHILOSOPHY (1871 – 1873)

When we returned to College after the summer vacation of 1871, the New Era was begun. In the ordinary course, I should join the class of Rhetoric; but, as the finances of students and College were very much straitened, there was a tendency to shorten the course as much as possible; so it was easy to get permission to pass over Rhetoric into the Logic class – or to jump, as we called it in College slang. So I began the new year as a student of Logic, with obligation, in addition, to attend a class of French two or three times a week. The Professor of Logic was Mr. Hackett; whose course comprised Logic, for the first term, and Metaphysics and Ethics for the second. Dr. O'Rourke was the professor in French.

We had not all the students of the Logic class in our Division of St. Brigid's: not the freshmen, but only those who had been in the Rhetoric and Humanity classes the preceding year: about forty-five in all, I should say – a very small division. Our home was the Logic House; our grounds the small and very uneven field that lies between that House and the Junior Infirmary and the Gas-house, very cramped accommodation for young men, who, it must be remembered had no Christmas vacation, but, except when we went on a walk – every Wednesday that was not wet – were confined within the small area from the beginning of September till the end of June. It was little better than a prison as regards space. We contrived to enjoy ourselves, however; and I had a pleasant year enough. As summer came, we made complaint that we had no shade under which to walk; for the little wood between our grounds and the Parson Street wall was fenced in by a hedge, and it was out of bounds to be within that, under the trees. In reply to this complaint an opening was made in the hedge, and some rough walks were made in the little wood, near the gable of the Logic House. Whereupon some wag cut in the bark of a beech-tree, just inside, and opposite the opening in the hedge, the letters THE POUND, and the name stuck, it was recognized as so appropriate.

I began this second year of my course pretty much as I had passed the first – quite careless and idle, without, however, indulging in any great irregularity. Our textbook in Logic was a treatise compiled by Professor Jennings, Mr. Hackett's immediate predecessor in the chair. It was written in Latin, and as there was no translation here, one had to make oneself familiar with the Latin, such as it was, on pain of being considered unable to translate the text, which was the greatest reproach that could be made against a student. The language of the class, too, was Latin, which we spoke, of course, very badly, especially at first; but, then, we spoke it; and thereby acquired a familiarity with the language whereby we obtained a power over it – made it our own. Might not professors of Classical Latin and Greek take a hint from this?

During the first term, while we were at Logic, I took an interest in what was going on; had a textbook, which I studied; and though, as I now see things, the treatment was poor, yet it gave me a firm grip of the construction of sentences. It was grammar, as much as logic – and more. There were, of course, syllogisms, with their rules, and words and figures, with theirs; and sophisms; and certain criteria of certitude. I got through all this, and liked it; knew what was in the textbook, and was acquiring a new kind of command of Latin; all of which meant no little progress.

Things changed very much in the next term, when we began Metaphysics, on resuming class in January. We had a textbook in Logic; here we had practically none. The official textbook, I think, was a treatise which had been drawn up by one of the old professors of our College – Dr. Anglade, who had read in the Sorbonne. This text, however, was not followed in class – or not consistently followed; so that it was not necessary to have a copy; nor, as I think, were there many copies in the hands of the students. The great thing, we thought, was to have a good manuscript; by which was meant a record more or less verbally faithful, of lectures given in old times, and handed down from one generation of students to another, by scribes who copied the original record. As these scribes worked on the eclectic principle – of taking one lecture from one source and another from a different source, according as either was deemed the more satisfactory composition of the matter in question – the MSS. as a whole, were very irregular and unequal. Such as they were, however, happy was the man who had got a good and full one; so he judged himself, and so we all deemed him. When, afterwards, it became part of my duty to teach Philosophy, some old friend of my student days, hearing of my lot, sent me a MS. of this kind which had been deemed a treasure. I examined it, in high hope at first, but soon found that it was a very bald rehash of Tourneli's treatise *De Deo,* which in itself is not very valuable. What a pity it was to see students at this poor jejune stuff, instead of at a book, however poor; and above all, instead of a fairly good book – which might have been obtained rather easily.

Unfortunately – or fortunately – I had no MS.; nor even a copy of Anglade's treatise. As, however, the professor often referred to a little treatise in three volumes that had been prepared for the students of the Collège de St. Sulpice at Paris, by one of the professors in that institution, and as our professor not only referred to it, but gave us now and then dictates taken from it verbally, some of us, students, had a high opinion of it, and so I procured myself a copy. It was simple and easily read, but shallow, as I afterwards came to see. Whatever Metaphysics I learned that year, it contained; but as the work done in class was based either on Anglade's treatise or on some manuscript, what work I did was to a very large extent out of order and line. I had, moreover, begun to develop a critical taste; and, in discussions with fellow-students, tore to pieces not only the treatise of Anglade, but that of St. Sulpice, and even the sacred MSS., with the result that I did little more than criticize, and was in a very bad way when the midsummer examinations came round. There again, however, fortune favoured me. I was examined by Dr. Molloy, who had burst some of the biggest guns in the class – men who had got up the MS. by heart, but were allowed little rope by the examiner, who pinned them down to some one point to which he objected. It was just what suited my method of preparation, so that I came off with flying colours, to the delight, as I thought, of our professor, who saw one at least of his men stand to his guns and show some power of resistance.

This reminds me of another professor who used to examine the Logic class, giving the students – those, that is, who were looking on and listening – good amusement, by the facility with which he puzzled the ablest men. I refer to Dr. O'Hanlon, who was a diocesan of my own and one of my predecessors as Prefect of the Dunboyne Establishment; an office which he held for twenty-eight years, with a great reputation for ability and learning. It is curious how this character was made; for he published nothing; and, when examined, as an expert, in the famous Saurin case, did not make a grand impression. He certainly impressed the Dunboyne students; principally, I have been told, by the clever way in which he represented the theologians and pitted them against one another. It was said that he never told the students of his class from what book he drew his inspiration at any time; and that, if any of them happened to discover the source and show this, the Prefect fell back at once on some other author. A good while after his death one of his relatives put into my hands some of his literary remains; consisting, mainly, of some lectures on Ecclesiastical History, and disjointed notes on Canon Law. The history lectures I did not mind, as tradition said that his forte did not lie there; but I looked into the notes on Canon Law, which I thought elementary – such as one might find in any ordinary handbook. I found also about the same time, some specimens of Theses which had been defended by his best students at the end of the year, and which bore evident marks of his hand. They did not inspire me, and whether this was or was not due to some defect in myself, anyone can decide by taking up the Theses in question, which I took care to place in the College Library.

Of one thing Dr. O'Hanlon must have had a unique knowledge – the secret history of the Irish Church; for, as his reputation for learning in the Canon Law was very great, he was consulted on nearly all ecclesiastical matters, by the Bishops and priests concerned. It was said, indeed, that he was ready to advise both sides, as to how each might circumvent the other. When the annual endowment of the College ceased, the Dunboyne students were disbanded; those of them, that is, who had not acquired vested rights; which meant all but two or three. The Trustees then found work for Dr. O'Hanlon, by asking him to lecture on Canon Law to the students of the Third Year's Divinity Class, and what remained of those of the Fourth Year. These lectures he delivered with great éclat, possibly from the Notes afterwards submitted to me. He died, rather suddenly, in the academic year

1871-72 – my second year in the College.

To return to my own career. There must have been something very wrong with the way in which we were taught philosophy, seeing that it failed so utterly to interest one like me. For my whole outlook on life changed about the middle of this academic year – when we were engaged on the study of Metaphysics. I began to realize what I came to the College for; to say my prayers earnestly, and to observe the rule. My spiritual troubles began; first, as regards confession, wherein Dr. MacCarthy was very kind and fatherly like the good, holy priest he was. And yet, see how I worked at Metaphysics, criticizing, but doing little positive work. It was not all my fault, but was due in part – perhaps even in great part – to the system and the professor. If I had had a decently good book in my hands, it might have been different, or if the Professor had been able to handle the subject in an able, manly spirit.

I do not think Mr. Hackett can have been happy in his chair, for he did not seem to have any interest in Philosophy, or any sympathy with those who were engaged in the great struggle that was then going on – in Germany, France, and England. We used to hear a little of Mr. Mill, and I remember Mr. Hackett reading for us some articles by Dr. McCosh, also perhaps by W. G. Ward, but he read somewhat as a task, or to put in time, never as if the question discussed entered deeply into his own soul or affected his religious position. His one notion of teaching was to keep us to a dead grind of some old, traditional statements of doctrine, proofs, and answers to objections; all very bald and imperfect – very unlike what one meets in the real world. Darwin was then revolutionizing thought; but we overturned him in two or three brief sentences. Kant was a name of which we read in a paragraph of our books with Fichte, Schelling, and Hegel, all visionaries. Following in the wake of Darwin, in England, there was a school of Materialistic or Agnostic thought, captured by Huxley and Spencer; who, however, troubled Mr. Hackett very little. We were educated in a fool's paradise as if we were still in the eighteenth, or even the sixteenth, century.

I do not know that it was the fault of Mr. Hackett alone; the whole College was run in that way – as regards Philosophy; what was being done in Theology we shall see in due time. Take Dr. Walsh's book *De Actibus Humanis;* Dr. Murray's treatise *De Gratia;* Mr. Crolly's three volumes *De Jure et Justitia* – all deeply rooted in Philosophy – and you will see at once that, while there is a sufficient parade of opinions about this or that, there is little or no grip of fundamental principles. Utilitarianism is not mentioned by Dr. Walsh; nor would you, to read Crolly, ever suspect that the Social Revolution was at hand and that the principles on which it is based had been already proclaimed in Germany. The truth is that Philosophy was not one of the strong points of our College; and if that reproach holds no longer – as please God it does not – the happy change is due to a quiet revolution that took place among us.

Well, in his dealings with the students – Mr. Hackett was at once strong and weak; strong with the weak, dull men; weak with the clever ones and with the body. He took lengthy notes of the answers made in class and at the examinations, and was said to be severe on weak men in his official reports to the President, with the result that they distrusted and feared him. The cleverer men did not fear him; despised him rather; and he seemed to feel this – to be conscious that it was deserved, and that he was incapable of earning anything better. Hence he very easily gave way to pressure from the body; a pressure which was now and then applied to make him afraid – of something like unpopularity; with the result that I witnessed some very sad and painful scenes. He had a good deal of the manner and disposition of an old maid, particularly in his relations with the students. In after life I knew him to do one manly act, in circumstances when others of us were meek and quiet enough, as I shall relate in due time; and we used to hear it said that, before my time, he stood up, often unsupported, against Dr. O'Hanlon, who now and then brought pressure to bear on the members of the staff, to make them support some project in which he was interested.

Up to our time, the course of Philosophy, apart from Physics, was complete in one year; if that may be said to be completed which left Cosmology almost untouched, and did not even touch on Ethics. It was part of the new order that this Philosophy course should extend over two years; in each of which there would be half the number of classes per week that had been held previously – in the one-year course – while the course of Physics would be divided similarly and carried through the same triennial period. This arrangement took effect for the first time at the end of my second year in the College; during which, as I have said, we read as full a course of Philosophy, apart from Physics, as had been read by our predecessors. The result was that we had practically but a half-year's course of Physics, with compensation in the shape of one and a half year's course of the other branch of Philosophy.

The second year's course with Mr. Hackett was just a continuation of the first; indeed, not at all so profitable, as the Professor did not well know what to do, while the students were more familiar with his ways and feared him less. My recollection of what we worked at is very dim; some more Metaphysics, I expect; a little Cosmology; and Ethics. These last two subjects must have been treated very jejunely; as, though I was now very serious indeed, observing the rule strictly and working hard at whatever interested me, I took little interest in Mr. Hackett's course, though working at it sufficiently to make my position – of average student – quite secure. To my surprise, I was rewarded at the end of the year with a premium, though but among the thirds.

All this year I worked really hard at Mr. Lennon's course of Mathematics and Natural Philosphy; Algebra, Geometry, Trigonometry, Mechanics, Astronomy, and Physics. We ran through this long course so rapidly that it took one all one's time to keep up at all, even though one began with some little knowledge of Mathematics. The great bulk of the students were hopelessly behind. I suffered a great deal for lack of teaching; for, in Mathematics especially, the professor examined us merely, but did not teach; and many short cuts were unknown to me. I plodded along, however, in my own oldfashioned way, and was engrossed sometimes for days in the study of a problem, the solution of which would be rewarded to me in a flash, perhaps at Meditation or at Mass. There was much loss of time, as in the case of the rustic who made his watch; but there was excellent self-discipline also, which, I fancy, has stood to me ever since. Only why will professors examine their students so much and teach them so little?

Mr. Lennon had the character of an able professor, and certainly he worked hard, led a highly exemplary life, and made for us at times very interesting experiments in Physics. In this he inherited a respectable tradition, for his predecessor, Dr. Callan – who had passed away before my time – must have been a really able man. Mr. Lennon prepared his experiments carefully, and these lectures, though elementary, were very successful, or appeared so to men of our calibre: hence, I fancy, much of the reputation which he had. The philosophy of his subject he hardly ever touched on; or if and when he did, he showed how little interest he took in that aspect of physics and chemistry. Gravitation, for instance, was a fact, of which the cause was – gravitation. We were taught to wonder at the simplicity of a time when the rise of water in a pump was ascribed to some abhorrence of vacua felt by Nature; we must know better – that it was due to atmospheric pressure; but we were never told why the atmosphere pressed down, nor even set to wonder why it should be so; it was, of course, due simply – to gravitation. So, in Mechanics, we heard of potential and kinetic energy, of which the former was due, in some way, to position, while the latter was due to motion; but how position should generate energy we never asked, nor what was the relation between motion and kinetic energy. We knew that sound, light and heat were propagated in the form of waves; the light- and heat-waves being very rapid, comparatively, and being transmitted through what is sometimes called Space; which, accordingly, must contain ether. This we were taught to regard as very attenuated – if I may use that word; but we had not the least suspicion of the difficulty of propagating waves with very great rapidity in such a medium; nor had we any notion that it might be the store-house of all the energy of the universe – gravitation, chemical action, electricity, magnetism, and the rest. As regards matter, we were told that it was all made up of molecules and atoms, these last being of seventy different kinds, more or less; but we had no inkling of the deeper and subtler theories that Professors Thomson, Tait, Clerk Maxwell, and others, were propounding about the time; theories which coincided so remarkably with what we read in our books on Metaphysics, about First Matter. All of which means, or goes to show, that Mr. Lennon was no philosopher and had no turn that way – was in fact, teaching Physics as shallowly as we were afterwards taught Theology. He was a man of his time, in the College, in this respect.

During this second year of our Philosophy course, we began to hear lectures on Ecclesiastical History; which were continued afterwards till the end – a period of five years in all; the professor being Dr. Gargan. Of these lectures I really do not like to speak – they were so poor; we had no textbooks, the most of us; and we learned little or nothing. There were, indeed, in the divisional library, some Histories of the Church in French; sixteen or twenty-four volumed works, into which we dipped now and then – those of us who could reach French sufficiently well. But, as you may fancy, beginners at the subject were quite lost in forests of that kind. There was a short, one-volumed, History of the Church, in English, by Reeves – the same, I suppose, who had given us the History of the Bible in which I took such delight. This I dipped into occasionally, whenever I got a chance; and I know that it would have been very easy, at the time, to awaken in me a deep interest in the subject; but Dr. Gargan succeeded in stifling whatever might have been awakened otherwise. Not that he did not work hard; he was most painstaking, as the manuscripts which he left behind him prove. It was sheer lack of capacity – to take a grip of the subject himself or to hold our attention. What he seemed most to lack was what I may call perspective: every fact and date seemed of equal importance; and, in that great panorama wherein so many thought, and taught, and fought, and shaped the world, or lost it, and died, the date of Luther's grandmother's birth, or the number of bishops who were present at some session or other of this council or that, was as engrossing as the struggles of Augustine or of Hildebrand. This, of course, is an exaggeration; but it helps me to express what I mean. Great events were diminished to make room for little ones; or, if the professor dwelt on them – and he kept us for one whole year at the Reformation and the Council of Trent – they were thinned out so as to make all phases of the event of nearly equal importance. The principle of development, of course, was never mentioned – never suspected; and that wonderful growth of liturgy, dogma, and scholastic tradition, wherein we might have found such delight, on which, moreover, the great French historians of the eighteenth century had spent so much time and learning – this we had to discover afterwards. This last defect, I know, was due to the fact that Dr. Gargan, too, was a man of his time; for, as I shall have to record later on, the principle of development was not mentioned, in my time, in our schools of Theology. There is, however, no excuse for his lack of historical perspective and failure to awaken interest in so engrossing a subject as the history of the Church. We did not read it nor listen to it; nor did we care to read or listen.

Before passing away from this part of my College course, I may refer a little to the social side, of which the centre was the Study-hall. For, as our rooms were not heated during winter, in those days, except in the St. Mary's Division, where only theologians lived – and not all even of these – we studied during the cold months – from October till Easter – in large halls, which served as class-halls also. These halls were heated by great fires, around which those who were socially inclined used to sit before study began whenever the halls were open during recreation hours. We chaffed one another, told stories, sang songs, discussed Philosophy, and, of course, criticized professors and superiors. We were allowed such games as dominoes, draughts and chess, but not, of course, during study hours. I acquired some little knowledge of chess, which during the early part of my first year's Philosophy – before I began to settle down – I played, now and then, even during the time for study. We had tee-totum during that year, and lost or won our pennies as the letters turned up – A, H, P, or N; some losing more than they could afford. This, of course, was not known to the superiors. We played at hand-ball, in the ball-courts, the year round; and at cricket in the summer. Football and hurling were not then allowed; lest, it was said, an interdiocesan and inter-provincial faction-spirit should be raised, and we should kill one another.

Now that superiors have taken courage and risked the danger of strife, it has been found that the competition is not between province and province, but between class and class; so that these very games have been most potent to break down any spirit of provincialism there may have been among us; and which in my experience was very little. I had many close friends all this time, chosen from all the provinces indifferently; it was kinship of spirit, rather than geography, that determined the selection.

We had a short vacation of about ten days, after the Christmas examinations closed – that is, about the middle of January. During this time none but the Dublin and Meath students were allowed to leave the College; except, indeed, the Doctor sent one home; and many a scheme was laid to induce him to do so. He was a good, conscientious man, who was so accustomed to students shamming illness that it took almost a high fever to make him think one of us really ill. Yet he allowed us freely enough to stay a certain number of days in the Infirmary; where, though the diet was meagre, we could sit at the fire all day long and indulge in our simple amusements. The Infirmary was not a place for those who were ill – in those days. I found the Christmas vacations spent in College very profitable; for lack of other amusement, I read books which I should almost certainly not have read at home. The present arrangement may be better for the health, but I doubt whether it is as good for the education, of the students.

MAYNOOTH: THEOLOGY (1873–1876)

In September, 1873, I began my theological studies, and the fourth of my College course: it was the immediate preparation for the priesthood.

Under the Old Order, the course of Theology has for a long time extended over four years, so that, as one class finished each year, while another began, there were four classes; each of which had, almost up to our time, its own professor: Dr. Murray for the Fourths; Mr. Crolly for the Thirds; and so on. The year's course, in every case, comprised both Dogmatic and Moral Theology; which were taught by the same professor, who, moreover, traversed the same part of the course year after year, each of the four classes being taught separately. This meant as many as eight or nine lectures, or classes, in the week for each professor; too many, it was thought, to allow him to do any permanent work in writing.

To remedy this, a new arrangement was made a little before our time, whereby the classes were combined, two and two; the Fourths with the Thirds and the Seconds with the Firsts; and these doubled classes were taught by two professors, who still retained each his old share of the course. The result was that, at the expense of making the classes rather unwieldy, the number of lectures which the professors gave per week was diminished by half; so that as each man's course was comparatively short, they must have had abundant time for writing. Accordingly we began our theological course in this way, linked with the Second Year's Divines, and taught together with them, by Dr. Molloy and Dr. Walsh; both of whom had a course of part Dogmatic and part Moral Theology. During that first year Dr. Walsh lectured on Apologetics – *De Vera Religione* and *De Ecclesia;* and Dr. Molloy on Sacramental Theology. The latter did not remain with us the whole year; as, towards Easter, he became Vice-Rector of the Catholic University, Dublin, where he also gave a course of Physics. On his departure, Dr. Walsh took up the two courses, till the beginning of the next academic year; when Dr. Carr was appointed to the vacant chair, after a concursus, which took place during the vacation.

In our new course of study we had the advantage of definite textbooks: Perrone's *Praelectiones* in Dogmatic Theology; and in Moral, Gury's *Compendium*. We followed Perrone closely with Dr. Walsh, while reading *De Vera Religione;* but when we came to deal with the Church, we changed to a Compendium of Dr. Murray's book that had just appeared. This was more easily read than Perrone, besides being fuller, and more suited to the condition of these countries; so that the change had everything in its favour. The professor, moreover, gave us dictates, wherein the doctrine, the arguments, and the answers to objections were put more pithily, so that one could easily commit them to memory and make a better show at the examinations – if one were examined on the lines of the dictate. Dr. Walsh worked hard, and prepared us well for examinations such as they were. He did not merely examine, but teach; and, if the teaching was not very subtle or deep, perhaps we were not ripe yet for more than elementary principles. Finding that his dictates, which we had to write out in class, consumed a deal of time, he had them lithographed in our second year and distributed among us; so that he was teaching, practically, out of his own book. And yet these lithographs, though full, were not the same as a book, but were a kind of peptonized intellectual food, which one could assimilate without difficulty. It would have been better to teach us how to use books ourselves, without so much of this peptonizing.

Dr. Molloy was certainly a brilliant man who made things plain, or seem plain, though somehow it did not look as if his heart was in theology, or as if that was his line of study. He gave us a few dictates, not very condensed; which, however brilliant they seemed then, I found afterwards to be somewhat shallow. In his opening lecture, I remember, speaking of books of reference, he mentioned Bellarmine as the great storehouse; dismissing Franzelin in a few words as characterized by German fog. I do not think, somehow, that he had read much of Franzelin; his teaching certainly gave no proof that he had; nor, in Dr. Walsh's class, did we hear of Franzelin's classic work *De Traditione et Scriptura*. This and the no less classic treatise *De Sacramentis in Genere* may have been too difficult for us; though I doubt it, if the professor were able for his work and the classes were not too large. Certainly, the student who, as a result of one or two years at Theology, should be able to read such books with comfort, would be much better educated in the science than we were; though he might not be able to make so good a show at an examination conducted on the lines on which we were examined. It is not enough to impart knowledge, unless students are trained to gather it for themselves; for which they must be taught to read books, and not merely spoon-fed on notes and dictates.

Looking back now on the notions I acquired during the first two years of my theological course, I cannot recall having ever heard of the principle of development. We had Scripture authority for almost everything; and though, here and there, the testimony of Scripture might be obscure or lacking, there was no lack of patristic authority; as every doctrine which was set before us as Church teaching was known as clearly and definitely to St. Clement of Alexandria, Tertullian, Origen, or Justin Martyr, as it was to Fr. Perrone. It is not, I suppose, vanity on my part to say that I, who worked hard, was a fair specimen of the average student; yet I left the College, after a three-years' course of Theology, under the impression – not, I admit, formulated definitely – that if one could only ascertain what Origen and St. Clement knew and taught, one would have a perfect system of Theology. It was only when I myself came to teach, and read Franzelin's work *De Sacramentis in Genere,* I began to realize the growth of theological science; and on this matter, I hope, the students who read under me were left in no obscurity.

It was from Franzelin I first learned the doctrine of development; not from Newman, to whom so many ascribe it – as if it was discovered by him. Franzelin, I suspect, never read Newman's work, and was not influenced by it. Dr. Walsh, who was a student of the Catholic University in Newman's time, occasionally referred to him; not, however, to the essay on *Development,* but to some one or other of his *Lectures.* These we read; as also the *Apologia,* and *Loss and Gain,* but not the *Development,* which, indeed, may have been suspect, owing to its having been produced before the author was received into the Church. In fact, I think my own impression at this time was, that Newman, though a clever controversialist, as against the Church which he had left, was not a great theologian – to compare with our own Dr. O'Hanlon for instance or Dr. Murray. And in this, if I mistake not, I was in no way peculiar – among the Maynooth men of my time.

Another thing I notice now, looking back: that the only adversaries whom we recognized were the Protestants of these countries; Protestants, that is, of the old school – High Church men, Low Church men, Evangelicals, and so on; all, however, Episcopalians; with a shot, now and then, at the Presbyterians, but little thought of the Congregationalists or Unitarians; or indeed, of the new Rationalistic spirit which had begun already to wave over England, and which has since become such a mighty force in all Protestant, and most Catholic, countries. While reading *De Vera Religione,* we had our eyes on Hume; not heeding or recognizing Strauss, or the Tubingen school, or the subtle attack on supernatural religion which had recently been made, near enough to our own door, by Lecky and others. We went on arguing on the supposition that the Gospels, if not divinely inspired, were at least the authentic testimony of men who witnessed the facts described; which principle apparently, was not called in question by the unbelievers of the eighteenth century. And we did not notice how our position was being turned by the Rationalists, who ascribed the facts on which we relied partly to the imaginations of the witnesses, and in part to legends which grew up around what they had told and which became incorporated with their testimony. We were behind our time; slaying foes that had been disabled or killed long ago, and unaware of, or closing our eyes to, the new method of attack; with the result that, while we were not in the least danger of joining the Anglican or the Irish Protestant Church, some of us were painfully disturbed when we could no longer keep our eyes closed to the arguments of the Rationalists. This is true, at least, of one. Nay, so imperfect was the system which we formulated even on the old traditional lines, that it was turned inside out not many years afterwards by Dr. Salmon, whose work on *Infallibility* still remains without a sufficient answer.

Dr. Molloy, as I have said, was a brilliant man; who, however, seems to me to have frittered away his life on trifles – *Shall and Williana,* and such things. He took the greatest pains with the form of things; but he does not seem to have cared for deep thinking. We used to know that, being a poor penman, he took lessons in handwriting, even after he became a professor. He cultivated style; in conversation as well as writing; and no man in England, or elsewhere, with the possible exception of Professor Huxley could give a more brilliant lecture. He used to say that a lecturer should proceed as if his audience knew absolutely nothing of the subject. To judge from the way he sung High Mass, he must have been a poor singer, yet he made determined efforts. Before he got lamed by sciatica, he excelled in many outdoor sports; rode well, skated well, was an Alpine climber, and had no superior, or tried to have none, at ski-ing and tobogganing. His book on *Geology and Revelation* shows him at his best, I think; absolutely clear as to what geologists had already explained; and specious but not ultimately satisfactory, as to how the results obtained by them are to be reconciled with the opening chapters of the Book of Genesis. I remember hearing him say, not many years before his death, that he had been preparing a second volume, on the *Antiquity of Man;* but, having satisfied himself on certain points, thought it more prudent to keep his conclusions to himself. He had no taste for martyrdom.

His successor, Dr. Carr, I knew first as a professor, during the second year of my Divinity course; and, after I joined the staff, as Vice-President. He was not brilliant; steady, rather, and sensible. As a professor, he was very tedious – in my time; I was told that he improved afterwards. He was built for administration and rule, not for teaching; and I am not surprised that he should have proved a great success as a Bishop. He was amiable, and even jolly; could enter into a quiet joke or game; was even-tempered, but could be roused, as I shall have reason to show in time. He was a man of blameless life: a priest and a gentleman.

Well, in due course we passed on to the higher class, which was under the charge of Dr. Murray and Mr. Crolly; the former, in our case, teaching Moral Theology – Matrimony, and Justice – while Mr. Crolly had the Dogma – Trinity, Incarnation, and some of the sacraments. Both have left behind them so much evidence of character, in their works, that a student's impressions may well be spared. Murray was clear; but then, he did not go very deep; and when he tried to do so, was hardly impressive; not as one looks back now. He read for us occasionally, from the *Dublin Review* or some English book; and this he did beautifully. He was more ultramontane than the Pope; and lost no opportunity of venting his hatred of Bismarck, who was then enforcing the Falk Laws; and of Cavour, Mazzini, Garibaldi, and all the makers of United Italy. For United Italy he seemed to have nothing but hatred. He was a bigot, if there ever was one; and this trait in his character, I fancy, unfitted him to be a really great theologian; as he had not sufficient sympathy with error to realize an adversary's position. He was fond of boasting playfully; and said, on one occasion, that, as St. Thomas had received a privilege whereby he was relieved from temptations of the flesh, so he (Murray) had never had the least temptation against faith. This, though said in jest, showed the man's mind; he could not understand how a Catholic could have difficulty, not only about dogmas of faith, but even about received teaching.[1] Moreover, whatever view tended most to the honour and exaltation of the Holy See, or of the Church, or of God, the Blessed Virgin, or the saints, became, for that reason alone, to him more probable. He certainly was a Catholic.

He had a fine collection of books, not only on Theology, but on English Literature; and he rarely came from Dublin, whither he went every week, without adding to the store. His library overflowed to that of the Junior House; also to a reading-room sacred to the professors, which was then where the billiard-room is now. Soon after I became Librarian, this room being wanted for a billiard-room – which up to that time was part of what is now the Sacristy – it devolved on me to dispose of this collection of books; and I did so by turning nearly all of them into the Students' Library of St. Mary's Division.

Dr. Murray's room was quite bare of all but books, which were stored all round, in plain deal cases, well glazed. There was no carpet; nor pictures, that I remember, except one of Suarez such as may be found in the frontispiece of some old folio edition of his works. He read Suarez' *De Angelis* for Spiritual reading; also Lessins' *De Perfectionibus Divinis*. There was a rather long, narrow, deal table in the middle of the room; with a plain board-seated arm-chair at the head, towards the fire, where he sat at study. Plain unbacked forms ran at each side of the table; I do not remember any other chair. I was not, however, often in his room, even after I joined the staff. Shortly before his death, a servant asked me to go up, as the old man had left his bed and insisted on dressing and coming out to his sitting-room. I found him there, more than half dressed, and sitting in his chair; in the company of

1. In this connection, however, it may be noted that he himself advanced an opinion on divine co-operation which had not been heard in the Schools since Durandus' time.

angels, as he told me. We got him back to bed, and that was the last time I saw him alive. He was a holy man, even though a bigot.

Mr. Crolly I did not know so well, as he died before I joined the staff; so that my impressions of him are only those of a student. These I can set down the more freely as the books which he has left behind are evidence of what was in the man; for, to judge merely from the lectures which we heard, his character would be different. The Trinity is mysterious enough, however clear the professor may be; under Crolly it was awful. Even the Incarnation suffered; and when we came to deal with the redemption of Christ, one really could gather nothing, except that there was some kind of redemption. It was the custom for each successive class to ask Mr. Crolly to give a lecture or two on the principle *Lex dubia non obligat*. We asked, and received the lecture; of which I have no recollection except that it was one jumble. Crolly was at his best in his books. The portraits of him and Murray that hung in the College Parlour are very like the men, as I knew them.

Our course of Scripture extended over three years, I think, under Dr. MacCarthy, who has been already mentioned. The picture of Dr. MacCarthy in the College Cloister is not, as I think, a very good likeness; not near so good as a photograph at the Presentation Convent, Maynooth. We now came under him as professor, of the books of the New Testament, which he examined minutely – too minutely. To use a hackneyed expression, some of us did not see the wood for the trees; and we should, I fancy, have done much better if we had been made to read the text more, without note or comment; above all, if we had been examined without the text before us, and been made to read it so as to prepare for that kind of examination. We read Maldonatus on the Gospels, some of us; others of us A Lapide or MacEvilly; and Estius on the Epistles of St. Paul. We did not touch the Acts of the Apostles, as if it did not count; nor the second and third Gospels; and, so closely did we scrutinize the text, that we had not time to go through the Gospel of St. Matthew or St. John; the term being expired before we reached the history of the Passion in either case.

Dr. MacCarthy, like Dr. Murray and Mr. Crolly, has left such evidence of character, in his books, that the opinion of one who knew him merely as a student may well be withheld. He was just what he shows himself in the books – painstaking and conservative. He commented on the sacred text just as Maldonatus or Estius did, with the same undoubting and unsuspecting – one might say childlike – acceptance of the different books and every verse of them as the genuine writing of the pens to which they have been ascribed traditionally; and of course, as the word of God. He was acquainted, no doubt, with the new theories of the German Rationalists; but they seemed to give him about as much trouble as the doctrine of the Mormons, or of the Koran, or the sacred books of the Buddhists. They were doctrines which never could take root in Ireland or trouble any one in these countries. The prayers of St. Patrick, possibly, secured us that. In this respect he was simply a man of his time – in our College.

The great, strong, childlike faith of these men – *fides carbonarii* – was just the thing which a preacher requires; and, I have no doubt that they preached so well to us as to save most of us from any faith-troubles. But it was not scientific; nor, however they may have preached, can they be allowed also the fame of first-rate professors. A great world-shaking movement had been in progress for some years in Germany; had even found support in England, as witness the Colenso episodes; while our professors went calmly on their way, with a shrug at the most, or a sneer at a Church that could have any difficulty about dealing with the Colenso case. Dr. MacCarthy had a fling now and then at Dean Stanley, for throwing doubts on the inerrancy of the New Testament record; but we heard nothing of myths, or redactions or later insertions, or of the Synoptic problem, or of the many other commonplaces of modern Biblical criticism. Our strong, childlike faith kept us safe in the Middle Ages; which was well for such of us as could stay there always, but full of danger for any that could not.

There were two other men who influenced – or should have influenced – us during the latter part of our course, Mr. Tully and Fr. Gowan, C.M., both of whom deserve a word of notice. Mr. Tully was Professor of Irish, which he was supposed to teach to the students of the Second Year's Divinity Class; to all of them, that is, who were not exempted by their Bishops from the necessity of attending lectures in a subject so uninteresting and useless. As the Bishop of Ossory did not exempt us, I and my diocesans had to attend Mr. Tully's class. He was then an old man, white-haired and feeble; quite incapable of conducting a class. There was a notion current among the students that, owing to some private foundation, the chair of Irish was richly endowed; and that it was from this excess of income Mr. Tully used to provide the pious books, beads, scapulars, and other objects of devotion, which he distributed among those of us who sought counsel of him at his rooms. The truth is that he had no special endowment, and that he provided these things out of the income of a junior professorship, which was somewhat less than that of the deans and professors of theology. He was a pious man; zealous to hear confessions, and so he attracted people to him when he was younger, and used to give them these little gifts.

Being what he was, it was a pity he did not remain on the mission – did not do anything rather than occupy in our College a chair for which he did not seem to have any other capacity than a speaking knowledge of the Irish language. I may, of course, be judging him harshly, from what he was and did in our time, when he was old; though, perhaps he may have been quite different as a young man. Tradition, however, represented him as having always been uninterested in Irish, and not over-anxious to save it from decay. Some wag even said that he did more than all the Penal Laws to hasten the decay of the language which he was paid to teach and foster; and, certainly, unless his old age belied his prime, it would seem as if the sarcasm was not beside the truth. He came to us for the greater part of the year; during which he never did more than call a student's name, ask him to read, then to translate; and pass on to another man, to whom he gave the same commands. Once only I heard him teach, when he corrected what must have been a very dreadful mispronunciation of some Irish word; whereupon the man who sat in class immediately behind me, rose and gravely proposed 'a vote of thanks to the learned Doctor for the light which he had thrown on the subject'. This will tell you how the Irish language was taught in Maynooth College. I went into that class with an honest, though not very strong, intention of learning Irish; but gave up the effort after two or three lessons. Languages, however, were not my line.

A very different man was Fr. Gowan, who, by God's Providence, came to us at the beginning of my Second Year's Divinity, to instruct us in the art of preaching and teaching Christian Doctrine; as also generally, in the method of working a mission efficiently. He was then about fifty-five years of age, medium-sized, with a noticeable stoop of the shoulders; swarthskinned, spectacled, with iron-grey hair that was not divided or brushed back; dressed very plainly, in well-worn coat and hat, strong shoes, between which and his short trousers the stockings showed. The sisters of the Holy Faith at Greystones have a painting of him which is a very striking likeness. It was, I think, done from a photograph, by one who knew him. The Photograph in question, copies of which were common, is a very good one. I remember, the first time he appeared, how some of our fastidious young men despised him, while his being a Vincentian did not add to the warmth of his welcome, as the two Bishops of the congregation, Drs. Gillooly and Lynch, were not in favour with us. When, accordingly, Fr. Gowan proceeded to address us, in a strong, rough voice wherein there was no attempt to conceal the brogue, the first impression which he

produced was not favourable. Perhaps he never succeeded in win-
ning the esteem of those among us who judged a man by his clothes
and his accent – by his success in showing off, which Fr. Gowan
never attempted, but there were many of us whom he won over
late or soon, and who came to look on that iron-grey, rough, plain
man, not only with esteem, but with admiration and reverence. For
if ever man was in earnest in his work, Fr. Gowan was; and it was
that principally which won us.

Not alone, though; for we soon perceived that he was a man of
first-rate ability; and that, in particular, he preached not only with
great earnestness, but with true fire and eloquence. I never heard
him preach; but he read some of his lectures and sermons for us,
and they made a deep impression, even thus. His golden rule, on
which he insisted rigidly, was directness, terseness, brevity; few adjectives or adverbs escaped his pencil. He made us write six or
seven lectures or sermons each year, on lines suggested by himself; and he went conscientiously through all these, as the work of
his pencil showed; adding a little general advice at the end. Some
of our productions he read in class, as specimens; of what was good
and what was bad; pointing out how the bad might be improved,
the good made better. His aim was to chasten our style, by getting
us to avoid anything like fine writing; until, at least, we had acquired some mastery over Pegasus and could keep him well in
hand. He did us, I think, a deal of good; those of us, that is – and
we were the greater number – who grew to believe in him and
like him.

There are two other branches of our course to which I must refer: Liturgy and Sacred Music. The Liturgy was taught by the
Deans; the music by students who were members of the College
Choir, or by nobody. Both were taught execrably or not at all;
with the result that we left the College, knowing, indeed, how to
say the Divine Office and celebrate Mass; but with little or no
knowledge of liturgy, and unable, most of us, to sing a Preface.
Here, again, the Deans were at fault; as, in the Liturgy, they had a
splendid subject, in teaching which they could, as Mr. O'Kane had
done, rival the professors or even eclipse them. O'Kane, however,
had no successor; and the Deans of my time earned nothing but
contempt for the way in which they taught the Liturgy. As for
Sacred Music, so little attention did it receive that it is no wonder
the Requiem Office and High Mass for the dead should be the
abomination I have often heard; for which, instead of an honorarium, all concerned should of right receive a castigation. Art work,
surely, does no good and ought to cease, unless it is done with
some attempt at art – devotionally, and quietly, at least.

During all my time in the Senior House – four years – there was frequent disturbance in the students' Refectory, over the food-supply and kindred matters. After the first day, when I rapped a plate with my knife – a proceeding of which, almost immediately, I was thoroughly ashamed – I took no part in these disturbances. My fellow-students had many and varied complaints; that the bread was made of bad flour; that it was unbaked; that the tea or cocoa was bad, or the butter; that the plates or bowls were soiled or dirty: these are specimens. The students did not always agree as to the cause of the disturbance; some ascribing it to the bread, some to the butter, some to this or that other cause. The one great cause was that discipline was slack; not on the students' part alone, but on the part of the officials, who were careless in doing their work and paid little heed to the student's complaints, which, however, did not justify the measures which these took to make their complaints effective.

Seeing that I had but a student's opportunity of forming an opinion and apportioning blame, it would hardly be fair to say what I think now, looking back; but, as the Bursar of the time, Dr. Farrelly, lived in the College for some years after I joined the staff so that I had an opportunity of studying him at closer quarters, I am less afraid of saying that he was the kind of man that would be likely to give the students cause for dissatisfaction and to pay little heed to their representations. He was a large-framed heavy man, who seemed to have enjoyed rude health till a few years before his death, and who, while the finances of the College squared satisfactorily, paid insufficient heed to the refinements of our life. He worked through servants – stewards of one kind or other – over whom he used little supervision, and against whom it was impolitic to receive complaints; as that demanded supervision – which was just the nuisance. A perfectly straight, just man, according to his lights; which, however, did not show him that sour bread is either unwholesome or unpleasant, or that ill-washed plates are evils sufficient to set the world by the ears. In our refectory and kitchen the servants were all men and boys; almost all untrained, except for whatever training they gave themselves, in an institute where there was no one to train them. The upper-servants, stewards, or supervisors, had been promoted from the ranks; and, had, of course, all the habits and instincts of the untrained servant. Then, after the disendowment, there was less money going, so that the staff of servants was diminished and impoverished, with the natural effect on their habits and efficiency. This, I suspect, is why those outbursts of disorder took place just then. Two or three good women placed in authority in refectory and kitchen as at present, would have saved all the trouble; but it would have been thought too expensive then, if, indeed, women – religious or non-religious – would have been allowed to serve at all, even though they gave their service gratis. The admission of women – even religious – to the kitchen and refectories, was one of those reforms which have to be rejected two or three times before being adopted in our College.

I witnessed some sad scenes during these disturbances. The Deans were quite helpless, as the students saw, without growing in respect. On one occasion Dr. MacCarthy, then Vice-President and very unpopular, came to reason with us, but would not be listened to: was, indeed, booed in a shameful manner – the venerable, priestly man. The President, Dr. Russell, came to us on another occasion, to the refectory, and made a solemn and touching appeal, which had a temporary effect. At length the superiors took severe measures, rusticating five or six of those whom they deemed ringleaders; whereupon the students subscribed for a testimonial for the sufferers. This – as was hinted to me once by Mr. Hammond, after I joined the staff – very nearly got me into serious trouble; though I had hitherto taken no part in the disorder. For, as I was then Senior Monitor in St. Joseph's Division, those who were promoting the testimonial asked me to convene the students' meeting, and address them in favour of the project. I did not like the task, but yielded, partly from weakness, partly from compassion and kindly feeling for fellow-students in misfortune. We had the meeting, whereat I spoke, and handed in the first subscription; of which the superiors were informed in due course. They even considered whether they should take action against me; but fortunately for me, took a lenient view of the case, and let it pass without further notice. Looking back now, I see that I could not well complain if they had acted otherwise.

These disturbances recall Dr. Russell, our venerable President; a tall, spare, white-haired, scholarly, priestly man, whom everybody respected. He was one to be proud of, and we were proud of him. There is an excellent portrait of him, as I think, in the community dining-room; though his nephew – Fr. Matthew Russell, S.J. – who ought to know, said once in my presence, looking up at the picture, that there was something wanting in the likeness. I could never see the want. Dr. Russell spoke in a rather hollow voice, which most of us could mimic; not fluently, but often hesitating for a word; and at examinations he was not always happy in formulating syllogisms. Dr. Molloy could do this perfectly. We knew that Dr. Russell's *Life of Cardinal Mezzofanti* had been translated into two or three foreign languages; and that he was a scholar; but we had no idea that he worked then so hard as his nephew, Fr. Russell, afterwards made known. In many respects he was an admirable President; though he can hardly have been happy.

For it looks now as if, on becoming President, he committed the fault which so many men of his type commit – of giving up the line of work for which he was eminently suited, for one which did not suit him: a fault which always leads to misery, and not unfrequently to shipwreck. Before he became President, Dr. Russell had been Professor of Ecclesiastical History; and, knowing what we now know of him, through the revelations made by Fr. Russell, he must have been almost ideally suited for that chair and almost ideally happy therein. On the other hand, he had not some qualities which were badly needed by a President of our College in his time – and at all times. He was by nature very loth to interfere with any one, especially in a way to hurt one's feelings or cause pain; and, if the impressions recorded in this book are anything like correct, he was called on to interfere, in a way which would be very likely to cause pain to many people. With his knowledge of books and of modern life, he must have known what the Church had need of in his day, and how much of that was lacking in the College of which he was the head. He can hardly have been unaware of the shortcomings of the Deans; of the imperfection of the different courses of study; of the disorder in the Bursar's department, among the servants; and of the weakness of some of the professors. To remedy this, he would have had to admonish sharply, and even to report severely. This he could not do; so that one fears that the sad face which he almost always wore may have been due to a feeling that he was out of place – that he would be so much happier if he had remained in the chair of Ecclesiastical History. And if he had remained there, or if his successor, Dr. Kelly, had not been taken away so young, what a difference it would have made to the fame of either, and to the fortunes of our College! Good Presidents are very well; but good professors are so much more rare – and better.

I came into close touch with Dr. Russell but once or twice: on one occasion when he called me to his room in connection with some play or other on which we were engaged; and which he, very properly, forbade, by reason of its coarseness. Another occasion was just before I left the College for the last time, though I did not then know it was to be the last. He was organizing a penny-collection scheme, on cards, which he was trying to get the students to work; and, as I was then one of the most prominent of the students, he asked me to his room, where he explained his project.

He offered me, I remember, a glass of wine; but he – and I too, fortunately – was a total abstainer. He had taken the pledge from Father Mathew and kept it all his life, giving us all a good example. He spoke to me very simply and kindly; so that I left his presence with something of the same feeling of reverence, and even love, which Tom Brown felt for Dr. Arnold. It was the last time I saw Dr. Russell's face.

During the three years of my Theology course, I read a good deal of English literature. Books circulated among us freely; poetry, history, essays, but not novels. At that time we used to appoint some students as agents, to deal with the booksellers for books, which the agents sold to us; and as these agents were supplied freely, and we had free access to their rooms, while they did not press for payment, we bought books, or borrowed those which had been bought by others. Anyway, we had a fair supply; and some of us made use of them. The credit system on which we worked led, of course, to very unpleasant results, as the agents were not able to meet the booksellers' bills. And so feeble were the superiors, that, when this was brought to their notice, they could think of no remedy, except to forbid those agencies in future. If they had given notice that no book-agent would be called to priesthood who did not present either clear receipts from the booksellers or a list of defaulting students, the whole matter would have been arranged, and the fair fame of the College preserved. For the students would not have complained if agents returned the names of those who had not paid their bills; nor would these, when returned, have failed to pay, if their call to priesthood depended on the payment. It is fair to add here that a tradesman who supplied the students a great deal, and gave them no little credit, told me once that all paid him some time or other; as one might expect of priests. I hope the same holds of the bills that were due to booksellers.

All this time, the library at the disposal of the students was poor and uninteresting. It contained Suarez, De Lugo, Billiart, the Salamanca Course; besides many volumed Histories of the Church and such things; but then, we did not read much of Suarez or De Lugo, except here and there on some easy moral question; nor were we able to read them with interest: I remember, in this connection, when we were engaged on the Incarnation, borrowing De Lugo's treatise, with intent to read it carefully through; but was not able to get very far. Even now, to say truth, I find many pages of works of that kind quite uninteresting, if not quite unintelligible; they are based on a theory of physics so different from that of the present day. I read Carrière's treatise *De Matrimonio* with interest and profit, right through; till I came to the rules for applying for dispensations; where I stopped, as our professor, Dr. Murray, told us that part of the subject was only for Bishops, Vicars-General, and others – such as we should not be for a long time. So, too, when beginning the treatise *De Incarnatione*, with Mr. Crolly – who followed, or professed to follow, Perrone's *Praelectiones* – we passed summarily over the prophecies with which Perrone's treatise opens, on the ground, as the professors said, that the modern Jews have given up belief in prophecy. I mention these things – somewhat out of place – to show how scrappy our course was.

To return to our divisional library: I found it of some use for purposes of Ecclesiastical History; of very little use for Theology; and of none, practically, for general reading: this, at least, is the impression which I have at present. There was, of course, in addition, the College Library; which, however, few students ever entered. At the end of my Third Year's Divinity, as I was under age for ordination and so was supposed to be returning for another year, I was appointed to the charge of the sacristy of the Senior House Chapel: a position of great trust. The sacristan was bound to remain in the College for the retreat of the clergy of the Dublin diocese, which took place during the first week in July. Accordingly, I looked forward to at least two weeks of a stay in the College, with no company except that of books; and I went to the Librarian, Dr. Whitehead, for permission to enter the College Library and read there; thinking my request most reasonable, in the circumstances. Dr. Whitehead, however, was not of that view, but told me it was unprecedented; evidently fearing that it was all over with the Library, if a student, even though alone in the College and in a position of trust, were allowed to look at the books. There are some people who love books so much that they do not like to see them used; and it was, I fancy, by some feeling such as this that Dr. Whitehead was moved to preserve the Library from the profanation of being used by a mere student.

As regards this part of my life, I will add merely that some time – I think it was during our Second Year's Divinity – a few of us purchased a football and began to kick it in St. Mary's grounds, one evening after dinner. Soon, of course, the whole division were engaged; and we had a good time. Word, however, was brought to the superiors, who were at dinner, and who came out earlier than usual to see what was going on and wonder what they should do. They did not interfere that evening; but, when the bell rang for study and we were safe in our rooms or in the study-halls, they held a council, at which it was decided that football was an innovation – a dangerous one, too – and should not be allowed; a decision which was duly announced to us, at night-prayer. My lifelong friend. Dr. Sheedy, of Altoona, Penn, U.S.A., had the ball in his possession, or got hold of it and kept it in his room for twelve months; when he or some one else produced it again, one evening, on St. Mary's grounds, and had the entire division after it once more. This time, however, the superiors were not content to look on, but took up and confiscated our ball; and that was the beginning and end of the football game in the College in my time. I wonder are there many other things now banned as innovations and dangerous, which would turn out harmless enough on trial.

Such was my life at Maynooth, as a student; almost ideally happy, especially after I grew serious, and began to work hard and to observe the rule. I was blessed with a good constitution; enjoyed the plain, wholesome food; lost no minute of the eight hours, out of twenty-four, that were allowed for sleep; took part in all the games and most of the chaff; and had a friend in almost every one of my class-fellows. It would have been perfect happiness, were it not for some religious troubles now and then. A slight shadow of the future fell on me in my last year, in the shape of loneliness, when, on my being appointed monitor in St. Joseph's Division, I was partially separated from my class-fellows. The independence of the life at Maynooth had a charm for me. I knew no fear, whether of professor or dean; and if called on, would have spoken truth, however unpleasant, to the College of Cardinals; for I had no notion that an honest, well-meaning man could be injured by any one, and especially by any ecclesiastic. I was very innocent; but I loved my Alma Mater, and was proud of her.

KILKENNY ONCE MORE: PROFESSOR (1876 – 1881)

At the time of the disendowment of Maynooth College, as the income of the establishment was very much reduced, the course was cut short, so that only three years were allowed for Theology; except for such as were under age for priesthood, who might return for another year, to read, practically, what they had read already. This was my position. My Bishop, however – Dr. (afterwards Cardinal) Moran – wanted some help just then for the diocesan seminary at Kilkenny – called St. Kyran's when I was there as a boy, but now written St. Kieran's: a spelling which I shall adopt in future – and not thinking, perhaps, that I had much further advantage to gain from Maynooth, appointed me, though but a deacon, to a position on the staff at Kilkenny; whither I went on the 14th of August, 1876, to begin life in earnest. When the students returned, at the beginning of September, I was in the position of dean, with general charge of the whole College, under the President; and with special charge of the lay house. I was professor also, of Philosophy; with, I think, a class of English. I had, I know, a class of English afterwards; and I think it began with my first year as a professor.

Does unhappiness, I wonder, always begin with life; that is, with real life; which itself begins when one leaves the shelter of one's home, or what may have served as a home, and faces the world for the first time on one's own account? My first year at St. Kieran's College was very lonely; and, in that sense, very unhappy. Hitherto I had had plenty of companions, whose amusements – even thoughts – I shared; now, in the midst of people, I was quite alone. The President – Pro-President was his official title – did not wish me to mingle with the professors, lest I should be taken away from my duties as dean; so that even while walking in the College grounds, if they took one walk, I had to take another. I could not make friends of the junior boys, of whom I had special charge; or, perhaps they could not make a friend of me; difference of age and of position kept us apart. The two Houses had different refectories; and I took all my meals with the juniors, seated at a table apart, in grandeur, perhaps, but very solitary. It was an awful change from Maynooth. Three or four times during the year I went to my uncle, who was Dean of the Diocese and Parish Priest of St. Canice's parish, in the city – to beg him to ask the Bishop to remove me somewhere – anywhere – to the Mission; but was sent back to my duty with whatever patience I could muster. The Bishop applied to Rome for a dispensation in age; so that I was ordained priest on October 14, the feast of St. Teresa, when I was twenty-two years and four months old. In one way the College authorities were specially kind to me; as I was allowed the small salary of a professor from the beginning, even before I was ordained priest; though men who had joined the staff previously, after their ordination to priesthood, had to serve without salary for a year or more. This special kindness to me was due, probably, to my uncle's position in the diocese; but was, in any case, a mark of appreciation. The salary of a professor at St. Kieran's at that time was £ 50 a year; on which I was far richer than the Vicar of Wakefield.

I began my teaching career with Logic, using as a text Jennings' treatise, which had been our textbook at Maynooth. I was discussing it as minutely as we did under Mr. Hackett, meaning to devote the entire first term to Logic, but the Bishop, meeting me one day and inquiring how I was going on, insisted – very wisely – that I should hurry through formal Logic and begin business much sooner than I had intended. Indeed, I thought that no business could be more important than formal Logic; and, I believe, there are some of that opinion still.

Trouble began with me when I had done with formal Logic and got to work on Certitude and its criteria; a subject of which, as I very soon found, I knew just nothing at all. Finding Jennings unsatisfactory, I had recourse to the St. Sulpice treatise already mentioned (see Chapter 5); and as my students had not this in their hands, I began to put it into the form of a dictate for them; but I soon thought that even the writer of this great treatise gave but a confused exposition of his subject; whereupon I threw down his book, and never, as far as I can remember, looked into it again. It was the first of my stars to disappear in mist.

I found then, as I thought, that I could not do better than adhere closely to my textbook, which was a compendium of Fr. Tongiorgi's *Institutiones Philosophicæ* and was exceedingly terse and pithy, so that almost every line needed a comment, and often for beginners, a translation. It was splendid exercise, both for professor and students, and if the philosophy would not satisfy me now invariably, it was not at all a bad presentation of the teaching of the School, modified by what were then regarded, except among a few of the very foremost men, as the latest results of physical and chemical science. It was old, with a flavour of modern physics and chemistry, and that suited me; it was my first real introduction, in any case, to the Philosophy of the School. I retained the office of Professor of Philosophy during my five years' stay at St. Kieran's, working throughout on the compendium of Tongiorgi, which I used to translate – and comment on for the students, doing my best to teach them how to use a book for themselves. As time went on, I dipped into other sources; Fr. Tongiorgi's large book; Fr. Liberatore's treatise; a compendium of San Severino's *Philosophia Christiana,* and anything else I could lay hands on. My theological studies helped me; Franzelin's *De Deo Uno,* as also his treatise *De Habitudine Rationis ad Fidem* (at the end of his work *De Traditione et Scriptura*), and Newman's *Grammar of Assent,* which I read in connection with the last-mentioned work of Franzelin's. There may have been other books which I forget, but I read hard and criticized what I read; loth to reject, or even question, whatever came to me, as I conceived, with the authority of the School. Moreover, I passed over nothing in the textbook, however imperfectly I understood it, and, in my two-years' course finished out the treatise.

It was part of my duty, as dean, to lecture the students every Sunday morning, during the time allotted for meditation – about twenty-five minutes. At first it was arranged that my lectures should be given to the students of the lay house only, while the President took those of the Ecclasiastic House, but as, for some reason or other – pressure of business, perhaps – he was not in position to fulfil his part of the arrangement, my weekly lectures were given to all. The subjects were arranged beforehand, with the President, and I prepared the lectures carefully, working out a fair copy of each, which I kept permanently in a book. I had also to preach, in my turn – seven or eight times a year – in the Cathedral, and these sermons also I wrote out with care, making a fair copy of each in a MS. volume, just as in the case of my Sunday-morning lectures at the College. It was good exercise, which I needed, as is shown by the fact that when, a year or two after I left Kilkenny, I took down my MS. volumes of sermons and lectures, to glance through them, I had not gone far when I was so disgusted that I threw them into the fire.

After my first year on the staff of St. Kieran's, I was relieved of the office of dean – it was a relief – and put in charge of the class of Dogmatic Theology, and the two classes of Philosophy and Theology. I continued to teach for the remainder of my time in Kilkenny – that is, for the next four years. The two subjects went well together and helped each other, as those who know them know.

My theological course began with Apologetics – *De Vera Religione et Ecclesia* – with Fr. Perrone's *Praelectiones* as a text-book, which I read through with the students to the end, without passing over a page, according to my method and in conformity with the rule laid down by the Bishops. When I came to the section *De Analogia Rationis et Fidei*, at the end of that volume of Perrone, I told Dr. Moran that I could not teach it, as I had never read the question myself. He, however, would not listen to me, but made me teach it as best I could. And I did teach it very badly. To guide and help me in the treatise *De Vera Religione,* I had Notes taken from Dr. Walsh, when I read it under him; and when working on the treatise *De Ecclesia*, I read Murray's large book, plodding through it till I reached about the two-hundredth objection against infallibility, when I threw up the volume in disgust. It was another star set in or obscured by mist.

I had placed great hopes in the Notes which I took in class during my theological course at Maynooth, and which I had had bound up carefully in six or seven goodly volumes, but these hopes were completely disappointed, for I found the Notes of very little use when I came to teach the subjects with which they dealt, which shows that the exercise of my critical faculty had already carried me far beyond where I stood in my student days. These Notes, however, I kept till after my appointment to the staff of Maynooth College, when they went into the fire, together with the collection of lectures and sermons to which I have just referred.

It was during this first year of my career as Professor of Theology, while I taught the treatise *De Ecclesia*, that I first made acquaintance with the works of Franzelin, which, for many years I read assiduously, deriving therefrom great profit, as I conceived and still think. The treatise *De Traditione et Scriptura* was a revelation, so different from the interminable string of objections which wearied me so in Murray, and withal so full and strong. The treatise *De Sacramentis in Genere* also was delightful; it was there I got a glimpse for the first time of the principle of Development – the 'expositio doctrinæ' on which Franzelin insists so often, in that and other works of his. But it was, I think, the treatise *De Deo Uno* in which I delighted most of all, and from which I derived most profit. It seemed to take me for the first time into the heart of Scholasticism, and to make me feel at home there; when, that is, I got to read the volume with ease. For, at first, I found it technical, and in so far difficult; but, fortunately, there was among my colleagues on the staff of St. Kieran's one, Father Michael Cody, who had studied in Louvain, and who gave me considerable assistance. When I found a very technical passage, I usually brought it to him, and we read it together, discussing the various possible meanings, so that in the end I came to read the volume *De Deo* quite freely. It was an enormous advance; and what I read there threw ever so much light on what I had been trying to explain to my students in philosophy. Since then, I have gone beyond Franzelin, and do not now accept much that I then swallowed eagerly, but still I recognize him as a Master of theological science, regarding his works – especially the three which I have mentioned – as classics, and feeling ever grateful to him for the assistance which I then received.

Now I began to realize the imperfections of the course which I had read at Maynooth. It was not merely that the notions I took away from there, on what I had read, were often shallow; but, what was worse, there was so much that I had not read at all and on which I had not even shallow notions. We had not done the treatise *De Deo Uno;* nor *De Deo Creatore;* nor *De Gratia;* nor *De Virtutibus Infusis,* while in the treatise *De Incarnatione* we had passed over the prophecies as well as the questions *De Scientia et Gratia Christi,* and had made hash of the question *De Redemptione.* Some of the sacraments also we had done very scrappily. Those who have ever taught, or even looked into, the treatise *De Fide Divina,* will realize the difficulty of the position of one who had to teach the question *De Analogia Rationis et Fidei* without having ever read the treatise *De Gratia.* Yet I did it – so badly. I read Franzelin, as I have said, *De Habitudine Rationis ad Fidem;* with little profit, however, except to raise certain questions for myself; nor do I wonder at this now, as there is much in that treatise which, though intelligible, is quite unacceptable. At that time, I was prepared to accept almost anything, if I could but understand. Newman's *Grammar of Assent* was not much better – except for the fine apologetic argument towards the close – nor is it still. The philosophy is not true to nature, as I think, except for the doctrine of real assent – if it means anything like realizing one's belief, which counts for little in apologetics. One recognizes Newman's work, however, as an honest, downright effort to grapple with a question which is at the basis of faith, and which has been pressing ever more and more for solution in modern times. From his different volumes of Lectures I derived great assistance in my reading on the Church, and once, dealing with Unity in Fundamentals, when I had read and read Murray, without deriving any settled comfort, a sentence or two of Newman's gave me, as I thought and still think, the true key to the difficulty in his own life, and so had the right, living word to say.

Meanwhile our English studies progressed, regularly but slowly, as might be expected under a professor who was himself sorely in need of guidance. The great thing, I saw, was to provide books and get them read, so, with permission of the President, I got the students of the Ecclesiastic House to form a Literary Society, the members of which paid a small sum annually, wherewith to purchase books; and in that way we got into the Library some English classics, and other, perhaps more attractive, works in English. What was even better, the students gave up some of their recreation to read what was thus provided. Soon after this a Parish Priest of the diocese of Dublin, Canon Smithwick, died, leaving by will all his books to our College at Kilkenny, and as he had a very fair collection of the English classics and other interesting works, the bequest was a great boon to us. For I had his books placed at the disposal of the students, who made good use of them. It was through this bequest, I think, I first became acquainted with Thackeray, whose works have since been so often in my hands. About this time, too, I began to read Tennyson, who was for many years a support and solace.

For exercise in writing, I had my sermons, which were prepared with care; with constant remembrance, too, of Father Gowan's warning against fine writing – against exaggeration and untruth of every kind, so that I kept down the adjectives and adverbs pretty well. I wrote a short story at this time, in competition for a prize offered by some journal or other, but did not get the prize, or deserve it, for my story, as I now recall it, was unimaginative and poor. Carlyle's *Lectures on Heroes and Hero Worship* led me to write an essay on Mahomet, with a view to showing how differently the Gospel and the Koran were propagated. The thesis took me to Gibbon, and gave me no little trouble. About this time, too, while I was engaged on the Church and the relations between Faith and Reason, two articles appeared in *The Dublin Review*, on 'The Assent due to Certain Papal Utterances', which I read eagerly. The articles were by Rev. Dr. Butler, a Kilkenny-born priest of the diocese of Dublin, who did not convince me; nor have I ever since been able to understand how an assent can be infallibly secure while not true infallibly – which was Dr. Butler's basis of defence, taken from Franzelin. I prepared an article in reply, and sent it to the *Dublin Review*, but it was not published, as I am now glad to say. Our Literary Society, moreover, had at least one public debate – on the Inquisition, I think – at which I, as President, summed up the arguments and propounded my own views. This, as far as I remember, was the extent of my writing, though I may have done fugitive exercises not meant for publicity.

In this way I worked hard at Theology, Philosophy and English; reading, not only during the day, but well into the night, and as, when relieved of the duties of dean, I was appointed chaplain to the Loretto convent, where I had to say Mass every morning at 7 a.m., I had altogether too little time for sleep, with the result that, during my fourth year in St. Kieran's, I began to suffer from insomnia, a malady with which I have been troubled ever since. My nerves were shaken, with the further result that I became timorous as regards the foundations of faith, as also with regard to errors and contradictions in the Bible. These fears also have haunted and troubled me all my life, making it at times such a torture, as those only can realize who may have gone through the ordeal. Those who have been spared it – who have been and are satisfied with the traditional defence of the Catholic position – may well thank God for having escaped the anguish of suspicion, and fear, and doubt, which I have gone through, but – and this thought, perhaps, should make them modest as well as thankful – as they have not fought with lions, they did not realize the lion's strength. It is all very well to say that this or that is the traditional Catholic view, and hence must be satisfactory, until its unsatisfactoriness has been burned into you, when you may not be so ready to insist on every letter of the tradition. Dr. Murray and Dr. MacCarthy, who taught us at Maynooth, knew – or seemed to know – but one side of these questions, which strikes one very differently when one realizes the other side. I say now, very solemnly, that the conservatism in which I was trained very nearly drove me out of the Church on many occasions, or into a mad-house, and that the good, easy men who, for the honour of God would in the interest of religion, insist on these traditional views – making dogmas of what are but school traditions – are tormenting souls and driving them out of the Church.

Apart from these religious troubles, my life at St. Kieran's was, on the whole – after the first year – a very happy one. I worked hard, but it was at work which suited me and which I liked; I got on well with the President of the College and the Bishop, though both were small and irritating at times. My fellow-professors were company, as were also the priests of the city, whom I met occasionally, especially after my health began to give way, and I had to relax my efforts. These social meetings of ours were simple, such as we could afford, nor did we seem to need anything elaborate. Such as they were, I enjoyed them all the more that I was a total abstainer, whereby I was saved at once from danger of grave excess on my own part, and of being misunderstood by the senior priests and the diocesan authorities. I retained the same spirit of fearlessness and independence that I had at Maynooth, conscious that I was working hard and with at least average success; and having no ambition except to acquire knowledge, I had very little conceit of myself and, after my unsuccessful effort for the *Dublin Review*, had no thought of publishing, neither did it occur to me to compete for a chair at Maynooth, which in any case, seemed beyond my reach, so that the prospect before me was to go on teaching at St. Kieran's till I should be appointed to some parish, first as a curate, and then as Parish Priest. With this I was content.

During all my time at St. Kieran's as professor, Dr. Moran, afterwards Cardinal, was Bishop of the diocese, and, as we at the College were brought into close touch with him, the impression which he made on me may be not without some interest. He was tall and dark, of medium weight for his size, held himself very straight – if anything, inclining backwards; he seldom raised his eyes, and sometimes joined his hands in front and rubbed them together softly. He was reserved and shy, so that, when we met at his table, conversation was forced, and he seemed as glad to get rid of us as we were to get away. He worked constantly, taking no recreation, except a walk before dinner to the College, and thence, often to an orphanage which he had founded and placed in charge of the Sisters of Charity. His house was unpretentious, as was his whole style of living, though his table was well provided with china, glass, and silver. He had an old phæton, for which, when he went into the country, he used to hire a horse and driver, the turn-out being very modest indeed. He cannot have spent two hundred a year on his household, yet it was well known that he laid by no money, as he spent on books and gave freely to convents and other religious organizations of the diocese. He was a Churchman born, very much respected, a good deal feared, but little loved.

I have said that he was narrow at times. This led him, now and then, into conflict with some of the laity, who did not always fall in at first with his semi-religious, semi-social projects. It also tended to gather round him a number of good but narrow-minded priests, who stood by him through thick and thin, however the laity might grumble, as well as the more broadminded of the clergy. He multiplied curates, who, in some parishes, had very poor incomes; the Bishop seemed to think that it did not take much to support a priest. He seemed jealous of power, and also of reputation, and, at least in the case of the College, interfered in petty matters, receiving all kinds of stories from the President, who once asked him for permission to dine with some family in the city – a permission which the Bishop gave. He distrusted the professors and required them to send the examination-papers of their students to himself; used to go into class now and then, though after a visit or two to mine, he left me alone.

As showing what the priests were like whom he gathered round him, I remember an occasion when Lady Ormonde had a ball at Kilkenny Castle, to which some of the Catholic citizens were invited, and the question arose whether their ladies could dance waltzes and wear evening dress. For the First Synod of Maynooth, which had been held not long before, had, in a Pastoral Address, warned the faithful against 'the improper dances which have been imported into our country from abroad, to the incalculable detriment of morality and decency'. 'Such dances', the address proceeded, 'have always been condemned by the pastors of the Church. This condemnation we here renew, and we call upon all to whom God has entrusted the care of immortal souls, to use

94

every exertion to banish from our midst what is clearly of itself an occasion of sin.' There was more to this effect, and in one of its decrees (n. 216) the Synod enjoined on all priests, secular and regular, to endeavour with all the zeal at their command to prevent these 'fast dances'; while confessors are warned, in the same decree, that they shall not be doing their duty if, on any pretext, they permit such dances or excuse them. By 'fast dances' it was understood, were meant waltzes, polkas, and such, and as it was well known that these would be danced at the Kilkenny Castle ball, the good priests of the city had to bestir themselves to save their people. They admonished the ladies – that it was a mortal sin to dance a waltz, in evening dress especially, but as these ladies insisted that they, who had done this often, without thought of sin, ought to know better than even the bench of Bishops, a very ridiculous compromise was suggested. The ladies were told that they might go to the ball, provided the dress they wore was merely cut in a V-shape at the throat; and that they might dance waltzes, provided the gentlemen held both hands of his partner in front! The ladies, I think, solved the question – many of them – by dressing and dancing as usual; with the approbation of some of the more broad-minded clergy in Kilkenny and elsewhere.

Cardinal Moran grew more broad-minded afterwards, we have been told, in Australia. In Ossory he was rather a hard master, who, however, had one great redeeming quality, that in his own life he gave an example of work and self-denial, and that he required nothing from his priests which, if he were in their place, he would not have done himself. One tolerates a good deal, in the way of harshness, from a superior of that kind.

There is one man to whom – though I merely saw and heard him – I cannot but refer, as he impressed me greatly: Mr. C. S. Parnell. He came to a Land League meeting which was held on the Parade at Kilkenny, the platform being erected outside what was then called the Athenæum. Mr. Parnell was on the platform before the speeches began, very handsome, faultlessly dressed, reserved, almost haughty, listening, but speaking little. When called on to make his speech, he took off his overcoat; and, as I was near him – a little behind and at his right, so that I could see his eye – I had a good opportunity of studying him while he spoke. He was very nervous; not, however, as if he were afraid of the audience or doubtful of his own powers, but as if he were one seething mass of energy, striving to burst into violent eruption, but kept under firm control. He spoke a good deal with clenched right hand, and one could see the nails digging into the flesh, while up along the back his tightly fitting frock-coat showed the muscles playing as an instrument. It was the occasion on which he proclaimed himself a moderate land-reformer, who held a middle place, between some landlord-champion at one extreme, and our Bishop, Dr. Moran, on the other. For the Bishop had written to the meeting a letter which said, or seemed to say, that the landlords of Ireland were bound to make restitution to the tenants – of rack-rents received.

There was no great volume in Mr. Parnell's voice, but it was so distinct and cut so sharp that it could be heard all over the Parade, as one could see by the attention of the people who filled the place. While he spoke I could see his eye, which glinted with a cold blue-green light, not a flame, but like the glint of a bayonet. I have seen three men with remarkable eyes: Archbishop Croke, Fr. Tom O'Shea, and Mr. Parnell. Dr. Croke's eyes twinkled, or sparkled, with humour, but I never saw him angry, or even excited. Fr. O'Shea's eyes flashed – even blazed, with mere sheet lightning, however, which you felt was not very dangerous. Parnell's eye, when he spoke that day, did not flash or blaze, much less twinkle; or, if it did flash, it was no sheet lightning, but the true forked kind, blue-grey, cold and steely. It showed a devil in the man, and made you fear him.

I saw him once again, many years after, a short time before his death, when he joined, at Sallins, a train on which I was travelling. He had been at some meeting, and was attended by an ill-dressed rabble, while he was so changed from the handsome young aristocrat I had seen before. I was sorry for him.

MAYNOOTH AGAIN: ON THE STAFF (1881 – 1888)

When the summer vacation came, in 1881, and the students left St. Kieran's, I proposed to enjoy the two months, as usual, according to the modest means at my disposal; and did enjoy myself for three or four weeks. Then, however, my uncle, the Dean, sent for me, to say he had had a visit from the Bishop, who asked him to tell me that it was his – the Bishop's – wish that I should compete for a chair of Theology that was then vacant at Maynooth. The concursus would be held in September – about five weeks from the day my uncle sent for me. Here was a trouble, cutting across all my vacation plans; indeed, across whatever life-plans I may have had: for I had no ambition, and not the least thought or hope of anything higher than a curacy, and then a parish, in my native diocese. Moreover, I had a very poor conceit of myself, and did not think I had much chance of success in any competition such as that which one had to face in a concursus at Maynooth. However, I did not like to go against my uncle and the Bishop; and so, after a day's consideration, agreed to set about preparing for the fray.

There were, as I have said, just five weeks left to prepare; or, possibly, a little more, but not quite six; so there was no time to lose. I wrote immediately to ascertain the programme of examination, which comprised the whole course of Dogmatic and Moral Theology, with the whole course of Philosophy, including Physics, and some elementary Mathematics. To a class-fellow and friend, Father (now Dean) Connington, of Achonry – who had been a candidate three times at a similar concursus – I wrote for any useful hints he might be able to give as to the method of preparation; and, from what he and others told me, I made up my mind to concentrate on Moral Theology. For Dogmatic Theology and Philosophy I resolved to depend on the habitual knowledge which I had acquired as professor of these subjects, while for Physics and Mathematics, which, I learned, were not deemed essential, I could rely on whatever remained to me of the knowledge I had acquired as a student. So I worked away on Moral Theology almost exclusively, confining myself to Fr. Gury's *Compendium* out of which the questions were to be taken, and studying at least twelve or fourteen hours out of every day that remained for preparation. It was a hard pull, but, then, it was not long.

As a result of the concursus – of which, and others of its kind, I shall have something to say later on – I was appointed to the vacant chair. That was in October, 1881, after five years spent as professor in Kilkenny, where, though I was glad to leave for Maynooth, I had had a pleasant time, and made good friends among the clergy. It was, however, a relief to get rid of the two long courses, besides the great number of classes, for, with as many as twenty-one hours or more per week for lectures, as I had had for some time at St. Kieran's, it was impossible to make progress in one's own studies. Professors, if they are to be happy or efficient, must have plenty of time for private reading – and writing, too.

When I returned to Maynooth, Dr. Walsh was President, Dr. Carr Vice-President; the Dunboyne Establishment had been restored two years previously, with Dr. Murray as Prefect; Drs. Healy and O'Donnell were my fellow-professors in Theology; while Dr. Macauley held the chair of S. Scripture and Dr. Gargan that of Ecclesiastical History. We had not much intercourse, except at table, and in walking round the College grounds after breakfast and dinner, when the same few kept together always. We rarely went to one another's rooms. At table we always kept the same places, in order of precedence, not of seniority on the staff; so that I sat between Dr. O'Donnell and Mr. Lennon, with, opposite me, Drs. Murray, Macauley, Gargan, Hackett, and O'Rourke. They were troubled times, in the political world, for new doctrines had been broached by the Land League, and Mr. Parnell had initiated a line of Parliamentary action very different from the old Gladstonian Liberalism which had satisfied the aspirations of the men – even the agitators – who were now passing away. Dr. Macauley and Dr. Farrelly were professed Gladstonians, as Dr. Russell and Mr. Crolly had been, and would have been still, it was supposed, had they lived; Russell and Crolly were friends of the O'Hagans, and Macauley and Farrelly clung to the Russell tradition. Murray had been associated with Gavan Duffy, which shows that he was more advanced than the Russell group; but he was, before all, an ultramontane, who hated the Italian revolution, and thereby came to hate all revolutions; while it was plain that the Land League meant social revolution in Ireland. Murray accordingly denounced the League almost as fiercely as if it were aimed against the Papacy; ignorantly, too, I must say, for he read the newspapers very little. He was essentially a bigot. Dr. Farrelly joined in denunciation almost as ignorantly; for though he read the newspapers, he was the slave of what he deemed the old tradition of respectability. No one loved a lord more than Farrelly; and, if he could not get a lord to fawn on, he fawned on any of the gentry whom he met – even in print. Dr. Macauley also joined in smacking his lips, in the pompous way he had, and disdaining to listen to anything that might be said by an uneducated plebeian like Davitt, who had the audacity to set himself up against Mr. Gladstone and all the education, wealth, and respectability of the British Isles.

Dr. Healy – who sat at my side of the table, immediately above Dr. O'Donnell – not only applauded the denunciations of the Whigs, but very often set on these gentlemen, by his own flings at the agents and the methods of the Land League. He had joined the staff of the College two years before, and had already assumed a certain air of authority which the old men were not strong enough to restrain, but to which those of the younger generation were not prepared to submit. He was, certainly, a man of ability, which, however, was not over-refined or cultivated; nor was he restrained, by any sense of delicacy or consideration for another's feelings, from securing his object, whether it was a passing dialectical triumph or a more permanent and substantial prize. He was tall, blond, rough, strongly-built, though inclined to waddle in his gait. The portrait in the Cloister of St. Mary's House is not a bit like him, in the sense that it refines away to drawing-room smoothness all the rough strength that gave the man his character. It makes him effeminate, in so far as that could be done. He had imagination enough for an orator, and did speak well on occasion; though on anything like a prolonged flight, a pinion would give way, and he would fall into the mud. As a Conservative, he was out of place. He should have been a mob orator, and he seemed to know it.

He had ability, as has been said, but was indolent, not in the sense of spending his time away from books, but in the sense of not criticizing what he read, and not going with sufficient care into details. Hence his history, I am not surprised to hear, is unreliable; and history was his line, rather than Theology or Literature. Apart from D'Arcy McGee's poems, his conversation did not show much knowledge of English literature, and he had not sufficient sympathy with error to be a profound theologian. Self-confidence he had in abundance, and assertiveness, as he displayed in his conflict with Newman, wherein he showed no appreciation of the difficulty, and no sympathy with those on whom it pressed – and still presses – so heavily.

Against this combination of old-fogy Liberals and a Demagogue-Conservative, there were allied: Dr. O'Donnell, handsome, well-bred, polite, but firm, as became a friend of John Dillon's; Fr. O'Leary, sharp, independent, fearless, somewhat indolent; Fr. Boylan, good-humoured, honest, weak; and Fr. Scannell, Professor of Ancient Classics, a man of wonderful memory, who seemed to know Greek and Latin well, and who had little respect for Dr. Healy's knowledge of these languages. Dr. Hackett gave the Land Leaguers what assistance he could, principally out of opposition to Dr. Gargan, whose sympathies were on the other side, though he interfered very little. Dr. O'Rourke also sided with rebels, now and then; as did also Mr. Hammond; while Mr. Lennon was neutral or uninterested; and the President and Vice-President held aloof, though occasionally showing that they sympathized with the older school. Fr. Browne, who was a dean, and afterwards became Bishop of Cloyne, was a satellite of the President's, though, in his heart, I fancy, he had some weak kind of sympathy with the younger men.

Such was the community in which I now found myself. In politics, at this time, I thought myself a Tory, not, however, of so high-and-dry a kind as to exclude leanings towards a struggling democracy, so that, later, when Lord Randolph Churchill developed his policy of Tory-Democracy, I used to proclaim myself – half in jest, but a good deal in earnest – a follower of his. The democrat in me prevailed so much as to make me approve of the Land-League movement, with reserves, of course, as to the crimes committed, which, like other Land Leaguers, I regarded as accidental, such as will occur in war, however justly waged, and revolutions, however carefully planned and conducted. Before long, therefore, I found myself siding with Dr. O'Donnell, Fr. O'Leary, and the younger men, against the Gladstonians and Respectables; and, as Dr. O'Dea, who joined the staff within a year, took the same side, the balance of power was maintained pretty even.

I set down these political differences, because, now that I look back on that period, they are what strike me most in the lives of the College staff. We worked away at our books, but in this respect there did not seem to be much communication – whether sympathetic or antipathetic – between us. Whatever theological tradition may have been in the College was broken, practically, as, though Dr. Murray remained, he had lost grip of things, while of the other professors in the faculty, Dr. Healy, the oldest, had begun to teach theology only two years before. Dr. O'Donnell had been teaching one year, so that I, though their junior on the staff, had the longest experience as a student and professor. Besides, our courses were different; and as each of my colleagues had much more than he could do to make up his own subject, they could give little help on questions that may have been puzzling me. There was, of course, the Professor of S. Scripture, Dr. Macauley, who had been three years at a subject in which I was deeply interested; but, so little sympathy had he with my difficulties that, if he had been at it fifty years, I should not have thought of approaching him for help.

There remained Dr. Walsh and Dr. Carr, the former of whom had been a professor of Theology, appointed during what may be called the old regime, and therefore in a position to converse freely with O'Hanlon, MacCarthy, Crolly, Molloy and Murray at his best. Dr. Carr also had not only studied in the old school, but had been appointed to the staff on the retirement of Dr. Molloy, six years before MacCarthy was made Bishop, and before Crolly died. These two, you would think, might preserve the tradition unbroken. On the other hand, however, they had given up teaching and occupied themselves with administration; and, as far as I know those who did that in my time to become Presidents or Bishops, with their teaching office they resigned any deep interest they may have had in theological science. It was so with Dr. Carr, and even with Dr. Walsh, both of whom continued, of course, to dabble a little in theology; especially in the questions of Canon Law that are usually discussed in connection with morals, but had lost any living interest they may have had in questions of science and of history. I doubt, indeed, if either would ever have been of much assistance to one who was plagued with modern difficulties. Dr. Carr certainly would not, as he had not that kind of mind: was built for administration rather than for books or science; while Dr. Walsh's line was legal or political, rather than scientific, as his whole record shows.

This, perhaps, is the most convenient place to put on record my impressions of Dr. Walsh (his portrait, by Gagliordi, in the cloister of St. Mary's House, is a good likeness, except for the eyes, which are sleepy on the canvas but were not so in the man), under whom I read, as a student, for two years, when he was a hard worker and a successful professor; and whom I had now an opportunity of observing more closely, as, for the next five years, I was one of those who walked with him after breakfast and dinner round the grounds. Apart from these walks, he took little or no recreation or exercise, but read or wrote in his rooms all day, except when he went to Dublin. He was interested in the working of the Intermediate Education Act, which had begun to transform the secondary schools of Ireland; while the Royal University, established still more recently, received no small share of his attention. He had, moreover, given very important evidence before the Bessborough Land Commission, and he was still interested in the land question. I notice, too, on looking over *The Irish Ecclesiastical Record* from 1881 to 1885 – when he became Archbishop of Dublin – a number of articles from his pen on all kinds of subjects, some strictly theological, as; on 'The Fruits and the Efficiency of the Sacrifice of the Mass'; on 'The Hour of the Crucifixion' and, 'The Numbering of the Hours in St. John's Gospel.' With these there are articles on 'Gregorian Music'; on 'The Recent Changes in the Ecclesiastical Calendar'; on 'The Law of Charitable Bequests in Ireland', and other such. This shows on what lines his mind was moving at this period, when it was almost quite at liberty to follow its bent. It will be noticed that he does not touch on any question that would be likely to occasion religious trouble, with the exception of the numbering of the hours in the passion of Our Lord; as to which he recounts and classifies the different opinions that had been already set forth. It was the kind of question that was sure to interest him, but only speculatively, just as if it were a matter of profane history, and presented no difficulty in the way of faith.

As President of the College, he was eminently constitutional, never pressing his own views unduly at the councils, though their decisions were very different, at times, from what he would have done if unembarrassed by their advice. He was fair, too, and always showed a sense of justice, public justice especially, which, in his case, was the more easy, as, with the possible exception of Dr. Browne, he had no friends. He did not, indeed, seem given to friendship – to have much heart. I regard his administration, on the whole, as successful – more so than any I have known, while, of course, he had a much greater career before him as Archbishop of Dublin, yet I doubt whether he would not have been a happier, more efficient, and even a more famous man, if he had remained at his books, as professor of Theology. Not that he would have become a profound theologian; but that while there is great work to be done for the Irish Church – and, through her, for the sister Churches in all English-speaking countries – in the way of reforming the Canon Law whereby she is governed, there is not much likelihood of its being done unless some man like Dr. Walsh devotes his life to the production of the book which points out the lines of reform and prepares men's minds for its acceptance. Whoever will write these books will make himself a monument *ære perennius* whereby he will be known and honoured long after Dr. Walsh has become little more than a name on the list of presidents of our College and of Archbishops of Dublin. He had it in him to do the work that was needed, but chose to fritter away his time on the University question, Bimetallism, public addresses, and letters to the newspapers. He allowed himself to be drawn away from the line of work that suited him – the greatest mistake one can make in life. It is all the greater in proportion to the importance of what one renounces, and the capacity which one has to do it; both factors, in Dr. Walsh's case, being very considerable indeed.

In my new surroundings I worked away pretty much as I had been doing, except that now the programme set me was much narrower, so that I had time to make a deeper study. For three years I was engaged on Grace and the Sacraments, with the Junior Class of Theology – First and Second Year's Divines – till, on Dr. Healy's appointment to the see of Clonfert, Dr. O'Donnell became Prefect of the Dunboyne Establishment, and I took charge of the dogmatic course in the senior class – de Deo, de Deo Creatore, de Trinitate, de Incarnatione, and perhaps some of the Sacraments. Recognizing that dictates wasted a deal of class-time, I gave none; but instead had expositions printed and put into the hands of the students, a system which Dr. Walsh had initiated in our College. I produced in this way Notes on the Sacraments in general, on the Eucharist, and on God (I kept copies of these Notes till about ten or fifteen years ago, when, on looking over some of them, I was so much ashamed that I threw them all into the fire: lest any of the students should have preserved them, I should like to let it be known that they do not represent my present views), based, for the most part, on Franzelin, whom I now read very carefully; also in the case of the Sacraments, on De Lugo, of whom, at this time, I had a very high opinion. Together with these I read all kinds of books, those specially of the later Schoolmen. St. Thomas I had not yet begun to read very much, nor did I ever make much use of Petarius, as the history of theological development has never had much attraction for me – apart, that is, from the development that took place in the first hundred years or so after the foundation of the Church; apart, also I must add, from the development of sacramental theology. All this time, my own religious difficulties haunted and plagued me; and, to allay them, I dipped now and then into whatever modern works on apologetics – against the German Rationalists – I could find. This, however, was spasmodic: my regular course of reading and study went on traditional lines.

I find, on looking over *The Irish Ecclesiastical Record*, that I had not been a year in Maynooth, as professor, when my first published essay appeared in that periodical – on 'Tennyson's Philosophy'; showing what was then the bent of my mind. It was followed by other articles, more or less of the same trend: on 'Remission of Sin', 'Eternal Punishment', 'Wood's Philosophy', and 'Mivart's 'Defence of Theism''. I have not courage to read over these productions now, for, when I did dip, here and there, into the essay on Tennyson, it was bitter reading – calculated to take the conceit out of me. Thank God, no one is likely to collect these essays and publish them in book form; and yet, I have no doubt, writing them did me a deal of good.

One evening, somewhere about 1884, as we started for our usual walk round the grounds after dinner, Dr. Walsh, who had been in Dublin that day, produced from his pocket a little volume – entitled, I think, *A Primer of Philosophy* – which he had found on Gill's counter, and which he now presented, mockingly, as the quintessence of all philosophy. I took it in the spirit in which it was offered, expecting to find in it some amusement, and I put it in my pocket till I got to my room. It was written, I should say, by Mr. St. George Mivart, with whose works, apart from some articles in the reviews, I had till then been unacquainted; and this little volume, though published by Messrs. Burns and Oates, had the appearance of one of the science primers which were produced at that time for Messrs. Macmillan.

On reaching my room, I began to examine the Primer, and soon found myself taken to the very heart of things, by one who had been there. It was a revelation – not so much because of the questions raised, as by reason of the way in which they were handled – by one who seemed to have had to face them in his own life and in the conversation of his friends. The authors whom I had been reading hitherto wrote as if the errors which they refuted made no present appeal, at least to a man of sense and good faith; and very often what the opponents of religion held was presented in such a way as to make one wonder – if one deemed the whole thing worth so much attention – how anyone out of Hell or Bedlam could have said anything so silly or so malicious. Here, however, was what was being said, every day, quite near us: not by lunatics, or demons, but by men of great scientific attainments, who deemed it a duty to say what they said. You felt that philosophy had entered into the life of this man – had been, indeed, a matter of life and death for him and for his friends. Hence, small as was his Primer, it stimulated me in a way I had never felt before. It was the beginning of a new life – the life which I have led ever since, and which I am likely to lead while I live at all: the only life worth living, apart from the service of God, which may be found in any life to which He calls us, were it only, in Milton's phrase, to 'stand and wait'.

Having been introduced to Mivart in this way, I got other books of his – *Nature and Thought* and *The Genesis of Species* – which I read with avidity; I even got a copy of *The Cat*, thinking it something of the same kind. Of *Nature and Thought* I made a special study, which has stood to me ever since; as may be said, too, of *The Genesis of Species*, which, though now, of course, behind date in many details, sets forth clearly the main principles of Evolution. This, no doubt, is largely due to Darwin's unsuccessful effort; but that it should be done so soon, and in face of the consensus of approval with which Darwin's work was then received, is proof sufficient, and even abundant, of Mivart's genius. It was he who made me realize the fundamental principle, that all Metaphysics, including Psychology and Natural Theology, is based on Physics – understanding thereby, not only Physics proper, but Chemistry, Astronomy, Biology, in all its branches: in one word, what is now called Natural Science. It is because Aristotle knew this that his Philosophy is so true, essentially, and it is because their knowledge of Nature was so imperfect that the

Schoolmen, who were content to depend on Aristotle for their knowledge of Nature, drew from him so many blunders in Metaphysics. If our knowledge of Nature has grown since the time of Copernicus, be sure that our system of Metaphysics needs to be reformed on parallel lines; and, of course, reform in Metaphysics reacts at once on Theology. Few things pained me more than that Mivart, to whom I owed so much in the way of religious and scientific instruction, should, at the close of his life, have had such a struggle and have suffered such eclipse; that he did, throughout, what he deemed his duty, I cannot for a moment doubt; neither, however, do I doubt that he was wrong objectively, in attributing to the Church, as definitive, what she never taught definitively; but that such a man should be plunged into such misery by non-definitive teaching – a fate which I myself barely escaped, if by God's Grace, I do escape it – shows how good men, by ultra-conservatism, may be doing the devil's work when they are most zealous for God and religion.

Another somewhat similar book which I read about this time was W. G. Ward's *Philosophy of Theism*. Mivart opposed Huxley, Spencer, and their school, while Ward's antagonist was J. S. Mill, whom he combated along the whole line, but especially as regards Intuition, the Universal, Freedom of the Will, Causation, and the nature of Right, and Wrong. On the last three, Causation, Free-will, and Right, I did not find Ward convincing, but on Intuition, the Universal, and Necessary Truth, I do not know how he could be beaten. And as these notions are at the root of all discussion as to the spirituality of the human soul, I conceive that it is to Ward I owe whatever grasp I have of the basis of proof of that fundamental doctrine.

Meanwhile, something occurred in our community life in which I had a part which I regretted very soon, and which I have since regretted even more deeply. The Royal University had been recently established, with a certain number of Fellows as examiners and teachers, but it had not been arranged, when I came to Maynooth, how the fellowships should be distributed or where the Fellows should teach. On this aspect of the question there was some public controversy and no little wire-pulling; our President, Dr. Walsh – then a man of great influence – advocating a policy of decentralization, as against Dean Nevill and the Jesuits, who wished to have all the Fellows teach in Dublin, either in the College at St. Stephen's Green or in the Medical School at Cecilia Street. As against this, Dr. Walsh advocated the claims of our College at Maynooth, and of the Blackrock College of the Fathers of the Holy Ghost. On mere grounds of successful teaching in the past, Blackrock had a strong claim indeed; and it was, perhaps, to show what our College could do, that Dr. Walsh prevailed on the Trustees to allow those of our students who were reading Latin and Greek to present themselves for Matriculation in the new University. The experiment was made, with very great success, proving, it was maintained, the right of our College to its share of the Fellowships, should the students continue to read for the University examinations. Looking back now, I cannot say that I regard the proof as conclusive; for the experiment, in so far as it went, was fortunate, though in no way unfair or questionable; and it was well known, within the College, that the class on which it was made was a good deal above the average; and that years might elapse before we should have two students as able and well-prepared as Scannell and Keane, to whom scholarships were awarded on the occasion in question.

Well, our President had his way so far as to get some of the fellowships – three, certainly, perhaps four, for my recollection is not good – allotted to our College; whereupon a difficulty arose as to who should have them. There was one in Mathematics and Physics, which was at once allotted to Fr. Lennon, whose teaching of these subjects was deemed satisfactory. Naturally, the fellowship in what was called Moral Philosophy would fall to Dr. Hackett, and that in English to Dr. O'Rourke; but, whether it was that their teaching was not deemed satisfactory, or that the wires were pulled successfully against them, they did not receive the appointments, which were given to Dr. Healy and Dr. Browne, the former getting the Philosophy, the latter the English fellowship. This happened, I think, in 1882, the year after I joined the staff, when I had not the least notion that any professor could push himself or intrigue; so that I paid very little attention to what was going on around me. I know now that the appointment of Drs. Healy and Browne must have caused a good deal of jealousy, which, in a way, was justified, as neither had done anything for the subject in which he was to receive a fellowship. The President might plead, no doubt, that he could not recommend the appointment of Drs. Hackett and O'Rourke; but why did he recommend Dr. Browne? And though Dr. Healy's ability was unquestioned, he had shown no turn for Philosophy, till this chance appeared, when he published some flimsy articles in *The Irish Ecclesiastical Record*. But perhaps the appointments were not made on Dr. Walsh's recommendation, for both Dr. Healy and Dr. Browne were likely to have other strings under their control.

To add to the jealous feeling, the new arrangement depressed the Faculty of Theology, comparatively, as the salary attached to

106

these fellowships in the Philosophy and Arts courses was £400 a year. Already Dr. Healy deserted for what was now the sunny side of the College, and the professors in the Faculty of Theology, whose position had hitherto been the most desirable after those of the President and Vice-President, did not see why they should now take a back seat. To meet this objection, Drs. Healy and Browne were understood to be prepared to apply part of the Fellowship salary to some College purpose, not so much, however, as would leave their income at its previous level, else why take on the labour of the new position?

The new arrangement was conditional on the students of the College continuing to present themselves for examination in the University, and the Trustees, who had allowed them to do so once, as an experiment, asked the opinion of the College Councils – the Administrative Council and the Council of Studies – before making the arrangement permanent. In both Councils, as well as I recollect, the majority were opposed to the change: in the Administrative Council on grounds of discipline; in that of Studies, for reasons which I cannot recall. But though the reasons on which the majority professed to vote, no doubt, influenced their decision, subconsciously – if even so – they were influenced strongly, if not more strongly, by the motives which I have indicated. However this may have been, the Trustees refused to allow the body of the students to present themselves in future for examination in the University, and so the scheme fell through. As a professor of Theology I had a seat in the Council of Studies, and went with the majority, which, as I have said, I very soon regretted, and have regretted ever since. The part I played, it is true, was very small, and I allowed myself to be influenced by others; but it is unfortunate that, while open to influence on either side, I actually moved in the wrong direction, so that, though there may be some palliation, there is no excuse, for the little that I did.

This recalls another, though dissimilar, incident, of which, thank God, I have no cause to be ashamed. The See of Galway becoming vacant, on the transfer of Dr. MacEvilly to Tuam, our Vice-President, Dr. Carr, was first on the terna presented, as usual, to the Holy See for appointment to the vacant diocese. At the same time there was a movement in the political world to collect money for presentation to Mr. Parnell, then at the height of his popularity with the great majority of Irish Catholics, though very much distrusted and even hated by a minority – among whom were some influential clergymen – and by the British Government. The opponents of the Land League moved the Vatican to issue the circular *Quidquid de Parnellio,* which Mr.

Timothy Healy, M.P., some time after dubbed an 'idiotic circular'; and, whatever may hold of this criticism, the action of the Roman authorities was deeply resented in Ireland. Its immediate effect was to stimulate contributions to the presentation fund; and five members of the College Staff – Hackett, Boylan, O'Donnell, O'Dea, and myself – forwarded a joint contribution, over our names. In this there was no formal disobedience to the Holy See; as, though the circular was issued with a view to preventing contributions, it did not forbid them.

On the publication of our letter, in the *Freeman's Journal*, Dr. Carr was very much annoyed, and showed it, going so far as to say that we should hear more of what we had done. And, sure enough, the matter came up before the next meeting of the Trustees, who passed a resolution to the effect that members of the College staff were to abstain from taking a side on public questions as to which the Bishops of Ireland were divided. This resolution was not entered, as usual, in the Minute Book, which is kept in the College for the use of the staff – that they may be in a position to see the acts of the Trustees whereby they are affected. It – the resolution – was to be read, privately, by the President to each of the five of us, but not otherwise communicated to us. This, of course, was lest it should be forwarded to the Press.

Well, the President, Dr. Walsh – whose hand we thought we could trace throughout, in the form of the resolution and in the precaution taken to keep it secret – came separately to each of the five, soon after the meeting of the Trustees, with the resolution written on a scrap of paper which he proposed to read for our benefit, telling us that he did so by order of the Board. Four of us listened to it; not, however, Dr. Hackett, who, before the resolution was read for him, asked might he have a copy, and on being told that copies were not to be supplied, said to the President respectfully, that he refused to accept or listen to a resolution that was not given to him in writing. There was some grit in the man.

This, I think, was the first occasion on which I knew – or felt – that an act so solemn as that of the Episcopal Body could be drawn up on false pretences; for none of us could believe that we were reprimanded in this way merely for taking a side in a matter of public interest in which the Bishops were divided. The resolution was passed, we felt sure, at the instance of Dr. Walsh and Dr. Carr, who feared lest Dr. Carr's appointment to Galway should be jeopardized by so many of the College staff subscribing publicly to a testimonial which the Vatican had discountenanced. The papal circular was falsely coloured, striking at the testimonial without daring to strike openly, just as the episcopal resolution struck at us, not for the reason assigned, but for one which had to be kept concealed. When poor Dr. O'Hickey got into trouble afterwards, it never occurred, even to their Lordships or the President of the College – who was not the man to miss a point – that, in publicly advocating what has been called 'compulsory Irish' in the National University, he – Dr. O'Hickey – took a side on a public question on which, as was notorious, their Lordships were not agreed, if they were not to a man opposed to what Dr. O'Hickey advocated. Yet he was assured, as was the whole country, by a formal letter of Cardinal Logue's, that he was as free as air to advocate 'essential Irish', provided he did so temperately and respectfully. So little did anyone think of the crime of taking a side. And, indeed, why should not a professor at Maynooth be at liberty to take a side, publicly, on such a question, even though some of their Lordships might have advocated the contrary opinion? Think of a professor in Trinity College or Oxford being forbidden to avow himself a Liberal or a Conservative as long as the members of the Board were divided in their allegiance.

Yet another incident of those days. On Dr. Murray's death he was succeeded by Dr. Healy as Prefect of the Dunboyne Establishment; though, if I do not mistake, as there were no students, or almost none, on the Dunboyne during Dr. Healy's single year in that office, he continued to act as professor to the senior class of Theology. When he was made Bishop, after a year, there was some difficulty about supplying his place on the Dunboyne, as Dr. O'Donnell, the senior of the three professors of Theology, had been himself a student only four years before. We – the three professors in question – learned that the President, Dr. Walsh, had written to Dr. Murphy, at that time professor of Theology in Carlow College, practically offering him the vacant position, if he would take it; and while we deliberated on the news, Father Boylan a staunch friend of ours, urged us to write a respectful letter of protest to the Trustees. We did so, claiming, rather cheekily, that, as we had won our chairs by concursus, we should not be passed over except for one who had given the same proof, and demanding that, if none of us was appointed to the vacant office, it should at least be given by concursus, at which one of us would compete. This protest resulted, as we hoped it would, in the appointment of Dr. O'Donnell. That Dr. O'Donnell – who, certainly, at the time, was very young and inexperienced – should have made such a protest, shows what manner of man he was, even then; and ever since his life has been consistent – full of pluck.

I do not regret my share in this transaction, though Dr. Murphy has been all my life a friend of mine; but there was a principle in question, and private friendship should not count. I do not know, indeed, that Dr. Murphy would have come among us, even though the President's offer had been endorsed by the Trustees. Since then I myself have recommended the appointment of professors without any concursus; but this should be only on the recommendation of the Faculty which he would join, the members of which, moreover, would not be empowered to recommend for the vacant chair anyone who had not given proof, by published writings, of his fitness for the position. I know Dr. Murphy's ability very well – that he is capable, if he wished, of producing admirable works in Theology; but, as he never produced any – not even an article in *The Irish Ecclesiastical Record* – I should regard even his appointment as the introduction into our system of the thin edge of the wedge of favouritism. On the very occasion on which our protest was made, Dr. Owens was appointed Professor of Theology, without concursus; and whatever one might think of him – who was my confessor and true friend, and for whom, as Dean and Bishop, I have the highest respect – one who knew his capacity as a theologian could not but regard his appointment to the chair of Theology as a job. We should have had more of its kind if the principle of selection without concursus or public proof of capacity were admitted, however excellent its results might be in a particular case.

Whatever political differences or other struggles and rivalries we may have had during these early years, interfered very little with our friendship, and our modest social enjoyment, at least among the younger members of the community, including Drs. Boylan, Healy, and Browne. We had many pleasant meetings and some good excursions by car and at least once on foot. This was when a party of five of us – Healy, Browne, O'Donnell, O'Dea and myself – drove to Saggart and there took the hills, walking to Glencree, Lough Bray, and Enniskerry, whence we went by train to Dublin on a fine May day. Dr. Healy was splendid on a mountain, which seemed to set his fancy free and ennoble him: he became a patriot and a poet. At that time there used to be a ladder, in the summer months, in the keep of the old castle outside the College gates, whereby one could get up to the top, and there, lying on the grass with which the old wall is covered near a certain angle overlooking the town, I spent some pleasant evenings with Dr. Healy, who told stories from Irish history, which he illuminated by snatches of the poetry of Mangan and of D'Arcy McGee. Sometimes, indeed, on these social occasions, he kept us – O'Donnell, O'Dea, and myself – in our places by reminding us of how young we were and inexperienced; yet he was pleased to admit that we were men of promise who might yet make some mark. Yes, we were good friends, as, please God, we are still, those of us who remain, though some of us have since had differences, and are not now so frank or innocent as we were in those early golden days. I, certainly, retain very tender recollections of the friendly intercourse that took place between us then, and especially of the sympathy shown me and mine when I nearly died of fever, and of some pleasant evenings we had in my rooms during the time of my convalescence. These are things one would not like to forget, and though they can never happen again, one blesses God that they did once happen and that they can never wholly pass away.

There are a few things which I will put on record here, so that old College doings, of little importance in themselves, may not pass altogether into oblivion. When I joined the staff, our entertainments were simple. Port and sherry were served during dinner, that is, when there was a guest at table and on examination days. Claret came later on, and fruit on greater occasions, when we had a large number of guests. Even so, fruit seemed to be a novelty, due to Drs. Molloy and Walsh, and perhaps to Dr. Russell: I could not imagine men of the type of Murray or Gargan giving fruit. The tendency was, at that time, to have dinner in the priests' refectory, with a little plain wine or punch after, and then to retire to the entertainer's room, where there was a finer wine – Madeira, claret, or champagne on greater occasions – with fruit. The billiard-room had been established long before I joined the staff; but smoking came much later. I never saw cigars handed round, even in the rooms of the professors, during those early years.

Our dinners, even when guests were at table, were plain, but good – quite in keeping with our office as seminary priests. There was soup – always the same – and joints, the same too, always in number and kind. We got sweets – a pudding and a fruit pie – when there were guests, but only then. The joints came to table, and were carved by those who sat to dinner: boiled leg of mutton at the top; ham, fowl, and roast mutton towards the centre, and roast beef towards the end. Except the boiled mutton, which was always carved by the President, the other dishes were carved now by one and again by another of those few who sat in the region where the dish was placed. It was somewhere in the time of Dr. Gargan's Presidency, as far as I recollect, that the carving came to be done by the servants, principally, I think, owing to the advocacy of Dr. Mannix, and very much, as I well remember, against the wish of Dr. Fogarty, who always maintained that we were fools to do away, as he used to say, 'with our fine joints'. Looking at it now, I do not know that he was not right, though I was of the number of those who came under Dr. Fogarty's wild lash for advocating the change.

When I joined the community the old fashion was maintained of asking guests to have the pleasure of wine, and as each of the community thought himself bound to show this mark of respect to each of the guests, you may fancy how many challenges there were at times. Fortunately one could escape by merely raising the glass towards one's lips. A new professor was challenged in this way on his first appearance at dinner, by all the staff in turn, beginning with the President; and on examination days, the President of each board of examiners, day after day, while his examination lasted, asked each member of the board to have the pleasure of wine.

This reminds me of another custom which we had on examination days of having lunch in the rooms of the president of the board, who provided us with some meat, as a rule, a little wine – champagne occasionally – and now and then some fruit. We had a speech, too, from some member of the board when the examination came to an end, the students flocking in from all parts, and cheering lustily. Mr. Crolly, I remember, told funny stories on these occasions, but, as a rule, the speeches were poor. They were discontinued soon after I joined, and to some extent, I am glad to say, through my influence, in the sense, at least, that I was one of a few who dared to give them up. No one, however, made any difficulty when we put our resolution in practice: even the students seem to have tired of the drivel they had heard.

I have said that our dinners were plain, though good; and our breakfast was plainer still. There was tea, bread-and-butter and boiled eggs: no meat. Sometimes, indeed, we would have reserved, from the roast beef served at dinner, some slices for breakfast next morning, the butler getting charge of the provisions. I remember how one morning, having heard that Dr. Gargan, then Professor of History, had made this arrangement, Fr. Boylan, who was Bursar, ordered the servant in charge to produce the store at tea, when it was consumed by three of us in a spirit of simple mischief – Dr. Carr, Fr. Boylan, and myself. We three retired to Fr. Boylan's room, where we had a glass of wine. It was, as I remember over Dr. Gargan's room, and we made some noise, and even danced a step or two, to show how we had enjoyed his provisions. This was very extraordinary, but it may help to show the kind of amusement in which the members of the staff would indulge at that time.

Boiled eggs, it should be known, were not served at breakfast from the beginning, as, when I joined the staff, there was quite a fresh tradition of a time when eggs were supplied only when a guest was present. He had to get eggs, at the very least, and, that there might be no peculiarity, every one got the same treat. The resident medical attendant of this period – Dr. Edward T. O'Kelly – was a pious man, and came into the College Chapel very often to hear Mass; and I used to hear that when some of the staff wanted an egg for breakfast, he invited the Doctor to the meal – with unselfish hospitality. They were simple times. When I said we had no meat for breakfast, I should have made an exception – of examination times, when there was a large joint of spiced beef at the lower end of the breakfast-table, and each one could cut off what suited himself. This may have been provided at other times – Christmas and Easter: my memory for such things is not very good. There was no luncheon till later – when, owing to the addition of classes, the dinner-hour had to be postponed. When I joined the staff it was, I think, at 4 p.m. It was later, too, that we could get cocoa for breakfast and supper, a change largely due to my weak nerves. China tea came much later, and was introduced, I think, principally by Dr. Sheehan. I have never seen a cigar smoked at the public table in the College, but that, too, may come, even before I pass away.

PREFECT OF THE DUNBOYNE ESTABLISHMENT
(1888 – 1894)

On the appointment of Dr. O'Donnell to the See of Raphoe, I became Prefect of the Dunboyne Establishment: that was in June, 1888, nearly twenty-five years ago. During this quarter of a century I may be said to have lived my life: done the work that it was given me to do, and enjoyed the supreme good of doing it and of suffering for it. After my appointment, my uncle, the Dean, writing to congratulate me, said I had now the most desirable position in the Irish Church; which was not the whole truth, as I now think, after the experience of so many years. He should have designated it the most desirable position in the Irish Church or in any other; always, of course, provided you are able for its duties and not afraid of its responsibilities; when you will be likely to get into trouble, as I have done, but need not be unhappy. Or if all trouble implies unhappiness, it is such unhappiness as is made easy to bear by the consciousness of having done one's duty: 'work, be unhappy, but bear life, my son'.

On the morning of the day on which I was appointed, I asked the Archbishop of Dublin, Dr. Walsh, to propose the resolution of appointment at the meeting of the Board; and I asked the Archbishop of Cashel, Dr. Croke, to second it: which they did. Before consenting, however, Dr. Walsh asked me why I did not get my own Bishop to propose the resolution, and I was able to inform him that Dr. Brownrigg would not be at the meeting. This was the only occasion in my life when I asked anyone to recommend me for promotion, and I have since regretted – as I do still – that I asked then. Nor should I have done so, were it not that I felt assured there was no question of appointing anyone but me.

At the beginning of my career as Prefect of the Dunboyne, I followed, or tried to follow, what I understood to be the tradition of my predecessors, who, we used to hear, did little more than preside at disputations conducted by the students, interfering only now and then in the discussion. Dr. O'Hanlon, we were told, used to lecture in Ecclesiastical History, and possibly in Canon Law; but taught Theology by the method of disputation, as described. Fortunately for me, as I thought, I was relieved of the duty of lecturing in Ecclesiastical History, which, when I was appointed Prefect, was assigned to the Professor of that subject; but, as against this, I was expected to teach a more formal course of Moral Theology, which, however, was much more to my taste. I continued to lecture in Canon Law for some years, till we were empowered to confer degrees in Theology; when, as the Dunboyne students, in preparation for the degree of Licentiate, were expected to make a more profound study of Theology, both Dogmatic and Moral, it was deemed advisable to keep me to these subjects, giving Canon Law, like Ecclesiastical History, to the professor by whom it was taught in the ordinary course.

In this way, the curriculum on the Dunboyne was greatly remodelled; for whereas, in the old times the students had had but one professor, practically – not counting the Professor of Hebrew, who lectured once a week – now they had several; and, besides, if they did not take Theology or Hebrew, there was an option of something else. For, when I was appointed Prefect, an arrangement was made for teaching the Dunboyne students Modern Languages – French, Italian, and German; though I do not know how this arrangement succeeded, or whether it still holds. Dr. Browne had a tendency – shared by many men who never taught – to set students many different tasks and so make a show – on paper. He wanted, similarly, to bind us on the Dunboyne, to hold one of those dreary public disputations every month; so that I had to make a protest to the visitors, or whoever was making the new arrangements. The result was that, on my guaranteeing that each one of the students would take part every year in some one public disputation, we were let off with one at the end of each term; and as regards the languages, though the students were still over-burthened, Dr. Browne's programme was curtailed. Opportunities of learning – languages or anything else – are good; but to force students of Theology, while pursuing a post-graduate course, to learn in addition several languages, is to make them attend lectures in which they take no interest and for which they make no preparation – the very worst thing you can do with a man.

Well, though I carried on the classes in Theology by way of disputation, at first – appointing as subject of discussion for each day some Question or Article in a textbook, which we followed regularly – I soon felt it necessary to interfere constantly, to make the students face the really important points. Often they did not know what was important; and sometimes, for lack of preparation, they found it easier to spend the hour on some old-time wrangle, of no bearing whatever on modern life or thought. As the course was long and the class-time at our disposal comparatively short, and as I wished to let no question of real importance go unconsidered, I had to confine the discussion in Class to the more difficult questions, leaving easier ones for private study. This brought myself forward more and more, as I got a firmer grip of these difficult questions, with the result that, after some years, the disputations developed into conferences. We still have some formal disputations, towards the close of each term, but, as a rule, we make the class-hour a conference, wherein the students are encouraged to propose any difficulties they may feel. And as difficulties are so common, and so much more easy to propose than to solve, the Prefect, whose duty it is to find a solution for all, has his work cut out for him; especially if he should be resolved, as I have tried to be, never to ride off by confusing the issue or throwing dust in the eyes of his hearers.

As, moreover, the solutions which I proposed and advocated, differed sometimes from those which the students had heard and accepted previously, I have had to disabuse them of some old notions, and to supply them with others, against which they were at times deeply prejudiced. This implied a certain amount of mental friction, which was good for both sides. Few professors, I fancy, have had anything like the advantage I have had, in hearing my teaching criticized in this way, year after year, by a number of clever young men, who, if they accepted it at all, did so only with great reluctance. I have always welcomed this criticism, and tried to profit by it, lopping off or modifying any part of my teaching which I could not defend to the satisfaction of my own conscience. No doubt, like the students, I have passed over questions which others find important, but which did not appeal to me. In the books which I have written will be found the best evidence as to how far this has been so; but the students, I expect, will testify that they were allowed and exercised the fullest liberty of opinion. They were, moreover, allowed to defend their opinions and criticize mine with perfect freedom; and if, at times, their arguments were met with undue ardour on my part, they understood, I hope, that the heat which I showed was evoked, not by any feeling of resentment, so much as by love of truth, joined to keen dislike of the old-world prejudices, whereby, as I have long believed, progress in philosophical and theological science is so much retarded.

For, the science of theology, as I understand it, derives from three sources: the deposit of faith once for all committed to the keeping of the Church; the history of certain events connected with divine revelation; and philosophy or knowledge of nature. There has been no litte ignorance, and even error, in the Schools, as regards all three branches; as would be admitted at once, I fancy, with regard to history and philosophy; though most theologians, I expect, would not allow that, even as regards these, ignorance and error have prevailed so much as I think. There would, I take it, be much greater reluctance to admit the existence of error, or even ignorance, as regards the meaning of the deposit of faith; though, were the most conservative Schoolman to reflect on the difference of opinion there is as to the interpretation of many parts of Scripture; also that, as the most conservative will hardly deny, considerable light has been thrown recently on certain passages – (the early chapters of Genesis, for instance) – as to which the theologians of a hundred years ago were, surely, not in ignorance only; he – the above-mentioned most conservative Schoolman – would, perhaps, not complain of the statement that a hundred years ago there was no little error, in the schools of theology, even as to the content of the deposit of faith, and, of course, what was true of one century may hold of another; and, in matters of this kind, is likely to hold; though, of course, the mass of error diminishes with each century by the amount that in each may have been cleared away. It is only the definite teaching of the Church that may not be in error; and there is comparatively little defined even as to the content of the deposit of faith.

Accordingly, as years went by on the Dunboyne Establishment, I realized more and more that is was not for me a question merely or learning what had been taught; but of harmonizing it – as much

116

of it as would harmonize – with itself, and with other truths which one has to accept as such. And as I could not begin with exegesis, history, and philosophy, all at once; not at least, with all those equally, extensively and minutely; I took up what came readiest to me; which, owing to my bent of mind and previous studies, was philosophy. I found, that is, that quite a great part of the conclusions of the science of theology – dogmatic and speculative – though, no doubt, deriving to some extent from the revealed word of God, was deduced as much, if not more, from other premisses known by reason – from philosophy. Finding, moreover, on pushing inquiry further, that these philosophical premisses, however metaphysical or psychological they seemed, derived ultimately themselves from knowledge – real or supposed – of nature, I perceived that good part of our traditional theology depends for its truth on natural science. And as the natural science of the School, from which it derives, was in many parts quite different from and opposed to what are now the received conclusions of the same science; I saw that theologians – myself among them – have got to choose between some of the received conclusions of modern physical science and equal number of those of speculative theology.

If, of course, it came to a choice between definite teaching of the Church and any scientific conclusion, however widely received, the duty of a Catholic theologian would be clear, in peril of ceasing to be a loyal Catholic; and as I was resolved to stick to truth, wherever it led; while, with God's help, I have remained a sincere and loyal Catholic; I managed to get over any difficulties that arose, partly by satisfying myself that the conclusions of physical science, in so far as they are opposed to any definite Church teaching, are not such as commend themselves to a prudent man; and, in other part, on the ground that, when such conclusions cannot be rejected in prudence, even though they seem opposed to traditional or even official Church teaching, the teaching in question may be regarded as non-definitive, and may, in such circumstances be rejected without disloyalty to the Church.

This implies no doubt, that there were parts of the traditional philosophy and theology which I rejected; as, indeed, I did – more and more as time went on. And yet I must say, I found – or seemed to find – that the main lines of the traditional arguments and conclusions could be retained; in many cases, modified, no doubt; that when so modified, they received a new strength from the now so much clearer teaching of natural science on which they depend. Instead of rejecting incontinently the new knowledge of nature, I strove to see whether it might not be retained as a handmaid; and I satisfied myself that it could. How far this satisfaction was justified my writings must be left to show. But, of course, as I rejected any part of the traditional teaching, I was bound to come into conflict with the more conservative body of theologians; and as a pioneer in a humble way, was bound to suffer. That was anticipated, as part of the day's work; and as such, I hope, has been accepted.

So far for the conflict, sometimes real, between the physical sciences of our time and the theological science of the Schoolmen. It remained to deal with the apparent conflict between modern science, allied with historical criticism and the content of the deposit of faith; or, to put it in another way, with the question of error in the Bible. I have already placed it on record that this question caused me the gravest anxiety for years, as I could not be satisfied with the traditional solution of the difficulties raised; with the result that it was only after much trial and by God's great mercy I did not altogether renounce the faith; as, I fear, I might have done, ultimately, had I not at length satisfied myself of the truth – or the tenability of more liberal principles than those in which I was brought up. If these new principles were published, perhaps I should suffer more for them than I have had to suffer for my rejection of some of the conclusions of theological science. I may, possibly, have been – and be – out of harmony with official teaching; as I certainly have departed from the traditional view; but then, I find it comparatively easy now to keep within the pale of the Church, which would not be true if the traditional view were taught definitively, as, please God, will never happen. And perhaps, moreover, I could show that the tradition is not consistent; so that, while there is one line of it which I do not accept, there is another – more fundamental – on which I insist, and which is rejected by those who would blame me for departing from the other.

This double conflict – of science with traditional and official teaching and of criticism with the Bible – absorbed my attention for years, so that I had little time for history; except, indeed, to keep myself satisfied, as a kind of outsider, with regard to historical reliability, in the main, of the books of which the New Testament is composed. Keeping myself so satisfied, I devoted almost my whole attention to the science of theology, as such; and my progress therein was accelerated greatly, as I have always thought, by a method of procedure which I adopted very unwillingly at first. It was a rule in the Dunboyne Establishment, in Dr. O'Hanlon's time – the golden age, of which we were so often reminded by those who survived it – that some of the students made a public defence of certain theses. This exercise was very formal: took place, as the concluding act of the year, before the assembled students, professors and trustees; the objections being put by the professors, or by any of the Bishops who might be willing to break a lance with the students. In my own student days there were some strange traditions amongst us as to conflicts that took place on some of these occasions, between Dr. O'Hanlon and some of the other professors. Such legends grow nowhere so luxuriantly as in the atmosphere of a theological seminary, wherein the students have little else to talk of. Anyway, these disputations – which, since the revival of the Dunboyne Establishment had, practically, not been held – were ordered anew by the Trustees, when I became Prefect; so that every year we had to draw up a body of theses such as we might hope to defend against all comers – professors and others.

Now, if I had been cute – as I never have been – and cared merely to stand on the defensive, I should have advised the students to cull a number of propositions from the ordinary handbooks; and, in defending these, to depend on the traditional answers to objections. Bear in mind, however, that I had myself now reached the stage at which I was dissatisfied with much of the tradition – its conclusions, arguments, explanations; and I felt it cruel to expose young men to the ordeal of a public bombardment, against which, as I felt, they could no longer defend themselves on traditional lines. Such an exhibition, moreover, would be, I thought, a disgrace to the Dunboyne Establishment and to the science of theology of which it ought to be the home. And so, rightly or wrongly, I deemed myself bound in love of truth and honour, to have recourse to no chicanery or subterfuge; but to propose Catholic teaching such as I should represent it to real inquirers and adversaries, and to defend it only by such arguments and explanations as I should advance in conversation or controversy with them. This meant putting my own conscientious view of the question – whatever it was – before the students; and, to leave no room for doubt, I drew up the theses, doing my best to outline therein the arguments wherewith I should defend them and the solutions that I should give to the main difficulties which I felt myself. These collections of theses, sometimes amounting to near three hundred, were published regularly in the College Calendar, till the publication was interfered with by an event which I shall have occasion to record later on. They show the stages which I had reached in some of my convictions from the time of my appointment as Prefect of the Dunboyne to June, 1895.

The preparation of these theses I have since regarded as a very potent influence in the development of my theological views. It necessitated – or I thought it did – consideration, not only of the deposit of faith and the physical sciences, but of the science of theology; on which the objectors were most likely to fall back for most of the difficulties which they would propose. In this way I was led to harmonize theology with itself – to see that no part of the system which I held was in opposition to any other part; and where I found – as I did – that the tradition of the schools could not be brought into harmony with itself, I had but to choose what seemed to me the more fundamental or better part. This I did vigorously; with the result that I got farther away from teaching which, as it has become more and more common in the modern schools of theology – those in which the prevalent influence has been that of Suarez, De Lugo, and other great Jesuit theologians – had come to be regarded in our College as part, almost, of the ordinary magisterium of the Church. My defence was, and is, that the Jesuit theologians themselves departed from an older and more fundamental tradition; or that their teaching was and is in irreconcilable opposition to the same.

After we got power to confer degrees, these public disputations ceased; or, rather, were replaced by others no less formal and public, wherein the candidates for Licentiate in Theology – of whom we have had one or two every year – defended twenty-five theses for that degree. And as it was an exercise for the degree, I thought it right to let the candidates select their own theses, as well as the lines on which they would defend them. And so the theses which I prepared were published for the last time in the Calendar for 1893–4; though in the next academic year I prepared an elaborate set, *De Gratia,* which were not published for reasons that shall be set forth later on.

For years after this (1894–5), my attention continued to be devoted mainly to the science of theology – harmonizing it with itself and with the physical sciences. With what is now called positive theology, I dealt very little, as I did not feel the necessity of it in my own life; for, with me, during all my time as a professor, theology has been a science, not merely to be known, but to be cleared of error and to be developed – just like chemistry or physics; nor could I indulge in the luxury of history till the more pressing need, of harmonizing and developing, had been satisfied. I felt indeed, the urgent necessity of establishing the credibility of the books of the New Testament, and to this I gave attention; though I did not go into it much in class, as I deemed it better to leave that duty to the Professor of New Testament Scriptures. So, too, I realized the force of the arguments that can be drawn from the history of the Jewish people, for and against the credibility of the New Testament; as well as those which the history of the Christian Church supplies for and against the same. These also I deemed it well to leave for discussion in class to the professors of Old Testament Scripture and Ecclesiastical History respectively; the more as, on my appointment to the Dunboyne, I had been relieved of the lectures hitherto given by the Prefect on ecclesiastical history; whilst, later on, when the Dunboyne students were being prepared for the Licentiate in Theology, it was arranged that they should get lectures on the Scriptures of the Old and New Testaments from the professors of these subjects.

Almost the only need I felt for dabbling in positive theology was to find some basis of support for the opinions which I advocated: no doubt a woeful need. Not that, as far as my own convictions were concerned, I cared very much for such confirmation, or that I deemed it confirmation at all; for, if theological science may develop, just like that of physics or chemistry, it makes little matter what St. Augustine, or St. Anselm, or Duns Scotus, may have held on a certain point, more than it matters what Paracelsus may have held on a certain point in chemistry, or Ptolemy about the relation of earth to sun, moon, and stars. You do not find chemists or astronomers writing whole libraries of positive chemistry, or astronomy; because of course, they really believe in the development of their sciences. Which confirms me in the view that, if Catholic theologians have begun to take example of their Protestant fellows, and instead of further developing the science of theology, inquire into how it was developed so far; it is because they have some kind of notion that either there is no science of theology, as Protestants now seem to think; or that the possibility of development has ceased, for whatever theological science there may be; or that, by developing it, one is likely to come into conflict with authority and to lose one's chance of preferment. Naught remains, on each hypothesis, but to cultivate the history of opinions; for which, of course, we have the shining example of the Protestant schools.

There is, indeed, one branch of positive theology which I have always regarded as of the utmost importance – the story of the constitution of the Church and of the development of her institutions during the apostolic and sub-apostolic ages; which story is to be gathered – in so far as it can be gathered at all – from the New Testament and a very few other brief documents. Of the questions raised in this connection the most important, perhaps, is that of the position of the See of Rome, especially during the first centuries. For my part, I put off this branch of theology till

I should have acquired some kind of mental satisfaction as to what I deemed the more pressing questions of harmony – such as I have described them; but of late, I am glad to say, I have been able to make up my mind as to much of the early history; and the conclusions which I reached, with the evidence that convinced me, may be found in my volume of *Essays on Religion and the Church*.

I have not had any soul-trouble about Pope Honorius, Pope Virgilius, the Council of Constance, Galileo, or such matters; the distinction drawn between provisional and definitive teaching having settled all that. I own, however, to some suspicion of trouble over what is hardly ever mentioned by the adversaries of the Church – the seemingly definitive teaching of the Council of Vienne as to (1) the relation of the human soul to its body and (2) the unlawfulness of usury; and I wish that I had time to go into these questions thoroughly. Of late, too, I gave some thought to the development of the theology of the sacraments; not, however, primarily as history, but in aid of a theory of sacramental efficacy. My researches in this connection will be found in a volume of *Notes and Queries in Sacramental Theology*.

Besides these works, and in addition to essays contributed from time to time to the *Irish Ecclesiastical Record* and the *Irish Theological Quarterly*, there are in existence four other volumes to show the nature of my researches: *The Principles of Moral Science; On Motion; On Virtues;* and *The Theological Virtues of Faith, Hope, and Charity*. The three last-mentioned works contain my theory of the supernatural; which, indeed, has been almost fully, though incorrectly, formulated in the collection of theses which I prepared for the Dunboyne Disputation in June, 1895: the theses that were not published in the Calendar. I mean, should God spare me, to recast these theses, so that they may correctly set forth my present notions; but the great body of these notions may be gathered from the three volumes I have just mentioned; on which, mainly, I stake my reputation as a theologian.

POLITICAL OPINIONS: THE PARNELL CRISIS

In Chapter 8 of these Reminiscences, I have referred briefly to some of the changes that took place in my political opinions; recording the fact that, in the stirring days of the Land League, I used to class myself as a Tory Democrat. I was not then emancipated from the Tory tradition in which I had been brought up;

and yet my sympathies were with the people of Ireland in the revolution which, as I could not deny, they were conducting with regard to the tenure of land. I used to distinguish carefully between Democracy and Liberalism in these days.

To many, if not most, of those who are acquainted with the almost unremitting conflict that has been waged since the Union between Irish Nationalists and the English Tory Party, it may appear strange to hear one like me say that he was brought up in the Tory tradition. What I mean is, that, in spite of our opposition to official Toryism, Irish Catholics have been more Tory than the Tories — in some important respects. There is not, as far as I know — and there has not been since the Union — a Tory leader in England who would not advocate the principle of rebellion, given, of course, sufficient cause and a reasonable chance of success. As against this, so conservative have we been in Ireland, at least in our theological schools, that we have denounced as immoral in every possible case rebellion against authority, once properly constituted. The most we have allowed is what we have called 'constitutional agitation' — casting votes, but not firing bullets; and as any votes which we might cast could be overridden by the House of Lords and the sovereign, who must not, as we have held, be forced into compliance by anything stronger than a vote, we were bound by our principles to go cap in hand to ask them to be pleased to sanction the reforms which seemed good to us. If this is not Toryism, I do not know what the term means.

The question became something of a national issue with us towards the end of the Repeal agitation, when O'Connell came into conflict with Young Ireland as to whether political demands could be legitimately pressed by threats of physical force. He denied that they could; and in this he was supported by the great body of the senior clergy, including the Bishops and the staff at Maynooth, all of whom would be deeply offended to find themselves classed as Tories. Many of them, however, did not hesitate to pronounce the Young Irelanders infidels, of the French revolutionary type, thereby proclaiming themselves Tories, as it is in the French Revolution the Liberal idea has culminated.

Later came the Fenian movement, which, surely, was opposed by the great body of the clergy, not merely on grounds of pity for the young men who were about to sacrifice themselves in hopeless conflict with the British Government, but out of regard for the claims of that Government, which was deemed legitimate; while we were instructed that against legitimate government it is never lawful to rebel. It is possible that I may have picked up these extreme views without hearing them from those to whose training I was committed; but that I held them there can be no doubt, any more than there can be of the fact that I accepted them at first unwillingly; because, however they conflicted with my feelings as an Irish youth, they came to me, as I thought, with the authority of the Church. Cardinal Cullen, at that time, gave the tone to the thought of the Irish clergy; and the Cardinal was very much misunderstood if he believed that rebellion may be permissible – if he was not a Tory of the strictest type.

The conflict between O'Connell and the Young Irelanders, Cardinal Cullen and the Fenians, was renewed at the time of the Land League; which was, confessedly, a movement wherein reliance was placed on unconstitutional measures – the modern substitute for physical force. I do not refer to outrages – murder, maiming of cattle, and the like – which were charged against the League, but only to the boycotting and refusal to yield possession of holdings – which the members applied, against the letter of the law. Moral force can be quite as strong and effectual as physical – even as bullets; quite as unconstitutional likewise; and it was by unconstitutional moral pressure of this kind the revolution in Irish social conditions was accomplished. This was opposed at the beginning by nearly all the senior clergy, including the great majority of the Bishops; among whom Cardinal McCabe took the place which Cardinal Cullen had held against the Fenians. In opposing this agrarian revolution in Ireland, they were acting quite in conformity with the Catholic tradition, which had opposed the revolution in France, Italy, and elsewhere. The Catholic schools of theology are almost the most Tory bodies in the world; and, strange as it may seem, Ireland is the most conservative country in Europe, through its being so much under the influence of the Catholic schools.

You may fancy, then, what a struggle there was, at least subconsciously, in a mind like mine, which had been trained in that Tory school and reverenced the Catholic tradition above all things, when it came to decide whether it could sympathize with the people of Ireland in their unconstitutional struggle. A tenant-farmer's son, all my natural inclination was to act with the class to which I belonged; but, as against this, it was being constantly dinned into us by those who opposed the League – some of them with claims to rank as theologians – that the methods of that body were revolutionary, and the revolution in any shape was opposed to the Catholic tradition. I sympathized with the people and approved their methods; not, as I have said, the outrages which were committed, not the excessive and unreasonable boycotting that took place here and there, but the principle of moderate boycotting in cases where strict or even equitable rights had been violated, as also the moderate, though illegal, resistance that was made to eviction for the non-payment of unjust or even of inequitable rents. As for the revolution argument, I satisfied myself that the movement was not revolutionary – that it was strictly constitutional; and I regretted throughout the fact that the Irish people, in their struggle for freedom, found support only among the Liberals of England, whose theory of government, civil as well as ecclesiastical, I had been taught to dislike. The ecclesiastical or religious question, indeed, – of which the education question was no small part – was mixed up with the political; and, like most Irish Catholics – perhaps more than most of them – I disliked Liberalism in religion.

It was natural, accordingly, that I should be glad, in a way, of the first opportunity that presented itself of breaking with English Liberalism, while safeguarding Irish national independence; and the opportunity came with the result of the divorce proceedings taken against Mr. Parnell. Before the English Liberals interfered, I was of opinion that he should have retired, that he owed this to Irish religious sentiment. Hence I was surprised and grieved when, at the meeting of the party held in Dublin, he not only did not resign the leadership, but was supported in his determination by practically the whole of the Irish Party. It was on this occasion, if I do not mistake, that Mr. T. M. Healy, who soon became Mr. Parnell's bitterest opponent, uttered the warning of 'Do not speak to the man at the wheel'. The Bishops were not consulted: they were silent, but they were biding their time.

Very soon they and the leaders of the Liberal Party in England protested simultaneously: with the unfortunate result that some of us in Ireland were left under the impression that negotiations took place between the hierarchy and the English Liberals; and that the Bishops resolved to protest only when they were satisfied that they would have the support of the Liberal Party. This, as it seemed to me, was to subject to a foreign party – in many respects hostile to Irish Catholic interests – not only Irish politics but Irish religion, a thing which I found it hard to stomach. If the Irish people had not at Dublin expressed their resolve to retain Mr. Parnell, there would be no question of toeing the line chalked by the English Liberals. Or if the Bishops had spoken out before that unfortunate Dublin resolution had been taken, they would have prevented it, and all would have been well. Nay, if even after the Irish Party and its supporters had expressed their resolution at Dublin not to allow Mr. Parnell to resign, and before the English Liberals had assumed the attitude of dictators the hierarchy had spoken out independently, in the interest of morality, whatever might be the political issue, one could respect their motive and more easily accept their decision.

For me, at least, who had an intense dislike for Liberalism, it was very galling to find not only our nation but even our Church dominated in this way by the English Liberals; and I made little secret of the disgust which I felt. Moreover, to tell the full truth, I could not restrain a suspicion that, though the Bishops claimed to speak merely in the interest of morality, this was not their only, nor even their strongest, motive. It was convenient for them to say so, as their pronouncement was thereby raised above hostile criticism. And some of them – their leaders – as I suspected, knew this well and calculated on it; putting it forward as a very efficacious shield to cover the real, or at least, more prevalent, motive, which was political. Not, of course, that even these leading Bishops did not think public morals in some danger; but that their concern was much more to weaken or even destroy Parnell. It was not the only occasion on which, as I thought, a pronouncement which seemed likely to call forth criticism, was made to wear a religious or moral aspect, so as to make criticism appear anti-clerical; which, in Ireland, is the same as making it ineffectual.

Mr. Parnell's supporters in Ireland fell into the trap. Their strong point was that it was not wise for the Irish Party to allow itself to be dominated in one of its most important functions by any foreign influence; least of all, by the English Liberals, to whom we were so much opposed. Hence the leader's own cry: If you wish to sell me, demand a decent price. That sting of selling their chief went home to many an Irish heart. The mistake was to deny that there was any moral question involved, or that the Bishops had any right to interfere with authority. This was ground on which a party could not escape defeat, among a people so obedient to hierarchy as the Irish. It was part of the Liberal creed which I detested; and, of course, I never used it, but lamented its use in Ireland.

The position I took up was this: The question of Mr. Parnell's leadership was a mixed one, with a serious religious and moral aspect, but not without a political aspect perhaps no less serious. It was, moreover, I thought, for politicians rather than priests or Bishops to measure the political consequences involved. If, indeed, the Bishops could say that, however great the political danger, it could not balance or prevail against the loss which would accrue to religion – should one who had been convicted of adultery be allowed to remain at the head of affairs – if this broad principle could be advanced, then there was nothing more to be said. But surely, the principle in question is no part of Catholic ethics. Would any Catholic writer hold the English people guilty for placing Nelson in charge of their fleet, at a time when his genius was necessary for the national defence? It was, accordingly, a question as to whether the political services of Mr. Parnell might not, in the circumstances, be so necessary as to counterbalance the loss which would accrue to religion from the fact that a man of his character occupied a position so prominent. His followers in Ireland would have it that there was no moral question at issue; while the Bishops, and those who followed them, acted as if the issue were purely moral and religious. Both were, as I thought, wrong. The Parnellite defence was based on the Liberal principles which I detested; and their opponents advanced an ultra-clerical claim which was sure to result in Liberalism – by repulsion. The greatest danger to religion, I thought, was likely to accrue from any serious attempt on the part of the clergy to deprive the laity of their political rights, under pretence that such rights counted as nothing when weighed against danger to faith and morals. Such a principle would hand over the nation to clerical rule; and no nation consents to be ruled for long by clergymen, except in matters religious.

I felt all this very keenly at the time; and, being of an ardent disposition, with little sense of fear, I expressed my views, sometimes with unjustifiable warmth, and often with too much freedom. At the time of the Kilkenny election, which was the first trial of strength between the rival parties, I could not but regret the use which the clergy made of the influence they had over the people; and, as I did not keep my thoughts quite within the barrier of my teeth, I gave offence to the Bishop; to whom whatever I said, may have come in a very distorted shape. Passion was high at the time, and few of the clergy would take trouble to realize the distinction which I, who was something of a canonist, deemed of so much importance. The Bishop made no formal reproach or complaint to me; but I understood from others that he thought his authority slighted. As a matter of fact, I never at any time said more than I have condensed in the last paragraph. On one occasion I gave considerable offence by maintaining, at a clerical dinner, that the priests were not the natural leaders and guides of the people in political matters; and that the position which the clergy had so long occupied in Irish politics was justified only on grounds of necessity, which was passing and would soon be altogether past. Stated thus, the principle would, I hope, now be received pretty generally, even among the priests themselves; though, when the occasion arises – as it may, in connection with the management of the National Schools – there is reason to fear that their Reverences will assert once more that laity have no right to interfere in mixed matters of that kind.

With the College there was some little feeling, and some division and friction, over the question of Mr. Parnell's leadership, most of the members of the theological faculty expressing fears that the clergy who opposed him were pressing things too far, and depriving the laity of their right to have a say in the matter. Others took a different view; and there were jibes – though, possibly, that is too strong a term – at the theological faculty, for the position taken up by its members. This position, I think, was never understood; for we dare not explain, and had no opportunity of explaining. Those who opposed and answered us could be very open; as, the more open they were, the more surely would they find favour.

I deem it fair to say, before closing this chapter, that of late years I have not been, and that I am not now, so much opposed to Liberalism as I was: that is, in politics. If asked for a word whereby one may distinguish Liberal and Tory, I think I should give Faith in Development – that is, in development of the organ or seat of political power. This means, or implies, belief in the lawfulness of revolution, whenever the time is ripe for entrusting the people, or a part of them, with a larger share of the governing authority, and when this is opposed – as it is likely to be – by the King, nobles, or whoever may have had possession hitherto, I am prepared to admit that in England, for instance, the barons were within their right in wresting the Great Charter from the Crown; that the Parliament was right in curtailing the Tudor's and Stuarts' power of taxing; and that the Commons were right in threatening reprisals if the King refused to create peers in sufficient number to overwhelm the Tory House of Lords. Similarly, as regards France, I do not think the House of Bourbon could reasonably expect to retain for all time the rights exercised by Louis XIV. Which means that the people were justified in wresting from Louis XVI the great part of the power possessed by his predecessors; that he was not justified in resisting; and that, for the unjustifiable resistance which he made, he could have been duly punished. I do not say that the French people did not go too far at that time – that the crown was not left too weak, or the King and his consort punished unduly. That is a question of degree, with which I confess myself incompetent to deal.

As for the Dissenters of England, whom for a long time I disliked so much, I now see that I did them less than justice, even in their ecclesiastical policy; not appreciating as it deserves the fight they made for freedom of the Church from State control, as well as for freedom of conscience. Not that error – religious, or even scientific – is not wrong; but that the rulers of a body such as the modern State are not fit to be trusted with the right of appointing to offices in the Church, or deciding which religious tenets are, or are not, immoral. I honour the Dissenters also for the manly way in which they have built and endowed their churches and chapels out of their own pockets, without dipping into the public purse and so compelling the adherents of other sects to help them. Even as regards education, there is, I suspect, no small share of truth in the Dissenters' view that in England at present no sectarian religious teaching should be endowed by the State. I disagree with this entirely, if propounded as the ideal policy – of the perfect State; but in a country like England, where Christianity is so fissiparous, it may be well that in the interests of economy, and even of religion, sectarian instruction should be banished from very many of the State schools. This, as I understand the Liberal theory, is the ideal state of things; whereas in the Catholic view, which I heartily endorse, it is a very undesirable necessity.

Catholic publicists, I fancy, would serve religion best by claiming State aid for sectarian schools only in such places as the sect in question could supply a number of pupils sufficient to constitute a thoroughly efficient school, while leaving another ample supply of pupils to constitute a no less efficient school for those who do not belong to that particular sect. In this way there would be in every place an efficient unsectarian school in which the children of what I may call minority sects would obtain a good secular education.

REFORM IN STUDIES

'In April, 1885', Dr. Healy writes, in the *Centenary History of the College* (p. 528), 'a large number of Irish Bishops – about seventeen in all – were invited to go to Rome to confer with some of the Cardinals of the Propaganda regarding certain points of discipline affecting the Irish Church. A summary of the subjects to be discussed in Rome was furnished to each of the Bishops. The very first heading on the schema contained a series of suggestions for the improvement of the studies and discipline at Maynooth College'. The man who took the leading part in these conferences, at least as regards studies, was Cardinal Franzelin, as we learned afterwards.

The deliberations resulted in a number of directions (normæ), somewhat general in character, but together forming a rough plan or schema, in accordance with which the studies of the College were to be conducted in future, details being left to be filled in at Maynooth, where, though we might modify the schema to suit our needs, we were not quite free to depart from it in its essential features.[1]

As many of these normæ as had reference to studies were published afterwards in the *Record of the Centenary Celebrations*, where they may be found at p. 239.

'It was proposed', as Dr. Healy writes, 'to have two schools, or classes of the theological students – one containing the students of the First Year, who were to learn, under distinct professors, the fundamental theology, dogmatic and moral; the other, containing all the students of the Second, Third and Fourth Year's Divinity, was to have three professors – two for dogma and one for moral theology, the latter being the professor who had charge of the same subject in the junior class'. There would thus be three professors of dogmatic and but one of moral theology. The whole tendency of the Roman schema, in fact, was to emphazise the necessity of dogmatic theology as compared with moral; and this I thought the principal reason why the schema was so modified at Maynooth as to be scarcely, if at all, recognizable when returned to the Holy See for approval. I opposed nearly all the changes that were made; but we had a weak President and Vice-President, who sided with those who bewailed the threatened departure from the Maynooth tradition. The schema, as ultimately approved at Rome, was practically the same as that on which we have been working ever since; and though an improvement, no doubt, on what it superseded, is, in my opinion, very imperfect, and needlessly so – far less desirable than that which was outlined in the Roman conferences.

One good result was the introduction of a class of canon law into the ordinary course. This change, however, has been carried since to such extremes as to make it doubtful whether, as canon law is now taught in the College, it is not doing less good than harm. There is reason to fear that we may be pouring too much into the bottle at once, with the necessary result that the entrance

---

1. The Roman authorities . . . admitted that in minor points their scheme might be modified, according to the special needs of Maynooth – *opportune attemperanda sunt.*'—So Dr. Healy (*Centenary History*, p. 532).

is more or less choked by the superabundance of the supply. I have myself taught the class of canon law, and believe that it had better be left an optional subject; as also the scriptures of the Old Testament. If, with such attractive questions to discuss, the professors of these subjects were not able to attract from our students a fair number of hearers – well, they should be cashiered as unfit for this position. What we want is, not that all our students should be learned in canon law or Old Testament critics, but that we should turn out a few such, who might serve as centres of such learning among the clergy. What is wrong with Maynooth, and has been wrong with it while I know it, is, that we aim at producing good average men. The worst of it is that we succeed; for, while our average man is very good, our best men are poor – as compared, that is, with those who are trained elsewhere; or if you object to that, as compared with what might be made of our best men if they got a training directed to raise them above the average. I, who say this, have more acquaintance with our best men – far more – than any other man in Ireland.

The schema devised in Rome for the improvement of our theological course was to be applied also to that of philosophy, with such modifications as might be necessary. The Roman authorities prescribed a three years' course of philosophy, beginning with physics – the natural order. We kept to our old two-year course, with physics and metaphysics taught concurrently. The Trustees had established an additional chair of philosophy – first, whether before or after they had received invitations to attend the conference at Rome, I know not. They went to Italy in the spring of 1885, and the new chair was established six months previously – in September, 1884. Efforts were made to fill the new chair by concursus; but the candidates were not deemed sufficiently qualified for a chair of higher philosophy, as we called it then. Ultimately the Trustees appealed to Cardinal Zigliara, I think, to send us from Rome some one whom he thought qualified; and, on his recommendation, Fr. Esser, O.P., was appointed. As far as I could discern, he had little acquaintance with, or appreciation of, modern physical science, and taught 'higher philosophy' as it might have been taught by Soudin or John of St. Thomas. Since then a third professor has been appointed, and much greater care is now taken to make the students acquainted with the physical basis of metaphysics; though, I fear, our philosophical school, like the Catholic schools elsewhere, has still much to learn – or, at least, to put in practice – in this respect.

In the Propaganda schema it was suggested that, after our theological course was reformed on the lines suggested, and when it was found to work satisfactorily for a sufficient time, the Pope would authorize us to grant degrees in theology. Acting on this hint, the Trustees, in June, 1893, commissioned the Professors in the Faculty of Theology, with the President and Vice-President, to report as to the conditions on which such degrees might be conferred. The Commission presented its report in October of the next year,[1] and, as the College Centenary was approaching, the Holy See was asked to grant us authority to confer degrees. The grant, though not made at the time of the Centenary celebration, was not long delayed, as it came in March of the following year, with power also to confer the degree of bachelorship in philosophy, but with the obligation, moreover, of drawing up new statutes for the regulation of studies in the College. We were instructed to provide in these new Statutes, among other things, for a Prefect of Studies, as well as for some one to preside at the examination boards.

In connection with the new offices thus instituted I got two little bits of preferment, neither of which I retained very long. At a meeting of the Faculty of Theology we decided that the Dean of the Faculty – to which position I, as senior professor and Prefect of the Dunboyne Establishment, was appointed for three years, by the votes of my colleagues – should preside at the examination Boards. The arrangement, however, had to go before the Trustees, by whom it was cancelled; the office in question being given to the President of the College, in the first place; and, in his absence, to the Vice-President. So that, in reality, I never held the position at all.[2]

By way of compensation for this little disturbance, their Lordships, on the same occasion, appointed me Prefect of Studies. There were no emoluments – only trouble – attaching to the office; else, perhaps, I should not have got it. And I should have respectfully declined accepting it, if their Lordships had consulted me before making the appointment; not, however, because of any labour or trouble it would bring, or because there was no remuneration; but because I felt that to fulfil his duties a Prefect of Studies should have what I lacked – the confidence of the Trustees. Having been appointed, I felt it would be ungracious to decline; so I retained the position for a few years, during which increasing pressure was being put on me, by the Vice-President, to note and report on certain little irregularities in some of the

1. It is published in the College Calendar for 1896–7, p. 228.
2. See letter addressed to the Cardinal Prefect of Propaganda, and published in the College Calendar 1897–8, pp. 167 ff.

classes. If I excused myself on the ground that he knew as much about these matters as I, he called my attention to the Statute, in which the obligation was laid on the Prefect of Studies. This I could not deny; but as I did not relish the duty – which, I thought, was specially difficult for one like me, who alone of all the professors in the College, had been reprehended, not only by their Lordships the Trustees, but by the Holy See – I thought it best to divest myself of office and responsibility alike. I resigned, accordingly, somewhere about the time Dr. Mannix became President or Vice-President, when he was appointed in my place. The duties sat lightly on him; so much so that, on his appointment to Melbourne, his office of Prefect of Studies was either forgotten altogether or allowed to remain unfilled. I, at least, have not heard of anyone having been appointed to succeed him in that capacity.

Having got what we deemed a good thing, we thought we could not have too much of it; so, on the advice of a majority of the professors in the faculties concerned, Dr. Gargan and Dr. O'Dea wrote to Cardinal Ledochowski a joint letter, which was approved by Cardinal Logue, asking for power to confer additional degrees – licentiate and doctorate in philosophy and the three degrees in canon law.[1] I was opposed to this, as I thought it required a larger staff than we could provide. Besides, the scheme which was proposed contemplated the partition of the Dunboyne students – seven or eight in all, as a rule – into smaller fragments; as, while some would study theology, others would take up philosophy, others canon law; and there was no reason why classics, mathematics, and other subjects should be left without possible devotees. Not that I did not, or do not, ardently desire that those of our students who have special taste or capacity for any of these subjects should get an opportunity of specializing in them at the end of the ordinary course; but that, as I thought and think, the place to specialize in canon law is Rome; in classics or mathematics, some university; in philosophy, Louvain or somewhere else.[2]

However, the proposed arrangement was recommended by a majority of our College councils, and we duly received from Propaganda authority to confer the usual three degrees both in philosophy and in canon law. There was some difficulty about

1. This letter may be found in the Calendar, 1900–1, p. 172.
2. I have sometimes thought that the Dunboyne Establishment is a mistake altogether; that a College or University, however excellent, in which one has already spent six years or more, is not the place in which one would derive most profit from a post-graduate course – of theology or any other science.

satisfying the Propaganda authorities that we had, or could have, a sufficient supply of professors, especially in the faculty of canon law; and a more or less sham arrangement was devised whereby our two professors of moral theology became professors also of canon law; thus making, with the special professor of canon law, three professors in that faculty. The result of which is likely to be that these two professors will be neither theologians nor canonists – that at least, if they are canonists, they will not be theologians. Since then we have been conferring degrees of bachelorship and licentiate in both faculties; but, while there is provision for a course in preparation for the doctorate in canon law, there is no doctorate course in philosophy.[1]

The canon-law course, moreover – until the candidate begins to specialize for the doctorate – runs concurrently with that of theology, the same students as a rule, preparing for bachelorship in both. This, together with the weakness of the professorate, seemed to me to make it inadvisable for us to confer all these degrees in canon law; and experience has confirmed me in that opinion. In the faculty of philosophy, wherein no students are prepared for the doctorate, nor has any provision been made for doing so, the professorate had to be strengthened before the Senate of the National University would recognize it as capable of preparing students for degrees; though, before this was done, the professorate in the faculty of philosophy had been stronger than in that of canon law. But then, no secular corporation, such as the National University, has any interest in seeing that we provide adequate means of preparing students for degrees in canon law.

The new system, of teaching with a view to degrees, has been working now for nearly twenty years; and though, no doubt, it has led to some improvement, I do not think the progress made such as it ought to be, and as it easily might be. This, I know, will be unpalatable reading to many who love our Alma Mater dearly and are jealous of her fame. I do not, however, admit that their love for her is greater than mine, or that any one of them – or any man living – has had as good an opportunity as I of knowing how much progress has been made in this respect within the last twenty years. Neither has anyone else as much personal interest in making out the progress to be greater than it is.

Seeing how long our students are in training – all of them remaining with us four years, and the best of them six or seven, after taking their degree in the National University – why is it

1. So far – up, that is, to 1913, when I wrote this – one student only has read for the Licentiate in canon law, none for the doctorate.

that, when leaving us, they are not better than they are? Is there not something wrong with our system? You may, of course, deny the fact – that the results achieved in these four or six years are so small, comparatively; in which case I can reply merely that I wish you were present at some of our examinations. Anyway, I, who am in position to know, insist that the results are meagre, comparatively; so that there must be something wrong with our system of teaching. And in saying this I do not at all mean to imply that priests, as a rule, are not better educated than the members of other professions, but only that, considering how priests are educated, they are not so superior to others as we might expect. For it is not merely that they have a much longer course than others, but that the studies to which they devote themselves – philosophy, theology, and history – are much more perfect instruments of education than is either law, or medicine, or engineering, or any of those branches of physical science in which men are trained in the secular universities. And when, in addition, one bears in mind the fundamental excellence of the system of philosophy in which priests are trained – of which no one is more convinced than I, however I may insist that the substantial excellence of our system is impaired and almost neutralized by accidental errors, which reverence for tradition prevents us from discarding – when I reckon up all this, I am all the more firmly convinced that there must be something wrong with us. Does it take four years to teach university graduates to make an examination such as we listen to, or to write an essay in theology such as we read? I do not read or hear the sermons of our senior students or young priests, but I think I know what they are, I hear it, in any case; and I ask myself whether that is all we have a right to expect from four years of study after men have taken their university degrees.

What I am about to say, in this connection, will, I have no doubt, be regarded as half-treason by those who are responsible for the course of study in ecclesiastical seminaries everywhere; and, if I speak out, I only ask men to believe that I do so out of sheer love for the seminaries, for our own College of Maynooth in particular, and for the system of religion which they are devised to serve. And I say that I am convinced that our lack of success is due, in very great measure, to the use of Latin in our schools.[1]

1. This chapter was written before June, 1913, when I sent to the *Freeman's Journal* the article for which, in the following October, I was admonished by the Trustees. The admonition did not, and does not, change my views with regard to the use of Latin.

Mind, I do not advise seminarists, whether students or professors, to take the law into their own hands and discard this old dead Latin, in spite of the Bishops, their superiors: we are under obedience and must act accordingly. But I have yet to learn that obedience requires us, not only to do as we are told, but to refrain from making known the inconveniences we suffer; making this known, not merely to our rulers – who, if we stop there, will pay little heed to us – but to the great world, whose opinion they heed so much. Neither do I deny that the daily use of Latin, in class-books and in class, has considerable advantages. I merely insist that these advantages are purchased at the price of much greater efficiency in our schools. Think of what you might expect from a medical school in Dublin which would teach medicine in French or German. Not that a young man may not do very well who learns medicine in French or German – in the schools of Paris or Berlin. There his professors and fellow-students will speak their own language, so that their faculties, at least, will have free play, and he, though himself hampered for a time, will participate in the good results which they obtain; while, as this language of theirs is in constant use, not merely for study but for all manner of social intercourse, he gradually makes it his own, and not till he has done so can he derive advantage from his studies. If one of our students, similarly, were to go to some college or university in which Latin was the language, not merely of class, but of social life, he would do as well there as by going to Paris or Berlin and making his studies in French and German. To use a language for purposes of study – the study, that is, of philosophy, theology, or any other science – one must make it one's own.

Why not, then, it has been often said, make Latin our own, as was done in the Middle Ages, and is still done in Rome? Simply because it is no longer the Middle Ages, not even in Rome. Do as we may – as we may ever hope to do – the language of our daily life will be the vernacular, wherein we do our thinking, especially when called on to deal with abstruse and difficult things, such as must occupy us in philosophy and theology. Latin is a dead language, even to those who speak it best and most fluently – even in Rome. It is a well-known fact that in all the courts and offices there, one gets on ever so much better by speaking Italian; and, if Latin is the language of the schools, may it not be that this is a necessary evil where the students are of many different nationalities? Who will assure us that the teaching of those Roman schools would not be ever so much more effective if it was given in Italian, to men for whom that was the language of their daily life? I know nothing of the Roman schools except that I gather from the books published by the professors who teach therein; which seem to me to be out of touch with some of the best results of modern science and research. I do not think that books of the kind would continue to be published, if they were written in a language which could be read and criticized by every one, including the advocates of different views or systems. I insist, in other words, that the teaching of Italian professors would be very much improved if, instead of Latin, they used the vernacular; and that their Italian students would then derive ever so much more profit from their seminary course than they do at present. The use of Latin as a school-language is one of the most potent of the causes that have been retarding the progress of theological science in Rome as elsewhere.

But, it is said, is there not compensation – in the fact that Latin provides a necessary means of communication with the centre of unity; besides keeping us in touch with the great minds of the past? If we give up speaking Latin in class, all textbooks will soon be written in the vernacular, and then St. Thomas, De Lugo, and the others will be literally on the shelf.

I hear this said constantly, by men who are unable to read with intelligence an article of the Summa or a chapter in De Lugo. You would think, to hear this kind of talk, that the average priest now reads Latin freely; whereas the fact is that he is unable to read Lehmkuhl, and that to read even Gury is unpleasant and uncertain work. As for St. Thomas, Suarez, and the others, no one reads them but professors, who may be depended on to do the same no matter what language they speak in class. Does the use of the vernacular in their lectures and books keep professors – of history, let us say – in the secular universities from reading the much more difficult Latin of the mediæval documents? A professor of theology now must read French, German, and English, at the very least, because it is in these languages the best modern books are written. He will take care to read Latin also. What priests on the mission want is well-written theological books which they can read freely; and they have no comfort in reading Latin texts. No wonder that there is such a break between the College course and the life to which it should be a prelude.

And as for communication with the centre of authority, it is well known that if you can write in Italian or French you had better do so than in Latin. Is it too much to expect the centre of unity to provide itself with a few clerks who can read English and German? How many lay people are there who may have need to communicate with Rome; and must they, too, learn to write Roman Latin? Which is easier: to have sufficient clerks in Rome to handle communications in the principal vernacular languages, or to have all the seminaries of the world hampered by the use of a dead language in order to facilitate communication with the Holy See?

There remains an appeal for unity; which, it is argued, is made so much closer by the use of the same language everywhere, at least in official acts. And I certainly should be the last to question the efficacy of a common language as a bond of union; what I do question is the necessity of that particular bond, while I insist strongly on the evil which results from it, and which I regard as more than counterbalancing any good which it effects. The need for special bonds of union with the Holy See has been greatly diminished by the decrees of the Vatican Council, whereby schism is practically excluded for those who retain the faith. The danger would now seem to be, not schism or even discussion, so much as excessive centralization. In any case the need of a common tongue, to serve as a bond of union, is no longer so great as it was; while the evils that accrue from the use of a dead language in seminaries are daily growing, with the progress of science and history, both of which are now taught exclusively in the different vernaculars. Would either, I ask, be what it is if those by whom they have been developed had continued to teach and write in Latin? Does not the era of progress date from the time when the questions raised by both began to be discussed in the language of everyday life? Here I may be reminded that theology is not like either physical science or history, but does best when it makes no progress: when it just discerns the mind of the Schoolmen and takes their authority as decisive of any question that may arise. This – however it may be denied when put so bluntly – is, I honestly believe, at the back of all the objections that are raised to the new developments that some of us have advocated in theological science, as well as to the means which we have recommended as calculated to lead to further progress now undreamt of. Theology is regarded as an unprogressive science; or if it did make progress at one time, that was long ago – in the earlier or later mediæval schools, wherein the science reached its full stature; dwindling later except in so far as it is preserved in books, so that the best theologian is he who is best acquainted with the school tradition and is most ready to accept that as true.

Against all this, my whole life has been one long protest, which will be continued while breath is left to me. The deposit of Catholic faith, it is true, was closed with the last of the apostles, but there never was and never can be any such closing of the science either of theology or philosophy; which must either make constant progress or become fossilized. The more one admires the fundamental principles of the scholastic philosophy – which may be reduced to this one, that scientific truth is objective, to be dug out from nature – the more one is convinced that, as we progress in knowledge of nature, we are in position to advance in philosophical science: and who is it that does not realize that the science of philosophy and that of theology go hand in hand? Why should the progress of theology cease with St. Thomas or any other man?

If, indeed, you do not wish for progress, in theology and philosophy – if what you desire most is to have us know as much as St. Thomas knew – then indeed, you are consistent in denying us the use of any other language than his. But, oh! how he would scorn you and your stagnation – he whose whole life was spent in pressing forward the confines of both sciences, which he loved and served so well. If, however, you desire that we should keep abreast of the times, but think we can do so while using Latin only in our schools, I can only give you the assurance of one whose whole life has been spent in those schools that, hampered as we are with this dead language, we cannot attain or keep the position which you wish us to occupy. We are behind the times in many ways; mainly because our thoughts, from being clad in old-fashioned garments, have become themselves old-fashioned. You may not find this assurance comforting, and you may be displeased with me for giving it, but it is given out of pure love of the sciences in question and of the schools in the service of which I have spent my life.

OTHER COLLEGE IMPROVEMENTS

When preparing to celebrate the Centenary of the College, we considered whether it might not be possible to do or institute something which might signalize an occasion so auspicious, and, possibly, serve as a memorial. The number of free places for students was increased out of College funds; rather too liberally as I have often heard since, when we needed money for strengthening the professorial staff. Then, of course, there was the Chapel tower and spire, which appealed to the sentiment of the majority. I was opposed to this, as a profitless waste of money that was badly needed for pressing reforms, and I said that, if a sum of ten or fifteen thousand pounds were obtained, it would be put to a much more profitable service if invested as a library endowment than if spent on a showy but useless tower and spire. Few, however, had any interest in our library, so my appeal was little heeded. I was told, that, whereas we should get fifteen thousand pounds for a tower and spire, we should not get one-fifth of the sum for library endowment. I did not think this true, and am still of the same opinion. There would, no doubt, have been a certain unwillingness to provide what was regarded as a rich corporation with so large a sum, but there was not much heart in the response to our appeal for a tower and spire. The money for this was supplied because the Bishops pressed for it, and it would, I feel sure, have been provided just as willingly, if the same pressure had been exerted for library purposes. Besides, we could have appealed openly for the library, whereas the tower and spire had to be euphemistically represented as 'the completion of the College Chapel'.

Among other projects mooted at the time was that of a Catholic Congress to be held in Dublin or some other Irish city. I was in favour of this, as a means of getting the educated laity to take an interest in what I may call the intellectual service of the Church. They serve her at present, and have done so for ages, most devotedly, by their cash; were they not capable and worthy of something higher? The Intermediate School System and the Royal University had given us a fine body of highly educated young men, who, thank God, were full of the religious spirit, though it was to be feared that their interest in the intellectual side of their religion was not very keen. This, some of us thought, should and could be remedied, and we dreamt of getting them to work for a Congress and so interesting them in the defence of religion, besides initiating them into a higher and more honourable service of God and the Church.

We had many conferences and discussions on the Congress project; the Vice-President, Dr. O'Dea, who had to do most of the organizing for the Centenary, being afraid to undertake it, lest we should not be able to find men to read a sufficient number of papers, or to make them sufficiently interesting. This raised the question as to what kind the papers should be, with regard to which I thought it better to allow a certain amount of latitude to those who would undertake to write. The Vice-President, however, was afraid, so I had to draw up a formal programme for the Congress, dividing it into sections, and suggesting for each section a number of subjects on which papers might be written. The programme was afterwards published in the *Centenary Record*, where it may be found at p. 232.

It did not allay the Vice-President's fears – possibly added to them, the papers suggested seemed so difficult; and as I maintained that, by pressing into service the young laymen who had graduated in the Royal University, all the papers suggested, or others as good, could be made out without difficulty, I was further asked to draw up the greater part of them in outline, so that the Committee might be able to judge. Being very simple then, as well as very anxious that the Congress should be undertaken I, did actually write out a draft of nearly all the papers on the programme; to find that, when it was presented to the Committee, the members had already made up their minds that we could not, or would not, undertake the labour of a Congress. It was for me a lesson in the art of shelving things.

There remained the idea of an annual reunion of former students of the College, which an old class-fellow of mine, Provost Lynch of Salford, had been pressing on us for some time. To him is due the credit of having first suggested the association which afterwards became known as the Maynooth Union; this title having been copied from that of a similar association – of priests educated in Rome, I think – which had been in existence for some years in England. Even the project of the Union was regarded as bristling with difficulties; what would the Bishops think of it? What should we do with the former students when they revisited the College? How long would they stay? By whom and how would the Union be proposed? These are samples; I verily believe that it would never have been begun, or even proposed, had we not been more or less committed to a three-day Centenary celebration, and had there been any other project to fill up the programme for the third day. As so often happens, the difficulties which had seemed so formidable, vanished or were surmounted easily, when the Union was started and began to work. It has, I think, been the source of no little good to the College; not only in putting us into closer and more sympathetic touch with our old students, but in bringing us more into the open, so that the world can see more of what we are and of what we think and do.

There has, I think, been a considerable change in the character of the meetings which we contemplated at first, and especially in the academic part, the papers and discussions – which, according to the original notion, were not to be nearly so political – if I may call them so – as they have become. The academic committee, moreover, was at first quite an active body; so much so that, when I was asked to read a paper at the first meeting, I found it difficult to fix on a subject which they deemed safe enough to discuss. I think I had to submit the paper for censorship or revision, harmless though the subject was: on 'The Intention Requisite on Singing the Divine Office.' It was a decided failure, which, perhaps, is why it was the only paper of the kind that the Union called forth. A few years afterwards – in June, 1903 – Dr. Sheehan read a paper on 'Maynooth and the New University', then a burning question; the aspect under which it was discussed by Dr. Sheehan being whether some of our students might not read in the university, residing at some hostel to be provided in Dublin. The paper, I understood, had to be submitted to the Bishops – or some of them – before being read, with the result that the lecturer was asked to modify the conclusion to which he had come, so as to reverse it almost completely, and the paper – a very able one – presented the curious anomaly of a mass of arguments tending to one conclusion, which, however, was not only drawn but was rejected.

I hope it is needless to say that I do not regret the stricter censorship which we contemplated at first. The secretary of the Union must be trusted to find the best men to read papers at our meetings, and they are more likely to meet his wishes if left free to select the subjects that suit themselves – in which they take a personal interest – and if, in writing, they are left free to take their own line and are not bound to have an eye on one or more censors, who know little of the difficulties of the question at issue, and but too often realize only that they never read anything like this before. Any specially good paper is calculated of necessity to produce that impression; most of all on the safe man who is likely to be made a censor.

Neither do I regret the tendency that soon manifested itself, to discard questions of an academic character, and, in place of them, to take up some political or semi-political or economic question of the day. This change was due, I think, in large measure to the first secretary, Dr. Mannix, who did much thereby to ensure the success of our meetings. Even the laity, who read of the proceedings in the newspapers, were interested in what we said and did, and the Union grew in importance as a force in the country. This, of course, was not without a dangerous side – that the force might be applied in a tyrannical and narrow spirit, to increase the power of the priests at the expense of the laity, and so hasten the advent of the struggle which so many predict. This danger, I think, has been counteracted to some extent by the establishment of the Irish Catholic Truth Society, wherein lay Catholics can make themselves heard; though it must be confessed that, either because they are apathetic or because they are not invited to come forward, the Catholic Truth Society also is in some danger of being worked in the interest of the clergy – such interest, that is, as is not always identical with that of religion and the Church.

One of the first benefits which the Union conferred on the College was a contribution of fifty pounds to each of the divisional libraries, the money to be expended in the purchase of literary works. Besides the direct benefit of this grant, it had an even greater indirect effect, as it was the occasion of our getting from the Trustees of the College an annual allowance of fifty pounds for the purchase of books for the students' libraries. The Archbishop of Dublin it was who proposed and carried this grant; for, as he said to me in conversation, seeing that the Union had taken action, the Trustees could not very well refrain from doing as much. The happy result is that the students have in their own libraries – especially that in the Senior Hose – a very nice collection of works of literature, philosophy, theology, and the kindred sciences.

About this time – when the Union was established – some of us began to agitate for a better supply of reviews; for the staff in the first instance, and, after serving them, for the students. We had been getting a few such things: *The Times, Athenæum, Nature,* and some of the quarterlies. Nearly all of us, if not quite all, had been taking, in addition, some newspaper and reviews of our own, and it was proposed, in the first place, to pool a good part of the cost of these, and out of the fund so created to procure for common use a greater variety of periodicals, which would pass on to the students' libraries as fresh numbers were received. The proposal was agreed to by nearly all the members of the community, whereupon we applied to and obtained from the Trustees an additional yearly allowance for literature of this kind.

I was largely responsible for creating or procuring these funds; but when we came to draw up the list of reviews and periodicals which we should purchase, I was chagrined to find that others had little or no interest in the kind of review which I wished most to see. My notion was that the whole of the allowance made by the Trustees, as well as a good part of our own contributions, should go for the purchase of what I may call scientific periodicals; those – or the best of them – that were being published in the interest of the faculties to which we belonged. I wanted to glance over the principal Catholic – and even Protestant – reviews in theology and philosophy; to read carefully any article that I deemed of special interest, and to be brought into touch in this way with those who were working elsewhere. I wanted to have the best Catholic reviews of this kind placed in the hands of the students; to stimulate them, and keep them abreast of the thought of their time. Instead, we got the *Nineteenth Century,* the *Fort-*

nightly, the *Revue des Deux Mondes,* the *Saturday Review, Spectator,* and such things, all, no doubt, interesting and amusing, but very unlike what I had had in mind – for staff and students. Hence the movement has, as I think, been a failure. A number of the staff – though piqued at certain action that I took in connection with another matter – withdrew after some time from the pool, which was never lavishly supported, and I should not very much regret if the Trustees were to withdraw their allowance. I should prefer, however, that they would order a revision of the list of periodicals, with instructions that in future the allowance they make should be applied only to the purchase of such reviews as bear directly on the studies of the College. The community would, of course, be free to expend the pool as they wished, according to the vote of the majority, every one being free to join or to withdraw as he pleased.

As regards the students, the movement just recorded was hardly even a partial success. I had hoped to get them allowed, or even supplied with, not only scientific reviews, but newspapers. For the true principle of education, it seemed to me, was to train, as far as possible in the surroundings of after-life, so that, while monks, who did not read newspapers, should not have them during the novitiate, secular priests who read them regularly after ordination, should be trained to use them during the seminary course. The ideal seminary, I still think, would be the house of a Bishop or parish priest where the young clergyman would live as a son with his father, having access to almost everything, but with prudent and loving eyes to watch over him and keep him from excess. There are, of course, newspapers which a good father, though he might read them himself, would not like to see in the hands of even his grown-up sons, and so I should not dream of allowing seminarists to read everything which priests may read. But, surely, there are some newspapers which no priest would forbid a seminarist who might be staying with him. There is, I know, the objection of time lost, which one so often hears from those who ought to be at least as busy as seminarists, yet find time for at least one daily paper, besides other not altogether scientific journals.

When a question like this – of providing newspapers and reviews for the students – is first broached at Maynooth, those who bring it forward get no hearing. The second or third time you move in the matter, you may be asked to present a report, showing, among other things, what is done elsewhere. We do not seem to have courage enough to make up our minds independently, but must feel that we are moving with the crowd. So I remember writing to many prominent seminaries – in England, America, France, Belgium, and even at Rome, in nearly all of which, we learned, newspapers and periodicals were allowed the students, subject, of course, to certain rules. Strengthened by these returns, of which I had a digest made, printed, and sent to all the Bishops, we brought the question before their Lordships once more, and got them to give way a little. They allowed the *Saturday Review*, I think, but not *The Tablet;* nor would they allow the weekly edition of *The Times.* Of course they would not hear of *The Freeman's Journal*, but had no objection to *L'Univers* or *La Vera Roma*, which, on the contrary, they seemed to think rather advisable as enticements to read French and Italian. We got something – very little, and so the modest reform continued, till the authorities in Rome got frightened over Modernism, and we were thrown back, practically to the old order of things.

It was about this time, also, when the Maynooth Union was established, the students' literary and debating societies took anything like firm root in the College. There was no such thing during my time as a student. A few years later, while I was teaching in Kilkenny, the Bishop of Raphoe, then at the head of the house, started some kind of debating society, as I have heard, but it did not flourish, as was to be expected, seeing how badly the students' libraries were then supplied with modern literature, or indeed with readable books of any kind. When this defect was removed, the societies got a new start, with the blessing, this time, and encouragement of the Vice-President, Dr. O'Dea, who had turned his own class, of sacred eloquence, into a kind of debating society. The Gaelic League also helped, as it put a new spirit into the students, and, possibly, the new system of training in the Intermediate Schools and under the University had begun to tell. Anyway, these societies have been doing fairly well, I think. A year or two ago, I understand, the superiors began to fear that they were getting out of hand – that at times the members turned from art and letters to criticize their superiors. I do not know how much, if any, harm was done, and suspect it was very little. Fear of criticism, indeed, on the part of superiors, seems to argue a certain lack of confidence – self-reliance – on their part. Surely, the rulers of the State also are entitled to obedience and respect, and, no less surely, have they been improved since the time when no one dare criticize their actions, under pain of imprisonment, confiscation, or worse. It is just possible that the ecclesiastical state, too, might flourish even though the citizens, without usurping apostolic authority, were allowed to speak their mind more freely both as to men and measures. They cannot be kept from doing it in private caucus, and it might, possibly, make them more manly, and thereby more reliable, if they were free to publish what they say in private, always, however, within reason. Dr. Pastor tells us that Pope Alexander VI, however he may have sinned otherwise, took no notice of the many pasquinades that were posted up in Rome at his expense, and if he could afford to do this, with honour to himself, better men need not be so very sensitive. A debating society or journal that is kept in leading-strings will do little good to its members or readers, and very little service to the Church, State, College, or institute, for which it works – in fetters. If the Catholic Church has in her service hardly one strong, well-conducted newspaper or periodical, that is the price she pays for keeping all her journalists in bondage; no really strong man will continue to serve under the restrictions that prevail.

The reform in the faculties of theology and philosophy occasioned by the conferring of degrees in both, had another very considerable, though indirect effect – on the mode of selecting the professors. I have already, in connection with my own appointment to the staff, called attention to the many weak points of the concursus, as it was then and for many years afterwards. For a chair in theology it was little more than a competitive oral examination on twelve questions taken from Gury's Compendium; not, be it remembered, on any of the great principles with which his chapters or Articles commence; but on some Quæritur that follows and completes those principles, bearing usually on a matter of detail, as to which there has been some disputation. They were, as a rule, the kind of questions one would give an average or a weak student at a term examination. Dogmatic theology was so little regarded that I knew a man to be appointed who made no attempt whatever to answer the question – I do not think there was more than one – set him for his written examination.

In philosophy it was even worse, for as all professors of theology had a seat on the Council of Studies, which was the examining board, there were always among the examiners two or three who knew theology and could set proper questions, if allowed to do so. Since, however, at that time there was but one professor of each of the different subjects in the faculty of philosophy and that of arts – there was, for instance, but one professor of physics, of mental philosophy, of English literature, of Latin and Greek – the examination for these chairs had to be conducted by a body of men of whom not one was professionally connected with the subjects in question; on which, as was natural, the candidates were to be examined most closely. We selected questions for examination, not of students, but of candidates for chairs, on subjects of which the best of us knew little and some of us very little, and we reported on the answering of candidates who, if at all qualified for the chair, and if anxious to secure our votes, must have set themselves to talk down to the measure of our incapacity.

I witnessed some strange exhibitions in connection with concursus for these chairs – in choosing the questions especially; for in listening to the candidates reply, however little we knew, we manifested an appearance of profound scholarship. We had concursus for the chair of Latin and Greek and for that of English literature (the advanced course) which were very bad; but even in Mental Philosophy, of which we might be expected to know something, I remember, when selecting questions for a concursus for the higher chair, obtaining – by the process we used, of cutting in the College textbook – the question as to the essence of bodies; to which one of the examining board objected, on the ground that it was not discussed by our professor in his class. Whereupon the President, Dr. Walsh, took a vote of the Board, and the question was ruled out by a majority. When this occurred in mental philosophy, you may imagine how inept we were in ancient classics, English literature and ecclesiastical history. Fortunalety no vacancy occurred during this time in the chair of physics; when Dr. Lennon resigned, we had adopted a new and better system of appointment.

Bad as the system of concursus was, as applied by us, there was this to be said for it, that the votes of the examiners were given honestly, withour fear or favour, to the best of our knowledge, and that the Trustees almost invariably made appointments in accordance with the vote of the majority of the examining board. Our votes were cast by ballot, but, as most of us made little concealment as to what we did, we nearly always knew how the great majority went. Besides, the votes were read out for the Trustees, who almost all took a record, and through some of them we learned how the examiners voted, through I never knew the vote of any individual examiner to be revealed. It was all absolutely fair, as far as I ever knew; that is, of course, apart from the question of competence, wherein our deficiency must have told against really qualified candidates, outside theology. As for myself, I often felt quite ashamed to vote, and did so under compulsion, giving notice to the Trustees that I did not regard my opinion as of any importance.

There was one case in which their Lordships, as we understood, made an appointment against the vote of the majority of the examiners. It was on the occasion of a concursus for a chair in theology, and three of the Trustees who had themselves been professors of theology in our College, had attended the examination in Moral Theology, which, as I have said, was then regarded as the main thing. It so happened that the candididate who was ultimately appointed did well that day – perhaps slightly better than his opponent, who, however, in the opinion of the majority was superior all round. Those three Bishops told at the Board of Trustees what they saw and heard, and their report prevailed over ours, who had heard the whole examination. It was done in perfect good faith, without the least personal or provincial prejudice, and it was so characteristic of how opinions have been and are weighed at Maynooth.

Gradually, by constant pressure, as occasion arose, we got more and more importance attached to dogmatic theology and philosophy, in the concursus for chairs in theology. At first the written examination was made more searching; then candidates were required to present a hundred theses in dogmatic theology, for defence, their opponents being at liberty to propose objections to any one of these theses. This was in keeping with what was required for the doctorate in theology, and was suggested by the examination for that degree. I have no doubt that any concursus that may be held in future for a chair in theology will be a searching examination, by competent examiners, whose fairness will be above suspicion, as has been the constant tradition in the College.

Even at its best, however, the system of concursus for professorships is open to this objection, that it keeps away good men who may have made a name in the subject, and may, therefore, be unwilling to pit themselves against young men just from the schools with fresh memories and nothing to lose by being worsted in the contest. The concursus system may get you the best students in the sense of the Latin alumnus, but not the most qualified man. Moreover, as against a student trained in our own schools, a man who had read elsewhere, however qualified, would be very much handicapped in an examination conducted here, just as our men would be at no less disadvantage in a similar examination conducted elsewhere. That is why I have no hope of seeing many of our students appointed to chairs in the colleges of the National University.

To meet this difficulty, we had inserted in the new statutes, which were drawn up for approval by Propaganda, a provision to the effect that, when a chair became vacant, it could be filled without concursus or other examination, provided the members of the faculty in question, the President of the College, and the Visitors, were satisfied that a man could be found who had proved himself fully qualified for the vacant position and the President and the members of the faculty were exhorted to bestir themselves, whenever a vacancy occurred, to find some one who might be recommended for appointment in this way, on merits of which he had already given proof. This statute was approved by the Trustees and afterwards by the S. Congregation of Propaganda.[1]

As I am mainly responsible for originating and pressing this reform – as I deem it – it may not be out of place to say here that I was, and am, well aware of the abuses which it may be made to cover, unless the members of the different faculties are not only vigilant but independent. Indeed, I think I see some of these abuses already creeping in. It was very far from my mind to recommend any man for appointment to a vacant chair, except on grounds of a character which he has made by published work bearing directly on what he should have to teach when appointed. I should pay no attention to college distinctions, nor to university degrees, whether obtained at home or elsewhere, nor to recommendations of any professors or experts, however eminent. None of thes things, nor all of them together, mean very much – that is, of necessity. The one test that is fairly reliable – though even this can be secured by craft – is a reputation based on published work of exceptional merit, and I, for my part, should be deeply grieved and disappointed to find any man recommended for a professorship in any faculty on any other qualification.

In the statutes, as finally and definitely approved, another important provision was made, to the effect that, in future, as a rule, professors should be appointed temporarily at first.[2]

I originated and pressed for this reform also with a view to bringing pressure to bear on young professors to work hard at something which might be published and bring credit to themselves and the College. It was my notion that on the expiry of one's first temporary appointment, one should not be reappointed unless one had published some work of that kind, for I was and am convinced that professors are likely to continue as they have begun, so that, if during their first years they devote themselves to writing and publishing, they will, especially if successful, be even more prolific in after life. This, however, supposes that the probationary period is long enough to allow a man who has entered on a new sphere of duties to produce a work of the high character which I contemplate. I should allow at least seven years, and should appoint at first for a period of that length. Since the statute was approved, the

1. See the statutes published in the College Calendar, in their original form, 1901-2, pp. 180 ff., nn. 22, 23; in the form which was afterwards approved definitely 1901-11, pp. 164 ff. Stat. Generalia, Cap. II, n. 3.
2. See College Calendar 1910–11, Cap. II, n. 5.

Trustees have been appointing for a period of three years, which is not nearly long enough to allow of really good work being done. The result is to defeat the purpose of the statute, or if, at the end of the brief probationary term now allowed, the new professor can show no published work of sufficient character to justify permanent appointment, he can plead lack of time, with the result that permanent appointments are made now, as formerly, without any published work to justify them. This is very different from what I contemplated.

Another practice of considerable importance was begun at this time, and will, I hope, be continued, though the Trustees are in no way bound to do so. While we were preparing to celebrate the College Centenary. Mgr. (now Cardinal) Mercier, who had been commissioned some time before to organize at Louvain a special school for the study of nature according to the method and principles of the schoolmen, wrote to me to inquire whether we might not send him from Maynooth some of our more advanced students. In reply I said that if he would come over to our centenary and speak at one of our meetings on that occasion, we might be able to get something done to meet his wishes. He did so, with the result that Dr. Forker, who in the following October was appointed to a vacant chair of philosophy, was allowed a year's freedom from the duty of teaching, on condition that he would spend the time in study at the Philosophical Institute at Louvain. Dr. Harty, who was appointed to a vacant chair of theology at the same time, got the same privilege, on condition of spending the year in the study of theology at Rome. Dr. Walsh, Archbishop of Dublin, was mainly instrumental in getting all this accepted and approved by the Board, and ever since it has been understood that professors in the different faculties, either immediately on their appointment or soon after, get a year's leave of absence, for study in some foreign university. It was my notion that they should attend there as any other student, passing whatever examinations might be prescribed for others, and, if possible, taking a degree. Others, however, at first, thought this unworthy of professors in our College, but many of our staff have since graduated in Germany and elsewhere, without, I think, lowering our dignity in any way, and I should like to see this made compulsory, in so far, at least, as to require those who go abroad in this way to show some tangible proof of having made good use of the privilege allowed them.

As I am on the subject of appointments, and as I have something to say with regard to those which have been made in my own time, and must be made hereafter, to the higher offices of President and Vice-President, I may as well set it down here. Since, moreover, a good deal of what I am about to say is not flattering or likely to please, and may easily be ascribed to personal disappointment or pique, I will begin by protesting anew that I have never had the desire for any of these offices, that, if offered either, I should have refused it, and this on the ground that they are not in my line, that I am quite unfit for them, and that, if I accepted either, I should never be happy till I had got rid of the burthen. I have not the least touch of bitterness or soreness in this respect, recognizing that the Trustees read my character quite correctly when they decided that I was not a suitable man for either the Presidency or the Vice-Presidency.

Of course, one never finds a man – or anything else on earth – perfectly fit for anything; so that one should not be disappointed or complain if at any time some one is elected President who does not quite reach the ideal. It is one thing, however, not to be ideally fit for a position, and another to fall so far short of the ideal as to be unfit, and that this latter case is possible must be admitted, unless we hold that every one is fit for every position whatever. When, moreover, an unfit person is put into an office of command, those who are made subject to him have reason to complain of the appointment. And it will not be denied by the great body of those who know our College intimately, that we, whose interests are so much bound up with its success, have been severely tried by some of the appointments to higher positions that have been made since I became a professor.

I do not say, or even imply, that there has been anything like conscious partiality on the part of the Trustees, who alone are responsible for these appointments. I know well that no member of their body ever casts a vote on such occasions without having satisfied himself that the man for whom he votes is the best he can find for the position. While this, however, is true, it is also undoubted that personal friendships, the supposed interest of provinces, and other such considerations, have been allowed to determine the opinions of the voters, and thereby to affect the result, in the case of these elections to higher offices, as to which the staff are not consulted officially; much more than in the case of appointments to professorships, where the Trustees have been almost invariably guided by the opinion of the staff. And there can be as little doubt that, whereas the results of the elections to professorships have given practically no cause of complaint, the same cannot be said of the elections to the higher offices. Is it too much to suggest that, when these are being filled, the staff might be consulted, as diocesan clergy are before the appointment of their Bishop? Surely if the opinion of the staff had been taken on the occasion of some recent elections for the Presidency, their votes would have saved the Trustees from some very serious blunders.

It is unfortunate that, since Dr. Walsh became Archbishop of Dublin, no President of the College took any personal part in any form of literary work, and though the holder of the position has other work to do, he should not, in my opinion, be so completely divorced from literature. I have heard many sneers at the expense of Trinity College, Dublin – when Dr. Traill was appointed Provost, but we might have looked nearer home. And though, now and then, it may be necessary to place at the head of a literary corporation one who either has done, or is doing, no literary work, the necessity will be ever so much more unfortunate if it lasts so long that not one, but five or ten or more, such Presidents are appointed in succession. In Ireland administrators are as thick as blackberries, as are also politicians, clerical as well as lay. The tendency, moreover, is and has been that way towards local administration, royal commissions, public boards, the university senate, and such things, which distract one from steady literary work. Is there to be no honour for bookmen? Or, if we honour them, must it be only by unmaking them – taking them from books to administration and ecclesiastical politics? 'It is not reason', said the Apostles, on a memorable occasion, 'that we should leave the word of God and serve tables.' That is what our highest clergymen have been doing – mere clerks' work; while the great apostleship of the Press is left to underlings. Our Presidents and our Bishops are so much occupied – by clerks' work – that they have not time, they say, to write an article for *The Irish Ecclesiastical Record;* the most they can prepare is a speech on the education or the university question, or some such semi-political utterance. The Church that neglects the apostolate of preaching – which, in its highest form, is now worked through the Press – that Church is in a bad way, however it may seem to flourish.

One reform the Trustees would be well advised to make – to relieve the President of our College of all the merely clerical work which he does at present, and to require him to devote his time and abilities to something higher. The Vice-President, moreover, should rarely, if ever, be appointed President, as the qualifications for both offices are essentially dissimilar. Of recent years, men have been made Vice-Presidents lightly, whom the Trustees would not dream of appointing to the Presidency just then, for lack of proper qualification; but when, after two or three years, the Presidency became vacant, those heretofore unqualified men were found to have become fully qualified; or, though not qualified as fully as one would like, they were appointed, on the ground that now it would be too hard to pass them over. And so our rulers have their sport, while we, poor Greeks, are aggrieved.

The period of the College Centenary was marked by another change, whereby the status of the professors and other members of the staff was very much improved – as regards salary. When the College was disendowed, the Trustees resolved that in future those whom they might appoint to the staff should receive only two-thirds of the salaries that were attached to the various offices after the endowment was increased by Sir Robert Peel in 1845. This reduction of salary made the position of professor or other official of the College much less desirable, from the temporal point of view, than it had been, and as the emoluments attaching on the mission to such offices as members of the staff might reasonably hope to obtain, if they remained in their own dioceses, had increased, if anything, while salaries at Maynooth were diminished, there was reason to fear that the best men were, and would be, loth to join our staff, as also that, having joined, they would be looking forward to preferment outside rather than to spending their lives at the College in the service of religious science. Besides, it appeared reasonable that here, as elsewhere, long and faithful service should find some temporal reward other than transfer from one's field of labour, which, the more successfully one cultivates it, the more one dislikes to leave.

In view of all this, I had been suggesting for some time the advisability of asking the Trustees to increase our salaries, so that, at least after a lengthened period of service, they would come up to what was provided in 1845. After some time the community took up the suggestion, and we formulated and presented our petition, which, as usual, was not granted at first. The President, however, Dr. Mannix, pressed it on the Visitors and the Board, as did also the Bursar, Dr. Donnellan, and, as they had powerful assistance from Dr. Walsh, the Archbishop of Dublin, the proposed arrangement was ultimately sanctioned. It was reported among us that the strongest opponents of our scheme were two Bishops who had been members of the staff, and who, while here, were not remarkable, to say the least, for lack of push in securing any emoluments that might be going.

One more reflection before I pass from this part of my subject: it shall be with regard to College examinations. During all my time as a student, and for long after I joined the staff, we had long and tedious oral examinations, of all the classes, at the end of each term, with the result that the time available for teaching was curtailed, and the professors wearied out, in the interest of these almost useless exercises. When will the directors of ecclesiastical institutions realize that it is teaching not examination, that is important, and that, if there must be a test of some kind, as a means of ascertaining whether the students have the requisite knowledge for work, let it be a simple pass test. For honours, the only test that is worth a straw, or very much more, is the production of some original essay or book on the subject in question. By much pressure, we got the Christmas examinations very much reduced, so as to occupy but three days, and anyone who knows how useless they are must be glad, I fancy, whenever they are abolished altogether. Of what earthly use are they, seeing that the students are liable to be examined in the same matter at the end of the second term? Or why not, rather, ask whether they do not interfere with our examining at summer in the whole year's programme? if that, indeed, is to be lamented. Examination, like interrogation in class, is the refuge of humdrum professors who are unable to make their teaching interesting. The main thing in teaching is to give students an interest in their work, so that they may like to do it and may continue doing it in after life, and no man ever yet was enticed in this way by examinations, but only in spite of them.

Professors, as I have said, are simply worn out and disgusted by this monotonous and useless work. And this reminds me that it is absolutely necessary, if professors are to perfect themselves and write good books, not to overload them with official work of any kind – even with teaching. Give them few lectures and a long midsummer vacation – plenty of free time, and make them use it. If they do not make good use of it, then do not promote them. Do not even appoint them permanently, unless they have shown that they have been well habituated into the use of this free time, during the probationary period, which should be considerable. In this way you may hope to make some first-rate men, whereas according to the traditional method of our seminaries, you will secure at best but a decent average.

ATTEMPTED REFORMS OUTSIDE (1904)

I had sole charge of the classes of canon law in the College for a period of nine years, during which time, and especially towards its close, the feeling grew on me that it would be much better for the Irish Church if the common law were observed more fully, modified, no doubt, to suit the altered circumstances of our time, but not changed in substance, or so much as to be no longer saturated with the spirit of independence and fair play that characterizes the *Corpus Juris*. Not that, in Ireland at present and elsewhere, we – priests especially – are not subject to a very minutely detailed body of laws; but that, while we are made to feel all the burthen of a law, we are deprived of much of its benefit. The result is, as I think, a certain timidity – almost servility – in the inferior clergy, with its correlative spirit of time-serving and sycophancy, and, in general, a growing lack of that manly spirit of sacrifice and independence, joined to strict obedience, that have marked the greatest Churchmen.

Now, it was rumoured, somewhere about the middle of the year 1904, that the Roman authorities contemplated a reform of the whole canon law, and that they had written to all the Bishops of the Church to make known this intention and to invite suggestions. This move, I thought, though desirable in some respects, was in other ways undesirable, as many of the reforms which I deemed most urgent would tend to restrict the power of Bishops, and, for that reason, would not only not be suggested, but would be opposed, by them. I thought it desirable that, as the lower clergy, and even the laity, had a very deep interest in what was about to be done, they should speak out; not, in the least, as possessing authority or giving a commission, but merely as placing respectfully before the Bishops and the Holy See the principal inconveniences which they (the inferior clergy and laity) had to bear from the present system – or lack of system. And as, besides myself, there did not seem to be anyone in Ireland who would set the ball in motion, I resolved to make an attempt to do so. One of the strongest proofs that could be advanced for the need of reform was the fact that the great body of the clergy and laity were convinced that we were doing splendidly; and that, if any reform was needed, it should take the direction of strengthening the hold of the Bishops on the clergy and of both on the laity, especially in educational matters; while those who did not agree with this grumbled in private, but were afraid to take any public action. It was almost a forlorn hope to try and stimulate a mass of this kind into action; but I thought it a shame that at least some attempt should not be made; and, hopeless as it looked, I resolved to make it.

I planned three articles for the *Irish Ecclesiastical Record:* on Ecclesiastical Trials; on Appointments to Parishes; and on Finance. Not that there were not other evils, but that what evils there were, centred in these three, and would disappear before long if these were remedied. Besides, there was danger of confusing a fairly straight issue, and of frightening a number of people who were already but too timid, if one were to take up all the points on which reform was needed.

The first paper was on Ecclesiastical Trials. The *Corpus Juris Canonici* provides – and it is one of its most fundamental principles – that no one shall be held guilty and punished as such, except after proof of the offence, the proof to be advanced in open court, unless the crime were committed publicly. Even in this case – of notorious crime – the ecclesiastical authority was required, by the canon law, to prove the notoriety of the offence before proceeding to punishment: this, as it has been said, is the spirit of the whole punitive legislation of the Church; which, indeed, is the basis of criminal procedure in all Christian countries. Where authority can punish without trial, there is no liberty; and without liberty neither Church nor State can flourish.

Now, in Ireland, though priests were liable to be severely punished – of which no one could complain, and at which I should be the last, I think, to grumble – they had practically no protection against abuse of the power to which they were thus subjected. They could be deprived of a mission or parish without proof of guilt, and they had practically no appeal. For, though the Metropolitan could, in theory, hear their complaint, he had, practically, no court in which to try it; nor would an appellant have the ordinary means of presenting his case – an advocate, for instance, or witnesses. He might, of course, get advice from some clerical friend, whose interferences would be resented by Metropolitan and Bishop alike, and, if witnesses refused to attend – as well they might, if their testimony was likely to be displeasing to the Bishop from whose action the appeal was taken – there was no authority to compel them. No wonder that appeals were almost unheard of; or that, when they did occur, Metropolitans deemed them subversive of discipline, and gave them no attention. I remember hearing a certain Archbishop tell, with pride, how summarily he would deal with an appeal which, it was said, was being made to him from the decisions of one of his suffragans.

One was free, of course, to take one's complaint to Rome, where the complainant would not know the language of the court, and where not even one advocate was to be found who could speak English; where, moreover, it was practically impossible to produce witnesses. Even in Rome, at that time, there was no court of justice; so that one could not get, even there, a canonical trial, but only an investigation, at the hands of officials who were busied with the affairs of a world-wide Church, and had little time or inclination to go into the merits of a dispute between Bishop and priest in some unpronounceable Irish diocese. Besides, if they – the Roman officials – must needs look into the case, for appearance sake, they had practically no evidence, to set against the Bishop's statement, but the counter-statement of the appellant, with whom they were unable to exchange more than a word or two in Latin. Of what use was an appeal or recursus of this kind?

The simple truth is that, up to the time of which I speak – the opening years of the twentieth century – there was no justice to be had in Ireland – in the sense of a judicial trial, with rare exceptions. In the diocese of Limerick, a parish priest, against whom a serious charge had been brought, got the benefit of the canon law; as did another parish priest of the diocese of Dublin. These cases are mentioned in a spirit of fairness, and out of respect for the prelates to whose sense of law and justice these trials were due; also to show that there was no reason why the rulers of the Irish Church should not, in this most important matter, give their subjects the benefit of the canon law as administered elsewhere.

This unfortunate state of things has now happily passed away – or, at least, has begun to pass. Even while I was writing my first article, on Ecclesiastical Trials, the S. Congregation of Propaganda had approved the Acts of the Second Plenary Synod of Maynooth, wherein it is prescribed (n. 141) that in future, as a rule no clergyman is to be punished for a disciplinary offence, unless he had been found guilty of the same after having undergone the substance of a fair trial, in which he shall have had the benefit of an advocate to plead his case. It is prescribed also that minutes are to be kept of all the proceedings of this trial, so that, should there be an appeal, to Rome or elsewhere, the facts of the case shall be on record.

This, one would think, should at once remedy all substantial grievances as regards ecclesiastical trials; but it has not, though it will, in time. Some of the Bishops have not realized that the synodal decree was meant to be carried out; that, at least, punishments inflicted without carrying it out cannot in future be so easily sustained as heretofore. They have yet to realize, in particular, that the right of the accused to the benefit of an advocate implies the right of those who may be called on for advice or assistance to give it freely, without being held guilty of undue interference or attempting to subvert authority or discipline, no matter how serious may be the charge against the accused. Indeed, the more serious the charge, the greater the need of perfect freedom for the advocate. Now, however this may be admitted in the Irish Church in theory, we have not yet come to act on it in practice: as I know, who have lost an old friend for advising one of his priests as to how he should defend himself. Here I must be content to state that I know that priests who desire to live at peace in our Irish Church, and those in particular who do not want to put a bar to their chance of preferment, are afraid to come forward as witnesses, and above all, are afraid to become advocates for fellow-priests, when, as often happens, it is known or suspected that the Bishop regards such action as an attack on himself.

My second article on canon law reform dealt with Appointments to Parishes, which had hitherto lain entirely with the Bishops, whereby they could punish most seriously in another way – negatively – and this without giving the least chance of redress. Their despotic power was thus increased immensely: as men whose lives were so blameless as to afford no pretext for positive punishment could be left without preferment, or, if promoted to a parish, might get only a poor and backward one, whence they would see others less efficient, except at securing episcopal favour, promoted over their heads.

I must not be understood to imply that those who were invested with despotic power used it unjustly, as a rule, or even that, whenever they did deal harshly or inequitably with some one, they were conscious of the hardship they inflicted. No, it was a benevolent despotism, exercised, for the most part, fairly and in the interest of religion; and, even where hardship was inflicted, this was done conscientiously, by one who made up his mind to do it, not in self-interest, but for the public weal. Bishops and clergy would have gone to the stake rather than be guilty of a conscious violation of duty in a grave matter; but they lived under a system which fostered adulation, which, as the world knows, may too easily be disguised as reverence. The evil had developed long ago, and had been met by withholding from Bishops the exclusive right of appointing to benefices, as the companion evil – of servility – had been met by withholding from them the right to punish without trial. But persecution had had to dispense with law; and so, in the Irish Church, as well as in all Churches which took their tone from her, the Bishop had become dictator and could do as he pleased. This authority, though necessary in the state of siege, must lead to mischief if continued after the Church had settled down once more to her regular life of peace; though it was natural that dictators, conscious of their own integrity and benevolence, should not see this, but should think that, once they gave up the reins of unlimited power, all kinds of abuses must creep into the Church.

Here also the Holy See interfered, bringing pressure to bear on the Bishops to revive the old canonical system of appointing to parishes by concursus, a system which, as outlined in the common law, was open undoubtedly to very grave abuses. If benefit was to be derived from introducing it once more, it should be modified considerably; but the tendency of the Bishops was to modify it so as to leave them practically all the exclusive power of appointment which they had acquired. Hence in the United States of America, where some years ago the concursus system had been introduced for appointments to certain parishes, it was reduced to a mere sham; whereby appearances were composed and the Roman authorities satisfied, while the Bishops retained the power of appointing to all parishes whom they pleased.

Now, it was rumoured that the Holy See had for some time been pressing the Irish Bishops to comply with the law of the Council of Trent in this matter, and some of us had a suspicion that, if their Lordships yielded, they would do so only after copying, if not even improving on, the modifications introduced in the United States. The suspicion has been verified, as those who know what happened in Ireland a few years ago knew too well. It was mainly to obviate this that I wrote my second article, on Appointment to Parishes; for it was well known that some form of concursus could not be long delayed. I got no support, and my effort was fruitless; nay, I have been told that I am credited among the clergy with having been the main cause of introducing the sham concursus system under which we live at present, by reason of the article which I wrote and published with a view to preventing the sham.

So far, the Catholic laity were not concerned, at least directly; for, indirectly, they had a very deep interest in seeing that only guilty priests were punished, and only efficient, holy, independent, but obedient priests promoted to the best and most responsible positions in the Church. In financial affairs, however, they were interested as directly as the clergy, if not even more so; for it is the laity alone who have to bear this burthen. And as, on the one hand, the burthen is very heavy, and has been borne hitherto, not only obediently but cheerfully, by a poor but exceedingly generous people, while, on the other hand, the money which is supplied for the support of the Church has been the cause of nearly all the evils wherewith she has been afflicted during the long course of her history; I thought it time, now, that we had fully emerged from bondage, to provide the faithful with some protection against unreasonable exactions. Not that in Ireland there has been very much to complain of, or that there have been very many complaints, but that the occasion is there, from which complaints and causes of complaint have arisen in other countries; and which, now that we were growing in freedom, wealth, and comfort, are pretty sure, if not looked after, to have the same result with us.

Now, the only protection that is worth a straw in money matters is publicity – publication of accounts – as experience proves. There is, I know, a feeling of some kind, that the Church is different from the State in this respect: that, while Kings and their servants need to be watched, lest they convert the public funds to their private uses, such a thing is, if not inconceivable, at least so rare as to be negligible in the case of Churchmen. Would that it were so; but, unfortunately, the history of the Papacy alone proves that it is not. For, if the Roman Curia lost the hold on Europe that it had during the Middle Ages, it is mainly because of misappropriation of Church funds. Not only was the wealth of Rome the cause of all the scandals that shocked the conscience of Europe, but it was in itself, perhaps, the greatest scandal of all. In reading Dr. Pastor's history of Alexander VI – no very edifying Churchman – I was more shocked at the abuse of public money than at the personal irregularities of the head of the Church.[1]

And the worst of it was that, while Alexander and his vices passed away, the money abuses remained; until at length the Popes also were dethroned in some of their fairest provinces; while even those, like France, which remained true to their allegiance, suffered untold injury from the scandalous lives of too wealthy clergymen. There would have been no Reformation, as there would have been no French Revolution, if Church and State had had the good habit of publishing their accounts.

In advocating this reform, unfortunately, one could not, as in the matter of judicial procedure and of ecclesiastical preferment, fall back on the canon law itself; for publication of accounts never formed part of the Church's economic system. Nor can she be blamed very much for this, as long, that is, as it formed no part of the economic system of other rulers, from whom she might well be content to learn how best to deal with matters of finance. Now, however, that they have adopted a better way and that there is not a governing body, whether national or local, throughout the world but publishes its budget, so that the taxpayers may know

---

1. See vol. v, pp. 366–70 and ff., to the end of the volume. Roscoe (*Life of Leo Tenth*, I, p. 23) gives a list of as many as twenty-seven benefices, culminating in the Archbishopric of Amalfi, held by that clergyman in his youth, though son of Lorenzo the Magnificent, he was tonsured when seven years old, that he might be capable of holding benefices, and that he might be educated at the expense of the Church. And at what expense! Even the good St. Charles Borromeo was loaded with benefices from his youth in this way. Cardinal Mazarin received the income of twenty-seven abbacies, besides a number of bishoprics. These are but a few samples. *See Cath. Encyclopædia*, Art. 'Mazarin'.

how much is received and how it is spent; is it to the credit of the Church that her corporations should cling to the old, defective, and even corrupt, system? The Protestant Church of Ireland has, since its disestablishment, published its budget annually: why should we not do likewise? It is not that our budget is inconsiderable; for, calculating on a moderate scale, it takes £533,000 a year to provide the official stipends of the eleven hundred parish priests and nineteen hundred curates who are employed in the service of the Irish Church.[1]

This takes no account of other perquisites (State-fees); nor of what is required for the maintenance of more than six hundred religious men, besides Christian Brothers and nuns; nor of Catholic charities; nor of the erecton and repair of buildings. No Government, perhaps, gives details of the perquisites of all its servants; but surely the budget of the Catholic Church in Ireland is so large as to make it desirable that the taxpayers – for such they are – should be in position to know with ease and certainty what are its main items.

As against this I have heard it argued, by priests, that: (1) the people already know pretty accurately what stipends they are paying those who serve them in the Church; and (2) that, if they knew, they would not continue to pay what priests receive under the present system. The arguments are contradictory; and yet I have heard them both used by clever men of the world, who were also sincere and hard-working clergymen.

I do not know whether, if the Irish people knew exactly what it costs them to support their clergy, they would or would not curtail supplies; but I am sure they are willing to make not merely a decent but a generous provision – for clergymen, who, after all, can do little service unless they show in their lives, their homes, and their surroundings, something of the poverty and the sacrifice of Christ. Well-fed, well-groomed, and well-appointed priests are of little use in a contest with the world, the flesh, and the devil; nor is it enough to give up marriage and family life, if we are addicted to the pleasures of the table and fond of show. I verily believe that the Roman palaces, of Popes and Cardinals, have cost the Church something infinitely more precious than money; and while the Catholic world, as I am sure, is quite prepared to supply the Pope with what he needs for Church purposes, the history of the Papacy justifies the faithful in being on their guard

1. The calculation is based on an allowance of £260 a year on the average for parish priests and of £130 for curates. The numbers of both classes are somewhat greater than the round numbers in the text.

against maladministration in the Roman Curia. The very best way to induce the laity to give what is wanted for the central government of the Church is to publish a budget, like other governments; and let the taxpayers – for such, in effect, they are – see what is needed, how much is received, and how it is spent. At present, it is to be feared, the burthen falls very unevenly on different parts of the Church.

I do not say that the faithful have a right to be treated by the Church as they insist on being treated by the secular governments. It is not a question of right but of expediency. I should not like to say that those who are accused of crimes have a right to call the means of defence with which the canon law provided them; or that the diocesan clergy have a right to be consulted as to whom they would like to have for Bishop; or that they have a right that appointments to benefices should take place by concursus; yet the Church has thought it wise to make these and many other similar concessions. Neither, I repeat, do I wish to imply that in Ireland or elsewhere the clergy are overpaid or exacting, the people too highly taxed, or charitable trusts maladministered, or that the laity are complaining or have reason to complain. I insist merely that our present system makes it easy for such abuses to creep in, as they did before; and that Churchmen should be more prudent even than Cæsar's wife. I do not know how any man of honour can feel comfortable if he administers a trust, the accounts of which he is not prepared to submit to those concerned; or if he takes a stipend from people who have no means of knowing, and do not know, how much they pay.

Well, the three articles in which I advocated these reforms were duly published in the *Irish Ecclesiastical Record*,[1] to my own surprise, I must say. I am sure they would not be published now – over my name, at least. I did not hear much as to how they were received by the Hierarchy. One Bishop, I was told, was so wroth that he threatened – not very seriously, I fancy – to reply to them himself. The Archbishop of Dublin, on the contrary, I heard, said to some one that he had no objection to them. It is not at all likely that the editor of the *Irish Ecclesiastical Record* would have continued to publish them against the wish of the Bishops; so I take it that, if they complained at all, they did not do so very loud. The priests, I think, were pleased with the first article; but the second caused grave dissatisfaction, especially among the senior curates; whilst the third was regarded by almost all as sheer Quixotism, if not lunacy, or even Anticlericalism. The

1. In the Nos. for October, November and December, 1904.

162

articles, on the whole, evoked no support from the clergy; while the laity either did not hear of them or were too listless or too much afraid to press the demand for publication of accounts.

Some time after the articles appeared, the Roman authorities wrote to the Bishops for suggestions as to the reforms which it would be advisable to make in the common law of the Church, which was being re-cast and codified anew; and their Lordships appointed a small commission to look into the matter and report to them. The commission consisted of Mgr. O'Donnell, one of the Vicars-General of the diocese of Dublin; Mgr. Murphy, one of the Vicars-General of the diocese of Kildare and Leighlin; Dr. Luzzio, professor of Canon Law in our College; and myself. The commission which we received was limited in scope – to the part of the canon law which regulated the administration of the sacraments: a department in which I found comparatively little need of reform. The first meeting of the commission took place in Mgr. O'Donnell's house at Booterstown, and seemed to me of so little practical importance that it was my last, as well as my first, time to attend. I had by this time learned a little, from the result of my labours on the programme of the congress, as well as from the failure of my articles on Canon Law Reform. The Bishops, I thought, and the other members of the Commission, could be depended on to suggest any changes in sacramental law that might be needed in the interest of Bishops and vicars-general; as also such as might be needed by the lower clergy and the laity, provided they did not trench on the rights and privileges of the Bishops. The three points on which I had written, if referred by Rome to the Bishops, were withheld from us; and even though they had been submitted to us, I did not think I should be able to carry with me even one member of the Commission. So I took no further part in its proceedings. In due time it presented a report; which, I suppose, met the fate of all such documents: I do not think it had, or ever will have, much influence in shaping the legislation of the Church.

PROPOSAL TO MAKE TERMS WITH TRINITY COLLEGE (1904)

Though taking no part in public life as a rule, I interfered on two occasions: first, in connection with the Irish University question, and again with regard to the management of National Schools in

Ireland; and as on both occassions the policy which I advocated was misunderstood, perhaps because I did not explain it fully or clearly enough – it may be well to set forth here what I merely outlined then. For, though the University question has been settled since, on lines different from those which I suggested, it is possible that the present arrangement may not last for ever, while the management of the National Schools may become a subject of controversy before very long. I will take the University question, as it was in that I first interfered.

The twentieth century was little more than six months old when a Royal Commission was appointed 'to inquire into the present condition of the higher, general and technical education available in Ireland outside Trinity College, Dublin, and to report as to what reforms, if any, are desirable in order to render that education adequate to the need of the Irish People'. This was spoken of as the Robertson Commission, from its Chairman, Lord Robertson, one of the Lords of Appeal in Ordinary, three of the remaining eleven members being Catholics: to wit, Most Rev. Dr. Healy Archbishop of Tuam, Dr. Starkie, and Mr. Wilfrid Ward – all able men. The Report of the Commission, which was presented on the last day of February, 1903, was signed by eleven of the twelve members and suggested the establishment in Dublin of a college which would be practically Catholic, and which, with the three Queen's Colleges already in existence, would form a federal university. The suggested new college would have chairs of science and arts, but not of theology, nor, apparently, of philosophy, nor even of history, except in so far as it might be held to form part of the arts course. It would be governed, to start with, by a body of seventeen gentlemen, the great majority, if not all, of whom would be Catholics, and the professors would be appointed by this body, subject to the approval of the Crown. All chairs would be open to persons of all denominations, on condition, however, that they would not teach or publish anything contrary to the doctrine of the Catholic Church. What this doctrine is, on any point, would be decided by two Catholic Bishops, who would be members of the Board of Visitors. The Queen's Colleges of Cork and Galway would be reformed, so as to make them acceptable to Catholics. Our College of Maynooth was left out in the cold.

The Catholic body, sick and disheartened as regards the university question, was prepared to accept the solution thus outlined, and the report of the Commission was signed by their three representatives, two of whom made, in Notes, reservations of no practical importance, while Dr. Starkie could not recommend 'that practical effect should be given to the scheme'. The Chairman also declined, in a Note, to recommend its adoption, as did Viscount Ridley. Another member, Professor Lorrain Smith, of Belfast, declined to recommend a departure from the form of constitution hitherto provided in the Queen's Colleges; at least until this had been fairly tried and found intolerable, as, in the commissioner's opinion, it had not been. In view of these addenda, it is no wonder that the report fell flat, or that, when the question came again before Parliament, Mr. Balfour's Government declined to make any effort to give legislative effect to the proposed scheme. Some time after this resolution of the Government was made known, Fr. T. Finlay, S.J., speaking at a meeting of the Scientific Society of the Catholic University School of Medicine, took up the Sinn Fein attitude, advising discontinuance of agitation and the establishment of an Irish, or even an Irish Ireland University, by Irish resources and on Irish lines. Though this was anything but a policy of despair, it was an open profession of despair of our obtaining any satisfactory settlement of the question from the British Government – unless we changed our policy.

It was in these circumstances that Mr. John Dillon, M.P., was invited by the Catholic Graduates and Undergraduates Association, to address a meeting convened by them at the Mansion House, Dublin, on the evening of Thursday, December 8, 1904. He spoke 'On the Need of a National University for Ireland and how best to Construct it', and I was asked to second a vote of thanks. In the course of his address he demanded rightly, that the university should be self-governed – independently of any veto on the part of Dublin Castle. The university, too, he said, should be national in the broadest sense, open to students of all creeds and of no creed. It would be Catholic as long as Ireland remains a predominantly Catholic nation. There should be ample provision for the religious instruction of Catholics on Catholic lines; and moral philosophy and theology in all its branches, should be taught in conformity with Catholic principles. This implied a right of veto on the part of the Catholic Bishops, at least as regards the appointment of the professors of philosophy and theology, and as to the continuance of such professors in their chairs. As regards other professors, however – those of science and arts – as I understood Mr. Dillon, the only guarantee he would have for their neutrality in religious matters, would be the prevailing Catholic atmosphere of the university, at least in its early years.

Of the two policies thus recommended to the Irish Catholic public, by men who spoke with considerable authority, I could approve of neither. Our fathers had tried the Sinn Fein one and failed, at a time when there was in the land more of faith, and more enthusiasm for things purely Catholic, than there is now. They failed, it is true, mainly by reason of their poverty; they simply were not able to endow and support an independent university – and continue to support it. The enthusiasm with which they began fizzled out with years: could we reasonably hope to do better and last longer? Their line of action, if renewed, would attract, according to Fr. Finlay, more attention from the Government, than all the resolutions we could pass in twelve months. Perhaps so; the Government might attend, or even admire, but would they help? That I thought more than doubtful.

As for looking still to the Government – which was the policy just advocated by the man for whom I was about to bespeak a vote of thanks, and whose suggestion I must criticize, favourably or unfavourably – how could we go on hoping to succeed in that way? Had we not proved our case at the Royal Commission? With the result that the Government, whose chief members did not need to be convinced, told us plainly that they could not act up to their convictions for fear of revolt among the Orange section of their supporters. Should we go on hoping – to convince these bigots? Or, perhaps turn out of power a statesman who extended to us at least a barren sympathy, to put in, as Mr. Dillon wished, the sworn enemies of that denominationalism for which we had been so long contending?

Ah, but might we not give up the denominational cry, and so hope for redress from the Liberals? Was this really what Mr. Dillon meant, with his plea of a university for students of all creeds and of none, whose professors might, without danger of losing their chairs, sneer at and attack religion or proclaim themselves atheists or unbelievers, not only in books or newspapers, but even in the pulpits which they were paid to occupy. Not, of course, the professors of philosophy and theology, who would be subject to the Bishops; but could we hope that the Liberals would give us any university in which such professors would have a place? I was not so hopeful, and I thought that our people – clergy and laity – would never go back on their part so far as to accept a purely secular university, in which, if religion were taught, the teaching would not be under control of the bishops; while the professors of science and arts, whose teaching as we were wont to proclaim must, of necessity, have a great though indirect influence on faith and morals – were to be more independent of ecclesiastical authority than those of Trinity or the Queen's Colleges. If we were to go back on our part at all, why not aim at making terms with these institutions, where we had a right to enter and which we might hope to modify? This, in substance, is what I said in seconding the vote of thanks to Mr. Dillon.

Half a year after Mr. Dillon's address, the Most Rev. Dr. O'Donnell, Bishop of Raphoe, read a paper on the same subject at the Maynooth Union. The date of the meeting was Thursday, June 16, 1905. His Lordship advocated the policy of fighting on as we had fought, and suggested that redress would come, at the farthest, with Home Rule. I had gone into the hall without any intention of speaking, but, being called on by the Chairman, his Eminence Cardinal Logue, I spoke out my mind, as follows:

'I would co-operate with the body of Catholics in any policy on which they might determine, but I think myself that the true policy would be to go at once, in an organized body, into Trinity College. I admit that this course is not without danger, but is there not a greater danger – lest, for lack of proper university training, and consequent weakness of the Catholic Press, we may be losing more than we should lose in Trinity? There is leakage in the Church abroad, of which the Irish race is no inconsiderable part, and there is weakening of faith at home. If we can make Trinity a true centre of Irish literature and science, the stream of emigration might be diminished, the Catholic Press strengthened, and there would be no small gain to set against the loss that would be pretty sure to accrue'.

I went on to say that, in estimating the dangers of Trinity, we must not base our calculations on what has occurred hitherto, when to go there meant, practically, to take the Saxon shilling:

'Those who did so were the right material for renegades. Because some of them fell away, is it so clear that the same fate would befall the army of Catholic Ireland, if we were to march in a body, with the blessing of God and of the Church on our banners? Dr. Delany (who spoke before me) has referred to the position of Catholics in Oxford, but are a handful of Catholics there, or in Cambridge, to be compared, for security, to the great body of Catholic students whom we might send into Trinity? Besides, there is little or no danger of Irish Catholics becoming Protestant. 'There is danger of infidelity, but is there not less danger of this in Trinity College than in Paris or Bonn? And yet French and German Catholics are not content to sit on the bank, watching the drain on their people. Why, the very Protestantism of Trinity may be utilized as a breakwater against these waves of infidelity: the Christian faith is far from being dead among the Irish Protestants by whom the College is controlled.

'All this', I added, 'applies even more to Irish nationality. Are we to be told that the vast body of ardent young Irishmen whom we might send into Trinity, would lose their Irish spirit in the atmosphere of the place? Why do they not lose it in the Government offices, in the Kingsbridge and Broadstone stations, in the Grafton Street shops? There they are without any organization; whilst in Trinity they could organize themselves as they please. If the Gaelic League wishes to gain its most effective victory, it will saturate the atmosphere of Trinity with microbes of Irish nationality. Is it not possible to outline some scheme, such as is already working in so many of the German universities – the highest type of school of which we have any knowledge – to secure for Catholic young men in Trinity faculties of theology and philosophy, which might serve as nuclei for Catholic organization within the university? This is nothing more than Protestant Germany has conceded, nothing but what Irish Protestants must concede, if they are to retain, as I hope they may, the Divinity School in Trinity College. Could we not demand securities, if we need them, for the free development of the Irish national spirit within the university? If the claim is recognized, you will have the nucleus of a fine organization; if it is denied, you can ring the changes on the difference between the banks of the Liffey and of the Rhine'.

I set forth thus distinctly the policy which, at the Mansion House, I had referred to vaguely as 'making terms with Trinity'; and still I was misunderstood. It was said that I would have Catholics go into Trinity College and 'swamp' it; as if I held that we were in position to get control of that College at once. I had not, and did not hold out, any such hope, but insisted merely that if Catholic students went there in a body – the best of them, with the support and blessing of their Church – they would be well able to protect both their faith and their national spirit, especially if, as I did hope, we could get them from the beginning Catholic faculties of theology and philosophy, to serve as nuclei of organization and support, after the model of some of the great German universities. I believed, as I do still, that such faculties are, in modern times, practically the only means left of safeguarding Catholic students; nor should I have made with Trinity any terms that did not comprise the establishment therein of faculties of theology and philosophy under the control of the Bishops – as in the universities of Bonn and Freiburg.

Well, the Conservatives went out of office in 1906, and, to the surprise of many of us, the Liberals took up once more the Irish University question. Their first step was to appoint a Royal Commission 'to inquire into and report upon the present state of Trinity College, Dublin, and of the University of Dublin – and – upon the place which they now hold as organs of the higher education in Ireland, and the steps proper to be taken to increase their use-fulness to the country'. This is known as the Fry Commission, from its chairman, Sir Edward Fry, later one of the Lords Justices of Appeal. It had three Catholic members: Chief Baron Palles; Dr. Coffey, now President of the recently established Dublin College of the National University; and Mr. Kelleher, one of the Fellows of Trinity College. Dr. Hyde also was a member, and might be expected, from his position as President of the Gaelic League, to sympathize with the claims of Irish Catholics.

Those who thought, with me, that such terms might be made with Trinity as to render it acceptable to Catholics, could not desire a more favourable opportunity than was thus supplied for setting forth their view. As early as March 6, 1892, some Catholic laymen held a meeting under the chairmanship of Sir Gerald Dease, and it was proposed by Mr. Ambrose More O'Farrell, and seconded by Mr. Commissioner Lynch, that a number of gentlemen should be appointed a committee to make known to the Royal Commission (the Robertson Commission) the views of Catholic laymen who supported a solution of the Dublin University question on the lines of collegiate education within the University of Dublin. Over four hundred names are appended to the document which was drawn up and presented to the Commission in pursuance of the foregoing resolution, but it should be noted that there was no thought at that time of reforming the constitution of Trinitiy College, but only of establishing within the University of Dublin a second College, which should be for Catholics what Trinity College is for Episcopalian Protestants.

In December, 1905, however – just twelve months after Mr. Dillon's address at the Mansion House, and six months after the Bishop of Raphoe had read his paper at the Maynooth Union – Mr. George Fottrell wrote to one of the Professors of the Catholic Faculty of Theology at Bonn, to ask for information as to how the university question was solved there, and received, in reply, a detailed statement of the first importance, which may be found in the *Appendix to the Final Report* of the Fry Commission (pp. 408, 661). From this document it appears that the number of students at the University of Bonn was at that time 2,800, of whom three-fifths were Catholic, and two-fifths non-Catholic. All, or almost all, were drawn from the Rhenish Province of Prussia, which had then a population of about 5,500,000, of whom about 69 per cent. were Catholics. The conditions of the province were very like those of Ireland, as regards population and distribution of seats; and, as regards students and their creeds, the University of Bonn was very like what we might expect Trinity College to become before long, if it were so modified as to draw to itself all those who matriculated then in the Dublin College of the National University. Yet Bonn was found by experience to turn out a particularly healthy type of militant Catholic layman, though the Protestantism of the place is much more insidious than is likely to prevail in Trinity for very many years.

The question of making Trinity College another Bonn must have been a good deal in men's thoughts after the Fry Commission was appointed, for, towards the end of July, 1906, a 'scheme for widening the constitution' of Trinity College was submitted to that Commission by 'twelve Junior Fellows, one retired Junior Fellow, and eight Professors of Trinity'. The scheme was drawn up with the avowed object of 'modifying the constitution of the College, so that it may become the National University of Ireland'. There was to be an Advisory Committee of six persons, of whom four should be laymen, all to be nominated at first as part of the settlement, and vacancies, as they arose, to be filled by co-option. The duties of the Committee, which should be clearly defined, would relate to the faith and morals of Catholic students, and it was understood, of course, that all its members should be Catholics at first, or acceptable to Catholics, and that two of them would be members of the Catholic Hierarchy. Provision was made, further, for the appointment of second professors in mental and moral science and in history, subject to the veto of the Advisory Committee and under its supervision. There was a provision also, subject to the same control, for the religious instruction of Catholic students by clergymen of their own Church, and for the establishment of a Catholic chapel within the College. 'Should the Roman Catholic Bishops desire, a Faculty of Theology under their direction would be established in Dublin University'. Finally, as 'no settlement intended to make Trinity College a National University would meet with Roman Catholic support which did not provide for immediate representation of Roman Catholic interests on the Governing Body', it was proposed to replace the existing Board by a new Governing Body, which should be elected on the principle 'that Roman Catholics should be afforded an opportunity, within a reasonable time, of obtaining adequate representation on the Governing Body, according to number and academic merit'. The statement went on to suggest, for criticism, details of a plan whereby the election of the Governing Body would have that result.

As to the amount of support which their scheme had in Trinity College itself, the Provost, in his evidence before the Commission, gave interesting details. He 'did not call the Governing Body' to consider it, but he himself 'presided at all the meetings of Junior Fellows and Professors'. 'We kept a number of our staff here during vacation discussing the matter, and the reason the names put to it were not more in number, was that they all scattered next day, but the division was about twenty to four in favour of the scheme'. Asked by Mr. Kelleher, whether the men in the College would not suffer such violent resistance to the scheme that it could not be carried into effect, he replied: 'a very violent opposition would undoubtedly be offered by some of those of old-fashioned views, but I would hope that the majority of the whole body would be in favour of a scheme of the kind, if it would really solve the whole question' – that is, if it proved acceptable to the Catholic Bishops and their flocks. Asked, further, 'if the scheme were accepted by the Bishops, would it certainly be accepted by Trinity College as a whole, with some modifications, of course', he said: 'I should hope that a majority of the whole staff would be in favour of such a solution, if the Bishops went in for it'. The Provost himself approved. The Board, however, would be opposed to it. (See Note at end of this chapter.)

Meanwhile the Catholic Laymen's Committee were not idle. The Provost states in his evidence that the Committee of the Junior Fellows and Professors within the College 'were in communication with a committee of Roman Catholic Laymen, and they agreed in the main on the basis of a new arrangement'. The Catholic Committee drew up and circulated the following statement, which was signed by 467 laymen, of the class which provides university students:

'We, the undersigned Catholic laymen, desire to place on record our conviction that no solution of the university difficulty in Ireland, based upon Trinity College being constituted the sole College of a national university, can be accepted as satisfactory, as long as is fails to provide for: (a) A substantial representation from the start upon the Governing Body, with a power of expansion of such representation dependent upon, and fairly proportionate to, the number of students whom Catholics send into the College, and the academic distinctions which they may there win; (b) the establishment of dual professorships in at least mental and moral science and in history; (c) the religious instruction of our students by clergymen of our own Church; (d) the establishment of a faculty of theology on terms of full equality with those enjoyed by Protestants; (e) the establishment of a Chapel for our students within the College; and (f) the creation of a Council or other body to secure the practical efficiency of the safeguards provided for our students in religion, faith, and dogma'.

These conditions were, practically, what had been agreed to by the Junior Fellows and Professors, with the sympathy of the Provost and by far the greater part of the College staff, so that practical agreement had been reached, as regards a basis of settlement, between the College and the Catholic laity. The Catholic Hierarchy, however – a far more powerful body, as regards this question – had yet to express their view, and they did so in a statement issued by their Standing Committee on July 25, 1906 – the day after that of the Junior Fellows and Professors of Trinity College had been presented to the Royal Commission. The Bishops inform the Commission 'that under no circumstances will the Catholics of Ireland accept a system of mixed education in Trinity College as a solution of their claims'. That was decisive. The Commission reported – as they could not help doing, in face of the episcopal statement – that 'inasmuch as the Standing Committee of the Roman Catholic Bishops, in the document sent by them to us, have assured us that the Catholics of Ireland 'would on no account accept any scheme of mixed education in Trinity College, Dublin,' we cannot hope to render the College acceptable to the Roman Catholic episcopate by reasonable changes in its constitution. In the above the Commission are unanimous. The Bishops, in the document before mentioned, have in fact disclaimed any desire on the part of the Roman Catholic people to have changes made in the constitution of the College for their sakes'. 'Meanwhile', the Report proceeds, 'there is a considerable body of Roman Catholic laymen who would gladly send their sons to Trinity College, if they could do so with the approbation of their Church'.

The statement of fact made by the Bishops, that 'now no more than then (when Fawcett's Act was passed) do the Catholics seek to be allowed to enter Trinity College; they have never asked to have changes made in the constitution for their sakes', – this statement, however literally true, does not, I think, represent the state of Catholic opinion and desire at the time of the Fry Commission. I may be deceived, but I am satisfied that if the Catholic body were asked whether they regarded as a basis of discussion likely to issue in a satisfactory settlement, the scheme of reform submitted to the Commission by the Junior Fellows and Professors of Trinity College, and if they – the Catholic body of priests and laity – were allowed to vote uninfluenced by any authoritative statement such as was issued by the Bishops, the voting would show a very great body of opinion, lay and clerical, in favour of trying whether we could not make terms with Trinity College. When, however, the episcopal statement was issued, the Catholic body sided with the Bishops, as it always does, so that the Standing Committee were in position to make their own words true. Nor is there any ground, as far as I know, for complaint of this method of forming public opinion, if there were reasons, based on considerations of faith and morals, sufficient to justify the episcopal interference.[1]

I find a kind of academic interest in considering the reasons on which the Hierarchy based their refusal to make any terms with Trinity. The College, they said, is not popular, it is too expensive for Catholics, while its course of studies could with difficulty be brought into modern shape, so as to meet the actual needs of the country.

It was, no doubt, unpopular, and will remain so, as long as it remains unreformed on something like the lines suggested, but, if it were so reformed, would it remain unpopular? And if the Senior Fellowships ceased, while the endowment was increased by the sum that has been spent on the National University, would it not be possible to make study and graduation in Trinity as cheap as it now is for Catholic students in Dublin? Finally, as regards courses, those of Trinity and of the National University are not so very unlike; while if a great body of Catholic and Nationalist young men were to enter Trinity, it would be difficult to set bounds to the development which their advent would be sure to occasion.

The Bishops, in their statement, proceed to set forth objections which they represent as 'of more importance, because they touch upon principle'. 'For years', they say, 'it has been the wish of the Catholic Bishops of Ireland to give their ecclesiastical students the benefit of a university education. At the present moment, there is a regulation in force which requires all the students of Maynooth College to take out a degree in the Royal University, and it has been the hope of the Bishops that, sooner or later, they should have a university, or at least a university college, in which they might maintain a Theological Faculty. That would be impossible in Trinity College, Dublin. To Catholics, at all events, it is evident that their ecclesiastical students could not be sent to re-

1. On this occasion the question at issue was a mixed one, as to which the laity had a right to have their say; those especially of them whose sons were likely to go to a university. As the 467 signatories to the Statement submitted to the Fry Commission by the Catholic Laymen's Committee were all of this university-going class, I cannot help thinking that they were set aside rather unceremoniously. So many Catholic gentlemen, of the social position which they occupied, had, I think, a right to complain, at being treated as of no account.

side there'.

But surely it is no less evident that ecclesiastical students could not be sent to reside in any new college, whether of the Dublin or of any other University. They need not reside in either. They might have a hostel of their own, with regular ecclesiastical discipline, as they have at Bonn – and even at Rome. There is not, as a matter of fact, a Faculty of Theology in the National University, principally for lack of funds; while the Trinity offer comprised the establishment in Dublin University of a Faculty of Theology under the direction of the Roman Catholic Bishops, should these so desire. This offer, according to the Catholic Laymen's statement, should be understood to mean 'the establishment of a faculty of Catholic Theology on terms of full equality with those enjoyed by Protestants'. Besides, provision was made in the Trinity reform scheme, for dual professorships, subject to Catholic control, in mental and moral science, as also for the religious instruction of Catholic students by clergymen of their own Church, and to complete this, for the creation of a Catholic chapel in the College. In the National University, which we have accepted, the Professors of Philosophy are independent of episcopal control, whether as to their future appointment or as to the tenure of their chairs – as independent as are the Professors of Latin or Greek or Physics; while there is no chapel of the Catholic or any other religion, within the College, and there never can be. The University, as it has been denominated by Cardinal Logue, is 'a pagan bantling'.

The second of the more important objections set forth by the Bishops is to the effect that 'a college, whether for ecclesiastical or lay students, is a home in which the students, under a domestic discipline into which religion largely enters, complete the education which began in their parents' home. Public prayer, catechetical instruction, and the profession of a common religious faith, are the essence of collegiate life. It is so in the colleges of Oxford and Cambridge, and in Trinity College, Dublin, itself. The few Catholics who study in these colleges do not invalidate the argument. They are exceptions, and stand apart from the common life. Being a few, they are generally treated with special consideration, like guests in a family, but the college routine, with its religious practices, goes on independently of them. It would be quite another thing if, instead of being a few, they were equal, or nearly equal, in numbers to the others, and, instead of being ignored in the college discipline, provision had to be made in it for their religion also. A system of this kind seems to be a practical impossibility. You may have a Catholic college or a

174

Protestant college, but you cannot have a college which will be, at the same time, positively, both Catholic and Protestant; and the inevitable result of an attempt to set up, for the first time in the history of universities, an institution of the kind, would, as regards religion, be negative – that is the exclusion of all religions'.

To which the answer, supplied by time, is, that it would be, even though the prediction were verified, no worse in this respect than the 'pagan bantling' which, under their Lordships' guidance, Irish Catholics have accepted, wherein is no home, or domestic discipline, and no religion, Catholic or even pagan.

I never attached importance to residence in Trinity College as of use to Catholic students. If residence in any such place is of use – of which I doubt: it is practically unknown outside these islands – why not have hostels, or houses of residence, which could be made self-supporting? Neither have I ever regarded as of much importance the erection of a chapel within such places as Trinity College. The Catholics of Ireland, who have built so many churches and chapels, could be depended on to provide one, in some convenient place, where the great body of the students would hear Mass, pray, and receive instruction. What they need most, as I conceive, is instruction, suitable for modern university students, such as can proceed only, as an indirect result, from Catholic Faculties of Theology and Philosophy. There is no man or body of men, as far as I know, in so great need of strong, intellectual religious guidance, as are the university students of to-day – and, as it is hopeless to look for such guidance except to men of the intellectual standing of university professors, any university or university college which has not well-manned Faculties of Theology and Philosophy, is and must ever remain a serious danger to faith and morals. If we want, as we do, the National University to prove a blessing, not a curse, in this respect, we cannot too soon set about providing it with a well-manned Faculty of Theology, especially as the professors of philosophy are independent of ecclesiastical control and may be, one or all of them, unbelievers.

The one great argument that can be advanced in justification of the refusal to deal with Trinity, is the result – the fact that we have got something better than anything Trinity had to give. We have got an almost purely Catholic atmosphere. There is no denying this – for the present; and there can be little doubt but that it will remain so during the present generation of professors – and even outlive them. A generation, however, counts for little in the life of a university; we must look to future generations. Mr. Dillon, as we have seen, relies on the Catholicity of the nation to keep the air of its university Catholic: 'it would be Catholic as long as Ireland remained a predominantly Catholic nation'. I am not so sure that the university may not become the centre wherein the germs of disease are first sown and cultivated, to pass thence over the land and poison the atmosphere of what once was Catholic Ireland. It is the very function of a university to create an atmosphere; hence the anxiety of all parties to control these centres of thought. The Press is what the University makes it, and the atmosphere of a nation now is what it is made by the Press. Ballad-singers, it has been said, made laws in days of old. Now their function is usurped by Pressmen, who, in turn, are the product of the schools.

Let the Catholics of Ireland look to their university, if they would keep their Catholic faith. Tests are of little or no avail; nor can the present Catholic atmosphere of the nation be relied on to endure. The one great means of salvation lies in a Faculty of Theology worked by men who know their work and have courage to assert it, against the dogmatism of unbelief as well as against the no less killing dogmatism of a narrow-minded unscientific tradition. The opportunity of securing this was the main reason that induced me to advocate making terms with Trinity College.[1]

1. There were other reasons: reluctance to allow such a splendid institution as Trinity College to remain for all time in the possession of the Saxon and anti-Catholic garrison; and also, I confess with sorrow – a fear that in a self-governed democratic country, such as Ireland soon will be, Catholic faith and morals, being essentially conservative, would be exposed to less danger in Trinity, bad as it is, than in any new College which should be set up with a purely secular constitution – the only one we had any hope of getting. I withdraw that suspicion; but only on condition that a well-manned Faculty of Theology is set up in the Dublin College of the National University.
I may say here that I had no communication on this matter with anyone in Trinity College, except on two occasions. Mr. Stephen Gwynn took me one evening into the rooms of his brother Edward, where I met also the Rev. T. T. Gray, one of the Senior Fellows – a representative of the old school of Irish Protestantism. During the conversation I was told, and had to admit, that, as regards the Trinity question, I had little or no outspoken following. On another occasion, after the Catholic body had made up its mind to make no terms with Trinity, I was asked to speak to some address on the question at a meeting of, I think, the College Historical Society. I declined the invitation, on the ground that, as I wrote to the Hon. Secretaries – by appearing publicy at such a meeting, I should be giving some countenance to those Catholics who were entered as students of the College; thereby separating themselves

We have thrown away the chance, protesting that we did not need it – that we should provide as efficient a Faculty in any College which we might get and call our own. Unless we carry out this good purpose, I cannot restrain fears that a time may come when the Bishops of Ireland will find it necessary to exhort their flocks to send their sons to Trinity as the less dangerous of our university colleges.[1]

Inasmuch as it was, and is, natural to look to our own College of Maynooth for assistance – to say the least – in establishing a Faculty of Theology in Dublin, it may be well to record here

from the body of their Irish co-religionists, and opposing the policy which had been adopted by the great majority of our people.

1. Speaking in Galway, at a distribution of prizes in St. Mary's College, the Bishop, Most Rev. Dr. O'Dea, is reported to have said: 'This evil (the penalizing of religious studies) became much more deplorable because of its recurrence in the university. There, as in the schools, religion does not count in any official examination, and the penalty for its study would be a like failure. This is not so in Trinity College, as at Oxford, nor abroad. Worse still, there is no adequate force in our University to represent religion, or to press forward and defend its interests, in the intellectual formation of students and staff. When I go a step further and ask myself the effect in time upon the well-being of the nation, of this starting of what I may call intellectual religion among the educated classes of Ireland, I confess I can see no comforting answer. Our traditional piety, especially that of our women, will save us, I trust, for many a generation. But I recall that thought as ubiquitous to-day, because the Press is everywhere and all men read. How, then, I ask myself, can we hope that plausible anti-Christian and corrupting images will not find their way, in growing measure, even into Catholic Ireland? This is terrific evil, which experience shows to have been fatal to other countries. I can see no true and full antidote, unless in a Press profoundly conscious of the value of Catholic truth as man's greatest asset, and therefore intensely eager for its championship; and I see no sure hope of such a Press unless from close study at the University of the great principles of Catholic truth, and of their intimate bearing upon the essentials of human well-being. Only such study can raise up a long apostolate of the Press; without which Catholic truth will, I fear, be hard to guard as time goes on'.

This address is reported in the *Freeman's Journal* of December 16, 1915, a little more than nine years after the Episcopal Standing Committee had strangled the project of a reformed Trinity College in which we might have all that the Most Rev. Dr. O'Dea now desires. He was on the episcopal bench, and silent, when the proposal was strangled; and I was then half-excommunicated for saying, by way of warning, what the Bishop of Galway now wails, by way of lament, to the students of his seminary, the priests of his diocese, and the clergy and laity of all Ireland.

some of the efforts that were made in my time in that direction. I have in my possession a MS. 'Report on the Advisability of Connecting the Faculty of Theology at Maynooth with any new University or University College that may be Established'. It is dated February 2, 1907 – just three weeks after the report of the Fry Commission was handed in, when it was known that there was no question of Catholics going into Trinity as a body. The Faculty of Theology here were considering just then the advisability of working certain changes in their own programme, and the question arose as to whether we might not represent to the Bishops the interest which we conceived ourselves to have in the teaching of Theology in any new college or university that might be founded. We were not asked for a statement of our views, but gave one, of our own motion. Three members of the Faculty – of whom I was one – were appointed to draw up a report, which may serve at least for a basis of discussion:

'1. There should be some representation of Catholic Theology in the University or University College.

'2. It is advisable to establish as close a connection as may be possible between the Faculty of Theology at Maynooth and the teaching body contemplated in par. 1.

'3. As one means of securing this connection, it is advisable that the Dunboyne Establishment be transferred to Dublin so as to be in closer touch with the proposed new College. (This would enable Dunboyne students who may be qualifying for professorships in the diocesan seminaries to take a post-graduate course in Arts, Science, and other subjects.)

'4. In case it should be deemed advisable to have in the new College public lectures on theological subjects suitable for students of the other faculties, such lectures should be given by the professors who may remain at Maynooth as well as by any that may be transferred to Dublin.

'5. These lectures should be mainly apologetical, and should be open to all the students of the University as well as any others who might wish to hear them.

'6. It is deemed advisable at present to leave the number of these lectures to be determined afterwards, when it would be possible to estimate how many would be likely to avail themselves of them'.

This report was presented in due time to the Faculty, and adopted by that body; whether it was ever forwarded to the Bishops I do not know. We heard no more about it, but three years afterwards, in February, 1910, we were assembled to meet the Bishop of Galway, Dr. O'Dea, and take counsel with him as to what might be done for religious teaching in University College, Dublin, then established. As a result of the somewhat desultory conversation which we had, a committee of three was appointed once more, to go into the question more closely with the Bishop. I was appointed one of the three; later on, before the Committee met, I declined to act on it, and another was appointed in my place. What they did or advised, or whether they did or advised anything, I do not know; nor did I ever inquire, as far as I can recollect; certainly we in Maynooth remained as we were, without any connection whatever between our Faculty of Theology and the National University or University College.[1]

This result I consider altogether lamentable, as regards both institutions – University College and ourselves. The former is without any Faculty of Theology, and is likely to remain so as long as the Dunboyne Establishment is not transferred thither. It would, of course, be possible, without it, or any students from here, to have in Dublin a School of Theology which would be attended by some young clergymen, from the religious orders, All Hallows College, and the diocese of Dublin itself. However possible this may be, it is not likely to be realized as long as our students hold aloof. It is true, of course, that provision has been made for lectures in Theology to be given by a competent man, but lectures given now and then are no substitute for the work of a regular theological school – they cannot have anything like the same influence on the mind and thought of the University. It is as a science that theology must make itself felt therein, and sciences are not taught by occasional lectures.

As regards our own College and the education of the clergy, it is no less lamentable, as I think, that our greatest school of Theology should be cut away so much from the influence of the currents of thought that are shaping the minds of those who will soon be our educated laity. Theology is a synthesis of all the sciences. But how is one to synthesize who does not know the

1. There has been a slight connection between our Faculty of Theology and University College, Galway; where, some time after it had become a constituent college of the National University, our Professor of Ecclesiastical History, Dr. MacCaffrey, was invited to give a lecture or two on apologetics. Since then, other members of our Faculty have had the same honour extended to them. I have been always passed over; though I have heard the Dean of Discipline there – who makes arrangements for these lectures – was asked by some members of the College body whether it would not be well to ask me to come. As I heard the story, he put the matter before the Bishop of Galway, who did not think it prudent to invite me.

elements? and how is one to know the sciences who is out of living touch with them? There are books, of course; but does not every one know that one half-hour's talk with a man who is full of his subject is often worth a cycle spent poring over abstract books? You think you know something, until you meet one who does know it, or you think you can answer an objection till it is cast in your teeth by an able man who believes in it. Theology has declined steadily since it left the Universities of Europe, and it is still on the decline. Our books are stuffed with arguments based on principles in which no man of Science believes – which would be laughed out of existence if paraded, in the language of daily life, where men of science could hear what we say and ridicule us. I have as much opportunity as any man living of knowing the mind of our best men at the end of their course, and I assure those who may read these reminiscences that I find those students very much out of touch with real life and thought. And if here we are a kind of private school with all the defects of such establishments, what must they be in the diocesan seminaries and elsewhere? Not that we do not produce first-rate missionaries, but that men who can work parishes, or even dioceses, well, may be utterly unable to influence the higher thought that shapes the world. The Catholic Press, as I think, is a very good index of how feeble we are in this respect.

Why then, I may be asked, did you refuse to act on the Committee that was to take counsel with the Bishop of Galway? For more reasons than one, but principally because I felt that the deliberations would end in nothing. On the day on which the Committee was to meet, and before I had made known my mind, Dr. MacRory, not yet Vice-President, came to my rooms to talk over the matter with me, as I suppose. I told him of my resolve not to act on the Committee. As we were talking, the President, Dr. Mannix, came in, and he, too, was told. He asked for my reasons, and among other things, I said that I felt there would be question of transferring the Dunboyne Establishment, including myself, to Dublin, and that their Lordships, the Trustees, would not like that, nor did I want to go – in the circumstances. Dr. Mannix then said almost without reflection, that, no doubt, some of the influential Bishops were loth to make use of me. That was my justification.

This, remember, was in February, 1910, little more than a year after I had resigned my position on the editorial staff of the *Irish Theological Quarterly*, a step which I took in pure self-defence – lest these same influential prelates might seize on some article or expression of mine, hale me before the Holy See, and get me deprived of my chair. I felt myself under a cloud of suspicion; and surely one would need the utmost confidence of the Hierarchy to undertake the task of founding in University College a new theological school, which could do nothing but mischief if it did not deal openly and boldly with the religious questions of the day. If I were to do that, how long should I be allowed to retain my chair? It would be, I felt, sheer folly to draw down on any new school that might be founded in Dublin the cloud of suspicion attaching to me, and for this reason, principally, I made up my mind to hold aloof from the project.[1]

I know, of course, that as long as I remain Prefect of the Dunboyne, there will be this difficulty about establishing a proper theological school in University College. Should I clear out, then, and relieve the Bishops of the incubus which I am? Would they really found the school, if I were to resign? And, if they did, would it be to the advantage of the science of theology? If I could make up my mind on these points – that they would then act, to the profit of the science which I have striven all my life to serve – I think I should not hesitate to serve it still, by doing what to me would be little less than death, giving myself a death-blow for its sake.

STATE OF OPINION IN TRINITY AS REGARDS THE SCHEME FOR WIDENING THE COLLEGE

'It is well known', said Professor Culverwell, in his evidence before the Fry Commission, 'that the general approval of Statement III (that of the 12 Junior Fellows, 1 retired Junior Fellow, and 8 Professors) was not confined to its signatories'. Again: 'Statement III is not to be regarded as the mere act of those whose names are attached to it. It differs in an important respect from all the subsequent statements sent to the Commission, inasmuch as as it was not due to the action of a number of gentlemen who united together because they happened to be of the same opinion. It is in a sense the act of the staff of the University, because it arose in the first place from a meeting of the whole staff summoned by the Provost, on July 4, to consider the question of the attitude the University should take in regard to

1. This chapter was written before I was admonished for my teaching on occasion of the article which I published in review of Dr. Moran's book, as set forth in Chapter 23. That admonition proves conclusively, if proof were needed, that I was right in refusing to have anything to do with Theology in the National University.

this Commission; and at that meeting the following resolution was passed without any dissentient voice at all: 'That a Committee be appointed to draw up a statement of what Trinity College is prepared to accept, and to offer to make it acceptable to their Roman Catholic fellow-countrymen, and that they report to an adjourned meeting to be held on the 18th inst. at 11 o'clock'. The Committee, after a very practical discussion, was appointed to represent, as far as possible, all shades of opinion in the College. There was not one proposed on the Committee who was not elected: there was no desire to exclude any member of the staff. Anyone who thought he could give valuable assistance was placed upon it. That Committee met from day to day'.

When engaged on these Reminiscenes, I wrote to Professor Culverwell for an explanation of the fact that only twenty-one names, including that of Dr. Starkie, were signed in Statement III. 'I find', I said, 'by the returns, that there were at that time on the College staff, besides the Provost, 7 Senior Fellows, 25 Junior Fellows, and 69 Professors, Lecturers, and Assistants (non-Fellows). How is it, if Statement III had the support of the majority of the College, as is implied by the Provost in his evidence (n. 43), that only 20 out of 102 members of the staff signed the document'.

In reply to this query Professor Culverwell kindly sent me the following statement, with permission to quote it in full, as I do gladly: –

'If you complete your quotation from the Provost's answer, you will see the reason indicated why those who would have accepted Statement III as a solution, *if it were accepted by the R.C. Hierarchy*, did not wish to commit themselves to accepting it before they knew whether it would be accepted or rejected by that body. The scheme was revolutionary in character, and was bound to offend the susceptibilities of a very large number of friends of Trinity College. Many believed – and unfortunately, as I think, they were right – that it would be useless to put forward any scheme by which the youth of the country would be educated together; and if useless, why should they commit themselves to a scheme which we all felt was a surrender of much that we valued? But if the solution which we prepared had been discussed in a friendly spirit by the R.C. Hierarchy, then, as the Provost intimated, the position would have been altogether changed, and I have myself no doubt that it would have had the support of a majority of the staff, though not of the Board; just as happened in the recent case, when the staff desired to be put under the jurisdiction of an Irish Parliament in the event of Home Rule being established, though the Board had declared against it.

'With regard to your quotations from my evidence, if you read a little further you will see why Statement III was not to be regarded as the mere act of its signatories. It was the report of a Committee appointed by a unanimous vote at a meeting of the staff summoned for that especial purpose by the Provost, and at a meeting of the staff to receive the report which was embodied in Statement III it was adopted by about 20 votes to 4, but the meeting was a small one. I did not refer to this last meeting or the voting at it in my evidence, because my impression was that we agreed that, as the meeting was a small one, the numbers would be misleading. Most of those who were keen to support the project made it their business to attend; those who were undecided stayed away.

'You speak of 102 members of the 'staff'. No doubt yours is the technically correct meaning of 'the staff'; unless, indeed, it were extended to include all the administrative members of the staff. Your count includes the Provost and 7 Senior Fellows, who do not teach. But we use it – incorrectly, no doubt – for the Fellows and Professors only, not including Lecturers and Assistants. Thus your count is very much too high, when the word is used in its customary College sense'.

Deducting Lecturers and Assistants, with the exception of Archbishop King's Lecturer in Divinity, and counting only Professors, I reckon 26 such who are not Fellows. These, with 25 Junior Fellows, make 51.

THE MANAGERIAL QUESTION (1907 – 1908)

I now turn to the question of primary education, as to which, I fear, I gave grievous offence to many of the senior and more influential of the priests of the second order – those who are managers of National schools. And perhaps I may be allowed to premise that I regard those who took offence in this way as good men, zealous for religion, with not the least animus against me. They may not, indeed, have trusted me very much – may have regarded me as a dangerous man, whom they were not surprised to find allying himself with the enemies of the Church. They could not see that my action, too, might be dictated by love of religion and desire that it should hold its place in the schools, or that the weapons with which, as they thought, I was supplying the anti-clericals, might be much more serviceable than their own in the battles of the Church.

On June 27, 1907, the Rev. John Curry, P.P., Drogheda – one of the foremost members of the Clerical Managers' Association – read at the Maynooth Union a paper in which he discussed the claim of priests to the management of the National schools. He based the claim on the canon, and even on the divine, law. 'Where', he asked, 'is the canon law that priests are to be managers? I will give divine and canon law; and if our critics are sincere Catholics, let them hearken to it and cease their attacks on us'. He quoted Acts xx. 28; two utterances of Pius IX, who lays it down that the Church has authority over schools; and a decree of the Synod of Maynooth, 1900, to the effect that 'every care be taken lest the rights hitherto enjoyed by the Catholic school managers may be injuriously affected'. Then he proceeded: 'We will have no secular schools; we will have no State board school. We will have our National schools under the control of our Bishops and priests, or we will not recognize them at all. We won't surrender them to County or District Councils or to Parents' Committees; for, if we do, we know how long they could be used for Catholic religious purposes'.

He had said: 'As long as the attacks come from our hereditary and religious foes, we ignored them; but latterly there are attacks coming sideways upon us, from clever, persistent, though short-sighted Catholics, who, in newspapers and periodicals, are under-mining our position as managers. They encourage an agitation to prevent all clerics from having more than a chance voice and vote in educational control.'

Here was a bold proclamation of something like divine right of the clergy to oust not only the State but the children's parents from any share in the management of State-endowed schools. Is this, I asked myself, the law of God or of the Church? Is it the teaching of the Canonists? Is it even the best way to set about keeping religion in its present place in the schools? And was this uncanonical and politically foolish claim, made thus, in presence, as one may say, of the clergy of Ireland, assembled at Maynooth, in the presence of an Archbishop, who, though he spoke on the occasion, did not let fall a syllable to repudiate the claim – was the Irish Church to be committed in this way to so extreme and so vulnerable a line of defence? I could feel that this was in the air – that Fr. Curry spoke what was in the average priest's mind;

and I resolved that at least one protest should be raised there and then, at whatever cost to myself. I rose and said[1]:

'I agree with so much in Fr. Curry's paper that I am loath to criticize on the one point as to which, with the best will in the world towards the present managers, I cannot see my way to think with Fr. Curry. I am, however, open to conviction, and venture to express a dissenting opinion only with a view to getting the question discussed. Those who do not agree with Fr. Curry are, many of them, not only intelligent but sincere Catholics, who have at least a right to a hearing.

'For my own part, I have been wont to consider the managerial question from two points of view – the speculative and the practical. From the speculative point of view I ask myself what are the rights of Churchmen in schools endowed by the State; for the question arises only as regards schools which are supported entirely, or almost entirely, by the funds of the Irish nation. My reading of theology and canon law is that in schools of this kind Churchmen, as such, have no right to direct control, but only to indirect supervision – to see that the laws of religion and morality are observed. Those who provide the funds – the people, in all democratic states – have direct control, involving the right of appointing teachers, inspectors, and other officers, as well as of prescribing courses and textbooks. The Church has a right to see that in all this religion and morality do not suffer loss, the appeal being ultimately, of course, to the higher – the ecclesiastical – tribunal.

'From the practical point of view, I think the present managers have been doing the work pertaining to their office as well as it is likely to be done by any body of laymen who may for some time be got to succeed them; and there is true wisdom in not disturbing such men, in order merely to assert a speculative right, and reduce things practically to a worse condition. I think, however, it may be wise to let the laity manage their own affairs, even though for some time there should be mismanagement. The ultimate result, in the development of a higher and stronger character, of people accustomed to do their own business, may be worth no little loss in the early stages of the process.

'My advice is, that if Churchmen think it better for the nation that the management should remain as it is, they would do well

1. The speech is quoted from the *Freeman's Journal* of next day. Immediately after the meeting, if I mistake not, I went to my room, wrote out the speech, and sent it to the *Freeman*.

to base their claim, not on any inherent right that the Church has to direct control of State-endowed schools, but on the presumed delegation of the children's parents, who are also the taxpayers and the electors. It is these only who, in my opinion, have the right to direct control in this democratic country; and they are within their right in delegating this managerial authority either to a committee or council of themselves, or to those in whom it is vested at present'.

Never since the foregoing speech was delivered have I seen any reason to withdraw either its speculative teaching or the practical advice which it contained. On the contrary, another reason, which shall be set forth here, has appealed to me with an ever-increasing force, to persuade me that, in the interest of religious teaching, it is of importance that the clergy should not retain sole charge of the schools.

Anyone can see that not only is Home Rule coming, but that, when it comes, the government of this country will be absolutely democratic. The National Board, which is now nominated by Dublin Castle, will, under this new democratic government, be manned by the Irish Government of the day – the representatives of the majority of the Irish people. This change is surely coming. As long, of course, as the central government in Dublin is careful to please the Church, the newly constituted National Board will be content to rule the schools through the present clerical managers. But in a self-governed Ireland, there will be many causes of quarrel between the two powers – the Church and the civil government: it has always been so in every self-governed Catholic country. May it not be that, after some time, these conflicts will beget antagonism; if not so great as in France and Italy, at least sufficient to set the civil rulers thinking of how they may oust the clergy from the schools? If it ever comes to pass, as it may, that the central (civil) government wants to manage the schools from Dublin – more or less after the centralized French model – the clergy, I fear, will make but a feeble resistance. No body of mere priests can offer efficacious resistance to the grasping of a democratic civil power. If any effectual resistance is to be made, the civil authorities must speak for the people; for it is only the people in democracies that can effectually oppose the 'people's will'. The French Revolution should have taught us that.

Why is it that in France there is no religion in the schools, while in Italy, the central government, which is even more anti-clerical than that of Paris, is unable to do what is done in France, in respect of religious education? Religion holds its place in the schools of Italy, because they are under the control of the local people, who want their children taught religion, and who will have no bossing in this respect from the central government. In France, where government was long since highly centralized, there was no one but priests to resist the encroachment of the Paris anti-clericals; with the results that we see. If, indeed, in a democratic Ireland, or elsewhere, priests might hope to have more influence with the central government than with local councils, they would do wisely, in the interest of religion, to refuse control of the schools to these local bodies. But if the reverse is true, as I think it is – if the power that is likely to oppose the clergy in election matters is the central government, while the local bodies are likely to remain under clerical influence – then the policy of the clergy should be to strengthen these friendly local councils, so that they may be able to offer effectual resistance to the central government, should this ever turn out anticlerical – as it may.

All this, however, is policy – a thing which I dislike, except in so far as it squares with the right. What lovers of religion should aim at, in the first place, is to ascertain what is right, and then do that: to ascertain, in respect of popular control of the schools, what right the people have to share in the management, and give them that, though the heavens were to fall. To ascertain and do the right can never have but one result, and that a happy one – in the end, and in respect of religion.

Soon after the Maynooth Union meeting at which Fr. Curry's paper was read an offer was made to me by the editors of the *Catholic University Bulletin*, of Washington, to write for that periodical some articles on different branches of Irish education. I accepted the offer; and in due course there appeared in the *Bulletin* two articles of mine on 'Education in Ireland', having, as sub-titles, one 'The Catholic University Question', the other 'The National Schools'. The first appeared in January, the second in March, 1908. Both were afterwards published separately by the owners of the *Bulletin*.

In the paper on 'The National Schools', Section XII, I dealt with popular control. In the course of this section I said:

'The local managers are almost all clergymen of the various denominations. Though appointed by the Commissioners – who are themselves the nominees of Dublin Castle – and therefore independent of popular control, they are fairly representative of popular opinion, owing to the confidence the people have in the pastors of the various churches, especially in educational matters.

Few, if any, would wish to oust the priests and other ministers from a large share in the local control of the schools; and up to very recently, no one thought of associating with them lay representatives who would share in the management. Rightly or wrongly, however, there has sprung up within recent years a demand that local bodies of some kind, popularly elected, should mediately, or immediately, control or share in the control of the schools. There is so far no means of ascertaining with anything like an approach to accuracy how great the volume of this demand may be. I have no doubt that if the country were polled just now on that question alone, the great majority of the voters would record their approval of the present system, that is, of clerical local management'.

Going on to discuss two questions: '(1) whether it is so really necessary in the interests of religion that the clergy should remain sole managers of the schools; and (2) if this be so, whether it is necessary that the clerical managers should be appointed for all future time as now, not by popularly elected bodies, but by a Board nominated by Dublin Castle', I said:

'I should be the last to deny the inherent right of the Bishops of the Church to whatever is necessary to safeguard the faith and morals of the little ones committed to their charge; but I should not like to have to defend the thesis that direct control of the schools – implied in the present managerial system – is necessary to enable the priests to exercise their indirect authority... I doubt, moreover, whether, even though the claim to direct authority over the schools succeeded now, it would be admitted for long, or that a people who are prepared to maintain in the schools teachers whose lessons or example they have reason to regard as injurious to religion, would continue to endow the clergy with power not to appoint or to dismiss teachers for reasons of faith or morals. As long as religion keeps its hold on the people they will be ready, in the interests of their own children, to dismiss from their service teachers who can be shown to be of evil character or influence. When they refuse to dismiss on reasonable proof of this, it will be useless for the clergy to strive to retain their hold on the schools. They might succeed by the aid of foreign troops, but I, for one, have no desire to see the day when Irish priests will be dependent, for their hold on the schools or anything else, on the bayonets of the Saxon... I would have the board of Commissioners, or whatever the central body may be called, immediately or mediately subject to a really effective Irish popular control.

And as I regard such centralized popular control as highly danger-·
ous – witness what had happened in France – I should like to see
it held in check by local bodies, popularly elected and endowed
with real power, which they would be slow to resign at the bid-
ding of any central authority. I would depend on the people – the
local people – ultimately'.

Here, again, I stated – this time with the full deliberation of a
carefully written essay – the principle that the people had a right
to control State-endowed schools: that, if priests wished to retain
their present position of sole managers, they should do so as dele-
gates of the people; and that, in my opinion, religion would be
safer in the schools of a self-governed, democratic Ireland, if the
management were vested, not in priests alone but in the elected
representatives of the local people. This I honestly believed and
still believe.

My article appeared in the *Bulletin* for January, 1908; and in
the following April I was severely rebuked for the same in the
Irish Educational Review, a monthly Journal edited by the Rev.
Andrew Murphy, a Limerick priest, and really controlled by the
Bishop of Limerick. The rebuke was administered in the 'Educational Notes', which appeared towards the close of each number
of the *Review,* and were apparently written by the Editor. I was
taken to task for saying that 'there had sprung up within recent
years a demand that local bodies of some kind, popularly elected,
should mediately or immediately control, or share in the control,
of the schools'. I was reminded that 'I was quite singular in my
views amongst the clergy of Ireland, and almost as much out of
harmony with opinion amongst the laity'. This was all the less
surprising, as I had a 'tendency to think and write at a tangent
to the prevailing opinion of those whose cause I advocated' – a
failing which 'mars a good deal of practical usefulness of my
otherwise very valuable work'. 'We have good schools', my critic
went on to say, 'which, as far as educational principle goes, satisfy parents, teachers, and the public, and give the responsible
authorities of the Church the one guarantee which, as things now
stand, they regard as effectual for religion – and Dr. McDonald
would invite us to throw all this up and undo the work of sixty
years of anxious labour on the part of the Church in Ireland'.

This criticism, I felt, was quite beside the one important question; which was, not whether my view was singular in this or any
other matter, nor yet whether there was more or less of a demand for a change. It was convenient also for any critic, likely
to win applause from those who took his view – to parade my

189

isolation, which I could not deny[1]; as I could not but admit that much of my published work had been done in advocacy of unpopular opinions. Other views had advocates in plenty, who found their work both easy and profitable: there was no call for me to interfere. It made me look unpractical, too – what missionary priests think a dreamer like me – to represent me as inviting the Catholic body to give up the present managerial system, at once and unsolicited. The priests would take it that such was my advice, though I never advised any such thing.

Every one in Ireland – including the conductors of the *Educational Review* – looks forward to a time, perhaps not far distant, when the present managerial system will be assailed. It was not I who first called attention to this; nor was I the first to outline a plan of defence of religion in the schools. We have seen the principles on which Fr. Curry prepared to fight – the divine and canonical right of the clergy. Till I spoke, there was no word of protest; simply because, when I spoke, and afterwards, practically all the clergy in Ireland, priests and Bishops, agreed with Fr. Curry, and were prepared to fight on the lines indicated by him. I thought it a foolish plan of campaign – sure to end in defeat and disaster; and I said so: said that, when the time of struggle came, the Catholic body would do well to give the local people a share in the management of the schools. This, I insisted, was quite in conformity with the canon law: and I have never been seriously taken to task for that statement. If it is not the law, the fact can be easily proved.

My critic of the *Educational Review* went on to say: 'On this question (of the management of the schools) the position of the clergy is unassailable, because they have behind them a united Catholic people. But it is just the point at which English politicians hope to drive in a wedge of dissension between the priests and the people, and it is precisely because of its tendency to lend some countenance to those designs that Dr. McDonald's article is to be regretted'.

The danger to the schools, as I conceived, and still conceive, it, is not from English politicians, against whose designs the

1. He knows little of Ireland who does not feel that the Bishops, by reason of the power they possess over the lower clergy — to punish or promote them – are sure of their support for any line of policy which they – the Bishops – may adopt; while the clergy, in turn, are, in most cases, able to command the assent of the laity. Mr. Parnell was made to feel this, as also the Catholic laymen who wanted to make terms with Trinity College on the university question. It does not, however, hold in every case – as regards the subjection of the laity.

writer in the *Educational Review* was right in deeming the clergy entrenched quite safely behind the Irish people. It will be different if it ever comes to pass, that it is in the name of this very people and their leaders the clerical management is assailed. English politicians could never bring this about; but stress of Irish politics may. It is well to note, moreover, that should the question be raised in this way, it will not be put to the people as a straight and simple one, disentangled from other party questions, but will be complicated with others purely political, of which some affect the farmers, some the merchants, some the working-men. When a central government stakes its existence on some one question, votes are given, not merely on that one, but on the much more complicated question whether it is advisable to retain or dismiss the government just now. A referendum on any one issue, such as Home Rule, may appear very simple; but would not some vote against Home Rule on the ground that by turning out the Liberals we should save the Church in Wales; others because the Conservatives would then be in position to reform the House of Lords to their own liking; others because we should diminish the Irish vote in the House of Commons and so dish the Radicals; others because the Franchise Bill would lapse? So, be sure, it will when – if ever – the central government in Ireland raises the question of the management of the National schools.

I do not forget the admonition that by saying all this I 'lend countenance to the designs' of the enemy. Is it that I teach them how to go to work? But no politician needs a lesson in a matter so simple. Or is it that I advocate principles which the enemy can turn to account? The principles which I advocate are those of the canon law; and, if the reverse can be shown, I shall be the first to cry Peccavi. Perhaps I should keep silent, in any case? As, no doubt, I would have done, if false principles were not in the air: but it is, always has been, and ever will be, a keen pain to me to meet with a defence of religion based on untruth. Good may come of economic silence: but no lasting good, for religion, ever came from a lie. Besides, I insist that it is on the principles which I advocate and on the lines which I have traced the foes of religious teaching in the schools can be most successfully opposed.

The criticism of my *Bulletin* articles called forth some letters of mine which appeared in the *Irish Educational Review* for May, June, and July of that year (1908), and which were answered regularly in the 'Educational Notes' of that journal. The communications on both sides were bitterer than need be; and, of course, I had to defend myself from the charge of attacking the Bishops. The decree of the Synod of Maynooth was thrown at me[1]; but I refused to admit that the Hierarchy, while claiming the management as representatives of the Irish nation, and against the English Government, laid claim to any direct control of the schools as against their own people. It was a somewhat far-fetched interpretation of the decree, I admit; but I did not want to have even the appearance of conflicting with the Synod so far as to say that in passing that decree the Bishops went *ultra vires*. I did say, however, that, in case it were shown that they did mean to claim, as against the Catholic people of Ireland, direct control of schools which these people endowed, the synodal decree would be in conflict with a higher law – to wit, the common law of the Church: a possibility which I refused to contemplate.

This brought on me the severest lecture I had yet received. And as my position was unassailable, if the common law was as I said, while it was not so easy to show that I had misstated it, statements derogatory to the Bishops, which I never made, were imputed to me: a common trick of controversy. 'We are informed', my critic and – meaning informed by me – 'that the Bishops go beyond their rights and oppress their people'. 'Is it', he asked, 'competent for any individual to tell the Bishops that they are wrong, and to suggest that they are so manifestly wrong that their legislation conflicts with a higher and more sacred law'? I was represented as saying that 'the Bishops are not competent judges in this case, or authoritative legislators, when they make a statute according to their judgment'. And I was told that, in writing as I did, I had 'violated propriety and my duty as an ecclesiastic'.

Serious charges, were they not? Yet my critic seemed to have some latent notion that I might be right in my own way. In his last communication he said: 'We find, and note with considerable satisfaction, that Dr. McDonald all the time has been discussing the points at issue, including the original 'demand', in relation, not to the state of things actually existing in Ireland at the present time, but to altered position which will come into being when the Irish people get possession of the Government of their own country'. It was hard for me to get this understood. 'That', continued my critic, 'is what we used to call, in our Greek grammar days, the paulopost-future. When it comes, it will so revolutionize everything that we do not regard the discussion, at the present time, of one possible readjustment under it as of practical importance'.

1. No. 433, of the Synod of 1900. It had been quoted by Fr. Curry in his address. (See p. 542).

I thought differently – that a false principle, embodying a claim to direct control of National schools, as part of the divine or canonical right of the clergy, would avail under Home Rule as well as under the rule of the Saxon; and that, if it were made without protest now, it would be likely to take even a more arrogant form then; so that, as Home Rule was likely to come in the very near future, discussion of this far-reaching principle was not so much out of place. My critic, I noticed, kept clear of the discussion; and so the question remains.

We parted on good terms, I with a testimonial to my character which I did not deserve, and which modesty forbids me to reproduce. While the controversy was proceeding, the Bishop of Limerick let it be known that the Notes in criticism were from his pen. I have on many occasions found him sympathetic, and friendly; as, I believe, he continues. I on my part reciprocate these kind feelings. His criticism was honourable and open, and I got ample room to defend myself: I never want more than that.

1920. The Managerial Question has since become so critical that the Bishops have met to denounce a Government Bill that has been prepared on the matter, and to exhort all Catholic parents to make a solemn protest in defence of their rights. Of the teachers in the primary schools no small number have welcomed the measure; and what support they have in the country no one knows. So the 'demand' has come; and the clergy, led by the Bishops, instead of falling back on the principles of canon law set forth in my controversy with the Bishop of Limerick, have chosen to take the politician's way; objecting, apparently, to the fact that in the proposed new arrangement, two out of three of the supreme rulers of the schools will be non-Catholic and non-Irish. As if their Lordships would welcome a board of three Irish Catholic laymen! Why can they not muster up courage enough to depend on their own Catholic people?

Some time last year I had a visit here from a very well-informed Toronto priest, who told me they had gone through the same school difficulty in Ontario, the clergy being divided: some in favour of the proposed new lay management of schools, while others opposed it as destructive of religion. My visitor confessed that he had opposed, at first; but, seeing how the measure was working out all round him, had changed his mind and accepted the new order. 'And how has it worked out, in your parish'? queried I. 'Excellently', he replied; 'so well that now I should think it folly to revert to the old system'. So, in my view, it will be found to be here; when we brace, and humble, ourselves to rely on the fidelity of the laity, who, whatever else they may want, have no desire at present, nor do they seem likely to want in the near future, to oust either religion or the clergy from the primary schools.

'THE IRISH THEOLOGICAL QUARTERLY' (1905 – 1906)

I had long felt the want, in our College, of a journal wholly devoted to theological science in the best sense, a review, that is, in which the latest questions would be discussed, always with a reverent eye to ecclesiastical authority and scholastic tradition, but with a filial confidence, too, that one had nothing to fear from the authorities, even though one were to maintain, with a fair show of reason, that a school tradition, however venerable, could be no longer held. I felt that in Maynooth we were somewhat out of touch with life and were likely to remain so – to keep running on the old track made by our predecessors – unless we had a journal of our own to sustain by work and thought; that the very books that would come for review would be a constant source of light and a stimulus to work, and that, in exchange for ours, we should get almost all the theological and philosophical reviews, and thereby be kept *au courant* with what was being said and done in the schools of theology the world over. I hoped for immediate profit to our Faculty from this new supply of theological literature and the added stimulus to work, nor was I without assurance that in good time we should do something for the science of theology: that it would develop under our care, not so rapidly, of course, as other sciences, such as physics and chemistry develop in their schools, but however slowly, that it would be steadily evolved. Every other branch of knowledge – every science, at least, that was taught in universities – had one or more journals devoted exclusively to its service, and was advanced thereby. So had theology, too, in Germany, where there were a number of theological reviews. Why should not we have one in English for our own school in the first place, and for the other theological schools of the English-speaking world?

For some years before this idea took practical shape, I broached it from time to time in conversation with colleagues – those especially who had spent a year abroad after appointment to their chairs. They, too, felt the need, but it was another thing to meet it by starting a review of our own. There were, in the first place, the Bishops, without whose sanction it would be almost impossible to get on, and who would not be likely to sanction anything that was not under their own direct control. I felt very strongly that, if a theological review is to make for progress – for the development of theological science – the Bishops had better leave the control of it to others, and be content with intervention now and then, if necessary, to correct grave mistakes, if made, and take measures against their repetition. I would not work in leading-strings, being convinced that no really good work can be done in that way, and the question was whether we should be allowed the liberty that, as I thought, was necessary for a review.

Then there was the *Irish Ecclesiastical Record,* already in existence, with a large circulation, and ready to our hand for any purpose, of development or stimulation, we might want. In view of this, how could we maintain that another – special – review was necessary? And should we not, by starting and supporting a new one, simply kill off or weaken the *Record:* which was giving excellent service to the Church?

I had not the slightest wish to interfere with the *Record,* quite the contrary. I agreed that it was doing excellent service, and I would take care that we did not interfere with its circulation. The work which it was doing, however excellent, made no appeal to me. We should not deal with records, nor liturgy, nor canon law, nor the petty details of moral theology; and we should leave the *Record* the wide fields of philosophy, secular and ecclesiastical history (apart from the history of doctrine), literature, and science (apart from the science of theology). Here, surely, was scope enough, especially as the principal attractions of the *Record* were its documents, and the practical instruction it gave in moral theology and canon law.

At the same time, I did not think the *Record* a suitable organ for our Faculty of Theology: it was better than none in that way, but not much better. The editor, in the first place, was not a theologian; and no one but a theologian – and a good one – could take or awaken interest in the questions which I had before my mind. Then, even though he were a theologian, his hand was not sufficiently free. The *Record* was owned by Messrs. Browne & Nolan, whom a whisper from Cardinal Logue or the Archbishop of Dublin would frighten into refusal of any article or even dismissal of any editor, who must, therefore, always take care to please – or not displease – Ara Cœli and Drumcondra – no easy task, if one were, at the same time, bent on developing theological science. I felt this so much when the editor's chair became vacant on Dr. Browne's election to the see of Cloyne, that I refused to apply for the position, though the Archbishop, I was told, left it open for some time, to see would I, or some of the other professors of Theology make application. This, of course, may not have been true.[1]

In any case I had no notion of applying, or even of taking the position if it were offered me, as it would only bring me a lot of drudgery, without any compensating advantage – of serving the science of theology, in the way I wished. I should not have shrunk from the drudgery, if only I could do the service; but, then, I know that I should not be allowed this; and as, in all probability, I could not refrain from attempting it, my tenure of the editor's chair – of the *Record* – would be likely to lead to unpleasantness – which I did not want, and not to last long. I mention all this to show why I could not regard the *Irish Ecclesiastical Record* as an organ ready-made to our hands.[2]

With these thoughts in my mind I spoke to Drs. MacRory, Mac-Caffrey, and Toner, on two or three different occasions towards the end of the year 1904, about the advisability of starting a quarterly journal of theology, to be edited and worked by these three gentlemen in conjunction with myself. Dr. MacRory, as I thought, would look after the Scripture department; Dr. MacCaffrey that of ecclesiastical history; Dr. Toner that of the history of dogma; while I should take the theological science. In December of that year, however, I fell ill – got one of my nerve attacks – and did not think it prudent to undertake any fresh responsibility. So the matter dragged, till the beginning of Lent, 1905, when Dr. Mac-Caffrey asked me whether I was giving up the project. I had then regained a little of my courage, so we agreed to speak to some of the other members of our Faculty – others, that is, besides Drs. MacRory and Toner. Dr. MacCaffrey was to talk the matter over

1. Dr. Hogan, who afterwards got the position, came to me, while it was still vacant, to ask me whether I was about to apply for it. He said it would suit him, as he had not much else to do – in the way of work. Dr. Fogarty pressed me to make application, promising assistance in the conduct of the journal. I felt that the chair of the editor of the *Irish Ecclesiastical Record* was no place for me.
2. The *Record* – no doubt, wisely – has carefully abstained from taking any lead or giving any guidance on burning questions – of theology or of Church jurisprudence or policy. That would not suit me. A clerical wag – the Rev. William Murphy, of the diocese of Dublin, now Canon Murphy, P.P., Kingstown – used to say that only two organs of opinion in Ireland kept quite aloof and safe on the Parnell question: the *Lyra Ecclesiastica*, of which he himself was editor, and the *Irish Ecclesiastical Record*. To appreciate the joke, you should have seen a copy of the *Lyra*.

with Fr. McKenna, his diocesan, and I with Drs. Coghlan and Harty.

On approaching Dr. Coghlan, about March 25, I found that he looked forward rather to some project whereby the *Irish Ecclesiastical Record* would be made suitable for our purpose. I asked him to think over the matter and meet our colleagues. He agreed to do so. Dr. Harty also agreed to come. Accordingly, on the evening of Thursday, March 30, the following gentlemen met in my rooms: Drs. Coghlan, MacRory, Harty, MacCaffrey, Toner, and McKenna, with myself. There were two other members of the Faculty, Dr. Luzzio and Fr. Reginald Walsh, O.P., whom I did not ask to come, principally, I think, because, as I apprehended, those who were engaged in this enterprise would have to undertake some financial responsibility, which would not suit either Dr. Luzzio or Fr. Walsh, and also, I confess, because I did not expect any very valuable help from either, and therefore did not see why we should be hampered, possibly, by their counsels.

Two questions were proposed to the meeting: (1) whether it was advisable to start the Review? and (2) if so, what practical steps should be taken? The vote on the first question showed five for, one (Dr. Coghlan) against, and one (Dr. MacRory) not voting. For a first practical step, we elected a committee of four, viz., Drs. MacRory, Harty, MacCaffrey, and myself: the senior members of the Faculty, with the exception of Dr. Coghlan, who took no part in this second voting, nor had he any further connection with the Review. It was understood, I think, that the four who were elected should be a kind of editorial committee, and that all should have an opportunity of reading any article that bore a suspicious look. All six electors agreed to share the financial responsibility of the enterprise.

The result of the election was a disappointment to me, as I wanted Dr. Toner instead of Dr. Harty; for, whereas I myself could manage the moral theology department pretty well, Dr. Toner was necessary to look after the history of dogma, which was his special line of study. I called attention to this weakness, with the result that he was added to the committee. In this way our first number appeared under the names of five editors, an arrangement which I did not like but to which I had to submit. Dr. McKenna's name was added at the beginning of our second year.

While this was being done, I insisted more than once, in conversation with my colleagues, that the kind of work we should aim at was different from – higher than – what appeared in the *Irish Ecclesiastical Record* and similar journals; and that, as few but professors of theology, and not all of these, could do the work I contemplated, we should depend in the main on ourselves – for the articles we required. It was not, I said, a question of making known or popularizing what had been already done by others, but of doing something which had not yet been done – of extending the bounds of theological science, partly by the discovery of truth, and in part by the exposure of untruth. This, I admitted, would be likely to meet with opposition, even from those in authority; but if we published nothing but what was deemed orthodox by the six of us, and if, having once agreed that it was orthodox, we adhered to that view, until the contrary was decided by authority to which we were bound to submit, it would not, I said, be so easy to get a pronouncement against us. For my own part, I had engaged in this enterprise, not for money, nor for reputation, but for pure love of theological science, the borders of which I would enlarge, if I could; nor should I remain on the staff of the new journal one day, if I ever felt that it was not permitted to serve theology in this way. If we all stood firm, back to back, and were at the same time prudent, I felt sure that we should have our way, however people might condemn us in their talk, but if at any time I did not feel sure of support, my colleagues were not to be surprised or complain if I severed my connection with the review. This I made plain more than once, at the start of the enterprise.

The suspicion with which our project was regarded manifested itself soon. We issued a circular announcing our intention, and had some encouraging letters in reply from a goodly number of Bishops, but some of the more important members of the Irish Hierarchy were silent: this applies to Cardinal Logue, who was reported to have observed in conversation that our Review would be carefully watched. The Archbishop of Tuam wrote that he thought our project ought to have the approval of the Bishops as a body, and that he could give no definite opinion till he had an opportunity of taking counsel with his colleagues. What the Archbishop of Dublin thought will appear immediately.

For there was the question of censorship, with regard to which I wrote as follows to His Grace:

'St. Patrick's College, Maynooth,
July 14, 1905.

'My Lord Archbishop, –
'Some of the professors in the Faculty of Theology here have agreed to begin next January the publication of a quarterly journal of theological science. Those who are associated in the project have asked me, as the oldest amongst them, to lay the matter before

your Grace, as Bishop of the diocese in which the periodical is to be published.

'The journal will have five departments: (1) Dogma (scientific); (2) Dogma (historical); (3) Moral Theology; (4) S. Scripture, and (5) Ecclesiastical History. There will be five associate editors, each of whom will have charge of a department: Dr. MacRory, Fr. Harty, Fr. MacCaffrey, Dr. Toner, and myself.

'It is agreed among us that no article in any way suspicious or dangerous will be inserted, without having been submitted to each of the associates, and that no article will be published against the vote of any two of the body.

'In case your Grace should desire to have the articles submitted to the censorship of any other theologian, we should, of course, be happy to meet your wishes in every way. And if you wish for any further explanations, I shall do my best to supply them, either by letter or orally, at your Grace's convenience.

'I am, your Grace's obedient Servant,
'*Walter McDonald*'.

The Archbishop was away from home on diocesan visitation, when my letter reached him, and there was some delay caused by his having mislaid the reply, so that it remained unposted for about a week. In the letter which I received from him, and which was dated July 29, 1905, he enclosed a printed copy of diocesan regulations which he had just made with regard to censorship of books and other publications, and added:

'I do not think that I could make any special arrangement for the censorship of any publication without being deluged by applications for similar exceptional arrangements.'

On receipt of this reply, I wrote again:

'*St. Patrick's College, Maynooth,
August* 1, 1905.

'*My Lord Archbishop,* –
'I beg to thank your Grace for your letter of the 29th ult. and the enclosed printed document.

'I have to apologize for taking up so much of your valuable time, but I hope you will excuse my saying that the regulations for the licensing of publications in the diocese of Dublin, though admirable in case of books, pamphlets, and leaflets, do not seem to be so easily complied with in case of periodicals, unless, at least, there were some arrangement whereby only occasional suspicious articles would have to be submitted for special examination by the censor. Publications of this class appear so often, and must be published so regularly, that constant revision of all the articles would be intolerable for the censor and very inconvenient and expensive for authors and publishers.

'This is why, perhaps, nearly all the high-class Catholic periodicals dealing with religion – as far as I can lay hands on them – are published without either *Nihil Obstat* or *Imprimatur*. This is so in case of the *Revue Biblique, Museon, Revue Néo-Scholastique, American Catholic Quarterly, Washington University Bulletin, Month, Dublin Review, Civilta Catholica, American Ecclesiastical Review*. The last mentioned is published 'cum approbatione superiorum'; and, of course, it is well known that the same is true of the others, and that their publication would cease if it were objected to by the ecclesiastical authorities. Certainly, the five professors who contemplate publishing the new quarterly, would cease at once to publish, if their ecclesiastical superiors objected.

'I fear, moreover, that the public will think it strange that articles in which five professors who are empowered to examine for degrees in theology see nothing injurious to faith or morals, should need further supervision before being passed for publication.

'I will make bold, therefore, respectfully to ask your Grace to allow us to publish in the same way as, say, *Le Museon* and *La Revue Biblique* are published. In making this request I am joined by the only two of the five associate editors whom I have been able to consult.

> 'I remain, your Grace's obedient Servant,
> 'Walter McDonald'.

To this request I had a reply, dated August 7, to say that His Grace was constantly away from home, on visitation, just then; and that, before deciding, he would like to read the Apostolic Constitution again, which, he thought, made the censorship obligatory. As no further reply came, I wrote again, on October 19, as follows:

'My Lord Archbishop, –

'I beg to enclose a copy of the prospectus of our new quarterly, and to express a hope that we may reckon your Grace among our subscribers.

'It may be well to say that we do not think it likely that we shall injure the *Irish Ecclesiastical Record* in any way: certainly we hope not to do so. Our Review will appeal to a small class, even of priests. To succeed in making it what we hope in time to make it – a fairly representative organ of Catholic scientific theology – we shall need from the start the support, and the indulgence, of all lovers of theological science in the country. We have no very high opinion of what we can do now; but we hope in time to be able to do something for our science and for the Irish Church.

'About the censorship: I beg to remind your Grace that in your letter of August 7 you said you intended, before deciding finally, to read the Apostlic Constitution containing the new Rules of the Index. As you were so much occupied since then, I did not think it well to trouble you for a further reply'.

Next day, October 20, the Archbishop wrote me:

'Of course you may count on my subscribing. I can do this, as in a number of other cases, through Messrs. Gill's.

'As regards the Imprimatur, I should be very glad indeed if I could see any way of getting out of the obligation imposed by the Constitution. But I can find no loophole: 'scripta omnia in quibus religionis et morum honestatis specialiter intersit', would be an unmeaning clause if it did not apply to a professedly theological publication'.

Five days afterwards, on October 25, he wrote me again:

'Since I last wrote to you about the new Maynooth quarterly, I find that there is a difference of opinion amongst the Bishops as to the wisdom of issuing it. This being so, you will kindly see that my name does not appear in any list of subscribers. I should not wish to do anything that could be regarded as taking sides against the Bishops who disapprove of the intended publication'.

There was, therefore, not merely indifference, or lack of support, but positive disapproval, on the part of some of the Hierarchy, how many, and whom, we could guess pretty well. We persevered, nevertheless, and our first number appeared in January, 1906, under the censorship of Canon Dunne, the President of Holy Cross College, Clonliffe, who was uniformly kind while I remained on the editorial staff, as, I have no doubt, he has been ever since. We could not wish for a more courteous, obliging, or considerate censor. We remained of the opinion – at least I did – that the Archbishop might have dispensed with censorship in the case; and in support of this view, I could have quoted a very high official of the Congregation of the Index, who, however, said, naturally, that it was a case for the discretion of the Archbishop. I made up my mind that we were not to interpret literally His Grace's statement that 'he would be glad if he could see his way of getting out of the obligation imposed by the Constitution'. As we were under suspicion, and watched, nay, even opposed, by some of his episcopal colleagues, it was not unnatural on his part to subject us to a censor over whom he would have more control than, possibly, he thought he had over us. His attitude towards us was not unfair, but, then, it was not friendly or even favourable, which, of course, added to the difficulty we felt in bringing the quarterly up to our ideal.[1]

Within the month on which our first number appeared – that is, in January, 1906, towards the end of the month – the Episcopal Standing Committee met, as usual, with the result, on this occasion, that our President, Mgr. Mannix, received the following letter from their Lordships' secretaries:

'Bishop's House, John's Hill, Waterford,
January 25, 1906.

'My dear Dr. Mannix, –
'We are asked by the Episcopal Standing Committee to write to you and say that at the meeting of the Committee held in Dublin last Tuesday surprise was expressed that a theological journal should be published by the members of the Theological Faculty without seeking the consent and approval of the Trustees for the project, and that the Bishops expect that the matter will be set right at the next meeting of the Trustees.

'Faithfully yours,
'Richard Alphonsus, Bishop of Waterford.
'Henry, Bishop of Down & Connor,

Secretaries.'

I have no written memorandum of what took place when the associated editors met to consider this letter. I know well, however, what my own view was, throughout this whole period, that

1. On the desk at which I am writing this note is lying a copy of *Studies*, of which the secondary title is *An Irish Quarterly Review of Letters, Philosophy and Science*. It began to appear some time after the *Irish Theological Quarterly*. The first article in the number before me is on 'The Doctrinal Authority of Bishops'; the second is on 'Gibbon and the True Cross'; the third on 'The Catholic View of War'. There is a fourth, on 'The Historical Significance of Luther 1517–1917'. *Studies* is published in Dublin, without any *Imprimatur*.

to seek approbation of the Trustees was to recognize, implicitly, their right to direct control over the Review, and that this would deprive us of the freedom that was necessary for the kind of work we had put before us. So much did I feel this that, before the Review was published, I should have abstained from publishing, and, after it appeared, I should have discontinued it, rather than allow it to be directly controlled by the Bishops. It was meant for pioneer work, and, while, as I thought, Bishops should be glad to find such work being done, they should have no hand in doing it, but leave it to men like us, who had no position of authority. My colleagues must have agreed with me in this, for they authorized me to write to the President, and my letter in its original form, requesting that we should be told what statute or rule we had violated, was handed by me to the President. Afterwards it was withdrawn, modified somewhat, and again presented to him by me. In this new and final shape it ran thus:

'St. Patrick's College, Maynooth,
April 7, 1906.

'Dear Dr. Mannix, –
'My colleagues on the editorial staff of the *Irish Theological Quarterly* authorize me to say, in reply to the recent communication of the Episcopal Standing Committee, that, while we should deeply regret having done anything, especially of a public character, in violation of any statute or other regulation, or having failed in the least to exhibit towards the Trustees of the College the profound respect which is their due, we were not aware that we were bound either in obedience or in reverence to seek the consent and approval of their Lordships for the publication of the *Irish Theological Quarterly*.

'We beg respectfully to call their Lordships' attention to the fact that the journal has not been published by the members of the Faculty of Theology. The project was never even brought before that body. The five editors of the journal are, no doubt, members of the Faculty, but, as far as they are aware, such membership does not preclude individuals from publishing theological works on their own responsibility, subject, of course, to the laws of the S. Congregation of the Index.
　　　　'I remain,
　　　　　　'Faithfully yours,
　　　　　　　　'Walter McDonald'.

During the two and a half months that elapsed between the hand-ing in of the letter in its first form and in its second, the President of the College, Mgr. Mannix, we understood, was engaged in some kind of search for some statute or other regulation that would bind us to seek approval of the Trustees. We heard also that Cardinal Logue called attention to an old statute that bound professors to publish nothing without having first shown it to the President and obtained his permission to publish. I had looked up this before we wrote our letter in its first form and ascertained that the statute in question had been formally withdrawn. We should have held, in any case, that it was abrogated by custom, but the formal abro-gation made it difficult for the Cardinal to get the statute renewed by the Trustees, as he suggested – almost threatened – at that time, and at least on one occasion since.

Our letter, in its revised form, must have been before the next, quarterly meeting of the Episcopal Standing Committee – in April, but we received no further communication from their Lord-ships, till the end of June, when, during or after the meeting of the Board of Visitors of our College, the Bishop of Raphoe asked me whether I would not consent to ask the Trustees for approval of the review. I felt it very hard to refuse one who was not only an old and dear personal friend, but who had shown me great kind-ness and on one occasion done me considerable service. At the same time I felt deeply that freedom of action is as the breath of life to a review such as I wished ours to be, and that to seek approval was to put on the halter and acknowledge that we were not free. So with great pain to my own feelings, I refused to seek approval adding that, in case their Lordships disapproved, or wished us to discontinue unless we sought approval, I should withdraw from the project at once. They had but to say the word.

They said nothing, and so we continued to publish with an un-comfortable feeling that we were under suspicion and disliked. Much of the work which I had now to do was quite uncongenial, and soon became almost hateful to me, as it took me away from the peculiar line of study in which I had for many years found de-light. This applies not merely to the purely clerical work of read-ing and revising proofs and writing letters so as to secure articles and books for review, but to no small part of what I wrote for the periodical, and especially to my reviews of books. These I did con-scientiously, reading the books with care, even though I took little interest in many of them, and should have paid little attention to them if I had not to review them. Only those, of course, that had some connection with the sciences of Theology and Philosophy fell to my share, and in most of these I managed to find some point of interest, though, indeed, the reading of them was too often dreary and unprofitable, and I should have been very glad in some respects, to have done with the whole thing and get back undistracted to my own peculiar line of work. Certain articles, too, of mine made conservative people prick their ears, one especially on 'The Proof of Infallibility', another on 'Idolatry', and a third on 'The Ethical Aspect of Boycotting', so that my co-editors felt uneasy.

When applying to the Archbishop of Dublin for permission to publish without Nihil Obstat or Imprimatur, I had told him that 'it was agreed among us that no article in any way dangerous or suspicious would be inserted without having been submitted to each of the associate editors, and that no article would be published against the vote of any two of the body'. When our request was refused, and every word we printed had to be submitted to the censor appointed by the Archbishop, I did not consider myself bound by this agreement, as neither did my associates. When, however, remarks were made on my articles and reviews, and they began to feel uneasy, the agreement was revised, and, lest it should now appear to be aimed against me, we arranged that every article which any of us should write would be read by some other one of the associate editors, who should report to his colleagues anything of a suspicious nature that he might find. This regulation was observed for a little time, but soon I thought that it was only my writings that were under observation, and I confess it galled me somewhat to find myself looked after in this way.

On the whole it was not pleasant work; yet, irksome as I found it, I resolved to persevere, in the hope that we should promote the interest of Theology, of our Faculty, and of the College. The Review was making headway, its circulation was increasing steadily, and we were being noticed more and more by the Protestant journals. I had hoped to find readers among thinking Protestants, clergymen especially, and the hope was being realized more and more. From the financial point of view, not only were we not called on for any subsidy, as I had expected, but we made a profit from the beginning, and the net receipts increased steadily year by year. For my first year's work and share of the profits I received a cheque for £97 10s. 10d., and, though I have no record of what I received afterwards, I know that in my third and last year our position had become much stronger, and that, if we could continue to work with freedom, our profits would be very considerable and our influence more considerable still.

Towards the middle of November I heard in Dublin from one who was in touch with some of the entourage of the Bishop of Kildare, that the Bishops, or some of them, had delated some of my recent writings to the Holy See. Next day I called on the President and asked whether there was any truth in the rumour. He said there was not, as far as he knew. But, he added, the Irish Bishops were being pressed from Rome, for about twelve months, to proceed against me. He then read for me extracts from a letter which he had received from Cardinal Logue, in which it was stated, as I think – for I got no copy of the letter, and, though I took a memorandum of the conversation immediately after, my memory on this point was not clear – that the Bishops had been refraining from putting in force against me an authority which they had received, in the hope that things would improve, whereas, proceeded His Eminence, they were getting worse. This was stated, certainly, by the President to me, and, as far as I can remember – so runs my note – it was read from Cardinal Logue's letter. I asked whether the authority of which His Eminence wrote was the same as had been received towards the end of the correspondence about my book on Motion. He – the President – said he believed it was a new and distinct commission.

I then told him my reason for inquiring about the rumour I had heard, as, if it were true, I deemed it best to sever my connection with the *Irish Theological Quarterly*. He said I might do good work on the journal, if only I avoided certain subjects, as, for instance, Motion, which I seemed to have got on the brain. And, as a matter of fact, I had taken occasion, in reviewing some works on theology, such as Fr. Chr. Pesch's treatise on Grace, to show up some of the inconsistencies of the ordinary views. In reply to this remark of the President's, I said that I did not relish the idea of devoting practically all my time to the drudgery of a review, without a certain compensation. I was prepared for a good deal of slavish work, if there was some hope of pushing on the bounds of the science of Theology, but as the proposition before me left no such hope, further work on the *Quarterly* would be to me a servitude. Moreover, I feared that, if I undertook to give no further offence, I should fail, as critics who were on the pounce for heresy and disrespect to authority were pretty sure to find it. What has happened since has proved, if proof were needed, that, in this latter view, I was quite right.[1]

1. Those who have no pretensions to sanctity may find in the lives of saints not guidance only but consolation; and so I hope I am not very wrong in allowing myself to be comforted by the following passage in Francis Thompson's *Life of St. Ignatius* (p. 54): 'To be unlike others is the cardinal sin in the estimation of the multitude. How are you to

He – the President – read for me, by the way, a further extract from the Cardinal's letter, in which His Eminence said that the Bishops put me and other professors here to teach common things and to prepare students for the mission; not to investigate useless questions – useless for practical purposes. I had heard something of this before, direct from His Eminence, in an interview which I had had with him at the time of the Motion controversy. It was a revelation to me, as to what so exalted a Churchman thought of the duties of professors of theology in our College – including even the Prefect of the Dunboyne Establishment. I protested to the President, against this view of my duties in the College, and insisted that the questions with which I had dealt were of first-rate scientific importance. He then let out his own mind, which was that, even though my teaching were true, it was in many cases inopportune, as, for instance, in the case of 'The Hazel Switch'. The article, he said, was quite out of time and place, and he would not listen to my plea that it dealt with one phase of the great economic question, as to which we are the commencement of a social revolution, and that it was of the utmost importance that Churchmen – even in Ireland – should cultivate broader and truer notions on matters of this kind, if they were to avoid a greater mistake than had been made at the close of the eighteenth century by the Church in France. I shall return to this in the next chapter, but I little thought then that the working men of Dublin would so soon prove the truth of my prognostication.

On leaving the President, I went to Dr. MacRory's rooms and told him what had passed. He called in Dr. Harty, and the three of us discussed the whole thing again. They agreed with the President – that it was possible for me to work away on the *Quarterly*, and that this was the best thing to do even for myself. I had written a short time before quite a conservative article on the Pan-Anglican Congress, and Dr. MacRory asked me why I could not

know what such a man may do? How are you ever to feel at home and comfortable with him? He may be right and even wise in his fashion, but how are you to know it? And if you are to be continually investigating his sayings and doings, good-bye to all pleasant jog-trot tranquillity! Whereas the whole trouble could be avoided if he would only take the ways of other people. The procedure of the Spanish Inquisition seems almost to have crystallized this attitude into a dogma. Throughout it was Ignatius' one but intolerable fault that he would not be like other people. Sentence might turn on this point or that, but his distressing originality was the real offence'. It is an offence which every reformer must commit; and I had had the hardihood to think that even I might reform the science of theology – ever so little.

continue to do work of that kind. I said it was well enough to criticize those outside the Church now and then, if one could be fair to them at other times, and recognize whatever was of objective truth in their criticisms of our own system: otherwise it would not be fair. That, however, was what I was expected to do. Besides, I added, we did not start the *Quarterly* solely for work of that kind, but to develop the science of theology – the very thing that I was now told I must not attempt. I would not undertake the drudgery except for the only reward I cared for – the advancement of our science: the *Irish Ecclesiastical Record* was quite sufficient for the work they proposed to do.

A day or two afterwards I gave them my final decision, which was that they were to expect no help from me in preparing the next or any further number of the *Quarterly,* and we parted on the best of terms. They asked me to write at least a review of Volume IV of the *Catholic Encyclopædia,* the earlier volume of which I had brought under the notice of our readers. I thought it better to publish nothing at all for some time, nor have I broken the rule except on three occasions: once when Dr. Coffey wrote in the *Irish Ecclesiastical Record* something about Matter and Energy which, I thought, needed correction; again when, in fulfilment of a promise, I wrote for the *Freeman's Journal* a review of the thesis which Fr. Kelleher presented to our Faculty, when he sought the degree of Doctor of Divinity; and the third time when, in fulfilment of a like promise, I did a similar service for Dr. Moran. This last article brought me serious trouble, of which in its place.[1]

I say here merely that if, after nearly five years of silence, an article of that kind raised such commotion, how could I have continued to work on the *I.T. Quarterly* with anything like safety to myself?

We were unfortunate in the time at which our project was commenced, as the Modernists not only lamed but killed us. They aimed at progress, so did we; therefore we were Modernists. It was of no avail to disclaim Modernistic views: were not our whole aims Modernistic? If we were not Modernists, should we not be content with the *I.E. Record?* Is it not a strange, sad thing that I, who not only hate Modernism, but feel contempt for it, should be classed as a Modernist by so many, even highplaced ecclesiastics – as I

1. There were, in addition, as I remember, two public lectures, afterwards published: (1) on *The Manliness of St. Paul,* published by the Catholic Truth Society; and (2) on *Democracy,* published in the Kilkenny newspapers of the date January 4, 1913.

know I am? The Modernists have set back the hands of progress in the Church, dear knows how many years – far beyond my time, I expect. Were it not for them we might have been able to struggle on: is it any wonder that I dislike them? Though, indeed, it is not for any harm they have done to me that I dislike them primarily, but for what they teach, as well as for what they have done. It was hypocritical and mean of Loisy and Tyrrell to pretend to remain within the Church.

Since I severed connection with the *I.T. Quarterly* I have had no special means of knowing how it has prospered: I can only judge from the numbers, as they appear. It has not, I think, done much to advance the bounds of theological science, as was our object from the beginning, nor can I blame the editors for this. I, at least, am not sorry for having renounced my place among them. Instead of the drudgery of editing a colourless periodical, I have had the pleasure of working out my own views on *Religion and the Church, The Theological Virtues of Faith, Hope and Charity,* and *The Sacraments.* Even though I may not hope to publish these views, it is no small thing to have elaborated them. I have lost, but have not been altogether without gain, for which, as for everything else I have, I humbly thank the Giver of all good things.

ECCLESIASTICAL CENSORS (1908)

When released from the drudgery of the *Quarterly,* I turned to what I have been wont to call 'my own line of work', and produced three volumes: an Essay on *The Theological Virtues of Faith, Hope and Charity,* in continuation of my Essay on *Virtues: their Nature and Classification;* a collection of Essays *On Religion and the Church;* and a volume of *Notes and Queries in Sacramental Theology.* None of these three works are in print; all, however, are typed out fair, ready for the printer. I did not seek an *Imprimatur* for either of the first two volumes, knowing the *Nihil obstat* would be refused, as one or more commonly received opinions are rejected in each. I wrote the *Notes and Queries* in a disjointed way, with a view to avoiding altogether any subject which I could not treat with safety; and so I thought there was little danger of the volume being refused an *Imprimatur.* I did not, however, know censors fully, as the gentleman to whom I submitted this volume found unorthodox teaching, if not even heresy, in almost every page of it. This, mind you, though I wrote it throughout

209

with the set purpose of avoiding altogether whatever I could not treat with safety, and though a professor in our Faculty who read the MS. after it was returned by the official censor, asked me why I should have any hesitation in publishing the work.

I have said in the last chapter that two publications of mine which appeared – during the year 1908 – 'The Hazel Switch' and 'New Journalism' – brought – or helped to bring – things to a crisis in connection with the *Irish Theological Quarterly*; for which reason I must deal with them specially. 'The Hazel Switch' was a short article, contributed to an insignificant little monthly journal, the *C.Y.M.*, which was edited by a prominent member of one of the Dublin branches of the Catholic Young Men's Society: hence the title of the Journal. The article dealt with economics, under a phase which, though local and transitory, seemed to me to present in essentials, the one great fundamental question that demands solution the world over, with an ever-increasing urgency, which soon will not be denied. It is the question how far one is justified in using pressure, moral or physical – but especially moral – to compel others to respect not only strict but equitable rights.

Every one knows that an economic revolution has been effected in Ireland, as regards the land, but not without pressure – of the boycott; which can be justified only on the hypothesis that rents were inequitable, though not often strictly unjust. On this suggestion, not only the landlord who demands an inequitable rent, but the 'land-grabber' who co-operates with him, is an unjust agressor: in the sense that they co-operate to deprive the tenant of an equitable right. And the question arose whether such aggression could be resisted by moral force of boycotting, provided, of course, the inequitable attack could not be repelled otherwise and the boycott were kept within reasonable bounds. That question was answered, in Ireland, by the people in the affirmative, against the teaching of practically all the official lawyers and of many of the Bishops, and other lights of the Church. It is now being asked in another form, by the wage-earners: whether inequity as regards wages, and other conditions of labour may be resisted by working men, by means of the boycott of non-union labourers and of firms against which there is no other grievance than this – that they carry on trade with other aggressive firms and thereby help them to continue their inequitable treatment of the working man. It is the question of the right of trade unions to compel all labourers to join the unions, and of their right to refuse to handle 'tainted goods' and resort to sympathetic strikes in their battles with employers. Should these things be recognized as lawful, it will mean a revolution effected in an unbloody manner through the boycott. The struggle has begun, but who knows how or when it will end?

I thought, and still think, the question one of the utmost gravity, as to which the authorities of the Church should take no side till the controversy has proceeded for some time and we were in position to realize the force of the arguments of both parties; yet I felt in constant dread lest the Bishops would interfere prematurely with a decision against the working man. For, boycotting is a revolutionary weapon, and – unfortunately, as I think – the rulers of the Catholic Church have been opposed to revolution in any shape. Leo XIII condemned boycotting, as practised in Ireland, at the time of the Land League; towards which his whole attitude was so hostile, that it was a mercy he did not condemn its one effective weapon as unjustifiable absolutely – with whatever moderation it might be used. It may seem incredible that the same temper of mind is deeply ingrained in Irish Bishops and priests, but so it is, as anyone who knows them knows. And though sympathy with the tenant farmers from whom many of them spring, and on whom almost all of them depend, tempered their hostility to the boycott in the Land League struggle, it did not remove their suspicion or dislike of it, so that there was, and is, real danger that they would condemn it as immoral, if in any struggle their dislike of the weapon coincided with sympathy for the class against which it was being used effectively.

Now, these precisely were the conditions which were being realized at the time when the article entitled 'The Hazel Switch' appeared. It dealt with a certain remnant of the land agitation in Ireland, wherein the struggle lay, not between tenant farmers and landlords, but between men who had no land or too little and those who, having too much, were unable to use it except for grazing purposes; with the result that the best land of the country was devoted to feeding bullocks. It was not to be expected that men who could do little else than work on land, and who were in this way deprived of land on which to work, would not feel themselves aggrieved; and in the spirit of the Land League, which taught the farmers to right their grievances themselves, without depending on the law, or even though the law were opposed to them, these 'landless men', as they were called, took measures to prevent the working of the cattle ranches. They did no personal injury to anyone, neither did they injure the ranches nor the cattle, but they drove the cattle off the land, taking them quietly to their owners, who usually lived at a distance, and as the drivers often did their work with a pliable rod of hazel, which is plentiful in all parts of Ireland, their policy came to be known as the Hazel Switch.

211

It was an advance on boycotting, which left a man's cattle on the fields but refused to tend them there. But even the driving of cattle was far from being what it was represented by some high-placed ecclesiastics – a seizure and appropriation of the goods of those who owned the cattle and the land. It is one thing to appropriate cattle, and another to prevent them from feeding, on certain farms; just as it is one thing to turn in one's own cows on a piece of grass and seize on the grass in that way, and another thing merely to prevent the owner from using it, and so compel him to give it up.

Boycotting, if justifiable at all, is to be justified on the principle of resistance to unjust aggression; on the ground, that is, that one has a perfect right to compel another to abstain from treating one, not only unjustly, but even harshly or inequitably. Professional men are wont to enforce what is known as the etiquette of the profession in this way, by the boycott: nor does anyone find fault with them, as long as the etiquette in question is regarded as necessary for the profession. The same holds of trade-union rules; which are enforced by means of a strike – a form of boycott; nor does anyone complain of this, as long as the rules in question are necessary for the trade. It would seem then, that one may compel another by the pressure of a boycott within reason, to resign some right of possession, which, when resigned in this way, may be appropriated by another.[1]

Whereupon the question arises: why, if it is unreasonable or inequitable for a man to hold a certain farm, he may be forced to resign possession of it by a boycott, but not by driving his cattle off the fields? Or is it that cattle ranches are not unreasonable or inequitable, where plenty of people have no land – that the people of a country have no right, in equity, that they, rather than bullocks, shall get the benefit of its fields?

There may not be much in all this, but I thought it worth careful consideration, lest, possibly, in condemning cattledriving, we might commit ourselves to a principle which could be pressed, later, against the labouring class in their struggle with employers. If there had been danger that our bishops and clergy would denounce the pressure of boycotting, even when applied by the class from which they spring or with which they sympathized; how much

1. There is not a Bishop on the bench that does not some time or other squeeze those with whom he deals, to secure more favourable terms. The pressure applied is fear of losing this contract; perhaps others, too. This pressure is sometimes considerable, as every one knows who has experience of trade: it is the oldest and commonest form of the boycott.

greater was the danger of their denouncing the, seemingly, so much more unjustifiable pressure of cattle-driving, which was applied by men with whom they had little sympathy, against those with whom they had friendly relations? For, let the clergy say what they will about their being the poor man's friends, as they are; they do not spring from the labouring class, nor do they sympathize with labourers so much as with farmers and other employers of labour. This, of course, holds of what the clergy are by nature, not of what so many of them have become by grace.

'The Hazel Switch', accordingly, was published as an appeal to the clergy, high and low, to take care lest, in condemning cattle-driving, they should set themselves against the whole democratic movement, and thereby lose the people, as they have been lost in France and Italy. For, the whole democratic movement owes its success to pressure, of one kind or other, applied to aristocrats, oligarchs, and monarchy – to make them resign rights which had become inequitable. Here, of course, I had to suppose or imply that the political and economic revolutions which have taken place, and which we call the democratic movement, were, some of them at least, ethically justifiable; and this implication, taken with any toleration of boycotting and cattle-driving, was well calculated to bring a storm upon me. Worse still, the cattle-drivers and those who sympathized with them seized on the article, taking shelter behind me from the attacks of my brethren of the clergy, and it may be imagined how these latter felt.

Looking back now, I have no doubt, as I had not then, that cattle-driving was carried to excess in many places, just like boycotting in the days of the Land League; neither, however, have I yet heard any reason advanced sufficient to convince me that either form of pressure, can never be justified.[1] The older I grow, moreover, the more inclined I become to believe that the people of any country have an equitable right to the land of the country. Ranchers or graziers, no doubt, commit no strict injustice, and have a strict right to their estates and the proceeds of their sales. A strict right, however, may be an inequitable wrong, and the question always returns, whether one is allowed to resist, by force or pressure, violation of equity as well as of strict right.

'The Hazel Switch' appeared in January, 1908, and I was not without fears that I should be called to account for it at the next visitation of the College – in the following June; but their Lord-

---

1. Since that was written, I have gone into the question more carefully, and found that cattle-driving is unjust. The reasons will be found in my little book on *Some Aspects of the Social Question*, Book I, Ch. V.

ships, I expect, thought it well to give me a long rope, so they let me alone for that time.[1] The following summer vacation I spent in America, leaving Ireland at the end of June, and returning early in September. Soon after my return some one called attention to an article that had appeared in the August number of the *Irish Ecclesiastical Record,* under the title: 'The Causality of Creatures and Divine Co-operation; or, The Theory of the Flow of Motion'. It was by Dr. Coghlan, and was a renewal of his attack on my book on *Motion,* which for the purpose of this article, he calls *Le Mouvement* – and represents as having been published in Paris in 1898. It was in that year *Motion* was published; and as all Dr. Coghlan's references were to my book, there could be no doubt as to the object of his attack.

Now something like this was what I had been looking for ever since *Motion* was condemned by the S. Congregation of the Index – some public attack on the book, which I could criticize as publicly, and show how feeble and contradictory were the arguments of its opponents. I resolved at once to reply to the article in the *Record,* but, as its writer had stated that it was to be continued, I had to await the further development of the attack. This never came, nor, I suspect, was it seriously meant to come, for Dr. Coghlan who got the article published during the absence of the editor, must have known that when he returned he would not allow the assault to continue. The article, moreover, looked as if it exhausted all the writer's arguments, so that the promise to continue was mere bluff – as if he had ever so much more of the same kind of ammunition in store.

I allowed September to pass without communicating with the editor of the *Record,* but when even in the October number there was no appearance of the promised continuation of the article, I wrote to express surprise, and to request that what remained of the accusation would be published without delay, so that I might be in position to begin the defence which it was my intention to make. To this the editor, Dr. Hogan, replied with an assurance that, when the article was published, he was not aware that it was an attack on me. 'Having allowed the article to slip through', he proceeded, 'you may take it from me that the series will not be continued. I must add, however, that I certainly will not consent to have the *Irish Ecclesiastical Record* made the medium of further controversy on the subject. This, I dare say, will be the less inconvenience to you, as you have now an organ of your own'.

1. As the article had so much influence on my life, I deem it well to reprint it in Appendix, at the end of this MS.

I thought the letter cynical. Dr. Hogan knew well that I could not get my defence inserted in the *Irish Theological Quarterly,* yet he referred me to this impossible mode of remedying the injustice which the *Record* had committed. It was adding insolence to injury: he had not even the grace to apologize for the attack. If he had written in a straightforward, manly fashion, that the attack had been made unknown to him; that he regretted it and would take care that it was not continued; that he regretted also that there were paramount reasons, as he afterwards truly said, why he could not allow me to defend myself; and if he abstained from all reference to the *Quarterly*, I should have had no grievance against him, and should not have thought of calling him to account. He felt sure, however, that I could do nothing, so in reply to a further letter of remonstrance, wherein I stigmatized as calumnious the charges which he had published, and insisted that he was bound not only in honour but in justice to give me an opportunity of clearing my character – in reply to this he pleaded a higher and more imperative duty – not to continue the discussion. 'I would feel your grievance much more', he repeated, 'were I not aware that you have at your hand an organ of your own, founded by yourself, which reaches the same class of readers as mine. I think it is the natural place for you to defend yourself, but wherever it is done it cannot be in the pages of the *Irish Ecclesiastical Record*'.

This closed the correspondence. I had not written to him – the second letter especially – with any hope that he would accept an article from me, but I had resolved from the beginning to publish my defence, if not in the *Record,* then as a separate pamphlet, and, when writing the second letter, I had made up my mind to print the whole correspondence as an introduction to the pamphlet. When his letters appeared in this way, Dr. Hogan, I learned, felt sorry, but there was little sympathy for him, I understood.

There was even less pity for Dr. Coghlan, who, it was felt, did not get, in the remainder of the pamphlet, more than he deserved. He had made an attack which he felt sure I could not repel, for he knew well that neither he nor I would be allowed to continue the discussion either in the *Irish Ecclesiastical Record* or in any other publication subject to ecclesiastical control. For there was nothing the Bishops wanted so much as to stifle discussion on the *Motion* question, in regard to which they were uneasily conscious that neither they nor the Roman authorities had covered themselves with glory. Dr. Coghlan knew this well, so that his attack was directed against one whom he thought unarmed, for which reason no one regretted the chastisement which he brought on himself.

As regards myself, I was delighted with the opportunity which had been given me, not so much of refuting the arguments of my opponents – for however I might refute them, they were sure to be repeated – but of stating publicly where I stood in view of the prohibition of my book. I admitted that it needed correction, but only in matters of detail. The chapter which was deemed most surely unorthodox, – that on 'Vital Actions' – I myself had already corrected, by two articles, in the *Dublin Review*[1] and the *New York Review*[2]: so, however, that on this part of the subject, my teaching became much more advanced, towards mechanism, than it had been as set forth in the book on Motion; wherein I had made what I now deem the last and best – unavailing – attempt to defend the traditional teaching of the Catholic schools. While admitting errors of detail in the book, 'my belief', I said (p. 9) 'in the substance of the doctrine which it contains, had, if anything, grown more firm with years'.

'As far as I have been able to gather', I continued (p. 17), 'the basis of all these charges against me is, that, according to my formal teaching, as is alleged, there is no action that any finite agent can perform, and not the least tittle of an action, inorganic or vital necessary or free, natural or supernatural, morally good or bad; including any free consent, dissent, or self-determination of the will, there may be, to sin or service, and every positive tittle of the same; there is nothing at all in the way of action which is not originated by God in the agent, by a promotion as physical and inmediate – though, in the case of free acts, not so necessitating – as that of a carpenter on the saw with which he cuts. It is alleged, further, that, as a logical result, I have formally taught and do teach that no created agent, no matter how active, vital, or free, has any action exclusively its own; meaning thereby any action or tittle of action – consent, dissent, or other – really distinct from an action which God originates in the agent by the immediate physical premotion aforesaid; and which action he conserves by a continuation of the same premotion, as long and in so far as the action, free or not free, morally good or bad, retains a tittle of positive reality. Thirdly, it is alleged that, according to my teaching, no act of will is free at its inception, but only when continued beyond a certain instant, during a stage wherein the faculty can cease from acting.

'This, I understand, is the basis of all these charges. As this

1. July, 1902; January, 1903.
2. Sept.-Oct., 1906.

pamphlet has no *Imprimatur,* I abstain from stating whether the propositions in the last paragraph do or do not represent my views correctly. This only I will say, that whoever will sit in judgment on me must have made up his mind on fundamental questions like these; as also that, if the seal is taken off my lips, I will state very distinctly what I do hold on these and other questions'.

In this way I stated, plainly enough for even the poorest intelligence, my continued belief in the main doctrines which I had propounded in the book on Motion. I challenged anyone to call me to account for them, and, since then, I have never been called to account. Cardinal Logue, in a letter to Dr. Mannix, of this date – the letter has been already mentioned – complained of the scandal of two professors wrangling in this way. With me, however, it was not a personal question, but one of principle, and if I were to be deprived of my chair next day for asserting the principle, I hope I should have asserted it. I am not ashamed of nor do I regret the part I took in the dispute; neither, as I think, was I condemned then, nor am I now blamed, by the great body of the priests of Ireland for the defence I made.

I fully expected, however, to be called to account at the next meeting of the Trustees for the publication of *New Journalism* – on many counts: for having published it without an *Imprimatur;* censured the Bishops and the Holy See; reiterated opinions already condemned; and given scandal by quarrelling; and what not? The Trustees, however, did not meet till June, 1909, when they had Dr. O'Hickey before them. They thought, I suppose, that one such culprit was enough at a time; and so, I fancy, I owe to Dr. O'Hickey my escape from censure on that occasion. Their Lordships, perhaps, may have also taken into account the provocation which I had received – the wanton attack that had been made on me – and the fact that I had absolutely no other means of defending myself.

A last rumble – I hope it may be the last – of the controversy regarding Motion took place last June (1913) when Fr. Moran, one of the Dunboyne students, presented for approbation by the Faculty of Theology seventy-five theses which he proposed to defend as part of his examination for the Doctorate. Among the theses was the following: 'Deus totum actum supernaturalem physice in nobis operatur, nihilominus voluntas sub gratia efficace libera manet'. Dr. Coghlan objected to the thesis, as embodying the doctrine of activity to which he had taken exception from the beginning. He complained, too, of the hardship to which he was so often exposed in being compelled to renew a dispute of this kind.

I thought that the complaint would have more basis if it came from me.

There was very little discussion at the meeting. Dr. Harty agreed with Dr. Coghlan; in so far, at least, as to regard the thesis as capable of bearing the Kinetic meaning that had been condemned. He thought, moreover, that it was in this sense it was understood by Fr. Moran. The question was then put, with the result that the majority approved of the thesis, Dr. Coghlan and Dr. Harty voting against.

That was on May 29, and when the Visitors next came, on June 22, they had Fr. Moran's thesis before them, brought up I know not how. They receive, of course, for inspection at every visitation, the Minutes of the various Faculties, and it may be that it was in reading over the minutes of our Faculty they discovered the little controversy we had had. However that may be, they were, as far as I could learn, in a fix; having no enemies against me, and yet very much afraid lest Dr. Coghlan would report to Rome and they themselves be censured for remissness in stamping out the Kinetic theory. On the morning of June 23, which was Sunday, the Vice-President, Dr. MacRory, asked me whether I could show Fr. Moran's thesis stated in any book; and fortunately, I was able to put into his hands a volume entitled *Institutiones Theodiceæ*, by Rev. Joseph Hontheim, S.J., in which the impugned thesis was to be found almost word for word.[1] This, I expect, settled the question: at least I heard no more about it, and the thesis was presented at the examination next day, when one of the examiners took it as the subject of his attack.

Three months or more afterwards I heard from one of the professors in our Faculty, who had had it from the President of the College, that the episcopal visitors had tried long and vainly to lick the impugned thesis into some shape which would not smack of the Kinetic theory and yet would be safe. One expedient which they tried was to omit the word 'totum'; when the thesis would state merely that 'Deus actum supernaturalem physice in nobis operatur'; an almost colourless statement to which no one could object. But then it occurred to them that, colourless as the thesis might be in that shape if the word 'totum' had not been omitted, in the light of that omission it could mean only that God does not physically produce the whole supernatural action within us – a statement very closely akin to the Semipelagian heresy. So their Lordships decided ultimately that the safest thing they could do was to leave the thesis as it was, the smack of the Kinetic theory

1. Under Thesis 69.

notwithstanding.

I never denied that it did smack of that theory; indeed, in conversation with Dr. Harty – after the little discussion in the Faculty – I said that it had no other meaning; just as ever so much of the theology of divine co-operation could be understood only in the Kinetic sense. I had told the Trustees long ago that I was unable to distinguish much of the common teaching of the schools from the Kinetic theory as I had propounded it, and now, apparently, they found this true themselves.

But think of what we are come to in the Theological Faculty of Maynooth College, when a question like this is settled by one look at a passage in a work of a German Jesuit, which, as I, who have used it as a class-book, know very well, contradicts itself over and over, and is a very moderate production indeed.

MY LATEST REPRIMAND (1913)

I am writing this on October 21, 1913, just one week after being again reprimanded by the Trustees. It looks as if I were never to be out of hot water or to avoid giving trouble: this last escapade was occasioned by an Essay, on *The Government of the Church in the First Century,* which Fr. Moran, whom I mentioned in the last chapter, presented to the Faculty of Theology of our College with a view to obtaining the degree of Doctor of Divinity. He got the degree, but his Essay occasioned trouble, as I am going to narrate.

Fr. Moran, as I have said, was one of my students on the Dunboyne Establishment, and, naturally, I took some interest in his work. While his Essay was in progress, we had discussions about ways and means. The MS. was bulking large, and looked as if it would cost something to print, whilst the writer had never earned a pound and had no patrimony. No wonder he was anxious about how he should pay the printer's bill. My advice was, to make the book a good one and it would pay; and, to give more weight to this view, I promised him more than once that, if he made the book what I thought he could make it, I would write for the *Freeman's Journal* an article about it that would make it sell among the priests of Ireland.

I should, perhaps, say here that, apart from my wish to encourage Dr. Moran, I had not the least notion or desire of publishing any such article. I had resigned my place on the editorial staff of the *Irish Theological Quarterly* solely with a view to keep myself safe, for I felt that sharp and suspicious eyes were on the look-out for any statement of mine which could be distorted into heretical or unorthodox teaching, also that it is almost impossible for one who writes as frankly as I wish to write, to do so without giving such critics the chance for which they are on the pounce. Hence it was against my own interest and my own wishes that I wrote for the *Freeman's Journal* the article which I sent it on Dr. Moran's book.

Perhaps it may be well to explain also how it was that I sent the article to a daily newspaper like the *Freeman's Journal*. When we got authority to confer degrees, and had our first defence for the Doctorate, the clergy of the country, and many even of the laity, were expected to take an interest in the matter, and especially in the academic exercises. Hence the editor of the *Freeman's Journal* was anxious to secure an account written by some one who knew all that went on. Whether it was that I had already done some work for the paper, or that a friend of mine, Mr. Robert Donovan, was on the staff, I know not; but, for one reason or other, I was asked to write the desired account of the defence; which I did. I set forth the principal questions raised; and, as I did not think it well to give the answers, lest I should not be able in such brief space to put them in satisfactory form, the article was criticized, and I was told that it would have been wiser to say as little as possible of the points discussed. This criticism was not official; it emanated from some of my colleagues and friends on the staff.

Whenever, subsequently, we had a defence for the Doctorate, it was understood at the office of the *Freeman* that I would write an account of it for that journal, and I did so on every occasion but one, the reason for the omission being some little misunderstanding that had taken place between the candidate of that year and myself. And, as so many had represented it as unwise to call attention to the theses that were assailed, I used to eke out the articles otherwise; on one occasion by more or less commonplace observations about such defences, and afterwards by calling attention to the Essay presented by the candidate. I did no more in Dr. Moran's case than in ever so many others, either in the way of writing an article or in that of selecting the *Freeman's Journal* as the organ in which it was to appear. No doubt, in the article about Dr. Moran I referred to the use of syllogisms and of the Latin language, which I had not touched on previously, but then I had filled in previous articles with remarks of a similar kind.

As this last article, about Dr. Moran's defence and book has caused such a sensation – at least three of the Bishops described it to myself as a bombshell dropped in the midst of them – and as it has brought me a reprimand from the episcopal body, I deem it well to reprint it in the Appendix to these Reminiscences, that readers may see for themselves what it was like.[1] It appeared on the morning after the defence, that is, on Tuesday, June 24, 1913. As it was difficult to get an altar in the College that morning, I said Mass at the Presentation Convent, where I took breakfast, purchasing a copy of the *Freeman* on my way back to the College. I went at once to the parlour, for any letters that might be there for me, on the breakfast-table, and as I was passing through the outer room, Cardinal Logue, who was sitting on a sofa reading the *Freeman's Journal,* called me to him, and said he would have to refer in his speech at the Distribution of Premiums – it was Distributing Day – to this article of mine. He had been reading the article, and had got about half through. I said absolutely nothing, and he followed up his first observation by something more in the same strain. At length he said to me that in my writings I was always attacking the Bishops, whereon I replied that it was not true. He repeated that it was, and I said: If so, written words remain, and these attacks can be produced. Where, I asked, have I ever attacked their Lordships? He said that I had done so in the articles which I wrote some time ago for the *Irish Ecclesiastical Record,* wherein I represented the Bishops as tyrants. I said this was not true, the articles were there to prove it. To which His Eminence replied that, though my formal words might not be as he had put them, he had given quite correctly the substance of what I had said. This, I repeated, was not true.

Then he turned to the *Freeman* article, of which he complained, in the same manner, for the attack it contained on the syllogistic method and the Latin language, both of which, he insisted, were venerable to say the least, by reason of their connection with Church tradition. The use of Latin, moreover, had been commanded by the Holy See, which was itself attacked whenever one attacked its policy; while, as for the syllogistic method, it was absolutely necessary for exactitude of thought. In this connection he went on to ascribe to the disuse of the syllogisms all the confusion which he represented as prevailing in the universities. Here I protested that since then the universities had made extraordinary progress especially in natural science and in history, but he would not admit that any progress had been made. Outside our own schools, he was convinced, all was confusion. I said I could not see things in that way.

1. See Appendix, pp. 271–5.

He passed from this to the defence which we had had the previous day, whereon he assumed his natural conversational tone, and after a little while I left him, when he was apparently somewhat mollified. He had not, however, got yet through more than half of the article, for I learned afterwards that it was only by persuasion he was restrained from animadverting on it in his Distribution speech. As members of the staff are bound to attend that function I could not afford to absent myself, but, as I expected to hear myself denounced, and feared lest I might betray emotion under the whip, I attended in the gallery, where there was no one to remark how I took my punishment. The speech, however, to my surprise, concluded without any reference to me or my transgressions.

Soon after the Distribution the Trustees met, and, as I afterwards learned, the *Freeman* article was one of the first matters to occupy them. Apart from the meagre and vague rumours that reached me – for I do not pry into these things – I have no means of knowing what was said. Some one told me that it was proposed to inquire into the orthodoxy of Dr. Moran's book; and that, as against this, the Archbishop of Dublin reminded their Lordships that the book had had the approval of the Faculty of Theology; so that to call its orthodoxy in question would be equivalent to a censure on the Faculty. He suggested, I understood, that my article, rather than the book, should be made the object of inquiry, and this suggestion was adopted. A Committee of four – the Archbishop of Tuam (Chairman), the Bishops of Raphoe and of Galway, and the Bishop of Clogher (Secretary) – was appointed to inquire into and report on my article, from the point of view of doctrine as well as discipline, and under any other aspect which they might deem worthy of consideration. Moreover, they passed the following resolution: 'The Bishops desire to convey to the Professors of the College that they deprecate the discussion in the ordinary newspapers of difficult controversial questions of a theological character which may be easily misunderstood and lead to the disedification of the laity'.

This, of course, was a reprimand for me, as it implied that my article was such as they deprecated, for the reason assigned. I do not know to the present day wherein the danger consisted. Two of their Lordships told myself that it was wrong on my part to say that the Presbyterians had had some right on their side, one of the two adding that, even though they might have, it was a mistake to admit it, and so give them an opportunity of crowing over us. That, as I think, may be good politics, but it is not the scientific spirit, which does not hesitate to admit any error that has been proved.

222

No small part of the weakness of our theology is due to this, that we persist in maintaining positions, that have been long since shown to be indefensible, with the result that the adversaries of the Church, carefully avoiding us where we are strong, defeat us easily where we are weak, and are thereby able to crow over us, with justice and to our real disgrace. The General should be cashiered at once who will not withdraw his soldiers from a position that can be defended no longer.

Their Lordships' resolution, of course, was carefully worded, to express yet conceal what they really meant. I might have discussed Dr. Moran's book *ad nauseam,* if only I had made out that the episcopal office was from the beginning what it is now. That would be false; but, then, falsehood of that kind would not 'lead to the disedification of the faithful'. If their Lordships had expressed their mind frankly, they would have said that they deprecated any discussion, whether in the daily Press or elsewhere, that implied that Bishops were not always what they themselves now are; as this doctrine was unheard of, and its publication now could not fail to result in loss of reverence for the dignity of the Bishops and disobedience to their commands.

Well, the summer vacation passed quietly, and I heard very little of the Committee and its work, till the Visitors came again, in October. I was quite easy as regards the doctrine of my article, seeing that it was very little more than a correct summary of what was contained in Dr. Moran's book, which had got the approval of the Faculty. I knew that there were men in the Faculty who would take care that there would be no condemnation, by the episcopal committee, of what they had approved. If it were I alone who was concerned, I should not have been without apprehension, for though I regarded the doctrine of the book and of the article as so well founded as to be deemed at least probable by any unprejudiced student, still, I knew that it was opposed not only to what until of late had been the received teaching, but to the personal feelings of the Bishops, and my experience of *Motion* had taught me what to expect in cases of that kind. Not, by any means, that I contemplated foul play, or thought there was any special animosity against myself, but that a doctrine such as I have described could hardly escape condemnation, except by wire-pulling, a process in which I am not proficient and in which I would not condescend to engage.

When the Visitors came in October, the members of the Faculty of Theology had to report to them on the candidates for the chair that had been vacated by Dr. Toner, and, after we had handed in our votes to the President, Dr. Coghlan presented him with a second envelope in which, as we soon learned, was an indictment of Dr. Moran's Essay, which he represented as being plainly opposed to the doctrine regarding the Hierarchy which had been defined by the Council of Trent. There was, I understand, a further charge, that, at his defence for the Doctorate, Dr. Moran had maintained that one could not make an act of divine faith in what God had promised, and, when challenged to give the name of any theologian who held this, had said it was the teaching of 'the man who sits beside you', – meaning, added Dr. Coghlan, the Prefect of the Dunboyne Establishment.

What I hold on this question of faith in divine promises I have put very plainly in my unpublished work on *The Theological Virtues of Faith, Hope, and Charity;* that one may make an act of supreme divine trust (fiducia), but not of divine faith (fides), in the promises of God, as such. Faith is an assent, but one does not assent to a promise, as such; one accepts and trusts it. I will add here, merely, as regards this latest accusation of Dr. Coghlan's – who would seem to have attacked Dr. Moran only as representing my views – that it made little impression on the Visitors, who reported to the body of the Trustees that they had received the document, but did not think it necessary to read it for the Board.

Well, the Committee of four Bishops met in the afternoon of Sunday – the day after the Bishop of Raphoe had been speaking to me. I heard no whisper of the result, until near 1.30 p.m. on the following Tuesday, on which the Board met in the forenoon. As I was coming down to my rooms from luncheon, the Bishop of Raphoe met me and said he had been looking for me, as he had a message from the Trustees. We went up then to my rooms, where he told me that the report of the Committee had been adopted by the Board – with unanimity, I think he said – and that the Bishops commissioned him, as a personal friend of mine, to read the document for me. He then took it out of his pocket and read, while I listened.

It is not my fault that I cannot reproduce this report verbally, as, when I asked whether I might not have a copy – his Lordship having finished reading – he said he was not allowed to give one. And when I replied to the effect that I thought it strange that one who had received a solemn admonition of this kind should not be allowed a copy of the document, he said he did not think I had anything to complain of, as the Board did not want me to do anything.

The Committee divided my *Freeman* article into two parts; in the first of which I dealt with our method of teaching and examining, while in the second I gave some account of Dr. Moran's

224

book. Their Lordships found that in the first part I criticized un-favourably two things: the syllogistic method and the use of the Latin language; though the syllogistic method was traditionally interwoven with the Church's teaching in her schools; and though the use of Latin was enjoined by a statute of the College recently enacted, and confirmed by the S. Congregation of Propaganda – was, indeed specially insisted on by that S. Congregation; while, only last year, the statute was further emphasized by a special resolution of the Trustees.

Perhaps it may be well to comment on this – excusing or de-fending my conduct as best I can – before proceeding to the second part of the report. And first, as to the syllogistic method. 'I do not', I wrote, 'find many syllogisms in the *Summa* of St. Thomas, nor in the works of Suarez, Vasquez, or De Lugo'. My impression is that the method of putting arguments and objections into syllogistic form, and replying to their objections by distin-guishing the major, contradistinguishing and subdistinguishing the minor, denying or distinguishing the subsumptum, and other such apparatus, was developed at a comparatively late period, to suit the formal disputations that took place for purposes of show, in Rome and elsewhere, and that it is an excrescence on the tra-ditional method of the school. It has been discarded by – if ever they prevailed in – the school of natural science, in all its branches, the world over; in which alone any real scientific pro-gress has been made. Even the theological and philosophical schools of France and Germany – other than the mere diocesan seminaries – give us books constructed just as are those which proceed from the universities dealing with physics, chemistry, biology, political economy, archæology, and the rest. So that the truth would seem to be that the syllogistic method, as it appears in Disputations, is no part of the oldest and best method of Catho-lic teaching; and that it has been discarded in those modern Catholic schools in which any progress has been made. Outside Rome, and places that are under Roman influence, even the examinations of candidates for degrees, including that of Doctor of Divinity, are conducted pretty much as in the universities.

But, even though the Catholic tradition were as it is repre-sented in the Committee's report, may it not be time to make a new departure? His Eminence, Cardinal Logue, said to me, in reference to this part of my article, that he often saw and heard candidates for degrees examined in France according to the new method that dispenses with syllogistic forms; and that the results were indefinite – word-bandying, and confusion. I do not suppose that word-bandying can be prevented by any method of oral examination which the wit of man can contrive; and hence I am not surprised at his Eminence's statement. Only I knew what can be done by one who sedulously distinguishes majors and minors of the most obvious and truthful meaning; and I am confident that quibbling can be stopped much sooner and more effectually if the quibbler has not the advantage of the syllogistic method, as practised in formal disputations held at Rome. When the Bishop of Raphoe said to me something like what had been said by the Cardinal, I asked him to give one chance to the method which I advocated, and have all the Trustees there to see the result for themselves. I am sure it would be the death of both Latin language and syllogistic method in our schools of Theology.

It seems I had no right to say that; so the episcopal committee reported and the Trustees resolved – on what precise grounds I do not know. They appeal to the College statute, to the emphatic desire and command of Propaganda, and to a recent resolution of their own; all of which, if they prove that the advantages of using Latin are greater than its disadvantages, are decisive. But do they prove it? Not for me, who, though I know so little about many things as to which the authority of Propaganda and of the Irish Bishops is very great, think I have been in position to know as much as they about the advantages and disadvantages of the use of Latin in seminaries, being intent on maintaining it solely as an additional bond of union with Rome, while the Bishops are at once afraid of the Holy See, and suspicious of the more critical line of thought which would almost certainly result from the use of the vernacular in teaching Theology and Philosophy. What the real mind of Rome is as regards the advantages and disadvantages of the use of Latin is plain even to the purblind, from the fact that it is used only with reluctance in all the offices and tribunals of the Holy See; wherein, if you want to get business done expeditiously and well, you will speak or write in Italian – the vernacular of the place. No one realizes this more keenly or painfully than the Irish Bishops, none of whom speaks Italian colloquially, and all of whom, on that account, find themselves dreadfully handicapped whenever they have to do any business of a delicate kind in Rome. This, mind you, though many of their Lordships were at one time professors in Maynooth College, and as such, supposed to be able to converse freely in Latin, on every subject whatever, 'from the cedar of Lebanon to the hyssop that grows on the wall'.

But, then, did I not criticize a College statute, backed by the authority of the Bishops and the Holy See? And how could discipline survive, if those who are bound to obey orders were free to criticize the orders they receive? This was the burden of the complaint made by the Bishop of Raphoe, in the private conversation which we had about my article on the Saturday morning that preceded the meeting of the Board; and I have no doubt that it was what the entire body of their Lordships would insist on, if they were asked to analyse their thoughts. Priests – seminary professors in particular – have got not only to obey orders, right or wrong, but not to say or even hint that they are wrong, however hurtful they may be.

I told the Bishop frankly that I did not consider myself such a mere instrument, that subjects – including professors in ecclesiastical seminaries – have a right to make known the evils which long experience of working under any rule may show to attend it; provided always they criticize reverently and submissively, and observe the rule in question till it has been revoked. History, I said, proves that laws have been better made and better observed since subjects became free to criticize them. What! he exclaimed, would you criticize Propaganda? Yes, I replied, and greater than Propaganda; and there would be ever so much less for history to record, with shame and tears, if there had been more criticism, reverent but fearless, of those who occupied high places, even in the Church, in the past. This is my firm conviction.

I asked the Bishop what we were to do. Were we to go on silently, though convinced that things were rotting before our eyes? Why not, said his Lordship, send in a report to the Bishops, or even to Propaganda? And much attention it would get, I answered – from either body. I might have done that years ago, when I was younger and more hopeful, but not now. Besides, I added, some of our ablest and best men have criticized seminary discipline in published works: witness the Abbé Hogan's articles, afterwards collected and published in book form; also a very interesting volume entitled *The Training of a Priest,* written by the Rev. John Talbot Smith, LL.D., and published with an Introduction by that saintly man, the late Bishop of Rochester, Dr. McQuaide. In this work of Dr. Smith's there is a special chapter on 'The Language of the Seminary'; wherein, he says, most truly, that 'Latin is a hindrance to proper training' and 'ought to be laid aside, until that time comes when the Colleges send out graduates who can converse in it'. And 'to anyone so venturesome as to charge the writer with the design of doing away with Latin altogether, he has this reply: the methods of the colleges and the seminaries have already saved him the trouble. Latin was never deader at any period of its history as a so-called dead language than in America at the present moment. Its revival will be a work

227

of time. For the present the seminaries ought to refuse their countenance to its being made a hindrance to their own aims'. This, you may think, applies only to America; but I assure you it applies to the College of Maynooth.

Why, then, urged the Bishop, did you not publish your criticisms in a book, which would not be read by the common people, Catholic and Protestant; or in some periodical such as that in which the Abbé Hogan's articles first appeared: why publish in the *Freeman's Journal*? To this I answered at the time that I was called on to write for the *Freeman's Journal* and not for a monthly periodical or to publish a book. Apart from the call on me for the article which I wrote, I should not have thought of sending it, or anything like it, to the daily Press; but, as I had to write for the *Freeman* on Dr. Moran's defence and book, why should I not give my real views of both?

That, as I think even now, was justification sufficient for publishing my views in the *Freeman;* but there is another line of defence, which, though it did not occur to me when talking with the Bishop, did occur before very long, and which I should like to put on record here. It is, that, in case I put my criticism into book shape, I should find it hard to get an *Imprimatur;* and if I sent it say to the *Irish Ecclesiastical Review,* the editor, before publishing it, would probably submit it to some prudent ecclesiastic like Cardinal Logue, with the result that it would not appear. When I advocated canon law reform, his Eminence adjudged that I attacked the Bishops, and said that they were tyrants. The same, practically, was said by the Bishop of Limerick, when I criticized the arguments whereby the managerial system is defended.

So much for the first part of the Report of the episcopal committee. In the second part they complain of my saying that 'the Bishops have gradually *appropriated* the jurisdiction' which the cathedral chapters held at one time, and which had been held, before then, by the priests of the various dioceses. The report next animadverts on the implied conclusion of this part of the article which it represents, to the best of my recollection, as not being sufficiently established and therefore unsafe and irreverent. In this connection their Lordships find distinctly that the article showed lack of scholarship. Worse still, as they complain, the See of Rome was put on a level with those of Jerusalem, Antioch, Alexandria, and elsewhere, as if Rome had no primatial jurisdiction; while the statement that 'the monarchical (diocesan) jurisdiction which St. James held at Jerusalem would seem to have been very limited', and 'that the same would hold of the other great central sees'; this was as applying to Rome, so inconsistent with the primacy of that see as to make their Lordships think it likely that if the article were delated to the Holy See, this part would be condemned. I am not quite sure whether this last statement, about condemnation, was in the report; or whether it may not have been merely used by the Bishops in conversation.

I have but two brief observations to make on this part of the report. And first, as regards the term 'appropriated', I should be the last to use it, if I thought it bore or connoted any meaning disrespectful to the episcopal body. Even now I fail to see that it means or implies more than that the cathedral chapters – and before they were instituted, the diocesan clergy – were part holders of certain powers, which even the chapters hold no longer, as the Bishops have acquired sole possession of them, by prescription. That the fact was and is so is known to every one with even an elementary acquaintance with the historical side of canon law. There is even in the *Corpus Juris Canonici* a title (L. III t. 10) headed 'of the things that are done by a Prelate without the consent of the chapter'; wherein are specified certain affairs which Bishops could not transact alone, even validly. That was in A.D. 1230, when the title in question was drawn up, and long after; though by the time of Benedict XIV, as he himself testifies, the title had become a dead letter: 'in our day it is no longer cited in the courts'. As stated in my article, lower down, the power which the chapters then held was in course of time duly prescribed by the Bishops[1]; as, I hope, we may still say, though we must be careful to abstain from using the term 'appropriated' in this connection. 'Prescription,' however, and 'prescribed' are legal terms which one does well to avoid, as far as possible, when writing for the general public – for whom my article was intended.

Secondly, as regards the See of Rome, I deliberately abstained from touching on its primatial jurisdiction, as Dr. Moran also does, in the book which I had under review. 'As to the government of the Church Catholic', I wrote, 'Dr. Moran says little in his Essay, confining himself almost entirely to the diocesan jurisdiction': why should I deal, in a very brief article, on a great, broad question that had been left untouched by him? He does, indeed,

1. I have witnessed in my own day the prescription of our last fragment which two of the diocesan chapters in Ireland retained of their former power – the right to elect the members of their body, alternately with the Bishops. The Bishops of the dioceses in question simply ignored this right; and, when the chapter's turn came to elect a canon, made the appointment themselves, without even consulting the chapter. They did not, of course, 'appropriate' anything.

treat of the great central sees – of Jerusalem, Antioch, Rome, and the rest; and I summarized, faithfully, the conclusions to which he had come. Why should I deal with the primatial jurisdiction of Rome, which he had left untouched?

As for the complaint that limitation of the monarchical (diocesan) jurisdiction of the Bishop of Rome is injurious to his primatial authority, I can only ask why it should be. Pope Pius X has three different jurisdictions, which belong to him as Bishop of the city of Rome, Metropolitan of the Roman Province, and Primate of the whole Catholic Church. The first two are of their nature limited, as regards extent of territory; not the third. This third (primatial) kind of jurisdiction belongs to the Pope alone, not to the Cardinals; why should it be injured or diminished in any way, whether as to extent of territory or extent of power, even though the first, and last, of his jurisdictions were held in common by the Cardinals and by himself? They have certain rights now, which, of course, he could override, if he wished to override the canon law. So he could override their diocesan jurisdiction if they held it in common with him.

When the Bishop had finished reading the report, he added that he had an additional, oral, message to deliver from the Trustees: to inform me that some – or it may be many – of their Lordships were anxious and fearful lest, by reason of my teaching, I should be unsettling the minds of the students. They were, he repeated more than once, very anxious indeed in this respect.

When I had asked for a copy of the report and been refused, I told his Lordship he might say to the Trustees that I accepted their correction and bowed to their authority. He said it was not meant as a correction: their Lordships wished merely to let me know their mind; whereon I remarked that it made little difference: whatever they intended, as far as the report went, I accepted it and bowed to their authority. It was different with regard to the oral admonition that followed – about my teaching, as I could not modify this without being untrue to my convictions. I asked for no particulars, as to those parts of my teaching which were the cause of this anxiety. Perhaps I should have asked; and, very possibly, if I did, I should have got no particulars. I did not ask, but merely said that there was no cause for fear, that I knew, as I threw no doubt on any dogma, and was, perhaps, a stronger and more consistent advocate of the Scholastic tradition, in Philosophy as well as in Theology, than most professors in the modern schools of the Church. I did think that certain details should be modified, to bring our system into harmony with science and, to some extent, with history. But modification of this kind must go on always if the science of the school is not to stagnate and rot. Charges like this, I said, had been made against St. Thomas; whereon the Bishop retorted: 'Ah, yes, but I deny the parity.' And, of course, he had me there.

He expressed himself satisfied with my reception of, and submission to, the approved report; but asked me whether I could not say something more agreeable in reply to the oral admonition about my teaching; and when I said I did not know how I could, he urged me again to give him some message that he might communicate to their Lordships. I then told him he might say – I do not know that I remember what – that I should do my best to conform to their admonition, or that I should bear their admonition in mind. This, his Lordship knew, was no retractation of what I had already said – that my opinions were formed, and that I could not prove false to them.

For some time after the Bishop left me I deliberated with myself whether, as the Trustees had notified to me, officially, that some (or many) of them were dissatisfied with my teaching, and as I could not see my way to satisfy them, I was not bound, at least in honour, to resign the position which I held in their service. I cared little about the admonition they gave me for the *Freeman* article, as I need not write again; but I must teach these very matters as to which the opinions which I propound make their Lordships anxious. And as the opinions which I hold and teach seem to me the only ones which commend themselves to a man of reason, to satisfy the Trustees as I desire, I must abstain from discussing these questions – which means resign my chair.

This mood did not last long, not more than a few hours; after which I began to ask myself what it was precisely that made their Lordships anxious. Cardinal Logue, I thought, was one of those who complained; but I was certain that I had a right to teach many things that were a cause of anxiety to his Eminence. The Archbishop of Tuam also, I fancied, was assured that I was wrong on Motion; but, then, I have been teaching on Motion nothing that is not in accord with the best tradition – nothing that I cannot set forth in the very words of some of the safest theologians. The Visitors, I had no doubt, were dissatisfied, for instance, with that thesis of Dr. Moran's which was to be found almost verbatim in Fr. Hontheim's *Institutiones*,[1] and which could not be amended without danger of Semipelagianism. Surely I was not bound to relieve the fears of their Lordships the Visitors on that question. And were not all their other difficulties similar –

1. See p. 219.

the bogies of good men whose outlook was founded by the old, traditional horizon of this place – which sadly needed broadening? So I decided that, as my position is canonical, I retain it, till I am deprived of it in accordance with the provisions of canon law.

I am not in the least ashamed of the *Freeman* article, which, with God's blessing, will produce its effect – some time. I will not write anything of the kind again, as it either is not needed now or would do no good. Besides, it is now forbidden, at least implicitly. I do not, however, admit that it was in any way forbidden when the article was published, nor that any word of the article is disrespectful or injurious to Bishops, nor that it is an attack on them, nor that any part of its doctrine is unsound. It was imprudent, I admit – in the sense of being calculated to get me into a scrape; but my whole life has been an act of faith in such imprudences – a protest against the selfish prudence that will make no sacrifice for the right. It was a sacrifice, so I regarded it at the time; and its prudence or imprudence must be determined by the ultimate effect. For I do not believe in useless sacrifices, though even they may be called for sometimes, by way of protest and for love of the true and right.

THE O'HICKEY CASE AGAIN: THE LAST CONCURSUS
(1913 – 1914)

At the end of May, 1914, on the 30th of the month, Dr. O'Hickey wrote me that he had signed a memorial, drawn up by his advocate, wherein the Pople was asked for permission to take the case before the secular tribunals in Ireland, on the ground that a hearing had been refused in Rome, though Dr. O'Hickey had been pressing for justice since he came there in April, 1910 – that is, more than four years. He had no hope – so he wrote me – that the memorial would produce any effect; but he thought it his duty to present it, with a view to completing his case against the Curia. Neither had his advocate any hope of success.

What was my surprise, then, to receive, on June 6 – three or four days after the letter had come – a telegram, to say that the Holy Father had again sent on the case to the Rota. Next day Dr. O'Hickey wrote, giving what little details he had to give, including a čopy of a letter from Mgr. Bressan at the Vatican to Mgr. Sebastianelli, Dean of the Auditors of the Rota, who was informed that, rather than grant what Dr. O'Hickey had asked for, in his Memorial, the Holy Father had, 'by a quite special grace', arranged to send on the case again to the Rota, to be dealt with and decided by that tribunal.

Dr. O'Hickey – though elated, naturally, by this pontifical decision – was in doubt as to what he should do in the new circumstances that had arisen. To proceed again in the Rota would cost time and money: was the chance worth the cost? Had we any chance at all, considering the experience we had had of the methods and the mind of the tribunal? Dr. O'Hickey himself thought he had no chance – not the least; so did some good Roman friends of his who knew Rome and the officials pretty well. His advocate, on the other hand, thought he should proceed with the case; but, then, the advocate had miscalculated throughout, if he was not even guilty of negligence, and would seek naturally any opportunity to redeem himself. I was asked for advice as to what should be done.

At first I was in favour of proceeding; subject, however, to the better opinion of those who knew Rome personally, and who could, on that account, advise much more prudently than I. I wrote in this sense to Dr. O'Hickey, who, in his reply, said that he read my letter to one or two men who knew Rome well, and who assured him that he had not the least chance in the Rota. His own opinion continued to be in favour of withdrawal, after, however, writing to the Holy Father, to thank him for this new favour, and to explain why he could not see his way to accept. Bear in mind, in this connection, that he – Dr. O'Hickey – had not asked to have the case sent on again to the Rota, but only that he be allowed to take it into the secular courts of Ireland. Instead of this, he was now offered a favour which he had refused to ask, though pressed by his advocate to do so, and he proposed to excuse himself to the Pope on the ground of lack of time, and money, and because he felt that the Auditors of the Rota were prejudiced against him and would not give him fair play. When I got this second letter I replied at once, saying that it was better to withdraw, after writing to His Holiness in the sense proposed.

Nothing remained, then, but for Dr. O'Hickey to write to the Pope, and as the letter would have to be drafted with the greatest care, he was to take time. Meanwhile, of course, the news had spread in Ireland, and, though I heard few or no comments, I have no doubt that it was not at all pleasing to their Lordships the Trustees. They met, as usual, in Maynooth, at the end of June – on Tuesday the 23rd – and, of course, the Visitors had been here from the preceding Friday. All, no doubt, took stock of the new situation. I have no documentary proof that they took action, nor did I hear that they did until somewhere about July 23, I had a letter from Dr. O'Hickey, to say that the Holy Father had withdrawn the case from the Rota. A friend who knew Rome well had told him (Dr. O'Hickey) that Cardinal Vannutelli had been with the Pope and raised a row, with the result that the case was withdrawn by His Holiness.

I have no further proof that this was how the thing was managed, but neither had I any doubt that it was so. Bearing in mind that Cardinal Vannutelli had been over here with Cardinal Logue, and had had on that occasion friendly meetings with most of the Irish Bishops, I have as little doubt that the Irish Cardinal – acting, probably, on a resolution passed at the June meeting of the Trustees – wrote to Cardinal Vannutelli, asking him to present to the Pope their unanimous protest against the new reference of the O'Hickey case to the Rota. And so, once more, extra-judicial proceedings of one of the parties interested interfered with the course of justice in the highest judicial tribunal of the Church.

If they only knew that while they were priming Cardinal Vannutelli, and while he was proceeding to scold the Pope, Dr. O'Hickey was preparing a letter to His Holiness which would have had the effect of withdrawing the case, and so evading the whole difficulty! Their treatment of him was to be completed by this crowning act of interference with the course of justice. Almost while these proceedings took place in the O'Hickey case, a concursus was held for certain vacant chairs of Theology, and the result of the same decided here, all in a way, to make me, who had hitherto advocated the concursus – where no candidate of outstanding merit presented himself – conceive the hope which finds expression in the title of this chapter – that never again may I or anyone else see a concursus for any chair in the College.

Dr. Toner resigned his chair at the meeting of the Trustees held in June, 1913 – the same, it will be remembered, at which the orthodoxy of Dr. Moran's book on *The Government of the Church in the First Century,* and of my article on the same, in the *Freeman's Journal,* were called in question. I was of opinion that the author of that book should be rewarded and encouraged by getting the vacant chair. Other members of the Faculty of Theology were as decidedly opposed to him; some – Dr. Coghlan, at least – because they regarded his opinions as unorthodox; others, as they told me themselves, because they thought him (Dr. Moran) somewhat uncultured; others because, as his orthodoxy was now questioned, they thought it useless to propose his name to the Trustees.

When accordingly, at the approach of the October meeting of

the Board, the Faculty met (October 6, 1913) to consider the question of recommending one or more candidates for the vacant chair, there was no little diversity of opinion, all of which, I thought, was influenced by the feeling of the members towards Dr. Moran. Dr. MacCaffrey, I understood, supported him almost as strongly as I did: all the others, as far as I could learn, were against him. Some I was told – Dr. Coghlan, Dr. Harty, Fr. Boylan, and, perhaps, the President and Dr. Beecher – were in favour of recommending the appointment, without concursus, of Dr. Pierse, who was actually appointed in June, 1914, but only after the concursus of which I am writing. Some of these told me that the Vice-President, Dr. O'Donnell, and Dr. MacCaffrey – all from the province of Armagh – were manœuvring in favour of Fr. Maguire, a distinguished student from Kilmore, then on the Dunboyne Establishment. I could see no sign of this provincialism in the case of either Dr. MacRory or Dr. O'Donnell, and I have said that Dr. MacCaffrey strongly supported Dr. Moran. I have no proof that anyone was influenced by provincialism, but am of opinion that any tendency of the kind there may have been was manifested more by the Southerns than by the others. I certainly had no other wish than to see the author of *The Government of the Church in the First Century* honoured and rewarded as he deserved, and to see our Faculty strengthened by the addition of such a man.

Well, after manœuvring at the first meeting of the Faculty, we met again on October 9, when Dr. Harty proposed and Dr. Coghlan seconded the following resolution: 'That the Faculty report to the Visitors and Trustees by individual letters'. I proposed and the Vice-President seconded an amendment to the effect: 'That the Faculty report to the Visitors and Trustees not by individual letters, but by collective vote, on the question whether the Trustees be recommended to have a concursus on the present occasion'. The voting was five to four in favour of the resolution and against the amendment. The five were: The President, Dr. Coghlan, Dr. Harty, Fr. Boylan, and Dr. Beecher; the four: Dr. MacRory, Dr. MacCaffrey, Dr. O'Donnell, and myself.

The resolution, as I have said, and the amendment, were the outcome of the manœuvring that had been going on. The real question at issue was, whether Dr. Moran or Dr. Pierse should get the chair, without concursus. I thought that, whereas Dr. Moran had written a book that would do honour to any Faculty of Theology, and certainly could not be equalled by most of those who were now opposed to him, Dr. Pierse had done nothing out of the common, which, no doubt, he had done pretty well – when he stood for the doctorate. I felt, moreover, that Dr. Moran could be more easily depreciated, and Dr. Pierse's merits enlarged on, in private letters to the board, than in open voting of the Faculty. More important still, I thought, the general principle – of this voting by private letters – on the merits of candidates who stood no concursus calculated to lead to provincialism and jobs. Why, I said to myself, was it introduced now, except to oust Dr. Moran and give the chair to one whose work showed nothing of the quality of Dr. Moran's book? When, on October 7, 1905, we recommended either Fr. Boylan or Dr. O'Donnell for appointment to the chair of S. Scripture, there were no individual letters sent to the Board, as there were not, on June 20, 1909, when Dr. O'Donnell was recommended for a chair of theology – the only occasions, hitherto, on which such a recommendation had been made by our Faculty.

Another matter of which, I thought, we had reason to complain in these preceedings, was the vote of Dr. Beecher, who had practically no connection with our Faculty, and never attended our meetings, except on occasions such as this. He knew, and could know, little or nothing about the qualifications of the candidates, and yet his vote went, practically, to oust Dr. Moran from the chair. I could not make any formal objection to this, as, for some reason or other, Dr. Beecher had been made a member of our Faculty, and, as such, was within his legal right to vote. But I certainly think it objectionable that one who does none of the regular work of the Faculty, and knows little or nothing of its business, should attend our meetings and vote like the rest of us, whenever a position in the Faculty has to be filled up.

The same applies to one like the present President of the College, who, till he became President, was not a member of the Faculty, and who knows little or nothing of the qualifications of candidates for our chairs. As President, of course, he should be called on to advise the Trustees; but, then, let him do so as President, and let the opinion of the majority of the Faculty be determined independently of votes like his.

Well, as a result of the meeting of the Faculty, held on October 9, we sent individual letters to the Board, as after a concursus, and gave our opinion as to whether any of the candidates for the vacant chair should be appointed thereto without a concursus. I heard afterwards, that opinions were divided, as I expected: some were for appointing Dr. Pierse, others for making no appointment without a concursus. I advised the appointment of Dr. Moran, adding that, apart from him, no other of the candidates was of such outstanding merit as the Statutes required to justify their

Lordships in making an appointment without concursus. Dr. Mac-Caffrey, I understood, agreed with me.

And here I have to call attention to a change in the opinion of some members of the Faculty, which is characteristic in the sense of being at once surprising and yet very like what I had often noticed before. When we were engaged in drawing up the statutes of the Faculty of Theology, it was I who first proposed, and at length got the Faculty to accept, the arrangement that a man of outstanding merit in theology might, on the recommendation of the Faculty, be appointed without concursus to a vacant chair. I remember well the difficulty I had to bring some of the others to approve of this arrangement; it would lead, they said, to jobbery and all sorts of evils. It was certainly in my mind at the time – and I should be surprised if I did not state it publicly, at meetings of the Faculty – that the kind of outstanding merit we should take account of was to be shown exclusively in published writings, that I should take no account of College honours, or estimation of any kind that did not depend on published work. Where no such work could be shown, we should, I insisted, fall back on the concursus; nor would I be satisfied with every kind of published writing, except it were of first-rate quality, and original.

Now, to my surprise, it was I who had to stand up for the concursus system, against those who would not have recourse to it in any case, provided we thought some one of the candidates qualified for the vacant chair. They could not, apparently, maintain that Dr. Pierse's published work was of outstanding merit and original; so they spoke of his defence for the doctorate – when, as I thought, he answered fluently some commonplace objections – and, holding him to be qualified for the chair, they held that he must be qualified for appointment without concursus – a principle which would certainly have been scouted if proposed by me when we were drawing up the statutes. I have often noticed in our College that those who are most slow to accept reform when at first mooted, will press it to extremes later, when they find that it suits themselves.

Owing, I suppose, to the diversity of counsel which they received, the Trustees decided to fill the vacant chair by the old method of concursus, which, as they would not appoint Dr. Moran, was what I recommended. Another chair of theology became vacant when Dr. Harty was made Archbishop of Cashel, and we agreed, at a meeting held on February 9, 1914, to hold a concursus in May for the two chairs then vacant. This, accordingly, was proclaimed, in the usual way, two months beforehand, by the President, and between the date of issue of his proclamation and that fixed for the concursus, a third chair of theology became vacant by the appointment of Dr. Coghlan to the office of Assistant Bishop of Cork.

When drawing up the statutes for the Faculty of Theology, a new regulation was made, to the effect that the candidates at a concursus for any chair of Theology should each present a hundred theses: this was done with a view to securing a broader and more searching examination, by the competitors. Besides these theses I was of opinion that others should be chosen by the Faculty, so that candidates would not have it in their power to select the entire ground of examination in Dogmatic Theology. I had some difficulty in getting this further provision supported when we came to draw up the regulations for the concursus; but at length it was accepted by all.

At the old concursus, moreover, with which I was familiar, we selected the questions in Moral Theology and Philosophy by cutting in the class-book, immediately before the exercise at which the candidates were examined in either of these subjects. I was convinced that we did not secure suitable questions by the old method, and now proposed that the question should be selected beforehand by small committees appointed for that purpose. This, too, was agreed to, after some deliberation; so now, I thought, we were likely to have a concursus which would be something like a test. I do not know how I could improve on the system as now formulated, except, as we shall see, by limiting the number of judges who should vote.

Well, the questions were prepared by the committees, of each of which I was a member; so that I had an opportunity of securing, and did secure, that the questions should be testing. The candidates, I think, found them so. Unfortunately, however, many – if not most – of the examiners did not themselves know what answers to expect, and consequently were not able to judge of the value of the answers; unless, perhaps, to say that this or that candidate spoke fluently and used fairly good Latin, or the reverse. So that, after all our provisions, the test applied resolved itself ultimately into this – whether the candidate could talk in Latin fluently and without too much grammatical blundering, apart altogether from the extent and quality of his knowledge of theology. It paid a candidate to avoid deep things and difficult, since it was so much easier, and more profitable, to trot out commonplaces, which would remind some of the examiners – who knew practically no theology – of what they had heard or read before.

And so the concursus system of selecting professors proved a failure, even in case of chairs of Theology, and must prove so again and again, as long as any others than professors of Theology are allowed to judge of and report on the answering. At this last concursus the judges were: the President; Mgr. Hogan, who read no Theology since he was a student at St. Sulpice; the Vice-President, Dr. MacRory, who is an expert on the New Testament, but knows very little of the science of Theology, as such; myself and Dr. O'Donnell, who are professors of Theology; Dr. MacCaffrey, who is a professor of Ecclesiastical History, but has made no study of Theology since he was a student of the Dunboyne Establishment; Fr. Boylan, who, though very learned in his own department of the Bible, knows very little of the science of Theology; and Dr. Beecher, who, though a celebrated pulpit orator, would hardly claim to judge of the answer to a testing question in theological science. How could the majority of these men report on anything except the fluency of the speakers and their greater or less success in avoiding blunders in the use of Latin?

I have no hope of seeing the right of voting on these concursus limited to those who have expert knowledge of the questions proposed; nor, indeed, do I think it possible to find any body of examiners qualified to judge of the answers to questions taken from the whole course of Theology and Philosophy. The subject is too wide for any man; now especially, when the best of us has to devote his life to a few special questions. And as I have no hope of securing competent judges for such concursus, I agree at length, that they should be discarded – even for the selection of professors of Theology – and that professors should be selected, by the Faculty concerned, on their College record and their published work; this latter, if of good quality and original, to count most of all. To meet the abuses that are sure to arise on this system, I would throw the responsibility on the Faculty concerned, who should vote openly, so that the world may know who did the job, in case any job should have been done. And I would never give a man a permanent appointment till he had published something that, by its excellence and originality, proved the writer to be worthy of a chair of Theology.

That is why, in the title of this chapter, I have thought it well to express a hope that this last concursus which we held should be the very last of all.

I have only to add that Dr. Moran was not a candidate for the concursus in May, 1914. He had asked some of us whether he ought to stand, and we advised him that he had no chance of appointment. Meanwhile, he had sent a copy of his work to Rome, through some of the authorities at the Irish College there, who

239

submitted it to Fr. David Fleming, O.S.F. Somewhere about the end of May, Fr. Fleming reported – in a letter which he had no wish to keep private – that the book, in this opinion, was an excellent one on the subject. A copy of this letter was sent, I understand, to each of the Bishops of Ireland, and Dr. Moran notified our President that he was a candidate for the chair of Theology just then vacated by Dr. Coghlan.[1]

Our votes on the concursus were handed in on the morning of Saturday, June 20; and on the evening of the same day, at a meeting specially convened, we were asked by the President, on behalf of the Visitors, to say whether, 'on the supposition that two of the candidates who stood the concursus were appointed to the vacant chair, there was still a third sufficiently qualified'. We were not asked whether any of them was the most qualified – more qualified, for instance, than Dr. Moran, who had given notice that he was a candidate for the third vacant chair. He was excluded by the Visitors, and we were asked to report only on the five who had stood the concursus. As a result, the three vacant chairs were filled from among them, and Dr. Moran – for all his excellent book, and because it was so excellent – was left out in the cold. It is poor encouragement for learning, whether on the Dunboyne Establishment or in the Irish Church. If you wish to succeed, my students, you should take care either not to write at all, or to write good commonplace; above all not to do anything original, however excellent it may be.

It is, I hope, no harm to mention that Dr. MacCaffrey – to whom I spoke soon afterwards about Dr. Moran – told me he had had a talk about him with one of the most influential of the Bishops, and was told that there was no use in proposing Moran for any of the vacant chairs. That settled the matter.

---

1. It had a good effect, too; though it did not avail to clear Dr. Moran of suspicion – of being under my baneful influence, I suppose. The *Irish Theological Quarterly* made bold to notice his book, after deliberate silence of more than a year. Other journals did likewise. That a letter from Rome, from one who had given no proof of theological science more than a letter to the *Tablet* now and then, should be able to restore to orthodoxy a book which had won the doctorate from our Faculty of Theology, shows how little our Bishops and other high-placed clergymen think of the opinion of the Faculty of Theology in their own College – a Faculty of which so many of their Lordships were members at one time.

DEATH OF DR. O'HICKEY (November, 1914)

During the summer vacation of 1914, while at my old home in Emil, I heard that Dr. O'Hickey had returned to Ireland, and was staying with a brother of his at Portlaw, about three miles away. I wrote at once to say where I was, and that I should expect him soon, and the next day, I think, he came to see me.

There was very little change in his appearance. A trifle older, perhaps a little more subdued; but he seemed to bear his great disappointment well. He had been ill in Rome in the early part of the year, but he was blessed with a great constitution, and seemed to have completely shaken off the illness. He stayed to dinner, and made a hearty meal, I thought, as he did also later on when he paid me a second visit in the same place. He seemed in very good health – likely to live many years. Little I thought as he drove away after the second visit that it was the last time I should see his honest face, or grasp his manly hand.

On the occasion of the first visit I asked had he seen his Bishop – Dr. Hackett, recently appointed to the see of Waterford. He, Dr. O'Hickey, said he had not: had merely sent a line to say he had come home. I said, if I do not now mistake, that I thought it was not enough, and that it seemed due to the Bishop to call on him in person. Dr. O'Hickey then said, or indeed it may have been on the occasion of his second visit to Emil, that when he returned to Ireland, his best clothes were not such that he would like the Bishop to see him wear, lest his Lordship should take it for a cry of distress. When he got a new suit, as he hoped in a few days, he would call on his Lordship. The Bishop, whom I met about this time, expressed surprise – which meant dissatisfaction – that Dr. O'Hickey had not come to him in person. I excused my friend as best I could; but if I knew of the clothes difficulty at the time, I did not feel at liberty to mention it.

Well, in a few days' time, Dr. O'Hickey, duly apparelled, called on his Lordship, who received him kindly. There were inquiries about health, and then, after the usual commonplace, about Dr. O'Hickey's intentions. He had none, except to serve on the mission in any office to which he might be sent. The Bishop asked whether he had any spcial wish, as for instance, for the town or country mission. Dr. O'Hickey had none, would try to fit himself into any place that might be assigned him. The Bishop said he

241

had no place vacant just then, but would be on the look-out for something suitable. He evidently meant to treat the returned prodigal if not to a fatted calf, at least to something better than the portion usually assigned to beginners.

This must have been late in August, as I returned to College soon afterwards. I had an occasional short note from my friend, who did not complain of illness, but said he had not yet got an appointment. Fearing that he must be in need of money, I sent him a small cheque for his personal use; but it came back by next post with a word of thanks, but also an intimation that, though he had little money, he was in no need, and would prefer to get on as he was without such assistance. It was just like him.

The wife of his brother Maurice, with whom he spent a good deal of time at Carrick-on-Suir, told me after his death that every Monday morning, when episcopal letters making arrangements for priests are usually received, he watched the post, and that week after week he seemed disappointed and depressed when there was no letter for him. I knew how he must have felt to be dependent even on brothers; also how hard it was for him to meet others, priests and people, but especially priests, while he himself was without a mission. The Bishop meant well, no doubt; but it was a pity he did not provide some place, however humble, for this good man. It would have saved a tragedy.

One morning towards the end of November, I sat down to breakfast in the College, and opening the paper to find the latest news about the war, read a heading in capitals: 'Death of Dr. O'Hickey'. No one had heard of any illness of his: we knew him to be a man of powerful constitution. I myself had seen him, not three months before, apparently in excellent health. And now he was dead. He had been ill for a few days, of some intestinal trouble, which, as it was not remedied, led to blood poisoning. That was the immediate cause of death; but his friends believed – and who can blame them? – that he died of a broken heart.

We buried him at Carrick-beg, with his fathers, in the grave-yard attached to the Friary. The Bishop came to the funeral, as also a fair number of the diocesan clergy. There were two or three of us from the College, and two or three personal friends from among the members of the Gaelic League in Dublin. The clerical members of the League throughout the country were notable for their absence, as indeed were the lay members and officials also. All these must have known that the protracted suit in Rome cost a great deal. They had indeed, some of them, given something to meet this expense; but on his death, they never inquired whether he had received enough. I knew that he had not, that a goodly sum remained to be provided. In the earlier years of his stay in Rome he had been helped by an uncle; towards the end, he drew on one of his brothers, and one or two personal friends gave something. After his death, any of these who put in a claim were paid in full from the proceeds of a sale of his books, of which he had a large and valuable collection, so that a goodly part of the expense of the suit in Rome fell on him, as if it were his own interests he was defending. The Gaelic League, I thought, did not shine at his death, nor is it creditable to the members of that body that there is no monument – nor any talk of one – to the memory of a man who was not only its champion but its martyr.

In this connection certain recollections occur, which, however cynical they may be deemed, I cannot well omit to place on record. They are not without a humorous side, and throw some light on human nature as it is found in Ireland.

And first, with regard to Dr. Mannix, now Archbishop of Melbourne, who, it will be remembered – or will it? – was the prime mover in the proceedings whereby Dr. O'Hickey was dismissed from the College. On the same occasion, and for the same cause – of openly supporting the agitation for essential Irish – some of the ablest and best students of the College were withdrawn by their Bishops, which practically meant expulsion. This, of course, was done on the instigation of the same arch-enemy of the movement.

I should mention here that the men so withdrawn, or practically expelled, belonged to a students' society called the Columban League, of which the object is the study of Irish, the publication of books in Irish, and the promotion of all things antiquarian, literary or artistic, connected with the language. They produce and publish every year a fair-size journal made up of papers contributed by students on subjects of that kind, and in addition, they have had printed and published a certain number of manuscript works in Irish. One may fancy what they felt when not only Dr. O'Hickey, but some of the ablest and best of the members and officers of the League, were removed from the College.

Such feelings, however, may not last, especially among students of colleges who lose every year a good part of their number, getting in place others who knew not Joseph. So it came to pass that when Dr. Mannix was made Coadjutor to the Archbishop of Melbourne, and was consecrated in our College chapel, the students seemed as glad and proud as any of those whom he used to lead in the charge against essential Irish, and whom on two occasions he could tickle by inviting them to meet the King and Queen at Maynooth. The students at least – Columban Leaguers included – enjoyed the feast which the new Archbishop gave them on his consecration day, and repaid him by inserting a full-page portrait into the journal of the League for that year. The staff also – with two exceptions, of whom I was one – to show no doubt their appreciation of what their late President had done to secure them right of permanency in their offices, presented him with a gold chalice. They, with the exception of one who subscribed anonymously, had not given a farthing to help Dr. O'Hickey to fight his – and their – battle. How the common enemy must have despised them.

When next autumn I had a visit from two of the Columban Leaguers to ask for my annual subscription, I produced the journal and portrait, and asked whether the honour was done the Archbishop for the service he had rendered the Irish language by dismissing Dr. O'Hickey and the students? This while Dr. O'Hickey was fighting his case in Rome! They said, in justification or excuse, that, as they understood, it was a personal dispute with which they had no concern; to which, of course, I replied that they had made their case worse, and that I would not subscribe to any society such as theirs. Two or three years later, when the men of that time had left the College, some of their successors in the League came to plead that they had nothing to do with the offence committed, and that they hoped I would not hold them accountable. I said I would not; but I did not consider myself at liberty to subscribe to the League until it had made public apology for the offence of that time. There is little likelihood of any such apology being made now, as owing to his recent doings in Australia, the Archbishop is to-day – wonder to relate – one of the first, if not the very first, of Irish patriots.

Some months before Dr. O'Hickey's death, I made trial of another prelate, Dr. O'Dwyer, the late Bishop of Limerick, who had just then, or soon afterwards, been making himself a name as one of the greatest and most courageous and most patriotic Irishmen of all time. In my own difficulties I had had more sympathy from him than from any other Irish Bishop. Not indeed that I had had much from him; but then, a little may be very welcome where there is a dearth of any commodity. We had a controversy, it will be remembered, on the managerial question; but as far as I could see, this made no difference in our subsequent relations. He did me the honour now and then to ask my opinion on theological and philosophical difficulties that either occurred to himself or had been proposed to him for solution. He even submitted for my criticism – after he had made it – the speech he made in Limerick, when they gave him the freedom of the city, and though the criticism was unfavourable, and might even be termed severe, he showed no resentment, but contented himself with dubbing me a West Briton, in a letter to a mutual friend.

Shortly before his death, he sent me for criticism and something like a *Nihil Obstat* – Bishops, I suppose, do not require the real thing – a number of short lectures which he had delivered on the seven last words of Christ, the reading of which edified me greatly. They showed him to be full of simple faith and ardent love of our Lord and His Blessed Mother. I understood that he was to publish the lectures, and hope they will soon appear. Here and there I suggested little changes in the style, which he made with humility.

Well, to come to the trial which I made of him, I should say that when Dr. Henebry died in March, 1916, some of us thought it would be a convenient way out of the O'Hickey imbroglio if we could get our friend in Rome appointed to the vacant chair of Irish in University College, Cork. We felt that there could be little hope of this unless the Bishops of the province were to refrain from opposition, and so I wrote to ask Dr. O'Dwyer to use his influence with his episcopal brethren to get them to support our project.

'You will not', I said, 'take it ill, I hope, if I venture to put it a little stronger. That the Bishops would do well, in their own interest, and in that of the Church, to get him appointed. I will not refer to objective rights or wrongs, but am content to say, what I hope your Lordship will admit, that he fought straight in defence of what he deemed a principle, and that he is probably the most honourable and self-sacrificing priest in the Irish Church.

'There is more that I hope you will permit me to say, though you may not admit its truth. It is that there are a good many laymen and priests, not of the worst sort, who regard him as having met with hard lines, and who think an ugly question would be well settled if the Bishops would get him this appointment. Their Lordships would not lose by such generosity'.

Dr. O'Dwyer began his reply by assuring me that I need have made no apology – as I had done – for the letter I had written.

'But I must say', he continued, 'that as things stand between Dr. O'Hickey and the Bishops, I cannot interfere, and unless he puts himself right with them, I doubt very much if the Governing Body of Cork College will elect him.

'My idea is that even now Dr. O'Hickey ought to offer an apology to the Bishops, not for his appeal to Rome – for that was within his right – but for the language which led to his removal from his chair. I have not his exact words before me at the minute; but I remember that when I read them I thought them wild and unmeasured, and more like the utterances of a District Councillor than a priest and professor in a great ecclesiastical College; and although I have taken no active part in any of the proceedings against him, I hold myself fully responsible for them. Yet I am convinced that his fault, such as it is, is obstinacy, and perhaps a little pride rather than disrespect of authority.

'Why would he not now write to the Archbishop of Cashel, and withdraw the expressions of which the Bishops disapproved, and ask him then to support his candidature at Cork?

'No Bishop has any personal feeling against the poor fellow who has been severely punished, and as for me, I would be only too glad of a chance of helping him, but unless he withdraws frankly from the position which he foolishly, I think, took up at Maynooth, I would not interfere, and I should be greatly surprised if the governing body of any College in Ireland elected him under these conditions. After all, for a priest there is no humility or indignity in a manly and humble submission to ecclesiastical authority'.

In writing to thank His Lordship for this letter, I said I did not think Dr. O'Hickey would make the apology suggested.

To this his Lordship replied that he would be very glad to have an opportunity of reading the letter of Dr. O'Hickey to which I referred, and also the incriminating passages. Then he went on:

'Just consider the position. He has been dismissed from his chair in Maynooth by the whole body of the Bishops of Ireland for language which the Bishops regarded as so bad as to unfit him for professorship of ecclesiastics... Speaking from memory, I think there can be no doubt that Dr. O'Hickey's language was wrong. The Irish Bishops thought it so wrong that, under the penalty of dismissal, he should be required to withdraw it. But he point-blank refused to do so. I was present when he appeared before us, and I must say I thought that his attitude was unworthy of a gentleman and a priest'.

On receipt of this letter, I sent his Lordship a pamphlet which Dr. O'Hickey had had printed, containing a letter to the Secretary of the Trustees referred to above, as well as of the incriminated passages in his public utterances. With it I made bold to send a rather long letter, wherein I set forth some of the reasons which kept me and others from taking the same view of the case as the Bishops. The Bishop did not resent this long and very candid letter, which is very much to his credit. He sent me his reply:

'I have read your letter not only carefully, but with the fullest sympathy, and a desire to agree with your view of the case. Then I read the documents which you enclosed, and I must honestly say that their effect has been to cancel the impression which your pleading made on my mind.

'If it were a mere question of an appeal in a criminal case in which I happened to be the judge, I should allow that there is much in your contention, at least on technical grounds; but the action of the Bishops in removing Dr. O'Hickey from his chair was administrative, and taken principally in the interest of their students. Even so, Dr. O'Hickey had a right to substantial justice, and I really think he got it to the fullest extent.

'He complains of being taken short, and not getting time to prepare his defence; yet six months intervened between the notice he got through his own Bishop from the Standing Committee and the proceedings of the Visitors and his deprivation by the Trustees.'

'There was no question of fact at issue', continues Dr. O'Dwyer; 'he admitted and stood by his language, and the one point for the Bishops to decide was whether it was consistent with their duty to allow him to remain a Professor: was he a fit man to train ecclesiastics, and train them in habits of obedience and humility and respect for authority? As a juror, if I were on my oath, I should answer these questions in the negative. The very worst of his language was addressed in the College to the students, and we know what a seething spirit of insubordination existed among them at the time. Was it tolerable for him, a priest, to pour very foul abuse, and to heap at least constructively the gravest charges against the distinguished ecclesiastics who were on the Senate of the University, because, right or wrong, they differ from Dr. O'Hickey on the question of compulsory Irish. Every line in 2, 3, 4, 6, on pp. 10, 11, 12 (the references are to Dr. O'Hickey's pamphlet) is saturated with an insulting and contemptuous tone towards ecclesiastics, and the exception which he makes in 6 only *firmat regulam*. As to a number of extrinsic circumstances to which you refer, I can only ask *Tantæne animis cœlestibus iræ?* I am not much in the ecclesiastical *coulisse*, and my poor ears do not lend themselves to gossip; but unless your information is very direct and very authentic about the election of Vice-President, I should be inclined to doubt it. The two last elections were unanimous. No one was proposed in opposition either to Dr. MacRory or Dr. MacCaffrey, which makes the story you have heard rather improbable.

'Then on the whole case – technicalities, equalities and all –

Dr. O'Hickey has had his appeal to Rome, and we must conclude from the result that it was not a very sound one'.

No doubt Dr. O'Hickey had said hard things in the passages to which the Bishop referred about those who had opposed compulsory Irish. They were 'a worthless faction'; their policy was a 'dastard and foolish' one, a 'squalid and foolish apostasy'. 'They' – among them some ecclesiastics – 'would have the episcopate wantonly and recklessly seek to arrest the progress of Irish nationality', and thereby 'precipitate such a scandal as Irish public life has not witnessed since one of those who sold the country... successfully sought the suffrages of the burgesses of Athlone, leaning on the arms of two Bishops'. 'If the new university is to be West Briton, it will be made so by an act of treachery towards Ireland'... on the part of 'the University Senate... five of whom are distinguished Catholic ecclesiastics, two of the five being Bishops'. 'There have been centuries of national infatuation, for which Irish Churchmen are much more to blame than others'. 'My Lords and Gentlemen must be told... that, wily as they are, they will not be suffered to cozen and delude the Irish people'. 'In the clerical senators as a body I can repose little or no trust, though I cannot imagine how any body of responsible Irish ecclesiastics could embark on a more foolish or reckless course.' He makes an exception of the Archbishop of Dublin; but 'as for the other clerical senators, I shall say nothing further than to recommend them to your prayers'. 'The treachery of those who show themselves false to Ireland at this juncture must never be forgotten... A black list of the recreant Nationalist senators must be preserved, that in after times all men may know who were the false and vile'.

This is an exhaustive list of the hard sayings which the Bishop of Limerick, reading over them years afterwards, found to be such as to prove their author to be unfit to train 'ecclesiastics in habits of obedience, humility and respect for authority', and which, writing from memory, his Lordship had characterized as 'wild and unmeasured, and more like the utterances of a District Councillor than a priest and professor in a great ecclesiastical College'; Dr. O'Hickey's attitude, moreoever, when he appeared before the Board was 'unworthy of a gentleman and a priest'.

Some little time after the Bishop had pronounced these censures, he himself felt called on to use strong language about those whom he in turn deemed Ireland's enemies. They were not indeed ecclesiastics, but even laymen have some right to courtesy from 'a priest and gentleman'; all the more if the priest should be not merely a professor in a great ecclesiastical College, but Trustee of the same, and a Bishop. And perhaps it will be admitted that the supreme civil rulers of the country have special rights as holding their authority from God.

I might quote, from the Bishop's own language, many specimens of what poor Dr. O'Hickey might have said without failing to show himself priest and gentleman, worthy of a chair in a great ecclesiastical College, or even of mitre and crozier in the cathedral of Limerick.

Mind, I do not find so very much fault with the Bishop's language, though I should not care to use it myself. He had to put his views strongly, as he himself pleads; but so had Dr. O'Hickey. I ask myself, as others will ask, why one of the two should be deprived of his chair and made to die of a broken heart, and by the action of the other. Why should other Bishops, after dismissing Dr. O'Hickey for using language unworthy of a priest, eulogize Dr. O'Dwyer as if his pronouncements were worthy not only of priest and gentleman, but of a Father of the Church.[1]

And why should laymen – old Land Leaguers, Gaelic Leaguers, Irish Irelanders – forget what was said of boycotting and Essential Irish, and what was done to Dr. O'Hickey merely because one who was responsible for all this – and who was most responsible for part – had taken up Sinn Fein; not because he believed in the new policy, or thought the last insurrection justified – for he was a foe to Liberalism – but because he thought he could thereby pay a score which had been long overdue to his Land League adversaries?

These are some of the questions which one cannot help asking as one stands over Dr. O'Hickey's lonely grave and thinks over certain recent developments in Irish history.

1. The Most Rev. Dr. Fogarty, Bishop of Killaloe, a personal friend of mine, who preached at the Month's Memory for Dr. O'Dwyer. In a well-remembered letter, he once called the Parliamentary Party 'Ireland's Army and Navy'; but turned on them later on, when, during the elections of 1918, he referred to them in a public letter as 'spat upon as paupers' at Westminster, and 'coming back to us with empty hands or with a few crumbs from the English kitchen, garnished with rhetoric, but as always with the leprosy of Anglicization visibly developed on their person to the ruin of our national spirit' (see *Freeman's Journal*, November 30, 1918). The writer of this had voted to deprive Dr. O'Hickey from his chair for using language unbecoming priest or gentleman.

SINN FEIN; PROJECTED NEW STATUTES;
THE COLLEGE STAFF AND POLITICS
(1916 – 1919)

Two or three days before Easter, 1916, I went down to County
Kilkenny to spend the Easter holidays there, going first to Fr.
Treacy, P.P., at Conahy. I stayed with him till Easter Monday,
when he drove me into the city of Kilkenny, on my way to Emil.
He had some business to do at the Kilkenny post office, where we
heard that insurrection had broken out in Dublin, that the General Post Office had been seized by the insurgents, and that railway communication with Dublin was cut. With this news, which I
found it hard to realize, or even to believe, I made my way to Emil.

There I remained during Easter week, anxiously looking for news
every day, and receiving little. There were no newspapers, except,
I think, the *Daily Sketch,* which had a paragraph or two, passed
by the Censor. In Waterford, whither I went on two or three days,
there was, practically, only this *Daily Sketch* to be found; but there
was a plentiful supply of rumours of startling character. Dublin
was captured – it was burned; Cork and Limerick had risen; the
bridge of Waterford was to be broken down, as that city was but
waiting for the word, and might be up in any minute. The number
slain on both sides was enormous. The Germans had landed in
Galway, or at Cork, or somewhere in the North; or had sent plenty
of arms for the Irish volunteers of West and South who were
marching on Dublin. One knows how rumour exaggerates, when
fears and hopes are excited, and, apart from common-sense and
coolness, there is no means of testing the report. One knows this
vaguely, but to realize it one has to live through such a crisis.

One day, in Waterford, I met a lady who had a copy of the London *Times* of the preceding day. She had got it from another friend,
and gave it to me to read, as I did, with avidity. It contained but
a short paragraph or two about the rising, practically the same as
I had seen in the *Daily Sketch,* so the Censor was at work, and
one could not depend on anything.

Classes were to be resumed at the College on Low Monday; and
as my lecture hour was before noon, I should have to return in
normal times on Easter Saturday. On inquiry at the railway station,
however, I was told that there was no train going any way near
Dublin or Maynooth; so I had to stay in Emil – not very unwil-

lingly. On Monday I went down to Waterford to see whether perhaps the train service had been resumed; and was told I could get to Sallins. So I set out; but could get by train no further than Kildare. The price of a car to Maynooth being prohibitive, I stayed for the night with the Parish Priest of Kildare, Father Campion; and got by train next day to Sallins. Thence by car to Maynooth; where I heard pretty nearly the true story, as some men from the College had been to Dublin and seen the damage done to the City. Some young fellows, too, from the town, who had been out with the rebels, had straggled home, and before being arrested, had told something of what they had seen and heard. In any case the insurrection was over by this time; and, though rumour was still busy, one could make a pretty shrewd guess at the truth.

Some of the Maynooth lads, I have said, were out with the rebels. They had been drilling for some time, under Ted O'Kelly; a son of Dr. Tom O'Kelly, whom I knew so well. Hitherto Ted was good for nothing; had tried religious life and given it up; then taken to the family profession, of medicine, which he gave up also. He paid me a visit down at my rooms; and, when I proceeded to scold him, made defence so plausible that anger turned to pity. He had one great redeeming quality – temperance; and he looked a gentleman. They say he played the man in the rebellion, wherein he was wounded. Had he been captured afterwards, – and he had a narrow escape – he would most probably have been shot.

Though drilled and commanded by O'Kelly, the Maynooth commando, – Sinn Feiners were wont to take the style and titles of the Boers, – was influenced principally by Donal Buckley; – an honest enthusiast, trader of the town. On Easter Sunday, I was told, they had marched into the College, trying to find some priest to give them absolution, or at least a blessing. They knew of the pro-Germans and professed enemies of England on the staff; who, however, did not rise to this occasion. Whereupon the commando made for the archway under the President's room, and asked for that clergyman.

Mgr. Hogan, the President, came down; and, when told what they wanted, – a blessing, at least, in this hour of danger, said that he had not the least sympathy with their cause, and could not bless their expedition. As, however, they were kindly neighbours, now throwing themselves, like fools, into very great danger, he would bless them personally. Whereupon they knelt down, received the blessing, and marched off by a circuitous route to Dublin.

All that week guns could be heard thundering away. By day one could see the great columns of smoke rising from the city twelve miles off; by night it turned into a pillar of fire, and the whole inter-eastern sky was lit up by its burning. Frightened stragglers brought news of the conflict; one can fancy the excitement, especially among the pro-Germans; and the depression, when they had to confess that hope was gone, for the present.

I reached the College on Tuesday (after Low Sunday), and next day rode on a bicycle to Dublin, to see and hear for myself. There was no challenge till I got to Island Bridge, where a sentry was posted, who let me pass without difficulty. As I wished, above all, to see Miss Brennan, – an aged lady friend, who lived with a single maid at Charleville Road, off the North Circular Road, near Phibsboro, – my natural course would have been up from the Quay, by the Park, to the Park Gate on the North Circular Road. But hearing that about there somewhere there was a military barricade which it was difficult to pass, I went on into the city, and passed up to Phibsboro, through Church Street. There were bullet marks here and there along the way. A little above the Capuchins' Church there was a house from which bricks had been removed, to make loop-holes for rifles firing down North King Street; towards the Linen Hall Barracks, which had been burned. This had been a hot corner, and stories were told afterwards of domiciliary visits paid by the military, and of non-combatants shot in cold blood and buried in the cellars. That such men were shot, I can well believe; as also that they were buried by some one; but in a place where I myself saw bricks removed, plainly with a view to firing down the street, one should not, I think, be too hard on the soldiers exposed to such sniping, if on searching the houses, they found men and took them for their assailants. In the circumstances mistakes were pardonable.

On the North Circular Road, a little west of Phibsboro, there was evidence of an unsuccesful attempt to blow up a railway bridge, and where Charleville Road, – whither I was going, – branches off, sentries were posted. After a little parley, one of them came with me to Miss Brennan's; but must have satisfied himself that I meant no harm to the public peace, as he left me there, and did not challenge me on my return journey.

From Miss Brennan's I went down to Fairview; where my nephew, a young priest, was stationed. I met him somewhere at the city side of Bally Bough Bridge; but even though in his company, was not allowed to pass over the bridge without a pass; which, however, was freely given. Returning to the College, I passed through O'Connell Street, and saw the ruined and smoky buildings: sad sight enough; though, happily, there were no corpses. Passing along the Quays, I met some armoured cars, and thought what little chance the rebels had against such instruments of defence and destruction.

Foolish as it was, and without mandate, the result of the exececution of the leaders was to excite all over Nationalist Ireland a wave of sympathy that swamped the Parliamentary Party. When an opportunity came of testing public opinion, at by-elections, the result was an overwhelming majority for Sinn Fein. The Government contributed to this not only by shooting the leaders in the rebellion, but by retaining in prison those whom they did not shoot; and imprisoning others for continuing the agitation. No more powerful appeal could be made for a candidate than to say, with truth, that he was imprisoned by the British Government.

In those by-elections, as also in the general election that followed, some of the more enthusiastic members of our Staff took part; one in particular – Dr. Browne – who spoke, here and there, on public platforms, generally in company with Fr. O'Flanagan. This led to complaints on the part of the local ecclesiastical authorities; and Dr. Browne, I understand, was asked by the Visitors to satisfy them that he had not contravened the statute of the National Synod which forbids clergymen to appear at any political meeting without permission of the Parish Priest of the place. There were, I believe, some other questions put him, as to all of which, we were told, he was able to satisfy their Lordships.

The Trustees, however, at the meeting that followed, – of June, 1919, if I do not mistake – passed a resolution to the effect that members of the College staff must take no public part in discussing political questions on which Catholic opinion in Ireland is divided. (I have not the resolution before me, nor am I sure that I reproduce it quite correctly. Substantially it is as I have given it.) A not unreasonable regulation, as I thought.

This reminds me that, for some time previously, the President and Administrative Council, or some of them, were engaged in collecting and arranging the regulations of this kind that had been made from time to time by the Board, for the better ordering of the conduct of the Staff. The result was a pamphlet of fifty-six pages, giving (1) 'Acts of Parliament as now in Force relating to St. Patrick's College'; (2) 'Statutes Adjusted by the Trustees on the – day of – 191 '; the date to be filled in later; and (3) *Facultates a S. Sede Concessæ circa Gradus Academicos Conferendos*'. A copy of this pamphlet marked 'Draft' and 'Confidential', fell into my hands; having been left in my room by the Archbishop of Dublin. I did not consider myself bound in honour not to look over the proposed new Statutes.

Finding therein some points which I deemed of interest to the Staff, I spoke about the matter at the community table; saying that, in my opinion, we should ask to be heard before these Statutes were made binding. The idea was taken up; with the result that the whole Staff, with the exception of the President, met in the billiard-room, and appointed a small Committee to draw up a petition to the Board, asking them to supply us with copies of the proposed new Statutes, so that we might be in a position to make suggestions before they were finally approved. The Committee consisted of Father Mulcahy and myself; and, the form of petition which we desired meeting with unanimous approval, it was signed by each of the body and forwarded to the Secretary of the Visitors. The result was a resolution passed by the Board granting our request.

In due time – a week or two before the Board meeting of June, 1919 – members of the College Staff received copies of the pamphlet already mentioned, containing the proposed new Statutes; and, as senior member of the academic body, I called a meeting to consider the same. Practically all professors attended with the Bursar; the President and Deans did not come, as they had drawn up the Statutes. I was made chairman of the meeting, Dr. Beecher secretary.

We first passed a resolution of thanks to the Board for giving us an opportunity of making suggestions; after which we proceeded with the suggestions which we wished to make. Everyone, of course, was free to raise any point that seemed to him to need consideration.

The first point so raised dealt with the Statute Ch. II r. 14 on Residence; which all regarded as unnecessarily severe. It was proposed, and carried unanimously, to recommend the Board to leave the rule in this matter as it stands already.

We next considered the new proposals with regard to pensions: Ch. II r. 11, asking that they should be modified by leaving out the words 'have power to' as also the clause 'for such period and to such extent as they think fit'. The result would be to give rights of pensions to members of the Staff who may be disabled by illness or have given thirty years of service to the College. In determining the amount of pension, we suggested that, in the case of those who had given thirty years' service, it should be two-thirds of their salary, with two-thirds of the estimated value of their commons. And we added something to the effect that, in case the retiring official got another ecclesiastical appointment, the emoluments derived from this might be taken into account as part of his pension.

Some one proposed to ask for a present bonus in view of the depreciation in value or purchasing power, of the salaries we receive; but I and others said we could not see our way to make such a petition. I had no objection that others would get as much in this way as they could, but I would not ask anything for myself. Accordingly it was proposed that their Lordships should be asked to give a bonus to those whose salaries did not amount to £ 200. This was passed unanimously. I voted with the others, somewhat against my will; as I thought it somewhat petty to make this application.

Some one called attention to the Statute on publications: Ch. II r. 15: and it was agreed, unanimously, to ask their Lordships to omit this altogether, considering that we are bound very strictly already by the new code of Canon Law and the enactments of the National Synod.

I raised a question as to the mode of making appointments to the office of President and Vice-President; for which during all my time there has been what I cannot but deem unseemly canvassing, either – as usually happened – on the part of candidates themselves, or of friends among the episcopal body. It appeared to me unseemly for anyone to push in this way into an ecclesiastical office; but, unless we did so, as some very good men refused to do – one was left in the ranks. Personally I did not mind this in the least, as, had I been offered the Vice-Presidency or Presidency at any time, I should have declined the offer; but I felt that the system is not only unseemly but injurious to the College; which was being deprived of the services of the most independent, unselfish, and best men at its disposal.

I knew, of course, that there would be canvassing and pulling of wires under any system; but I thought there would be less of this, and that it would be less effectual, if the members of the staff were allowed recommendation. They, as it seemed to me, have more interest in the matter than any one else; they know the man better; and in all the recommendations which they made, in my time, on occasions of appointing professors, they voted regularly for the man they deemed best, without favour or bias of any kind. Whenever a job was done, – as happened, unfortunately, in appointing to the offices of President and Vice-President, – it was done by the Bishops; who allowed themselves to be swayed by personal or provincial considerations. Had the staff had a right of recommendation, this could scarcely have happened, and if it did, and the staff were responsible, we could bring criticism to bear on the delinquents.

Hence I proposed that, in future, when appointments were being made to these two offices, all officials who are personally attached to the staff would have a right to vote, in recommendation of candidates, as the Parish Priests of Ireland do on the appointment of Bishops. The suggestion was adopted by a great majority; three of those present voting against.

So matters were left on the first evening of our meeting; but that night, as I lay awake from toothache, it occurred to me that the proposal regarding dismissal of College officials, Ch. XVIII r. 3, is so loosely and badly worded as to place it within the power of the Trustees to dismiss even the best men – for 'example manifestly injurious to the discipline of the College or conflicting with the edification which all officials of our College are bound to give the students, public statements injurious to the interests of the College, grave violation of priestly obligations, conduct prejudicial to good order in the College, and the welfare of religion, as likely to be a source of disedification to the faithful'. I called to mind what had been brought against poor Dr. O'Hickey, in this connection. So I resolved to summon a further meeting to take this into consideration.

We met again in the same room; myself being chairman of the meeting and Dr. Beecher secretary. After reading the draft report which we proposed to send in, I called attention to the Statute regarding dismissal; and proposed that we should suggest the desirability of reconstructing the whole, so as to distinguish between two classes of offence; (1) those of so grave a nature as to merit dismissal on the first conviction; and (2) others for which the penalty on the first occasion, would be a monition from the Trustees; in the second a formal precept, given in writing by the same; while dismissal would follow only on proved violation of this precept. After some consideration, this was passed unanimously.

I forgot to say that at our first meeting some one called attention to the proposed Statute Ch. XVIII r. 21, as to the right of being heard in one's own defence; and it was proposed and passed unanimously that the Statute should be altered so as to allow one a right to a copy, in writing, of the charge against him, which should be furnished at least a month before the investigation would take place.

A LAST FLUTTER: VALETE! (1920)

I am going to write now what, to all human seeming, must be the last chapter in these Reminiscences. I have been told by medical and surgical experts that I am afflicted by an incurable disease, which may leave me a little more time for light work, but may incapacitate me any day. Welcome be God's holy will; which, if it has a dark side, bears also this comforting aspect – that I am likely to die in harness; without being laid up for years as an idle log. That is the fate which I used to fear most. Now

> The Bird of Time has but a little way
> To flutter, and the Bird is on the Wing!

What I have still to say will, perhaps, come with added force from one who has now no earthly advantage to secure or interest to serve.

My book on *Some Ethical Questions of Peace and War* appeared last Christmas, and got a mixed reception, in the Unionist and English press it was favourably reviewed, and the Protestants of the East and South of Ireland, – I do not know of the North, – read it with pleasure. Some of them sent me letters of thanks and congratulation. The Irish Catholic laity, moreover, – those, that is, of the business and better classes, who are still in favour of the old Home Rule policy, of Imperial union with Great Britain, – were pleased; and no small number of the senior clergy shared in this sentiment. Some of them assured me that they had read the book with delight and agreed with every word.

What the feelings of the Bishops were may be imagined. Cardinal Logue, I noticed, went out of his usual way, when here on one or two occasions, to pay some little attention to me. One or two more of their Lordships called at my rooms, to which I was more or less confined by illness; but did not mention the book. A colleague on the staff of the College told me that a certain Bishop had spoken of it to him, asking what had induced me to write the book. His Lordship, my colleague said, was kind enough to add that he was quite sure I did so to make what protest I could in the interest of what I deemed the truth.

The great body of the clergy were, undoubtedly, hurt and hostile – even those who were opposed to Sinn Fein. They had withstood Conscription; priding themselves that in opposing that measure they had done very great national service and achieved a national triumph. And here was one from their own ranks who denied, and even derided, either triumph or service, and what was more vexatious, made the arguments on which they relied look very silly. It was not pleasant to be shown up for fools or cowards just when they had taken such a fine pose as patriots. They were ready to explode with anger, but dare not do so, except in private.

A clerical friend told me that when somebody spoke of the book in a little assembly of Dublin priests, of whom he was one, the subject was tabooed; such a book should be allowed to sink into the oblivion which it merited, and which was sure to be its fate. This, apparently, was the cue, even among the lower clergy, who seemed to have adopted it by a kind of instinct. When I was among my own priest friends in Ossory, during the Christmas holidays, they did not even refer to the book, which was then selling rapidly and being much talked of in Dublin and London. They had made up their minds, I believe, that it was unworthy of me; and that, not only as an Irishman, but as a scholar, I had lost by the publication. A leader of their group had suffered eclipse; and they were sorry, for him and for the whole group which he used to represent.

Among higher churchmen, – the Bishops who had opposed conscription and were coquetting with Sinn Fein, and the satellites who orbed round their Lordships, – expecting, some of them, to become Bishops or high dignitaries themselves, possibly, – the word evidently had gone forth that the book was to be left severely alone; not to be written about, nor even spoken of, except in private; and not much even there. In a short notice that appeared in *The Month,* the writer said that the author's 'boldness was never so manifest as in this deliberate challenge to beliefs which are almost axiomatic among his brethren. He challenges them all, Bishops, Professors, Editors, Politicians – challenges them mostly by name, and no doubt the lists will soon be thronged by eager combatants. If his attack calls forth (as Sir Horace Plunkett's attack inspired that masterpiece, *Catholicity and Progress in Ireland*) a reasoned and temperate statement of Ireland's case, devoid of mere sentiment and 'sun-burstry', it will do much good'. Unfortunately I cannot claim credit on that ground, except for having done my best: there was no answering masterpiece, nor any answer at all! Must not the word have gone forth – to keep silent?

I had challenged the *Irish Ecclesiastical Record;* but they had not even a review of the book in return for the copy which was sent for that purpose. I was told that the Editor was offered an article in reply; not by Dr. Coffey, but by another colleague of distinction. The article did not appear; suppressed, it was added, by episcopal advice, or authority. I do not guarantee the truth of these reports; but is it any wonder we should credit them when there was not even a word of notice of such a book in such circumstances.

I had challenged the Editors of the *Irish Theological Quarterly;* who got a copy for review, but there was not even a word of notice. I had challenged the writer of an article in *Studies;* sent them a copy for review; but here again neither review nor notice. Not a word. Where were the champions whom the writer in *The Month* hoped to find crowding the lists in such ardour for attack? The Editor of that Journal, I was told, was himzelf very wroth with me for the attack I had made on Fr. Lehmkuhl, S.J., and through him on the moralists of the Society, for teaching folk how to defraud Governments; and threatened some terrible things in the next or some early number. I was told to look out; and did look; but either the Editor's courage oozed out, or he was restrained by less ardent members of the Society, who may have thought that it did not stand to gain by any controversy on the matter, and that it was better to let sleeping dogs lie. Any way, *The Month* did not take up the challenge.

Why did they spare me? Some, no doubt, those who had been challenged, had been old pupils, admirers, and friends of mine; and would, as I believe, hit me hard only with great reluctance. Would they not have hit me, all the same, in the interest of Sinn Fein; however sorry they might be to destroy my reputation? Some of their Lordships, the Bishops, I have no doubt had, and have, friendly feelings towards me; some of them in their day, were colleagues on the Maynooth staff; others read under me on the Dunboyne. This, however, did not restrain them, on occasion, from smiting me in worse way. Was it, then, some remnant of a grace of courtesy, or of ancient friendship, that bade them now suffer eclipse themselves rather than see my reputation injured? It would be nice to think so; but I do not believe it true.

If then, there was no answer to my challenge, it can have been only that it was felt that there was none to give; that the Professors, Editors, Politicians, Bishops, had put themselves in a hopeless position, making use of rotten arguments, bogus history, indefensible ethics. It was not pleasant; and no wonder it was deemed the wisest course to say just nothing at all. How, indeed, could Bishops, Canonists, Theologians, argue that the Imperial Parliament had no authority to enact conscription for Ireland, seeing that the Holy See had decided officially that the *de facto* government of this country is legitimate? To get at me, they must hit at Rome; and no one who knows the higher ecclesiastics of Ireland would ever deem them capable of folly such as that.

Their cue was to belittle me. If they could not answer the book, they might hope, at least, to diminish its influence by attacking the personal character of the author. And, quite characteristically, the attack was made with a bludgeon. 'No one who knows the erratic history of Dr. MacDonald heeds what Dr. MacDonald writes. As the author of the notorious work, *Motion,* condemned by the Church, he long since ceased to write or speak with authority as a Catholic theologian. That people who know nothing of Dr. Mac-

Donald's history may be inclined to treat him seriously, is a calculation that the firm of Burns and Oates no doubt duly made. Ignorance, flippancy, vanity and personal animus – and perhaps Episcophobia, to coin a word – are the marks of this shallow pamphlet. The Rev. Dr. Coffey, a brother-professor at Maynooth, and the Hierarchy generally, are the main targets for Dr. MacDonald's jibes... The vanity that makes the personal pronoun 'I' dominate every page is pathetic; but the ignorance that sets down falsehood after falsehood as fact, and on their basis founds an argument, is truly contemptible'.

Who could be expected to waste good paper and ink on such an author and such a production? In Ireland, we are inclined to plume ourselves on meeting an adversary with what we call silent contempt, especially when we do not feel that we can knock him down; and that was found the safest way to meet my poor self.

As Dr. Coffey's name appeared so much in these discussions, I deem it well to place on record here my sincere conviction that he had no part whatever in those anonymous attacks. He and I had had a controversy before; which was conducted, I am glad to say, in the true scientific manner. Dr. Coffey is not the man to attempt bludgeoning under protection of a mask.

Political prejudice seems to have blinded the Sinn Feiners to what I regard as a rather notable development in Catholic ethics; so notable that it would hardly be allowed to pass unchallenged by the Hierarchy in other days. For the second time I preached the doctrine of revolution, without being called to order; first when the article on 'The Hazel Switch' appeared. For this I should almost certainly have been carpeted were it not that the Trustees of the College had enough to do at the time in dealing with Dr. O'Hickey.

Some years afterwards – during the course of the Great War, I fancy – we heard that Cardinal Logue had written to the President of the College, in great concern over a report which had come to him, to the effect that some professor of Theology had been teaching that it was lawful at times to revolt from what had up to then been legitimate sovereignty, and that in this way we could justify the great French Revolution, or also that of New England under Washington. It was what the professor in question had learned from me on the Dunboyne, and which I have set forth, without protest, in this little book on *Peace and War*. Cardinal Logue, when he wrote that letter, did not, I believe, refer to me; but as he threatened to make visitation of our College, and punish severely all who should be found to have propounded doctrine so much opposed to the Catholic tradition, I could not hope to escape. Wiser counsels prevailed; or perhaps, changed political conditions in Ireland gave his Eminence more serious cause for anxiety, and so we were saved from the need of defending the new development. And as we could not, and would not, deny that it was a development and new – I take some little pride in being the first Catholic theologian, as far as I know, to proclaim the principle – we should have found our work cut out for us, and probably have failed, as I failed to justify so many other departures from tradition.

Now, I hope, there is no further danger, as the book on *Peace and War* has passed so many censors; and the Catholic Theology, for the first time, has found place for the doctrine that political sovereignty, which was quite legitimate and morally unassailable up to a certain stage of its duration, may at that stage become illegitimate, making it lawful for the subjects to throw off the yoke then, if they can, without doing greater mischief thereby.

Instead of thanking me for this, for their most valuable principle, Sinn Fein – as represented by its foremost exponents in the *Catholic Times* review of my book – shut their eyes, and relied on the old and foolish doctrine of no legitimate sovereignty without consent of the governed: false in history as it is in ethics, and almost no less opposed to the tradition of the Catholic schools.

Coming back to that charge of episcophobia, one wonders what did the writer, or his clerical inspirers, mean. 'Fear of Bishops', would be the natural translation; but was it I who feared their Lordships? – I, who, as the critic in *The Month* bears testimony, had challenged their Lordships into the lists? How often had I faced them, to tell them to their faces, what so few will dare to do, that they were reprehensible. Those colleagues of mine – who, as they pretended, were burning for a tilt with me – restrained this martial ardour in obedience to the Bishops: it is the one reason they give for their silence. Yet it is I, not they, who are characterized by 'fear of Bishops'.

Or is it hatred and jealousy of some kind rather than fear which they would impute to me? Soreheadedness, because I had no chance of becoming Bishop myself, or of obtaining from their Lordships the office of President or Vice-President in our College, which had been conferred, in my time, on so many of my juniors? This view, I know, is common enough with priests outside the College – those who can conceive of nothing better than being made a Bishop; and who, if they dare not hope for that, can look forward at least to the prospect of being made a canon, perchance even of being called Monsignor. It does not, I hope, prevail within the College, even among those who attacked me over *Peace and War*.

How little those good priests outside know of my view of life!

As if I cared for episcopal grandeur, or power, or as if I should not feel positively stifled by the petty details of administration whereby their Lordships are occupied. I pity Franzelin for being taken from his desk and pulpit to slave at the routine of Congregational pettiness. Had he been made Pope, the slavery – of audiences, administration, and ceremonial – would be even more intolerable. 'Ministering to tables', instead of dealing with the great fundamental problems of life and soul.

Think of Wiseman, with the genius for literature that produced *Fabiola* in scraps, at spare half-hours, and with the scholarship and eye for world-problems that gave us Lectures of so many kinds; think of the man whose article in the *Dublin Review* shook Newman's soul and at length converted him; think of him taken from his desk to work out the details of the re-establishment of the Hierarchy in England, and at the administration of a diocese like Westminster, poverty-stricken, in the metropolis of the wealthiest and most anti-Catholic people in the world! They took a round peg and put it into a square hole, and were surprised that he who could do so many hard things brilliantly was a failure in administration and died of a broken heart! If he was to have his English College, why did they not make him professor somewhere, and get some ordinary hack, with talents for administration, to do the work which was to be done in London? What a legacy he would have left us had he been allowed to remain at his books!

My office of College Librarian makes it part of my duty to superintend the administration of the small sum allowed for the Libraries. It is administration enough for me; I hate it. What on earth should I do if forced into the Presidency, or to become a Bishop? I should certainly resign. And yet these good priests find the key to what they deem my vagaries in soreness of head because I was not 'promoted' to the office of looking after all those petty details!

Is not the explanation much more simple, and, therefore, much more likely to be true, though creditable to me: honest love for the episcopacy and the Bishops, as also for the Papacy and the Popes, leading to sincere regret that Popes and Bishops should be taking up indefensible positions, in the line of Church diplomacy and even that of doctrine? Few professors, I dare to say – in all humility – have left in our College a record fairer than mine, of obedience to the rules and regulations made by the Trustees, whereever these rules did not, in my opinion, conflict with some more important and urgent principle. No President found me insubordinate or disrespectful, though I have resisted Presidents, as has been shown. So, too, I have stood up to Bishops, and even to the

Holy See, but reverently, I hope, and in the exercise of right. We are subjects, but not slaves, of episcopal and papal authority.

History has already judged some of these cases of conflict – that, for instance, over Mr. Parnell. Even their Lordships, I suspect, regret in their own hearts the precipitate and harsh measures they took with Dr. O'Hickey. As a result of our last conflict over the *Motion* question, they had to leave me alone, to teach almost formally the doctrine which they had insisted had been condemned in that volume. Many good judges now admit that it was a mistake not to have come to terms with Trinity College; and more still are being convinced that all is not right with the managerial question. The *Irish Theological Quarterly* has not been setting the world on fire since, despite my protest, it was taken under the protection of their Lordships; and the New Code of ecclesiastical law has left us with the old abuses of patronage, finance, and even of punishment without real trial. Parish priests may now be deprived of their benefices almost at the episcopal will, while Bishops are being appointed with increasing disregard for public opinion; and, should the new regulations for the United States be adopted here, as is to be expected, their Lordships can appoint their own successors practically, and the government of the Church will pass more and more into the hands of a ring. For having stood up against all that, reverently and modestly, to the best of the weak power allowed one in my position, I do not apprehend very severe judgment when I pass into the beyond.

That Bishop who asked my colleague why I wrote and published the book on *Peace and War* was good enough to add that he was convinced, from intimate knowledge of me, I did it altogether in the interest of truth. Right; but his Lordship might have added that I did it also in the interest of the Bishops, and of the Church which they govern. Since it is governed by them, not only in the domain of practical life, but in that of what we may call speculative thought, it is of the utmost importance that their character as thinkers should stand high; that they should not regard party shibboleths, only too often false; not compete with politicians for favour, by taking up whatever cry may be popular for the moment. I am not the man to deny the episcopacy, Bishops, and clergy a right to interfere in politics, especially where religious interests are concerned; but neither can I shut my eyes to the fact that their religious interests are too often used as a cloak, and that Bishops have acted merely as politicians while claiming to act in the interest of religion. Nothing almost could bring more damage ultimately to the Church and religion which we all desire to serve.

I saw, with disgust, Irish Bishops, both here and in the United States and elsewhere, use claptrap phrases – about self-determination, rights of nations, government by consent, and other such catch-words – good enough for President Wilson or Mr. Lloyd George, but unworthy of men who are supposed to have mastered the science of ethics as taught in our schools. In the use of these phrases, only too often in a sense which is false, our Bishops were competing for popular favour with political leaders: becoming, in fact, demagogues, while they should remain Bishops. By showing how false the position was, and how inconsistent with the teaching of their Irish predecessors, I hoped to apply some restraint, to do some little thing to keep the leaders in this kind of politico-episcopal agitation from making too great a display of the politician that was in them. You could not get them to write even the shortest article in ecclesiastical science for the *Irish Ecclesiastical Record*, for which they had no time, while they had time, and taste, to turn out letters and speeches on almost any aspect of the Irish Question. As if, indeed, they were members of Parliament. I hated all that, would have done so, even though the arguments they used were valid, but hated it especially for the error that was contained in these pronouncements, some of them emanating from the whole body of the Hierarchy. I need not specify which errors: they are set forth plainly in the book on *Peace and War*.

I had hoped that, after that exposure, there would be more caution as to the use of catch-phrases concealing falsehood; but the desire of shining in public, in the only way open to men who have given up scientific study, is not so easily restrained. While *Peace and War* was selling and being read, the Bishops – or some of them – practically forbade anyone on their side to attempt an answer: they met in Maynooth, towards the end of January, 1920, to consider the Education Bill then proposed by the Government. But first they must utter a pronouncement on the state of the country, wherein one could record 'the acknowledged right of every civilized nation... to choose its own government'; as also the principle that 'government by force, which was never right, is to-day wholly obsolete, and cannot hope to prevail for long against the democratic spirit now animating the world'. This from men boasting a divine commission to preach that the civil power 'beareth not the sword in vain'; and who must know that all through the Middle Ages, when Europe was ruled according to the mind of the Church, little heed was given to the consent of subject people!

I hated, and hate, all this kind of thing, as tending to degrade the Bishops to the level of politicians. I hate it, in the same way, as affecting professors in a College such as ours: men who, of all others, should cultivate accuracy and definiteness of thought. My gorge rose, for that reason, against the articles by Dr. Coffey and Father Finlay – that they, scientific men, should take up the clap-trap of politicians: false ethics and bogus history. I thought I should do one man's part to withstand the rot; and I did. Should it continue, despite my protest, I, at least, am not responsible. That is really how the book on *Peace and War* came to be written and published.

I am now passing through the Press a companion volume on *The Social Question*, mainly with a view to giving restraining advice to priests. How they will take it time alone can tell. Many, of course, will deem it impertinence on my part, and resent it. Others, possibly, may take it better. God grant that this be so. As for me, personally, it makes little matter. Even though I were to live I should not care much for their displeasure; which, as I am to die so soon, will have little effect when I have passed beyond the veil.

I am to die soon; and, perhaps, as Lochiel's bard thought, in the sunset of life we may be gifted with special insight into the future, somewhat akin to prophetic vision; or, at least, a dying man may utter warnings with more effect than if he had promise of many years before him. Anyway, I will say that I face death with much less fear than I should have had years ago – than I had when facing it in typhoid fever; though that was in the beginning of my course, when tradition still retained almost its full hold upon me. The arguments whereby my doubts were settled then, would, I greatly fear, no longer pacify: I am not so much under the influence of tradition.

Happily, for myself, I have found peace and confidence otherwise – by discarding such parts of the tradition as I cannot honestly harmonize with facts or principles which I can no longer refuse to admit. I do not mean to specify them; but apparently, they give no trouble in the Sacred Congregation of the Holy Office or to the Biblical Commission. To me, still, the Bible is God's word – the whole Bible; but I find therein no little of the human element, serving as crust or chrysalis to the word. How I reconcile things is largely my own discovery, set forth, imperfectly, in a paper on Inspiration in my unprinted volume of *Essays on Religion and the Church*. In other parts of the same book I have indicated how, in the last resort, I meet difficulties arising from official teaching, some of which, though enforced by anathema, honest minds may not be able to accept in the days that are coming.

There are, I fancy, plenty of men like me, not in Ireland, perhaps, but on the Continent of Europe and in America, who feel the pressure of these difficulties, as poor Mivart felt them in his closing days. And the number of such afflicted ones is growing, even, I fear, in Ireland, which, after all, though set out so far from the main currents of thought, yet cannot hope to escape altogether from their action. Those tons of literature which are landed daily at our quays will have their effect despite what Vigilance Associations may be established to resist them.

Comfortable Bishops, Cardinals, Consultors, and such – who became what they are because they never had a difficulty – will not see the danger coming, as their predecessors could not foresee the Reformation, and as the counsellors and parasites of the Bourbons could not imagine a Revolution. Congregations and commissions would have us depend almost altogether on tradition, and shut our eyes to difficulties which strike us in the face. Was St. Paul right in his outlook on the pagan world of Greece and Rome? Were these poor idolators as inexcusable as he represents them? His view, no doubt, is that of the old Hebrew prophets, in their judgment on the Philistine and other surrounding peoples; but did these really worship stocks and stones, or rather some occult supernatural power which they, however foolishly, conceived to dwell in, or be symbolized by, the material object which they worshipped, as a crucifix or a Bible enshrines for Catholics a hidden God? Was Samuel ethically right in pressing Saul with threats of Javeh's supreme displeasure, for not having put to death even the women and babes whom he had taken from Amalec?

Are we bound to the arguments for the existence of God set forth in the Book of Wisdom, or by St. Paul (Acts xiv. 16)? Was Cainan – who, in St. Luke's Gospel, appears among the progenitors of our Lord – a real personage; or did the authors of the Septuagint, from which St. Luke quotes, insert him by mistake? Is Razias praised for having committed suicide manfully and as befitted noble birth? Did the human writer or writers of Genesis mean to teach that the world was made in six days of twenty-four hours, that the deluge was absolutely universal and destructive of the life of land animals everywhere, that any species that survived did so through being brought into the ark, that all men of the time were present at the building of Babel, and that it was there and then diversity of tongues arose?

These are specimens. One knows that there have been answers, which satisfied our fathers: as that God could have placed fossils in the earth to try our faith. He could, of course; but did He? Can one now rely on such a possibility for explanation of the difficulty? So He could have allowed Razias to kill himself, and inspired the Septuagint authorities or St. Luke to correct the Hebrew text of the genealogies. Did He, though? Or is there not need of a more liberal explanation? Could even God command a King to smash the heads of all the babies he might find in the cities of his enemies? Or must we suppose that outrages of the kind were justified or even commanded by an erroneous ethic; which, for greater sanction, was ascribed to divine revelation? These are but a few of the questions that torment, and will continue to torment, honest students of the Bible, who dare not face the judgment beyond relying on the solutions that satisfied a Pereira or an A Lapide.

So too, in the early history of the Church, and especially of the Papacy and the Episcopacy: when there were no monarchical Bishops anywhere, can we believe there was one in Rome? Did Cyprian and Fulgentius, who recognized no 'Bishop of Bishops', believe in the Primacy of the Successor of St. Peter, as that doctrine is now set forth in the Vatican decrees? Did St. Augustine, with his belief in the necessity of divine charity, recognize the sufficiency of attrition to remit mortal sin? Or if charity was necessary, did he think mortal sin first remitted by the Sacraments? Were, in fact, sacraments of the dead instituted and administered for the remission of guilt, or only for that of punishment, and for the giving of graces to lead a purer life in future?

And, then, grace and virtues: supernatural qualities? But what is a quality, and how does it contribute to action? How does grace operate, and when is it given: before, or after, justification? Can human souls be supernaturalized in part – in the intellect, while the will remains in its natural state? Where does the supernatural begin in the roots of faith? Can faith be lost without formal mortal sin? and what is the testimony of modern life in this respect? What is mortal sin, indeed? How does it stand with regard to charity – in its commission and its remission?

When trouble arises, as it will, over certain Church definitions with anathema attached, the standard and great test case, I fancy, is likely to be that decree of the Council of Vienne, as to the human soul being substantial form of the body. That the Council taught it to be so in some sense I take as evident from the words of the decree; as also that the definition is one of supreme authority, claiming infallibility. Is it infallible? Is it even true?

In what sense is the soul a substantial form of the body? Or in what sense is the matter of which the body is composed –

chemical ingredients, such as are found in the inorganic world – in need or capable of a substantial form? Is it that the soul acts as a source of energy? But is there any smallest fragment of the energy of the human body – nerves or muscles – that does not come into it from the ether, as to any other machine. Conscious sensation, you will say; but is there any sensation that does not reside in the nervous system, consisting entirely of material motions, which, no less surely than the movements of a blacksmith's arm, arise chemically?

They tell us now, from Rome, that this difficulty has been cleared up, by discovery of the writings of John Peter Oliver; which, however it may have decided the question in dispute between Cardinal Zigliara and Fr. Palmieri, S.J., has left the real difficulty precisely where it was. In what sense, capable of being brought into harmony with modern biological science, is the human soul substantial form of the body wherewith it is united? Should we have to find a Liberal solution here, or with regard to Bible difficulties and those of early Church history, the wedge thus introduced will make fissures and pathways hitherto undreamt of in Catholic schools.

On these and many such questions I have found peace at length, on lines no little divergent from the tradition. I do not in the least suggest that I have been able to clear up all difficulties, or that the lines of solution which I have reached will stand the test of future criticism. Nothing stands entire – not even the theory of gravitation as propounded by Newton. All I know is that, whereas I could not face the judgment to come with any real confidence, basing on the old traditional answers to those questions, I have some assurance on the new lines, though I know well that the real solution, which it is revealed beyond, will be unlike in many ways to what I forecast here. I have reached peace, after mighty storms of fear and trouble; but how many other souls are still tossed on the waters, or have found peace of a kind only by abandoning all supernatural religion? The good, safe, comfortable men who rule our councils might think of these and have some pity. God does not deny grace, they say, to who does not willingly desert Him; but do not plenty deny and desert Him only after years of agonized effort to reconcile the irreconcilable? Why not face this significant and awful fact?

I have done my best, and the result will be found, in great part, in the unpublished books which I leave behind. Other part of the scheme of settlement is indicated vaguely, or not at all. For some such thoughts the time is not ripe, but it will come. I should dearly love to see these volumes published, but must pass away without hope of that. They might do a little to withstand the Revolution, which the official guardians of our religion will not see coming, or will endeavour to keep out with their broomsticks. Good men, animated by the best of motives, but so short-sighted, and so cruel, too, in their religious blindness to such as cannot shut their eyes. So God permits – no doubt for wise purposes; blessed always be His holy will.

Episcophobia! Yes, I have faced Bishops, and their Masters, being worsted in the conflict, and, as I believe, injured grievously. Not maliciously, however: the men who struck hardest at me did it in good faith. I do not blame them, nor desire to see them punished, however I may feel aggrieved. May they live long and rule happily, but may they be punished also, by having their eyes opened to the evil they had done unwittingly, not to me only – for that counts little – but to the cause of Truth. The shame of such revelation, when it comes, as come it will, is more than enough of punishment.

THE END

'THE HAZEL SWITCH'

(See page 241)

I have heard or read somewhere of a boy who took his whipping, though undeserved, in silence, but could not repress a protest against the lecture with which it was accompanied. This article is prompted by a kindred feeling. Some of us in Ireland could bear, and have borne, being skinned by foreigners: their added sermons are too much for our flesh and blood.

What, then, is your ethical creed, O Mr. Birrell, my Lord Clonbrock, and you pure-souled scribblers of the British and West-British Press? Tell us: is it always immoral to disregard the law? You lecture us as if you would have us believe it: do you believe it yourselves?

Who are they whom you delight to honour? and what have they done? Pym, Hampden, and Cromwell with his Roundheads; Trelawney and the Cornish thirty thousand; the Prince of Orange, Washington, Mazzini, Gambetta, Kossuth; not to speak of Mirabeau and those who bridled the French monarchy, or the wilder successors by whom the great Revolution was completed. Did they not one and all dance and spit upon the law? and is it not for doing so you hold them up for veneration? Yet you lecture us if in our poor, weak way we copy the models you present to us: wherein do we wrong you in deeming this hypocrisy?

Tell us, you mock Tories and canting Whigs: when and where was there a revolution, successful or unsuccessful, which you do not approve – outside of Ireland? Your own history is a series of rebellions: 'freedom slowly broadening down', one of your poets calls it. And through what precedents! One king's head lopped off; another hunted into exile – not with hazel; loyalist blood shed in torrents, you know in how many English and Scottish battles. The blood of your own fathers flowed: at Drogheda, Limerick, and many Irish towns; by the Boyne, at Aughrim, and on other Irish fields. It was your ancestors who shed it: you, their sons, approve of what they did – the substance, anyway; you swear that in like circumstances you would do the same; it is the lesson you teach your children – you who lecture us on the atrocity of hazel switches. No wonder that English spells hypocrite throughout the civilized world, outside of England: as you know it does.

You English Radicals, what political method do you believe in? Was it immoral to pull down the Hyde Park railings? and were it not for that threatened outburst and others like it, would your trade unions be legal now? You know full well that, if your masters could, they would put you in jail for strikes and picketing. And they could, and would, only that you learned to disregard their law.

Is passive-resistance moral, O ye righteous Dissenting ministers? And you again, O Mr. Birrell, was not it out of respect for lawlessness that you framed the Bill that sent you over here to fleece and lecture us? We could bear the fleecing, seeing that you do it tenderly as may be, and that you are under orders; but spare us, pray, the nausea of passive-resistance sermons on regard for law.

You ask us, working-men of England, to join you in a crusade against the House of Lords: but tell us how we may bring them to their knees. We know a little of Lords in Ireland; and our experience is – is it not the lesson of history? – that unjust rulers, masters, holders of every kind, laugh you to scorn unless you can take them by the throat. The Lords are in legal possession of what you would wrest from them – rights far more valuable than those of Irish ranchers. They cannot be made to yield legally without their own consent, and they are not likely to consent except under pressure. Admit honestly that you want us to join with you in applying this illegal pressure, to present pistols at holders of legal rights in England – you who object to the use in Ireland of the hazel switch.

Sinn fein, sinn fein, I hear you cry, you young Irish Catholics; it is for our own we care, not for the Saxon. It is our own fathers, the priests and Bishops of Ireland, that would have us renounce the hazel; and how can we turn a deaf ear to them? Are they not set over us by God to be our guides?

Yes, they are your guides and fathers, whom you do well to heed; but as you have proved dutiful children, you may surely ask them to have pity on you – to weigh your plea and think well of your condition before they condemn. What is it, then, that is denounced as wrong?

Is it, Most Reverend and Reverend Fathers, any part of the creed you teach us, that in the evolution of society the common weal may not demand at times that holders of political power and proprietorial rights should surrender part to those who have had no share hitherto? In England, for instance, the absolute power with which the Tudors ruled was wrested from their successors by the landlords and the merchants, who in turn were forced to share with the common people. The change was the result of pressure, which was always illegal and at times expensive: was it, however illegal, always unjust? So, too, in economics: employers everywhere have been forced to share with their workmen some of their most cherished rights and privileges; forced under pressure which the employers, without whose consent no law could be repealed or enacted, had taken good care to make illegal: was it in every case wrong as well? Are the Russians, however cultured they may become, bound for all time to autocratic Tsars? It is quite too childish to expect autocrats to resign their power, except under pressure, which they can make illegal – as they have done, and are pretty sure to do. If the United States had not thrown off allegiance, and England did not wish to release them – as she would not, if she could help it – would they be still obliged to take laws from Westminster? Had there been no revolution, would France be bound for ever to the absolute and spendthrift rule of successive Louis? All these changes meant or mean transfer not only of political power but of proprietorial rights, against the will of the holders, who were, or could only be, forced to acquiesce. Is it only the Irish people that are out of reach of this higher evolution law?

Those who denounce the hazel will not dare to tell you that the time is not ripe for the change we press for – the settling of the Irish people on Irish soil. They will say that our pressure hinders rather than helps the process, that the Government is benevolent and should not be embarrassed; and that it is only by conferences and policy we can succeed.

When the representatives of the nations go into conference, they succeed in so far as they have force behind them: that was to be expected, and is the lesson of history. Should you pronounce it immoral for a famished people to have recourse even to hazel switches? – where will you find the force to back your words in conference? And, mind, the hazel is symbolic of the force behind you, whatever it may be, which the Saxon will take care to render illegal, if that is all that is needed to make it melt away.

That is likely to be the cry of those who would smile to see you denounce your children: while it is in your ears let it not drown another cry. Listen to this as it rises from far-off cities: filthy, drunken, blasphemous yells, from lips that were as pure as cowslips while they breathed the air of the Irish hills. Much good it did them to beg for justice – with no force behind them to back the pleading. Is it among them you would send us, you who always counselled us to stay at home? Do you not see the famished cheeks and eyes of those of us who heeded you, for whom it is now a choice between the hazel and foreign slums? We have lived for you; we would gladly die for you – the death of the body: must we poison even our souls and those of our children, lest we disobey?

Think of all this, Fathers dear, ere you condemn us, and ask yourselves, before the great Father of the poor, what will avail Saxon promises or even Saxon gifts, if we, your children, are driven over sea? They will keep the promises – if you can make them: how many pledges have they not already broken? When you want force to back your words or keep them to theirs, where will you find it, if now you condemn as immoral what is symbolized by the hazel switch?

Walter McDonald

ACADEMIC EXERCISES AT MAYNOOTH

(See page 219)

Other correspondents will have set forth elsewhere many things which the public may wish to know of our proceedings yesterday; but, as there are matters with which they could not be expected to deal, perhaps your readers may welcome a few lines from one who should be more fully acquainted with the bearing and value of what took place.

And it may be well to bear in mind, in the first place, that the proceedings of yesterday were, to a very great extent, academic – in the sense of not being a real test, any more than they were a real contest. They were not meant to be either. The candidate, no doubt, might have failed to satisfy the Board of Examiners; and, in that case, would not have got the degree; but the likelihood of this was remote. Yesterday was a show day. Dr. Moran's work was tested much more closely, though so much less ostentatiously, last year, when he was recommended by the Faculty of Theology as a candidate for the Doctorate. The display of yesterday showed but very little of the work which he had done.

The character of display attaching to the exercises was emphasized by the use of a language, once virile and subtle, but long stiff and dead, as well as by the syllogistic form which the arguments were made to assume.

(I do not find many syllogisms in the *Summa* of St. Thomas, nor in the works of Suarez, Vasquez, or de Lugo.) Does anyone make use of a series of formal syllogisms in discussing anything in which he has a living interest – on which he feels his life, or his living, or his salvation, to depend? I do not refer to mathetics, where the argumentation is altogether analytical, but only to subjects such as politics, or social questions, or religion, wherein one must have recourse to the opposite – synthetic – process, and derive proof, sufficient to convince in prudence, from a mass of hints and circumstances many of which, taken separately, make but slight impression.

What a prig he would be who should attempt to prove by syllogisms the supernatural mission of Christ, let us say, or that of the Catholic Church. The most specious attacks on both have been made by those who, discarding forms, have piled up hints, suspicions, probabilities, unlikelihoods; ransacking history for evidence of failure in the results of Christ's mission and in those of His Church; as also for proofs such as we are wont to advance in support of all kinds of quacks and impostors. This is the kind of argument that tells, and is telling – the appeal to prejudice, which may not be reduced to syllogistic form. 'By their fruits you shall know them', it has been said; but how shall one show in a syllogism the fruits of a missioner or of a Church? Those who have had real difficulties about religion know how true is the main thesis of Cardinal Newman's *Grammar of Assent* – that is not by syllogisms, or logical and exact reasoning of any kind, such difficulties are met and removed; just as, I suspect, it is not in any dead language one can press the kind of argument that carries conviction where such difficulties are real. Newman could write Latin as well as most, if not better; but how straitened he would have been – that subtle wit of his and keen intellect made stiff and blunt – if he had had to express himself in any other language than that which he had been using from infancy. Think of the *Lectures on Anglican Difficulties* or the *Essay on Development* being written in Latin.

The use of a dead language in our schools and text-books is not, of course, without an advantage; but, as against this, the disadvantage is enormous. I remember reading with great interest the accounts which were published of the proceedings which took place some years ago – I hope they continue still – when a candidate was examined for the degree of Doctor of Divinity at the Catholic Institute of Toulouse. He presented no theses, and had to defend none, other than the book in which he had embodied his claim to the degree. This he had to defend against a board of examiners who parsed him very closely, in French, and without being hampered by syllogistic forms. Though Dr. Moran presented yesterday a very original book, wherein opinions are advanced which some of the examiners, I have no doubt, would be loath to admit, not one objection was raised to any of these opinions. I should have liked to see him tested on *The Government of the Church in the First Century* by some one who held more old-fashioned views than those which he propounds in his essay.

Fortunately for his character, the best of all proof of his qualification for the degree which he obtained yesterday is to be found in this essay of his, where the evidence may be sifted by all who can read English and take any interest in one of the most fundamental questions of theological science. The Church of to-day presents itself as a great world-wide or catholic organization, composed of smaller, local, bodies – dioceses and provinces – 'fitly joined together' so as to form an organic whole – one Church or Kingdom of God, just as the British Empire is made up of a number of cities, counties, nations, each with its own separate rights and government, but all bound together under the one imperial sceptre and acknowledging the one flag. Dioceses, provinces, and Church Catholic, go back to apostolic times, and were governed then, as now, by authority deriving from Jesus Christ. As to the government of the Church Catholic, Dr. Moran says little in his essay, confining himself almost entirely to the diocesan jurisdiction, which, in the Catholic Church, is held at present almost altogether by Bishops, the other clergy of the diocese being guided and ruled by them. It is known that this was not always so; that the cathedral chapters, and before they were instituted the priests of the various dioceses, held, with the Bishops, great part of the diocesan authority. The Bishops have gradually appropriated all this jurisdiction, and the possibility is suggested that the process may have been going on from the beginning; so that if we were to go back far enough – to apostolic times – we might find that the whole of the diocesan authority was held in common by all the priests of the diocese.

The Presbyterians hold that not only was this so, in every case, but that it was so essential to the divine constitution of the Church that it could not be modified; so that the monarchical episcopate or prelacy which was actually developed had no authority, as being opposed to the Divine ordination. As against this, the great body of the Catholic writers maintained that no modification or development was needed, as the diocesan jurisdiction was held from the beginning by Bishops who wielded it monarchically – a single Bishop holding it in each diocese. And so the controversy went on.

Recent criticism inclines to the view that both parties had some right – and some wrong, too – on their side; that, except in a few of the great central churches, such as Jerusalem, Antioch, Rome, Alexandria, and Ephesus, the diocesan jurisdiction was held, in apostolic times, by the priests of the diocese in common, but that this was altogether a matter of ecclesiastical arrangement; so that when great part of the power in question had been duly prescribed by the Bishops, it belonged to them alone, to the exclusion of the other clergy. Dr. Moran is inclined to accept this compromise as representing what held in the ordinary dioceses, to the exclusion, that is, of the great central sees.

As regards these, there can be no doubt that St. James held at Jerusalem some kind of place of his own, peculiar to himself, to the exclusion of the presbyters of that city. History and analogy lead us to believe that the same is true of Antioch, Alexandria, Ephesus, Rome, and, later, of Carthage and Lyons. St. Ignatius, Bishop of Antioch, calls himself Bishop of Syria: can it be that there was but one diocese in all that prosperous and extensive province? Or was it, rather, that the Bishop of Antioch held provincial jurisdiction over all the other dioceses of Syria? Similarly, the Bishop of Alexandria ruled over all Egypt, in which, as in Syria, there must have been many flourishing churches. St. James, at Jerusalem, held jurisdiction over all Palestine – perhaps, even over the Jews of the dispersion: is it that in Palestine there was no diocese but that of Jerusalem? The most likely view is that the provincial organization went back almost to the beginning, and that jurisdiction over the province was held by the Bishop of its central see, who, no doubt, was assisted by his presbyters, as the Roman Pontiff at present is by the cardinals. This, I take to be Dr. Moran's view.

There is, however, one point which, as far as I can see, he has not made clear: Whether the merely diocesan – as distinguished from the provincial – jurisdiction of the great sees was shared by the presbyters of the diocese. It looks as if that were so at Jerusalem, about which we have had many details in the Acts of the Apostles. St. James, no doubt, presided – and was entitled to preside – at the meetings of the clergy of that church; but, apart from this right to preside – which accrued to him, most likely, in view of his greater position – he does not appear to have had any purely diocesan jurisdiction that was not shared by his presbyters. So that the monarchical (diocesan) jurisdiction which he held would seem to have been very limited. The same would hold of the other great central sees.

So far, as regards jurisdiction; but there is a question also as to the power of order: whether in apostolic times all presbyters received the full character of the priesthood, which Bishops receive to-day, so that in the Apostolic Churches all the presbyters could, and did, ordain their successors. Or was it only the Bishops of the central sees who could then confer orders; or some other ecclesiastics, with special commission, and special powers, such as St. Timothy, St. Titus, and others had? Dr. Moran inclines to the latter view. Those who may be interested in the question will find it very fairly discussed in his book.

I have been looking forward a long time to the day when the entire question – of the powers of the presbyterate in the Apostolic Churches – would be fully and frankly examined in English by one who had read and mastered all that has been written on the subject, by the ablest and most recent English, French, and German critics; and now I am fairly satisfied. Not, of course, that the last word has been said; for Dr. Moran, I have no doubt, will make some changes in, and additions to, his work in future editions. I am satisfied that, even as it now stands, it is a first-rate presentation, at once learned and critical, of the Catholic position; and that nothing which has been put forward on the other side has been left unconsidered or unanswered. I am satisfied, above all, to let this essay stand as evidence of the kind of work that is being done by those of whose studies I have principal charge on the Dunboyne establishment of Maynooth College.

THE SYMPATHETIC STRIKE

(From the *Leader,* October-November, 1913)

I

From the Workman's Point of View

Having so often condemned the sympathetic strike, you will, I hope, allow one who does not think of it so badly, to say a few words on the other side. And let me commence by remarking that I am not a workman, unless in the sense that I have to work for a living, with my brains, and sometimes with a pen. I have never had any share in a sympathetic strike; neither am I likely to have. I have never, to my knowledge, set eyes on Mr. Larkin, or any other of the Labour leaders, in Dublin or elsewhere. I believe they and those who are led by them have made mistakes; like all other revolutionists. If they are Socialists, however, or Anarchists, or Syndicalists, as they sometimes profess, they do not, I fancy, object to all law, order, and proprietorial rights – for the present. I should not hesitate to entrust Mr. Larkin with my spoons, or even with my purse. We are all, I hope, Socialists, Anarchists, Syndicalists, of a type.

As for the sympathetic strike, moreover, I confess that I regard it as a dreadful evil, and that I hate it as such; just as I hate war and strife of every kind – including strikes, even when they are not sympathetic. Most wars, I fancy, are unjust, on both sides; as are most strikes and lock-outs; which is an additional reason for hating them. Yet I am no Quaker; but think wars and strikes may be just – as the less of two evils. You, I take it, will agree with this.

It is not, however, for every trifling, though real, grievance a State may go to war or a trade union go on strike: there must be proportion between the grievance and its remedy. Whereupon some logical Quaker asks us: How are we to draw the line? What you would say to the Quaker, you will, please, take as said in reply to the same question when put by yourself – as you have put it.

Few good things may not be pushed too far: is it any wonder that the same should hold of wars and strikes of every kind? Theoretically, we hear, the British Constitution is unworkable; and theorists, in France and elsewhere, would have us draw up lines for everything; but see how this theoretically unworkable Constitution does work, notwithstanding; and all the more smoothly and efficiently that British statesmen have wisely determined to draw lines only as questions arise. So, perhaps, it may be possible to say with a fairly safe conscience: A strike is or is not lawful now; without being able to give any cut-and-dry rule for determining whether it is or is not lawful in every case.

But the sympathetic strike is different: so I understand you to say. Do you contend, then, that it is never lawful? If you do not, then it is a question of drawing the line: and where does the difference come in between strike and strike?

I admit, readily, that the sympathetic strike, like all quarrels, may be pushed too far; that, even though it may be right to strike against the railway company A.B., as also against its ally, the shipping company C.D.; it might be wrong to strike against E.F., merely because he travelled or sent goods by either; or with M.N., for having a friendly chat with E.F. No quarrel should be allowed to extend in this way, indefinitely; nor, as far as I know, does anyone maintain the contrary: but may not such quarrels extend a little? Germany, for instance, goes to war with France over the lost provinces, and immediately Russia flies at the throat of Austria; both acting merely in sympathy with their allies. England might become involved, with the benediction of those guardians of morals, the Tory Press; or even far Japan. But while these great powers may, on grounds of sympathy, kill off hundreds of thousands, and starve even more than they kill by bullets, trade unions may not engage in a sympathetic strike. Do you really want the labourers to believe this? Or is it that sympathetic war also is of necessity unjust?

Have you thought out all this? And have you, in addition, thought out the kindred questions that arise in connection with tariff-wars: whether there may be fiscal unions, whose members would be expected to attack and defend one another sympathetically? Then there are questions as to contraband: where are you to draw the line at which belligerents may find a *casus belli* in assistance given to their enemies? And there are questions regarding blockades; which are of special interest in connection with our subjects, as strikes often, of necessity, take that form. You can fight some firms only by closing the paths for ingress and egress of the wares they handle. Are you prepared to say that sympathetic fights are immoral in all these cases? or that they may not be pushed too far? or that they must never be entered on, seeing that no one can draw the line at which belligerents may find a *casus belli* wrong?

If you hesitate why not give trade unions also the benefit of the doubt?

See how the employers have acted, in Dublin, and also in Manchester: they have had no qualms of conscience in having recourse to the sympathetic lock-out. I am prepared to applaud them; as, however I lament it, I applaud war, provided there has been sufficient cause. If the labourers of any city combine to force employers to grievously unreasonable terms; and if the combination can be met only by the sympathetic lock-out; why, then, lock them out, in God's name, and so bring them to reason by hunger; as any nation would, if it could, fight another grievously aggressive nation in the field. Only do not pretend that what is sauce for the goose does not suit the gander. Trade unions have the same right as employers to sympathetic help.

In all wars the real questions at issue are: first, is there sufficient cause for fighting? and, secondly, is there any less evil remedy? Whoever goes to war without grave cause is in the wrong, whether it be a nation, or employer, or trade union; and he is no less wrong who insists on fighting it out when he can right himself by milder means. And will you bear this in mind, in favour of unskilled workmen; that, as their places can be filled by labourers imported from everywhere, it is all the more necessary for them to have recourse to the sympathetic strike? If you do not agree this, will you tell your readers how, otherwise, tramwaymen or railway-porters can hope to force their employers to redress any serious grievance they may have?

I do not wish to take a side on the present lamentable dispute in Dublin; bot being competent, as I profess, to decide whether the lock-out there was or was not justified. An outsider like me had best accept the decision of the Court of Inquiry, which, with all respect to you and others, has not 'condemned the sympathetic strike'; though it holds that in Dublin that mode of warfare has been waged to an unjustifiable extent. I write this article with a single view to principle; nor do I pretend to infallibility. If you or any of your readers can show up my errors, I beg of you to do so; when, I hope, I shall prove of docile mind.

II

When Is It Legitimate?

I congratulate myself on having drawn from you – needlessly; if you will – so explicit a statement that you 'do not hold that a sympathetic strike by workmen is wrong under all conditions and circumstances.' This, of course, does not necessarily mean that you regard a strike of that kind as sometimes legitimate; but I hope I may take it that such is your opinion. So far, then, we are agreed.

I agree with you, moreover, that 'no community can live on a permanent strike and lock-out'; or, as you put it again, that 'a modern city cannot exist with the sympathetic strike as a permanent policy.' Mr. Larkin must be more foolish than I deem him, if even he would not agree to that.

When, accordingly, you state, further, that 'the sympathetic strike is an impossible plank in the labour platform,' I take you to mean that such a weapon while kept in stock, for use on emergencies, should not be employed daily; that it should not even be the ordinary resource of workmen when they disagree with their employers. Does not this, however, apply to every form of strike, the non-sympathetic as well as the sympathetic? The lock-out, similarly, whether sympathetic or non-sympathetic, should not, I take it, be the ordinary resource of employers, even when they and their workmen disagree. Strikes and lock-outs of every kind are war; and the ordinary relations between employers and workmen should be harmonious and friendly. When they disagree, about wages or any other condition of labour, they should discuss the question amicably, giving each other time for reflection, and, where necessary and possible, asking some tribunal or third party to adjudicate between them. They should strive to get on as neighbouring states get on, conducting their ordinary business by way of friendly intercourse and diplomacy, while maintaining an army – represented, in the case of workmen and employers, by the strike and lock-out – for use as a last resort. So reasonable is all this, that I do not suppose it would be called in question by any labour leader, including Mr. Larkin; as long, that is, as employers and employed are supposed to exist.

If, therefore, even the weapon of the sympathetic strike may be kept in stock, by trade unions, for employment in emergencies, the important thing will be to determine when it may be brought forth and used. And, though I do not pretend to have made out any cut-and-dried rule wherewith to decide this in every possible case, I hope to formulate some general principles which may be found serviceable when the time comes for any employer or union to decide.

1. The first condition, I should say, on which a sympathetic strike or lock-out is permissible, is, that what I may call the original strike or lock-out is justified. No individual or body of individuals, including nations, may assist another in unjust quarrel.

283

2. Supposing the original strike to be justified, a further strike, in sympathy, may be directed either (i) against the same opponents as those of the original strike – as when England joins France against Germany, or the guards on some railway strike in sympathy with the engine drivers of the same company; or (ii) it may be directed against a fourth party – as when, France being at war with Germany, Russia attacks Austria, or when the engine-drivers on one railway strike in sympathy with those on another. Let us take these cases separately.

(1) What would justify England in fighting Germany, for no other reason than to assist France? Obviously, if it were of great importance to England that France should not be defeated by Germany. As, of course, it might be, and is. So, I conceive, it may be of vital importance for one trade union to defend another, lest the two rods, taken separately, should be broken in succession. If nations have to cultivate alliances, in selfprotection, how much more necessary is it for smaller and weaker corporations? Alliances, however, whether among nations, trade unions, or individuals, suppose that the allies strike in sympathy in time of need. Accordingly, to justify the guards on a railway in striking in sympathy with the engine-drivers – who are supposed to have had just cause for their own strike – there must be such community of interest as would justify a defensive alliance between the unions. That such community of interest exists between certain unions, and especially between those which work together under the same employer, I have no doubt whatever.

(2) Coming now to the second case above-mentioned – wherein the sympathetic strike is directed against a fourth party, with whom the strikers have no special cause of quarrel – I will ask, taking once more the analogous case of war, what would justify England in fighting Italy, out of pure sympathy with France, should France and Germany be at war? Obviously some close connection between Italy and Germany, and especially if Italy were assisting Germany in its war with France: if, in other words, Germany could not be beaten unless Italy were beaten too.

Similarly, if the tramwaymen of any city were to strike against their employers, and were to get strike pay from the other workers of the city, it might be the interest and the right of the employers of these other workers to assist the tramway company, by locking-out these other workers and so depriving them of power to assist the tramwaymen. This is what has been threatened in Manchester and actually done in Dublin; justifiably, as I think, provided the original quarrel in both places was unjust on the part of the workers. But, then, the parallel is obvious with, and in favour of, the sympathetic strike, should it be on the employers' side that the original injustice was.

Nay, even where a nation is not assisting either of two belligerents, its commerce may be paralysed, legitimately, by one of the belligerents, for the sole reason that this is necessary for this belligerent's purpose. An example will illustrate what I mean. At the time of the American civil war, English commerce depended largely on imports of cotton from the Southern States; so that the blockade of the Southern ports was a severe blow at England, which had no quarrel with the North. So, too, if England went to war with Germany, and Germany were to succeed so far as to blockade Great Britain, it would be a severe blow at all those nations from which England draws her supplies. Would Germany and its allies hesitate to strike in this way at the United States or the Argentine; or even to go to war with them, if they attempted to raise the blockade. Is there not some analogy here with the case of transport workers, who, when they have held up a railway company, may, possibly, be entitled to compel a shipping company not to undo their work.

As against this, the shipping company pleads that it is legally bound to receive goods from the railway company; and that, in any case, it is not just to it to have, not only its trade with this railway company, but its whole trade held up.

To which, if I were acting for the blockading union, I should reply, that it was not the union that imposed the legal obligation of which you complain. If, then, the obligation in question is inequitable as against us – which is our contention – why do you not seek redress from those who bound you to what you have no right to do? Legal obligations are not so sacred that they may not turn out inequitable, or even unjust; and when this happens they are to be treated with contempt.

As regards your complaint that your whole trade is held up, we are very sorry; but there is no other way that we can see to defend ourselves against your inequitable interference with the blockade which we have rightly established. Do your duty, by refusing to receive goods from this railway company, and, as far as we are concerned, you shall be as free as air.

Note, however, in connection with the second form of the sympathetic strike – against a fourth party – that (*a*) there must be a certain closeness of connection between the striking unions, to justify the sympathetic strike; as also (*b*) that there must be some equivalence between the amounts of sympathetic assistance which the unions give one another.

(*a*) The carpenters of Dublin, I fancy, would not be justified in striking in pure sympathy with the bricklayers of Perth – for lack of a sufficiently close connection between the two parties.

(*b*) Neither, as I think, would it be wise policy – and whatever economic policy is unwise is thereby stamped as illegitimate – on the part of transport workers to take up as their own every quarrel of every other trade union, even of their own neighbourhood – carpenters, masons, bricklayers, and the rest. This would leave the transport workers in almost perpetual strike. Though the peoples are all brethren, no one expects England or any other nation to stand in war by every other nation whatsoever that may be unjustly attacked. If transport workers are wise, they will cultivate at least informal alliances, on the only true business basis of such relations – that of getting in time a *quid pro quo;* and they will strike in sympathy only with such other unions as can give them equal assistance whenever they themselves strike for reasons of their own.

It remains to say something about the limits of the sympathetic strike – in radius, as it were. Surely Germany might require the United States to respect a blockade of England, even though the republic might be at liberty to receive or trade with one who had run the blockade, or had bought a shirt made from cotton that had been smuggled into Great Britain. The common sense of nations keeps quarrels of this kind within reasonable limits, as a rule; why should not the common sense of trade unions be relied on to do the same – as a rule? Especially if, as is plainly advisable, strikes were not begun by any private individual, but only by the officials of the unions, after the resources of diplomacy had been exhausted.

HOW I HAVE STUDIED THE SOCIAL QUESTION

(A lecture delivered to the students of St. Mary's Division, Maynooth College, March 14, 1915).

Gentlemen,

You wish, I understand, to get some advice as to how you should
set about studying the Social Question. I do not know how to meet
your wishes better than by telling how I have myself proceeded;
though this, of course, exposes me to the risk of seeming to pose
not only as an expert but as a model. Hence I must begin by saying that I know very little of the question on its economic side.
There is, however, another side, the ethical, to which I have given
some attention; and as it is this alone which you are called on to
study, perhaps it may help you to know how one who lays no claim
to very special knowledge has proceeded in his investigations.

I began, like yourselves, with the treatise on Justice, as set forth
in the class-book of this College; which, in my time, was Gury.
I do not know of any better way of beginning, except, perhaps, to
devote more attention than we did to the title of Occupation; which
I now regard as the key to much of the question at issue between
extreme Socialists and ourselves.

Well, three years after the close of my College course, the Land
League was started; and it was not very long till we heard it argued
that there could be no private property in land, as 'the exertion of
labour in production is the only title to exclusive possession.' I
quote from Mr. Henry George's book on *Progress and Poverty*
(Book VII, Ch. I), which appeared about that time, and of which
we used to hear a great deal. I do not say that this was the official
teaching of the League; but it was certainly proclaimed from many
League platforms, by some of the most active of the new leaders,
who were wont to quote Mr. George, as I have done.

All this raised discussions in clerical circles about the titles to
property: whether one could own merely what one produced, or
what one received, mediately at least. from some producer. I
thought I saw, even then, that one may have a right in what one
occupies, even though one should not have it produced – provided it has not been occupied already; but it was some time before
I came to realize how little property we should have if we were
confined to the product of our own labour. For no one ever yet

produced the least bit of substance, or ever did anything more than change the location of something already produced; and this by means of energies which he does not give out so much as occupy.

'The pen with which I am writing,' Mr. George says (*loc. cit.*), 'is justly mine... because transferred to me by the stationer, to whom it was transferred by the importer, who obtained the exclusive right to it by transfer from the manufacturer, in whom, by the same process of purchase, vested the rights of those who dug the material from the ground and shaped it like a pen.' Alas, the miner who dug out the iron did not make that metal, but only found and occupied it, and then changed its position in space; using for that purpose a number of energies, none of which he produced, but only seized on or occupied; as holds also of the manufacturer, the importer, the stationer, and the rest. Allow them no right to what they occupy, in the way of substance or energy, and they can make, do, or own – just nothing; and if one can occupy and make one's own any part of the forces which God has produced, why not also the substances – including the land – of which He is no less, and no more, the Producer?

Another question akin to the foregoing, was much dilated on by Mr. George and his disciples – that of unearned increment; which, accordingly, was discussed at times in the little circle in which I moved. A strip of land in the City of London, which could be had for almost nothing in Caesar's time, would now make a prince's fortune; and it is not a hundred years since one might have bought for a few dollars all the ground on which the City of Chicago now stands. Some lucky people did get land in these places, and are millionaires in consequence – out of the sweat of those by whom London and Chicago were built up. *Sic vos non vobis fertis aratra boves:* are men like oxen, that they should not own the fruits of their labour? So we used to hear it said.

You should think well over this, as it is deep in many minds – even of those who do not belong to the working classes. It puzzled me for a long time; and does still, somewhat. I know, and have said to myself, that it was much easier to live in Rome than at London at the time of Caesar, as it was, a hundred years ago, to live in London, or even in New York, than in Chicago: it needed an allurement, in the shape of property, to draw men into these wildernesses. Chicago would never have been founded, nor work and livelihood provided there for so many millions, were it not for the attraction of property, just as it took the sheen of gold to lure men across the desert to California, as it allures them to-day to the frozen banks of the Yukon.

All this is most true, but I should like to see further proof that there would not have been sufficient lure to London or Chicago if the first settlers there did not get a right to the place and its increase – every possible increase – for ever. We need a lure for authors and inventors, who must, however, be satisfied with a comparatively short period of exclusive right to the fruit of their labour. Why not put a similar term to the rights of settlers, occupiers, landowners? In old days, the British Government used to reward its great military and naval captains by a pension that passed on for ever from sire to son; but now they give a pension for three generations, or a lump sum once for all; and they have commuted most if not all, of the never-ending pensions of earlier times. Perhaps what is good enough for a Marlborough or a Nelson should have sufficed for the early colonists of America? Or, if these needed a bonus, might they not have an additional generation or two without giving them rights to exclusive possession and all increase for ever and ever?

To come back to Land League days. The success of that body, as you know, was due to the weapon which it employed – the boycott; as to the morality of which there were many discussions, in the newspapers, and in my little circle; but not in books, or in such periodicals as the *Irish Ecclesiastical Record*. Our theologians seem afraid of the subject – afraid to approve of boycotting, and no less afraid to condemn it. They were afraid even to say they were afraid – that they could not or would not, either approve or condemn. In their published work they ignored absolutely a method of agitation of which the newspapers were full; which was fiercely debated in Parliament; and which, in spite of many bitter denunciations, was practised by some of the best and most loyal Catholics in the world.

In private, however, there was not the same reticence; and so, as has been said, the morality of boycotting came up for many a discussion – some heated enough – in the little circle in which I moved. It was contended, by those who denounced the practice, that it meant pressure applied to a man to keep him from doing what he has a strict right to do; for, surely, no one would say that landlords had not a strict right to evict tenants who paid no rent – even though it should be a rack-rent; that 'grabbers' had not a strict right to take the farms thus made vacant; or that dealers and working-men were not within their strict right in doing business for and with the 'grabbers'. To boycott any of these was to restrain them, by moral force, from the exercise of their strict right; and if this is not unjust, how is one to define injustice?

It was some time before I could meet this argument, to my own satisfaction, and perhaps I cannot do so yet; but neither was I allowed to remain blind to the extremes to which it carries one, if pushed to its logical conclusions. When I myself used it one day, in discussion with a friend, he asked me whether I did not see that in all bargains the best of men use pressure to make the other party do what he has a strict right not to do. You ask the price of a horse; fifty pounds, and you turn away, saying you will give only forty, thereby, of course, pressing the owner to sell for less than fifty – a thing which he has a strict right not to do. Here, then, is a case in which one may, without injustice, press another to do what he has a strict right not to do – unless, indeed, you would make all bargaining unjust.

This suggested other cases. Cutting people, or sending them to Coventry, is common enough in society especially, and implies strong pressure, as only those realise who mix in society. No one, however, thinks of insisting that one may cut a man only for doing what is strictly unjust – stealing or the like. This argument was common property.

Another case, to which I saw no public reference, was suggested to me, I know not how, by some incident in the book trade, I think whereby I first learned that publishers must not supply the public at a price which they charge booksellers. Not, surely, that the publisher may not do so without strict injustice; for is not the book his, to give away for nothing, if he likes? But that, though he does no injustice to any one by selling to the public at the price which he received from booksellers, they compel him, by a threat of boycott, to refrain from doing so. This, I soon learned, is a general rule of trade: that manufacturers and wholesale merchants must not supply the public at the price they charge the dealers, under peril of being boycotted by all the dealers in the trade. So that if it is a principle of justice that one must not prevent a man, by pressure, from doing what he has a strict right to do, it is one that is very much honoured in the breach throughout the business world.

When then, is pressure immoral? When is it strictly unjust? It is a question, gentlemen, which, one would think, should be raised in every even elementary treatise on Justice. Yet it is not; or if it is, one has to put on spectacles to find it. Perhaps you have been, or may be, more fortunate in this quest than I; but, if you can satisfy yourself as to the just use of pressure, you may feel pretty sure that you hold the key to a great part of the Social Question.

It was in this way I learned from the Land League – in the great University of life. The next stage in my course began, I think, with a talk I had one day, with a mason, who was engaged in building the MacMahon Hall in this College. The men had had a strike, because the builder had taken on some one who was not qualified according to trade union rules; and I did not then see why he was not free to employ any man he liked. As he alone was paying, was he not entitled to call the tune? I was pretty cocksure when I put this difficulty to my friend, the mason.

Without any attempt to solve it, he met it in the Irish manner, by a retort: why did not I and those of my cloth preach that to the doctors and lawyers? who take very good care to hold no consultation, and have no professional association of any kind, with any man, however qualified, who does not observe the etiquette of the profession; which, added my friend, is about the same thing as our trade union rules. What is moral for doctors ought to be good enough for artizans. I was not open or honest enough to admit the parity at the time; but the argument stuck in me, and I have since used it myself, in justification of some of the claims of the trade unionists.

Meanwhile I read little, if anything – except newspapers and speeches – on the Social Question. And yet I had, as you see, made no little progress by the simple and easy method of keeping eyes and ears open in the great school of the world; and, if I may say so, by a faculty I have – that has plagued and (I hope) blessed me somewhat – of observing with concern, that one part of our system of philosophy and theology does not hang well with another part; or with some fact which, however obvious, no one but myself seems to think worth noticing.

It was some years after my appointment to the Dunboyne before I was able to devote much time to the literature of the Social Question; and when at length I was free to do so, I began with some work on Socialism – Cathrein, I fancy – and was soon involved in Marx's Theory of Value and the Materialistic Conception of History. On the Socialist side I read the publications of the Fabian Society, I remember; but soon found that I was getting little profit from such reading – on either side. You all know of the Eastern poet-sage who

> When young, did eagerly frequent
> Doctor and Saint, and heard great argument
> About it and about; but evermore
> Came out at the same door where in I went.

That was my case pretty much. I do not think the working man knows anything, or cares a lot about Marx's Theory of Value; except, at most, a few prigs who, like so many of their kind on every side – love to parade the great names they know. I will even go so far as to say that, as I understand the theory of Marx, it adds nothing of real value to the old-fashioned principle that all increase of wealth is produced by the workers and should belong to them. That is what your robust working man can grasp – what he is disposed to believe, and to fling at you and me.

And as for the Materialistic Conception of History, of course many Socialist leaders advocate materialistic evolution, as do many of the apostles of Liberalism; but, as one may be a good Liberal without being a Materialist, so I can see no reason why Materialism or even disbelief in revelation, should be implied by Socialism. There is, no doubt, some danger that those who make profession of Socialism, frequent Socialist clubs, and read Socialist publications, may hear and see Materialistic tenets propounded; which proves, at most, that one must take care how one reads Socialistic literature or frequents Socialist clubs.

After some reading and considerable thought, I made up my mind that the speculative questions at issue between the Socialists and ourselves were these:

(1) Whether in the early stages of the development of our race it was necessary that occupation, rather than hired labour, should give a title to private property; and that it should be allowed the amount of value, as a title, which has been assigned it in the Catholic schools;

(2) Whether it is possible that, owing to the development of the race in the way of altruism, it might become reasonable, or even necessary, to socialize some things that previously had been held in private property;

(3) Whether this altruistic development might go so far as to justify, or even necessitate, the socialization of all private property in the same way; and

(4) Supposing some such development possible, what stage have we reached at present?

These questions I raised in the first number of the *Irish Theological Quarterly*, in an article under the heading 'About Socialism', to which I have very little to add, on the speculative side of the question. Now, indeed, I am more disposed to emphasize the rule that it is for men of the world – those especially who know business – rather than for theologians, to judge of the fact whether altruistic development has proceeded far enough in any country to justify the socialization of this or that kind of property – the railways, for instance, the land, the factories, or the mines. This day, on which I write this (March 11, 1915), the newspapers report the passage, without opposition, of a Bill authorizing the Government to take over the management of all the factories in these Islands wherein ammunition and such things may be made. It is a distinctly Socialistic measure; which, it should be noted, is advocated on the ground, not of our altruistic development, but of the reverse. So that a new question arises: whether it may not be development towards the universal strike, rather than towards perfect altruism, that will usher in and justify the Socialistic era.

The practical side of the Social Question is one of taxation and strikes; and taxation I have left – and shall continue to leave – to statesmen and economists; who alone, I think, have any claim to decide, or even advise on, the delicate and complicated matters involved. Economic science, like other handmaids of theology, had best be left to do her own business; of course, under the general surveillance of the mistress. So also with regard to wages – which are by far the most fruitful cause of strikes and lock-outs – it is business men, not theologians, who are capable of deciding or advising whether a firm or group of firms, can afford to pay a certain wage. Theology ought, in my opinion, to leave this work also to one of her handmaids.

There are, however, some general principles governing strikes which, as being more or less speculative in character, are best discussed and settled in the schools of ethics and theology and these I deemed it my duty to consider. Foremost among them is the doctrine of pressure, which I discussed in a second article, on 'The Ethical Aspect of Boycotting', that appeared in the third number of the *Irish Theological Quarterly*. Therein I advocated a considerable extension of the principle of self-defence; maintaining that it is justifiable to use a reasonable amount of moral force to ward off, not only strict injustice, but even inequitable treatment. The principle so extended, if sound, is of great importance; and the article in which it is set forth is no bad illustration of the method which I followed, and which I recommended to you: not to keep both eyes on books; but, with one on them – not necessarily old or classic books, but modern – to keep the other on the watch for every fact in the world around that may help to extend or correct your book-knowledge.

That article, on Boycotting, appeared in July, 1906; and nothing further of special importance occurred until 1911, when there was a strike in the Dublin timber trade, leading to a sympathetic strike among the porters on one of the railways. The question of the sympathetic strike was thus raised, but became much more prominent two years later, during the Dublin Labour Crisis, as I shall tell you.

Meanwhile, in 1912, there had been a kind of strike of medical men against service under the Insurance Act; and at a meeting of the profession, held in Dublin, the following resolutions were passed: 'That every doctor practising in Dublin be required to sign a pledge not to accept service with any Insurance or Benefit Society, or accept any medical appointment whatever, unless the local medical committee are satisfied that the payment is an adequate rate of remuneration'; and That a 'black list' be formed, on which the name of every practitioner who refuses to sign the pledge shall be placed, and it is understood that everyone who appears thereon shall be 'boycotted' by means known to the profession.' These resolutions were published, without a note of protest, in the *Irish Daily Independent* (May 22, 1912), which soon afterwards was conspicuous for the bitterness with which it denounced the boycott of 'scabs' by the members of the Dublin Transport Workers' Union.

I noted also, at the time, that two Conservative Dublin organs, the *Daily Mail* and the *Irish Times*, published a criticism to the effect that a 'doctor who, when his professional society decides that the conditions of service offered are degrading and unremunerative, goes behind the back of his society and accepts these conditions, is in the position of a man who agrees to undersell his comrades. He is a black-leg.'[1]

About a year later, in 1913, the great Dublin labour struggle began, when, on the men's side, there were sympathetic strikes, while over four hundred of the employers combined to dismiss every man who was a member of the Transport Workers' Union, no matter how excellent and faithful he might be otherwise. The reason assigned for this combination was, that Transport Workers could not be relied on not to engage in frivolous strikes; and, very probably, this did influence most of the employers, at the time; though, when it came later, to settling with the men, there was not, as we shall see, one word about frivolous strikes, nor about the Transport Workers' Union.

The men were led by Mr. Larkin and Mr. Connolly, the latter of whom showed himself thoughtful. Mr. Larkin, too, from the beginning had a firm grip of this fact, that unskilled labourers have no chance in a fight with their employers, unless they are supported by sympathetic action on the part of their fellows; not by way of supplying food, or even money, but by refusing to work with those who take the strikers' places, or to handle any goods that they make or forward. Mr. Larkin insisted throughout that the only way for English working men to enable their Dublin com-

1. This was first published in the *Daily Mail*, and copied in the *Irish Times*, February 2nd. 1912.

rades to win, was to refuse to handle goods forwarded by the strike-breakers, a method of warfare which, it is implied was justified by the fact that the strike-breakers were acting inequitably – towards the strikers. The masters denounced this as immoral; dubbed it Socialism, Syndicalism, Anarchism, and maintained that employers have a right to hire whom they like. The Press of Dublin sided with the masters, as did the great body of the priests.

By what principles these were guided, it is not easy to say: whether, that is, they regarded the sympathetic strike and the boycott of scabs as immoral absolutely; or whether they merely thought that both measures were being abused just then, in Dublin. Those of the clergy who either wrote to the Press or were reported therein, seemed to condemn absolutely, but it was not so clear that they meant this, or that they had thought out the question in that sense. If, however, they or others sided with the employers merely on the ground that sympathetic strikes, though not always unjust, had been frivolously, and therefore immorally, organized in Dublin, they were silent later when, as we shall see, the men were forced to pledge themselves, without any limitation, against taking part in any sympathetic strike whatever.

With all this going on at our doors for months, and with morning and evening papers full of it, you may imagine what discussions we had, with fellow-professors, diocesan clergy, manufacturers, shop-keepers, farmers. Everyone you met spoke of it; though, as I, unfortunately, did not meet very many labourers, it was only by close and constant reading of their journals I could learn what was in their minds. To me, an interested and unprejudiced onlooker, it seemed that, if the men's case was good in the main, they injured it in several ways; though I also thought that many of their opponents – manufacturers, shop-keepers, farmers, and others – had grown fat on methods which they now pronounced almost demoniacal, when turned by the labourers against themselves. It was comical to hear a farmer rage against a combination to boycott blacklegs, as if he had not had his own rent reduced, or even purchased his holding as a result of a similar combination – against land-grabbers. Or you might read in a newspaper a diatribe against the sympathetic strike, followed in the same column by an appeal to employers to lock out their men in sympathy with brother capitalists.

As in all disputes of the kind, many issues were raised; most of them irrelevant, or at least accidental, as could be seen quite clearly when the men were beaten and had to accept the masters' terms. Then the real question showed clearly, as it was open to the men to resume work on condition of signing an agreement to the effect that they 'would not take part in or support any form of sympathetic strike; that they would handle all materials, no matter from whom or how delivered, and carry out all instructions given them in the course of their employment; and that they would work peaceably with all other employees, whether they be members of a union or not; and would not interfere with or make any objection to work with those who had already signed any agreement.'

Not a word about Mr. Larkin's extreme measures; not a word about breaches of contract and sabotage, of which the men had been accused; not a word of the frivolous strikes, whereby, it used to be said the Transport Workers had made business impossible. Three conditions of employment, and three only, were insisted on: first, that the men 'would take no part in or support *any form of sympathetic strike*'; secondly, that they 'would not interfere with or make any objection to working with those who had already signed any agreement' – that is, with scabs or blacklegs – and that they 'would handle *all materials, no matter from whom or how delivered*' – that is, even though delivered by blacklegs of the worst kind; and thirdly, that they would work peaceably with all other employees, whether they were members of a union or not.' These conditions were absolute; no exceptions being made or allowed. No matter how reasonable a strike elsewhere may be, you must not strike in sympathy; no matter how an employer may have tyrannized over or defrauded his men, you must receive, handle, and forward the goods which he sends on by means of the scabs whom he employs; and you must work with any man whom we think it well to hire – non-union man, strike-breaker, blackleg, blackguard, or whom you will: nay, whom we will – we, the masters.[1]

That these, gentlemen, were the real questions at issue throughout is proved by the fact that any man in Dublin was free to resume work on signing the agreement just quoted. This was done in the open day – in the full light of the Press – without a whimper from any priest in Ireland. Does it mean that the clergy, to a man, approve of forcing labourers to work on these conditions?

Do not fancy that the issues were peculiar to Dublin, or that they will not be raised again. The question of non-union labour was raised within a month, in London, in the building trade, and

1. See a letter from Mr. J. Gibson, Secretary of the Dublin Building Trades Employers' Association, published in the Dublin newspapers of February 2nd, 1914.

threatened, just before the outbreak of war, to lead to a universal strike and lock-out all over these kingdoms. The same question was raised in Colorado about the same time, in a mine wherein the Rockefellers owned a controlling interest, one of whom, Mr. Rockefeller, jun., stated in evidence at Washington that his father 'was ready to sacrifice all the capital he had invested in the company, to uphold the right of non-union men to work for whom they please.' Not, mind you, to uphold the right of masters to employ non-union men; but to uphold the men against the tyranny of the unions.

The world over it is the same: the great body of the wage-earners and of the capitalists are divided on these three questions – of non-union labour, scab labour, and sympathetic strikes, which are sure to come up again and again – in America, England, Ireland, everywhere. They belong to your province: not like wage questions, which you had better leave to men of business; and when they do arise in your neighbourhood, you will be wheedled and pressed in many ways to take a side in the dispute. When they were raised in Dublin, the priests, as we have seen, sided with the employers: that, at least, I fear, is the opinion of the men of the Transport Workers' Union who were forced into submission. Mind, I do not say that the priests were not right: it depends on certain questions which I will now try to put before you briefly.

To begin with, there is a fundamental issue: whether men have a right to defend themselves, not only against injustice in the strict sense, but against harsh or inequitable treatment. I have dealt with this in my article on 'The Ethics of Boycotting'; and, though the discussion therein is by no means complete, I do not know where you will get the question more fully treated than in that article and those which it called forth. Mind, however, what I have said already; that, in studying questions of this kind, you may keep one eye on books; but you must hold the other on the watch for any facts in the world around you that may help you to judge, by analogy, of what working men may do.

If you decide that they may strike in defence of equitable as well as of strict rights, three subsidiary questions will arise; each more difficult than the fundamental one: – (1) whether men have a right in equity not to be forced to work with all blacklegs whatsoever – scabs of the worst kind; (2) whether they have a right in equity not to work with those who though decent otherwise, will not join a labour union; and (3) whether men on strike – when the strike is justified – have a right in equity that neighbouring firms shall not trade with the master against whom they struck, and so assist him in his fight with the strikers? You will find that on the answer to these subsidiary questions will depend what you are to hold on the matters that were really in dispute in Dublin; of which, depend upon it, you have not heard the last: scab labour, non-union labour, and the sympathetic strike.

How are you to study all this? Not out of books alone; for it is not to be found therein, except in general principles, which so far, have been very imperfectly developed. Not out of the letters, speeches and articles that appear in newspapers; though you must keep an eye on these, as stating one or other side of the question. The issues before you are new, and you must only study them as best you can in the light of old principles, which have to be extended so as to cover new ground, and in the added light of any analogies you may be able to discover in the world around you. It is no easy task, and requires no ordinary powers. Should your modesty tell you that you are not the man to face it, let it tell you also not to take a side hastily on questions so intricate and so little discussed; or, if you do take a side, not to be very dogmatic in your condemnation of others.

Perhaps you will allow me to propose, by way of illustration, some of the analogies which you may draw from the world around.

As regards the fundamental issue – whether one may use pressure to defend not only strict but equitable rights – the classical illustration, to be found in many books, is that of a father who presses his son not to marry a certain girl, by threatening him with disinheritance should he do so. May such pressure be legitimate, even though the son has a strict right to marry the girl? The recent history of Ireland suggests another case: whether tenant farmers may use pressure such as was applied by the Land League, to restrain landlords from exacting rents which, though harsh or inequitable, are not strictly unjust.

As regards scabs or blacklegs, you may ask whether, during the land agitation, the farmers of Ireland were entitled to use the pressure applied by the League, to restrain men from grabbing farms from which tenants had been evicted; or whether the doctors were within their right, three years ago, in threatening to boycott, as blacklegs, those of their profession who should take service under conditions which the medical committee regarded as degrading or unremunerative.

Dealing with non-union labour, you may ask whether retail dealers may boycott manufacturers and wholesale merchants who fail to observe the recognised rules of trade; or whether doctors may refuse to meet in consultation, or have any professional intercourse with, another doctor who does not observe the etiquette of the profession.

And as regards sympathetic strikes, you may ask whether employers may lock men out in sympathy with other employers whose men have struck; or whether, during the land agitation in Ireland, shop-keepers and labourers could take part in applying pressure to 'grabbers.'

These are specimen cases, which you may find helpful. They can be supplemented easily from your own reading and from your observations; that is, if you keep eyes and ears open, and are really interested in the Social Question.

Fiction

A Trilogy
by Francis MacManus

STAND AND GIVE CHALLENGE

A loving, living recreation of the life of the
hidden Ireland of the 18th century and particularly
of the life of one, Donncha Ruadh MacConmara.   6/–

CANDLE FOR THE PROUD

Once again we meet the wandering school-master,
rogue, poet, patriot, Donncha Ruadh MacConmara
who has already endeared himself to us.   6/–

MEN WITHERING

Here we have recorded the last days of an unforgettable,
proud man – his every desire withered except the
desire to live.   6/–

also

THIS HOUSE WAS MINE   5/–
THE GREATEST OF THESE   5/–
FLOW ON LOVELY RIVER   6/–

Short Stories

FIELD AND FAIR
Padraic O'Conaire   5/–

THE HORSE THIEVES OF
BALLYSAGGERT
Brian Cleeve   6/–

IRISH SHORT STORIES
Seumus O'Kelly   5/–

A MUNSTER TWILIGHT
Daniel Corkery   5/–

THE WOMAN AT THE WINDOW
Padraic O'Conaire   5/–

First published in the Netherlands 1967
Printed by Bosch, Utrecht